GW00535866

Navigating Colonial Orders

Navigating Colonial Orders

Norwegian Entrepreneurship in Africa and Oceania

Edited by
Kirsten Alsaker Kjerland
and Bjørn Enge Bertelsen

berghahn
NEW YORK · OXFORD
www.berghahnbooks.com

Published by

Berghahn Books

www.berghahnbooks.com

© 2015 Kirsten Alsaker Kjerland and Bjørn Enge Bertelsen

Library of Congress Cataloging-in-Publication Data

Navigating colonial orders : Norwegian entrepreneurship in Africa and
  Oceania / edited by Kirsten Alsaker Kjerland and Bjørn Enge Bertelsen.
    pages cm
  Includes bibliographical references and index.
    ISBN 978-1-78238-539-4 (hardback : alk. paper) — ISBN 978-1-78238-540-0
  (ebook)
    1. Norway—Foreign economic relations—Africa. 2. Norway—Foreign eco-
  nomic relations—Oceania. 3. Colonies—Africa—Economic conditions.
  4. Colonies—Oceania—Economic conditions. 5. Norwegians—Africa—
  History. 6. Norwegians—Oceania—History. 7. Entrepreneurship—Africa—
  History. 8. Entrepreneurship—Oceania—History. 9. Africa—Foreign
  economic relations—Norway. 10. Oceania—Foreign economic relations—
  Norway. I. Kjerland, Kirsten Alsaker. II. Bertelsen, Bjørn Enge.
  HF1566.5.A35N38 2014
  338′.04089398206—dc23

2014018761

British Library Cataloguing in Publication Data

A catalogue record for this book is available from the British Library

Printed on acid-free paper

ISBN: 978-1-78238-539-4 hardback
ISBN: 978-1-78238-540-0 ebook

☙ Contents

⚆⟫ Illustrations

Tables

Figures

ꙮ Maps

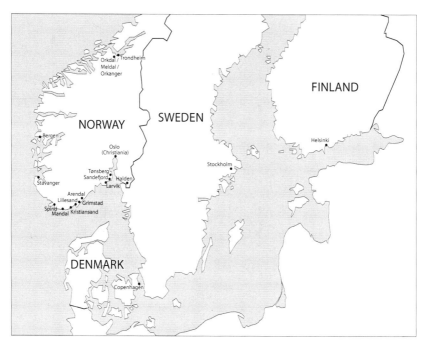

Map 1. Scandinavia, with relevant locations.

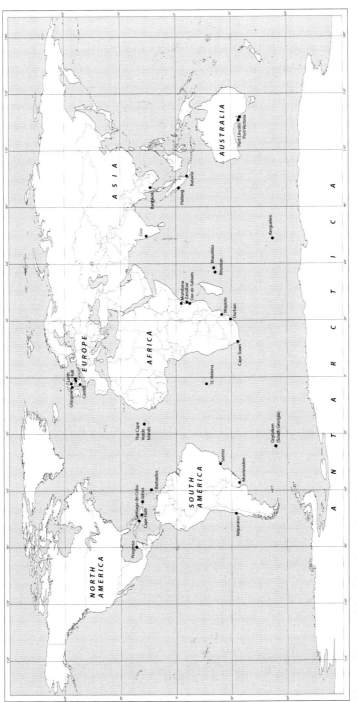

Map 2. The world, with relevant locations.

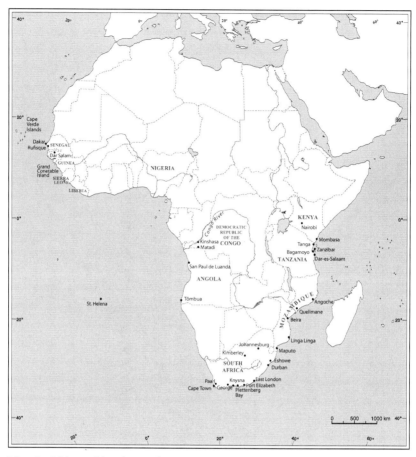

Map 3. Africa, with relevant locations.

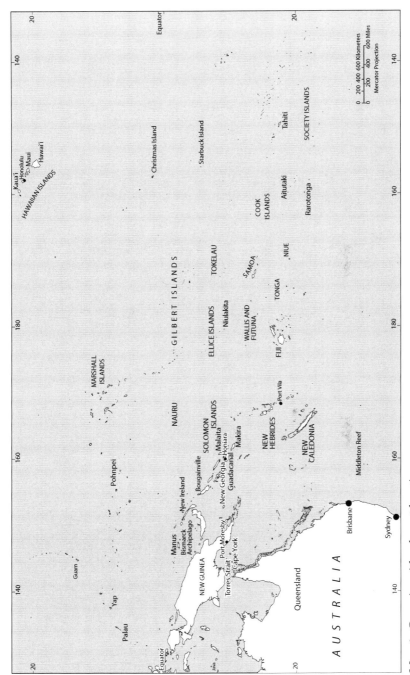

Map 4. Oceania, with relevant locations.

⊙⫸ Preface

Kirsten Alsaker Kjerland

A Norwegian in Africa – in the 1680s? What? Until a decade ago, such questions as well as the exchange of odd stories of a similar sort were the order of the lunchroom day between two Africanists at the University of Bergen. These stories were definitely sidetracks for both, whose respective PhD dissertations were concerned with Indian Ocean trade and Sufism and the struggle for land in rural colonial Kenya. Curiosity soon gave way, however, to academic obsession, and in October 2002 a popular science anthology about Norwegians in Africa and Africans in Norway was published, entitled *Nordmenn i Afrika – afrikanere i Norge* (Kjerland and Bang 2002). This anthology focused mainly on Norwegians in Africa, as well as a minor section presenting examples of some unfortunate few Africans stranded in the cold north.

We all know the wonderful sound of a positive review – not to mention the euphoria caused by several. To Anne K. Bang's and my own amazement, however, feedback primarily came in the form of numerous calls, letters and emails from accidental readers who had family connections with African histories, who possessed personal archives and photo albums or who wanted to know more about particular people or contexts mentioned in the anthology. In sum, all this led to our conviction that the story of Norwegians in Africa was a thoroughly underresearched area – a piñata calling out for a much more decisive strike, if you will. With this in mind, serious research efforts were soon focused towards challenging some well-established myths, centred on a handful of questions.

Why did a not insignificant number of Norwegians head towards Africa at a time when the United States of America was *the* magnet – a land of milk and honey that became the new home of some eight hundred thousand Norwegians between the 1830s and the 1930s? Who were those few who did not follow the mainstream? What were their motives, where did they end up and what did they do? Few indeed; in 1911 the official number of Norwegians in South Africa (where most

went) was some sixteen hundred persons, mainly men. The majority
lived in Natal, in and near Durban, where the only Norwegian settlement initiated by a South African government representative was
found. In the early 1880s some two hundred Norwegian men, women
and children arrived at the same time, on the same boat, in Port Shepstone. They settled nearby on forty equally sized plots (ca. one hundred
acres each) surrounded by Zulu grass huts. Thirty years later some were
still there, but at that moment most of the Norwegians (more than one
thousand people) lived in Durban itself. A city within the city included
a Norwegian church, a Norwegian cultural hall, a Norwegian school,
a Norwegian rowing club, a Norwegian choir and a newspaper in the
Norwegian language, not to mention the many Norwegian chandlers
deeply involved in shipping and trade. Given that the Norwegians in
this town had money in their pockets, Norwegian culinary specialities
of those days – *pultost* (a cheese made from soured milk flavoured with
caraway seeds) and *akevitt* (aquavit) – were easily accessible (Saxe 1914;
Semmingsen 1950).

Who created the notion that Africa was 'full' of Norwegian missionaries prior to the days of good intentions and merciful development
gifts? A slight rubbing of the surface suggested that this was at best
nothing but a well-established myth. The total number of Norwegians
working directly with missionary-associated work at any time in Natal,
South Africa – the stronghold of Norwegians wishing to convert Africa's heathens between the 1840s and 1950 – never exceeded more than
a few handfuls of persons. On the contrary, the majority of the Norwegians in Natal worked in every other business than the missions – primarily mining, joinery and in various kinds of trade. As for other parts
of Africa, the first group of missionaries that arrived in Tanganyika and
Ethiopia only did so some sixty years ago, around 1950. This made the
Norwegian missionaries here relative latecomers in comparison to earlier Norwegian ventures, as this book documents.

In Norway, a die-hard myth said (and still says) that Norway was
one of Europe's poorest countries before oil and gas was discovered a
stone's throw off the coast in the late 1960s. To this very day the narrative of historical Norwegian poverty is repeated, in particular by
Norwegian politicians embroiled in rhetoric linking prosperity to the
emergence of the welfare state after the Second World War. Such an
account problematically skews other facets of the Norwegian past,
such as, for example, the successful Norwegian history of shipping.
The mere fact that Norway had the world's third-largest merchant fleet
around 1890 more than indicates that Norwegian capitalists took an

active part in world business and thrived economically in the period when world trade expanded by 400 per cent between 1860 and 1914 (Johnsen 1998: 13, 35–36). Further, such an account also obscures the fact that this very merchant fleet was a major factor in Norway's withdrawal from the union with Sweden. As soon as Great Britain entered a policy of relative free trade by abolishing the Navigation Act around 1850, Norwegian ships began tossing their anchors in harbours around the globe and gradually became one of the major charterers of cargo. When modern whaling developed in the Southern Hemisphere around 1900, Norwegians were among the leading operators – an industry that brought wealth to many and in fact resulted in an extension of the Norwegian territory at the very start of the Second World War when Britain accepted Norway's claim on the Bouvet Island in Antarctica. This, by the way, was not Norway's first territorial expansion in the twentieth century: in 1923, thanks again to shipping, neutral Norway was awarded Spitsbergen for its assistance to the winning nations as compensation for its loss of tonnage during the First World War. According to Fritz Wedel Jarlsberg, Norway's negotiator at the 1918 peace conference, this was a very bad choice indeed. His suggestion for reimbursement was the German East Africa colony (Kjerland and Rio 2009a: 6; see also the introduction to this volume).

The initial research following the 2002 anthology dealing with Norwegians in Africa and Africans in Norway therefore provided a range of examples of how Norwegian traders, entrepreneurs and companies had gained from global trade between 1850 and 1950 and how they had worked and invested money in Portuguese, French, Belgian and British colonies in Africa (where labour and land was comparatively very inexpensive) during the colonial era. However, the deeper the initial few Africa-focused researchers delved into the material, the more it became clear that the maritime aspect of this Norwegian colonial history must be explored and acknowledged. The focus was therefore extended to include researchers with great knowledge of maritime and shipping history.

Interestingly, this extension to include, in particular, maritime historians also opened up a new geographical space – Oceania – in order to understand, at least from the outset, where all the derelict sailing ships ended up after being decommissioned from Norwegian shipping circles towards the late 1800s. However, while firmly rooted in maritime history, the research undertaken in Oceania also revealed other dimensions of large- and smaller-scale colonial entrepreneurship, long-term connectivities and untold colonial and postcolonial histories.

With a total of twelve scholars from the fields of history, anthropology, economy and geography, an application entitled 'In the Wake of Colonialism: Norwegian Commercial Interests in Colonial Africa and Oceania' (WAKE) was submitted to the Norwegian Research Council in June 2004. In November of the same year the WAKE group received almost NOK 10 million for research – a sum later to be supplemented by NOK 2 million from the University of Bergen, Bergen Museum, Bergen Universitetsfond, F. Meltzer Høyskolefond and Fritt Ord. The editors wish to thank all these institutions for their generous financial support.

WAKE ran for four full years and produced several monographs (Reiersen 2006; Bang 2008; Kjerland 2010), an anthology with thirteen articles (Kjerland and Rio 2009b) and an exhibition (also lasting four years) opened at Bergen Museum in June 2009. Several doctoral theses (one on shipping, one on whaling and one on Norwegians in South African trade and investment) are either finalized or in the process of being so. While the present book builds on all these publications, it seeks to present the scale, breadth and width of Norwegian colonial entrepreneurship. As demonstrated throughout the chapters and as contextualized in further detail in the introduction, such engagements spanned a wide range of activities, from liner shipping and plantation activities to beach trading, whaling and participation in warfare. With this book, the editors also hope to contribute to a truly international colonial history of Africa and Oceania by showing, precisely, the multiform and complex nature of the colonial system – and its many engagements, also by entrepreneurs from a small, cold Scandinavian country.

The editors would on behalf of the book project also like to thank the Norwegian publisher Scandinavian Academic Press/Spartacus Forlag A/S for being so supportive of an English version of this material. The editors also wish to extend their gratitude to Berghahn Books, where Marion Berghahn's support, insights and enthusiasm for the project has inspired us greatly. We also wish to thank Berghahn Books' Adam Capitanio and Elizabeth Berg, who patiently steered us through the different phases of production, as well as copy editor Caitlin Mahon who did a marvellous job in the final stages of manuscript preparation. Further, we wish to acknowledge the publication support kindly provided to the project by the Norwegian Research Council. We are also grateful for the help given to us by Kjell Helge Sjøstrøm in developing the maps in the book. Lastly, we wish to thank the contributors to this volume, who have taken part in the long journey of research towards, finally, this book.

Bibliography

Bang, A.K. 2008. *Zanzibar-Olsen: Norsk trelasthandel i Øst Afrika 1895–1925*. Bergen: Fagbokforlaget.

Johnsen, B. Eide. 1998. 'Rederstrategier i endringstid: Sørlandsk skipsfart fra segl til damp og motor – Fra tre til jern og stål, 1875–1925', PhD dissertation. Bergen: University of Bergen.

Kjerland, K.A. 2010. *Nordmenn i det koloniale Kenya*. Oslo: Scandinavian Academic Press.

Kjerland, K.A. and A.K. Bang (eds). 2002. *Nordmenn i Afrika – afrikanere i Norge*. Bergen: Vigmostad & Bjørke.

Kjerland, K.A. and K.M. Rio. 2009a. 'Introduksjon', in K.A. Kjerland and K.M. Rio (eds), *Kolonitid: Nordmenn på eventyr og big business i Afrika og Oceania*. Oslo: Scandinavian Academic Press, pp. 5–9.

Kjerland, K.A. and K.M. Rio (eds). 2009b. *Kolonitid: Nordmenn på eventyr og big business i Afrika og Oceania*. Oslo: Scandinavian Academic Press.

Reiersen, E. 2006. *Fenomenet Thams*. Oslo: Aschehoug.

Saxe, L. 1914. *Nordmenn jorden rundt*. Kristiania: H. Aschehougs & Co., W. Nygaard.

Semmingsen, I. 1950. *Veien mot Vest: Utvandring fra Norge, 1865–1915*. Oslo: Aschehoug.

 Introduction

NORWEGIANS NAVIGATING COLONIAL ORDERS IN AFRICA AND OCEANIA

Bjørn Enge Bertelsen

Many Norwegians cultivate an image of Norway as exerting a thoroughly benign global influence. Rhetorically, therefore, Norway's foreign policy is regularly presented as being steeped in humanitarian ideals of mediation and peacemaking rather than caught in the throes of Schmittian realpolitik ([1932] 1996). Reflecting this self-congratulatory position, in 2006 Jonas Gahr Støre, who was then Norwegian minister of foreign affairs, boasted in a public lecture, '[w]e have some advantages – as a state outside the power blocks in international politics, with no colonial history and no tradition for hidden agendas' (quoted in Simonsen 2010: 22; see also Smith-Simonsen 2011). Moreover, Norway's active branding as a nation of benevolence and peace is often referred to in domestic political discourse and scholarly analysis alike as conditioned by the fact that what became the country of Norway has historically lacked colonies. This claim is often asserted to be based in the fact that Norway itself was subjected to colony-like relations – first under Danish rule as part of Denmark-Norway (1521–1814) and then in a considerably more independent position in the union with Sweden from 1814, finally gaining full sovereign independence in 1905. In Norwegian historiography, this period under foreign rule has been referred to as *Firehundreårsnatten* – the 'the four-hundred-year night'.

The present book challenges this politically motivated and internationally marketed national stereotype of colonial nonpresence and nonparticipation. Its chapters demonstrate the ways in which Norwegians at multiple levels – private, commercial and national – engaged in and effectively navigated what are termed here 'colonial orders'. While the anthology comprises Norwegian engagements in Oceania and Africa, primarily between 1850 and 1950, this scope could have been expanded to encompass similar Norwegian colonial activities in the Americas, Asia and Australia. However, limiting the temporal and geographical scope of the anthology provides us with an opportunity to analyse and theorize key global aspects of Norwegian colonial engagements, their contribution to, and interaction with, local, national and transnational elites, and their emplacement in both colonial peripheries and metropolises. This approach results in an analytically rewarding empirical emphasis on the various hot spots, locations and contexts that comprised the colonial orders (Ittmann, Cordell and Maddox 2011).

This introduction will frame colonial Norwegian entrepreneurship in Africa and Oceania in terms of international debates on colonialism and the analytical and political challenges of colonial representation – both visual and textual. It presents the chapters in a context of emerging Nordic history, which encompasses various (and sometimes conflicting) approaches to colonialism and national history. In general, the aim is not to fully summarize the anthology's contributions per se, as these speak for themselves, but rather to resituate them within research on the colonial era in order to make sense of the phenomenon of Norwegians navigating colonial orders.

Flows, Formation and Noncolonial Colonials

Given the inherent heterogeneity characterizing colonial orders, the contributors to this anthology in differing yet complimentary ways analyse what may be termed *colonial flows* on the one hand and *colonial formations* on the other. Several of the contributors underline the crucial maritime aspect to these colonial ventures – a material dimension that concretizes the *flows* that characterized the colonial order. Geographically Norway has a long coastline, and historically it has been characterized by an expansive commercial and entrepreneurial seafaring orientation. Thus, in the era of white sails Norway was the third-largest nation globally in terms of tonnage in 1878, outranked only by the United States and the United Kingdom (Det statistiske centralbureau 1887), remaining a major sailing ship nation well into the 1900s. Unsurprisingly, then, Norwegian entry points into both emerging and more settled colonial orders – the Solomon Islands in Oceania being an example of the first order, and South Africa of the second – suggest that shipping, seaborne trade and agents, and a maritime labour force have held primacy. This mainly seaborne focus on flows also reflects how resources such as minerals, goods, manpower and foodstuffs – such as timber, copra, coffee, sugar and whale meat – were transported through the arteries that interconnected the colonized zones to the colonizing powers' metropoles. Maritime transportation and its shifting routes – according to markets, technological advances, geopolitics and collective or singular entrepreneurship – play significant roles in this volume. Equally important are the differentiated dynamics of expansion and penetration that contrast Africa and Oceania: the maritime trade replete with ports and agents serving a well-developed world trade that characterized the colonial orders Norwegians encountered in various African contexts contrasts dramatically with the pioneering spirit of rogue merchantry and beach trade within nascent colonial formations and local polities that comprised the historical contexts into which Norwegian sailing ships ventured in parts of Oceania in the mid- to late 1800s.

Beyond flows, any description of colonial engagements needs to grapple with the minutiae and localized unfoldings of colonialism – its sites, systems and spatial organizations. In this book, therefore, much attention is given to an exploration of the particular wider geographies and specific loci of Norwegian entrepreneurship: the physical emplacement of farms, whaling stations and whaling grounds, mines, plantations, warehouses, offices and trading posts. Such sites provide the empirical frameworks for narrative accounts and analyses that are rich in historical and ethnographic detail – often through presenting extraordinary individual biographies that were shaped by singular or multiple colonial contexts.

Of course, colonial formations also need to be conceptualized beyond spatialities in terms of polities, governance and the encompassing nature of colonial and imperial rule. For this reason, attention is also paid to the politics of identity; for instance, the Norwegians studied here were embroiled in a politics that sometimes cast long postcolonial shadows beyond the 1950s (Jonassen, chapter 9). Further, this book posits that any approach to Norwegians' colonial ventures must recognize the interlinkages of business and politics – of local, national and transnational kinds (Reiersen, chapter 11) – as well as the fact that Norwegian domestic politics in some periods were shaped by colonial aspirations and desires (Angell, chapter 6). Within some colonial orders these linkages materialized as Norwegians became part of local elites and were consequently involved in the unfolding, upkeep and, sometimes, implementation of colonial rule and domination (Rio, chapter 10). Arguably, then, flow and formation comprise key parts of colonial orders within which a wide range of Norwegian entrepreneurship was afforded possibilities for navigation – literally and metaphorically. In exploring colonial orders from the point of view of Norwegian entrepreneurship, individual chapters also debate the nature and representation of colonialism. Obviously, such writing – or, indeed, rewriting – of colonial histories involves treading a number of difficult paths.

The most obvious political-cum-scholarly danger is the risk of being perceived as fully deconstructing or radically revising postcolonial national histories. In many former colonies such national histories were usually, and perhaps necessarily, narrated with a focus on national liberation from plural or singular colonial forces, imperial regimes or repressive powers. Sensitive to such dimensions, in a recent broad assessment of global history Woolf points out that '[a] triumphal nationalist narrative of the advance of this or that former colony into a free and full member of the international community marked much of the new African historical writing up to about 1970' (2011: 445). Since the 1970s, however, the early era of unified postcolonial historical accounts has given way to positions on colonial representation and its imageries (and imaginaries), taking into account a new multipolar world order where narratives of postcolonial nations emerge as ever more complex and ambiguous: increasing difficulties in cultivating and upholding singular narratives of national origins, of the colonial order, of struggles against clearly demarcated enemies leading up to liberation, now seem to condition postcolonial national history writing (see, e.g., Werbner 1998).

Seeing Norwegian entrepreneurship in the colonial orders of Oceania and Africa in terms of 'noncolonial colonials' necessarily further complicates postcolonial historiographies while at the same time muddying the waters of sometimes overly unified and neat national histories of former colonizing countries. However, such an expansion or, rather, desingularization of the colonial order, which this anthology aims towards, also risks contributing to revisionism. This is because we afford voice, agency and – through photographs – a face to Norwegian settlers, middlemen, shipping agents, traders, peddlers, farmers, whalers, plantation owners and the jacks-of-all-trades who operated in the colonial domains. Through further emphasizing the Norwegian aspect, this particular volume risks being misconstrued as an expansionist and, perhaps even belatedly, imperialist tale of some forgotten late-Norse grandeur. Nothing could be further from our intention, as a key concern is precisely to counter the forms of histories that imbue colonial domination with a rosy hue, or rhetorically coat such repressive and often violent systems in nostalgia. Concretely, such a concern empirically and analytically implies an awareness of being integral to and complicit in European imperial expansion into Africa and Oceania. Further, the contributors hold that seeing Norwegians as noncolonial colonials provides a fresh and novel approach to the politicized, thoroughly researched and debated colonial pasts of two particular regions of the world. In order to develop this perspective further, there is a need to situate the argument about colonial flows and formation and its Norwegian dimensions in relation to key readings of colonial history and colonialism.

The Ambiguity or Disambiguity of Colonialism

In line with a common approach to defining colonialism, Reinhard (2011: 3) sees the 'colony' as a territory beyond the 'originating polity' that is characterized either minimally by 'settlement *or* rule' or maximally by 'settlement *and* rule'. Beyond this basic dichotomy, Reinhard develops a tripartite typology: *trading-based or military-based colonies,* which comprise colonial forms shaped by economic interests and/or military presence; *settlement colonies,* involving the permanent establishment and dominance of new people; and *colonies of rule* – being the supremacy over a majority of indigenous people by a minority, and often characterized by little interference in economic and social ways of life in the colony (2011: 3–4; cf. Krautwurst 2010 for a critique of this kind of approach). Reinhard further notes that colonialism as a form of domination implies one people's control over another, 'through the economic, political and ideological exploitation of a development gap between the two' (2011: 1).

Reinhard's systemic (and systematic) approach to colonialism has a long trajectory in historical and critical studies of capitalism – approaches that lend themselves quite easily to seeing the colony-metropole relation as constituting a near-totalizing form of political, economic and social order. This stance on colonial coherence had already been expressed, for instance, more than sixty years ago, by Balandier: 'It is in the light of these facts [from Asia and Africa] that we reaffirm the compelling need to consider the *colonial situation* as a single complex, as a totality' ([1951] 1966: 42). Following Balandier and others, the idea of the colonial situation as necessitating a systemic analysis, not least in terms of capitalist transformations, was developed in detail, especially by Wallerstein (e.g., 2004) and the so-called world system theorists. In general terms, he sees the rise of a world system emerging from the 1500s as built on the back of a nascent capitalist world economy. Having undergone a number of historical developments, this world system comprises a range of institutions, cultures and religions, for example, to form an interstate system that while nonunitary nonetheless constitutes a totality due to a division of labour serving a capitalist system, which gives priority to the accumulation of capital (2004: 23–24). In this *longue durée* approach, much inspired by the works of Braudel ([1987] 1995),

Wallerstein envisions colonialism as integral to the world system and to the production of colonial states that are, comparatively speaking, institutionally weak. Given such limited autonomy and sovereignty, the colonial state is therefore 'maximally subject to exploitation by firms and persons from a different country, the so-called metropolitan country' (2004: 56).[1]

The following chapters certainly illustrate aspects of Wallerstein's argument about the colonial state's frailty in terms of providing entrepreneurial opportunities in what were to become (or already were) French, Belgian, British, German and Portuguese colonies in Africa and Oceania. However, that Norwegians were involved in such orders indicates that not all colonial activities fit within an overly systemic, unified vision of capitalism and colonialism. Put differently, given Wallerstein's argument that the 'weakest form of state' was the colonial variety, one simultaneously needs to recognize its destabilizing effects and the possibilities it created to contest the relative sovereignty of the polities that such weakness afforded. Furthermore, this anthology illustrates the particular opportunities seized by entrepreneurs *external* to the metropole-colony link: for example, the Norwegian entrepreneurs involved in the control and development of a large-scale plantation in what was to become Mozambique (Reiersen, chapter 11; Bertelsen, chapter 12); the significance of numerous Norwegians' military engagement and ethnographic trade in the Congo (Wæhle, chapter 14); the establishment and development of large Norwegian-owned and Norwegian-run farms in Kenya (Kjerland, chapter 13); the Norwegian origins of entrepreneurial, spatial and political dominance of the town of Knysna in South Africa (Eidsvik, chapter 3); the intriguing career of a Norwegian timber merchant in Zanzibar (Bang, chapter 4); a Norwegian family's establishment of a vast sugar plantation in Hawai'i and its Norwegian workers (Rio, chapter 10); rogue traders of various goods in the Solomon Islands (Hviding, chapters 7 and 8); the personal and *longue durée* implications of identity politics at different levels of Norwegian trading in the Cook Islands (Jonassen, chapter 9); the long-haul tramp voyages of a Norwegian captain in Africa and Oceania and his dependence on global Norwegian networks (Sætra, chapter 2); the emergence of Norwegian shipping to South Africa (Nygaard, chapter 1); southern Africa–based Norwegian whaling and its dependence on South African and Cape Verdean labourers (Børresen, chapter 5); and finally, the political wrangles predating Norway's attainment of independence from Sweden in 1905 and the importance of colonial aspirations in this regard (Angell, chapter 6).

As the vignettes in the chapters indicate, these historical cases evade a strict definition of the term 'entrepreneurship'. Nonetheless, the editors have pragmatically chosen to employ this term as a conceptual and heuristic tool rather than a term fully informed by entrepreneurship theory per se. It encompasses a wide range of historical projects, from the Norwegian-controlled investments of transnational venture capital in colonial Mozambique and elsewhere (Reiersen, chapter 11) to rogue traders and adventurers plying copra and engaging in gunrunning between the Solomon Islands (Hviding, chapter 8). Thus, while some of the individual projects or collective engagements described here would fit classical definitions of entrepreneurship, as discussed by Eidsvik (chapter 3) in some detail, others would not. Entrepreneurship as it is employed here, then, needs to be understood as being located in this broad, commonsense meaning: individual or collective agents who seek out, create and/or exploit particular economic, sociocultural or political niches in attempting (sometimes unsuccessfully) to reap various forms of benefits within multiplex colonial orders.

Although noncolonial colonials are not the primary objectives of her research, it is along such lines of multiplicity and nontotalization that the influential historian of colonialism Ann Laura Stoler has argued. In one of her earlier works (1989: 135), she notes that '[t]he terms colonial state, colonial policy, foreign capital, and *the white enclave* are often used interchangeably, as if they captured one and the same thing. While such a treatment encourages certain lines of novel enquiry, it closes off others. The makers of metropole policy become conflated with its local practitioners.' Her words of caution can be taken even further: analyses of colonial orders in Oceania and Africa, as elsewhere, also need to recognize subjects who are not under the direct authority of metropolitan policy, as well as their role as 'local practitioners' in Stoler's sense. Certainly, there were tensions within what Stoler calls 'the white enclave', and many Norwegians were regarded (and sometimes strategically presented themselves) as different from imperial agents and the white majority population more generally. Cases in point are both Eidsvik's analysis of the ways in which the powerful Thesen family navigated dangerous political waters during the Anglo-Boer War (1899–1902) by strategically appropriating Boer and British identities (and oscillating between these), as well as Rio's and Jonassen's analyses of how Norwegians were integrated into and developed kinship systems, political orders and identity dynamics in Oceanic contexts.[2]

As the activities of noncolonial colonials have not been addressed to any great extent in major studies, this volume aims to further understandings of such colonial heterogeneity. However, while retaining the focus on the flows, tensions, contestations and ambiguities that are explored mostly empirically here (Stoler and Cooper 1997), we also maintain a wider, systemic and *longue durée* interpretation of the colonial and capitalist system (see also DeLanda 1997). That is, it is necessary to recognize both systemic and unambiguous readings and elements of the ambiguous and the contested to analytically account for the colonial orders in which Norwegian entrepreneurship was multifariously engaged. Such a dual totalizing and detotalizing scope assumes importance given the sometimes explicit (but often more implicit and complicit) colonial ambitions of Norwegians and other people from the Nordic countries.

Noncolonial Colonials: Or, Alternative Norwegian and Nordic Histories

It is precisely such Nordic ambitions that come to the fore in a text that Shirley Ardener has published: the manuscript of the Swede Knut Knutson who, together with fellow Swede, friend and business associate George Waldau, lived and worked as hunter, trader and adventurer in, on and around Cameroon Mountain between 1883 and 1895 (Ardener and Knutson 2002). It provides unique insights into the emerging German colonization of Cameroon and the multisemic relations among Europeans of various nationalities – effectively pluralizing 'the white enclave' in Stoler's sense. Importantly, it also evidences the adventurous and entrepreneurial presence as in no small measure relating to Swedish national and colonial interests. According to Ardener, Knutson's reaction to the imminent German imperial occupation of Cameroon at the time was to ask the Swedish Ministry of Foreign Affairs to set up a Swedish protectorate. While this colonial aspiration for various reasons remained unrealized, it underlines the presence of a colonial orientation and (perhaps) desire on the part of the Swedes (Ardener and Knutson 2002: 5, 8n2).

Similarly, it is important to recognize that during the first decades of the twentieth century Norway greatly expanded its territory: in 1923 Norway gained the right to govern Spitsbergen in the extreme north; in 1939, following a long international political struggle, it was awarded sovereignty over Bouvet Island in the extreme global south, greatly enlarging Norwegian territory (Chaturvedi 1996). While such territorial expansion has not usually been approached in colonial terms, probably because such domains lacked human inhabitants, the country's ambitions were *not* restricted to the globe's polar and unpopulated regions. A crucial event in this regard was the post–First World War negotiations at Versailles in 1919, during which the Norwegian chief delegate Fritz Wedel Jarlsberg launched the claim that Germany should recompense Norway's war-induced loss of tonnage by conceding one of its colonies to Norway (Bomann-Larsen 2008). His autobiography confirms such a desire for African colonial territory when recollecting having thought the following prior to the negotiations (Wedel Jarlsberg 1932: 368): 'Perhaps it would not be impossible, I thought, to obtain a colony somewhere in the overseas territories, to which we could direct the Norwegian emigrants and where we could produce goods that our Northern climate does not allow us to do but which are so vital for our industry and our agriculture.'[3] Wedel Jarlsberg also went further and concretized his plans for a Norwegian sovereign and institutional framework related to this proposed colonial (and territorial) expansion (Wedel Jarlsberg 1932: 370–71):

> I have to honestly say that I could not have thought otherwise than see the idea as sound and realisable by a Norwegian East African (or other) Chartered Company under Norwegian sovereignty. A small country [a colony] would in this way not annoy England and other major powers and beyond the goods we could gain access to, and the market for our own products that we would then control, a good colony could have offered new fields for that energy and sense of adventure which characterise our people, and which would in this way benefit Norway rather than be scattered all around the world.[4]

This most probably referred to Tanganyika (now Tanzania), but despite receiving some support from British negotiators, Wedel Jarlsberg's claim was not recognized (1932: 370–71). Of course, both Norway's postcolonial relation to the African world and its politics of representation would have been very differently configured had this large-scale colonial ambition been realized.

These examples – the first two directed from the colony towards Stockholm and the last from high levels of Norwegian politics towards the European colonial powers – are suggestive of how Nordic people were not exempt from the general European-wide nationalist discourse and the political ambitions of colonial aspiration.[5] These instances are instructive, however, as much research on Nordic relations with the wider world has hitherto been dominated by studies of the substantial out-migration and return migration, particularly in the period from the early 1800s to the 1930s. A major theme in this vast literature is the examination of migratory relations between, for instance, Norway and the Americas – especially the United States (Gjerde 2001; Norman and Runblom 1988) but also Latin America (Runblom 1987).

What this Nordic historiographic tradition eclipses, though, is the rich history of connectivities that transcend those to be made between, for instance, Norway and the Americas. As two contributors to this book have already asserted in a Norwegian anthology (Kjerland and Bang 2002), significant multifaceted Norwegian-African ties were forged during the colonial era, thus predating the era of aid and development that has since the 1950s conditioned these relations (Ruud and Kjerland 2003; Simensen 2003).[6] Importantly, there was also relatively substantial Norwegian migration to and links with Australia – a route that also comprised a point of entry into the world of Oceania (see Møller 1986). Another mainstay of historical research has been the exploration of shipping and seafaring as a means of documenting Norway's past 'oceanic presence' – as, notably, several contributors (Hviding, Nygaard and Børresen) to this anthology also argue. Recent studies analyse shipping and seafaring as expressions of Norway's long-standing history of providing regulatory frameworks catering for globalized business and labour (see Brautaset and Tenold 2008).

This anthology, then, explores the idea that connections between Norway and the wider world exceed both American and Australian geographical orientations and the thematically focused extant research on migration, development and seafaring. This kind of expansion is also reflected in recent historical research in the Nordic countries to the extent that one may talk of an emerging literature on colonialism (see also Kuparinen 1991; Wohlgemut 2002). Admittedly, this relatively new literature is varied in terms of scope and periods covered, some of it bordering on the counterfactual in dealing with and envisioning the potentialities of imperial aspirations in the precolonial past.[7] A case in point is Már Jónsson's (2009) work addressing how Denmark-Norway under King Christian IV in the 1620s emerged as an imperial force in the scramble to control whaling and fishing rights in the northern waters along the coast of what is today Norway, around Spitsbergen and Greenland. As Már Jonssón asserts, '[a]lthough nothing came out of any of these projects they could have been the beginning of a promising colonial empire' (2009: 22).

Why is this early imperial or, perhaps, protocolonial aspiration important? Primarily because colonial ventures should no longer be seen to pertain solely to successful colonizing powers such as England, France, Belgium, Portugal, Germany, Spain and the Netherlands, as mainstream contributions to the study of colonialism often suggest (see Wesseling 2004). Rather, the European colonial impetus was formed and emerged across a range of national, transnational and colonial settings – as both the Swede Knutson in Cameroon and the Norwegian delegate Wedel Jarlsberg contrastively testify to. Let us, however, briefly look at some of the possessions and ventures that *did* materialize from these Nordic ambitions – beginning with Denmark.

The Danish Gold Coast (today part of Ghana) is a key reference point, as it was here that Denmark-Norway (1521–1814) (and, later, Denmark) maintained outposts and some measure of control between 1659 and 1850 (see Nørregaard 1968 for a general history). Building and maintaining more than thirty forts, lodges and stations, the Danes shipped an estimated total of eighty thousand to one hundred thousand slaves into the triangular trade system between 1671 and 1802 (DeCorse 1993; Hernæs 1995). They also established coffee plantations and traded Akan gold for European commodities (see also Gøbel 2011).[8] The Danish East India Company was founded in 1616, inspired by the more famous Dutch East Indies Company (Jónsson 2009; see also Feldbaek 1978). However, after having largely reflected early European expansion, from the mid-1800s Danish overseas possessions were gradually discontinued: the trade stations in Tranquebar (today Tharambambadi in Tamil Nadu, India) and Frederiksnagore (today Serampore on the Hooghly River, West Bengal, India) went to the British in 1845 and Gold Coast possessions in 1850; the Frederik Islands (today the Nicobar Islands) in the eastern Indian Ocean were formally occupied by the British in 1869, and the Danish-controlled West Indian possessions (later the Virgin Islands) were sold to the United States in 1917 (DeCorse 1993).[9] Much recent Danish work, such as Jørgensen (2011), retains a critical and noncelebratory approach to the Danish colonial past, while also bringing forth refreshing perspectives on colonial and postcolonial entrepreneurship and hybridity in former Danish colonial spaces (see also Weiss 2013).[10]

Perhaps as already indicated by Knutson's late nineteenth-century aspirations in Cameroon, the impetus under the Swedish crown to acquire colonies and establishments overseas are as long-standing as those of Denmark (Schnakenbourg 2013). A well-known case in point is Carl Bernard Wadström (1746–99), who was a key advocate for Sweden establishing a colony in (what is now called) Sierra Leone, while simultaneously advocating abolition (Kent 2008). These aspirations did not materialize, however, although he set sail towards West Africa with a mixture of commercial and abolitional interests that were strongly and repeatedly voiced in writing (see Wadström [1794–95] 1968). Primarily his ventures show that Swedish aspirations did not reach the same scale as those of Denmark, despite attempts at establishing a colonial presence in the same location as the Danes: the Swedish Gold Coast consisted of a fortress in Cabo Corso, which was erected in 1649. Failing to fortify, secure and invest in the fortress, it was gradually lost to Dutch interests in 1663 (Jónsson 2009: 23; Thomasson 2014). Around one hundred years later (in 1785), following negotiations with France,

Sweden assumed sovereignty over the islands of Saint Barthélemy and Saint Martin, returning the islands to France less than a century later, in 1878 (Kent 2008). As emphasized in recent work on the business of slave labour and the treatment of slaves on Saint Barthélemy, the Swedish colonial overlords ruled in the same violent and brutal way as those of the larger colonial powers, such as the French.[11] While research on long-standing Swedish business interests outside Europe and North America exists (see, e.g., Nováky 1999), similar studies have delved into the politics of establishment (e.g., vis-à-vis apartheid South Africa) rather than colonial history (see Brundenius, Hermele and Palmberg 1980). Thus, Swedish colonial history remains somewhat underresearched, although a number of recent scholars are now addressing this issue (for an overview, see Fur 2013).

Compared to Sweden and Denmark, there is scant literature on Finnish colonial ventures in Africa in particular (see Hokkanen and Särkkä 2008; Särkkä 2007 for overviews). However, this emerging literature suggests that in the case of southern Africa, for instance, South Africa and Namibia were particularly important localities: the former was a key destination for sawn timber, and exports to the growing mining sector approached 1.5 per cent of all Finnish exports between 1925 and 1939 (Koponen and Heinonen 2002). Being part of a wider Nordic pattern of emigration to South Africa, it is estimated that around a thousand Finns migrated to work mainly in the mines prior to the First World War (Koponen and Heinonen 2002; see also Winquist 1978), although more recent research alleges that the numbers are higher (Särkkä 2012). Similar to Norway and Sweden, outright colonial aspirations also permeated parts of the political establishment. For instance, shortly after Finland's independence – and reflecting a long-term missionary history – '[a] delegation consisting of local notables turned up in the office of the State Secretary of the newly independent Finland, K. G. Idman, and proposed that Ovamboland [now Namibia] should be made a Finnish colony' (Koponen and Heinonen 2002: 20). While such ambitions for gaining colonial territory were dismissed, the example shows how the colonial mentality affected this country during this period. Moreover, as with their Nordic brethren, it is estimated that around 150 Finns worked (Koponen and Heinonen 2002: 20) in colonized Congo under King Leopold II; Nordic participation is estimated at around two thousand people from 1880 to 1930 – many were Norwegian (Godøy 2010; Tygesen and Wæhle 2007: 6; Wæhle, chapter 14).

Generally, historical and anthropological analyses of Norway's dealings with the colonial or postcolonial world have avoided the long-term critical scrutiny to which the major colonizing powers have been subjected. One may make the argument that a scrutiny (or celebration) of compliance with the colonial powers has instead emerged in the form of journalistic accounts, travel writing or novels. A case in point is Yngvar Ustvedt's (2001) work on Norwegian officers serving under Danish-Norwegian colonial rule in Bengal and the Coromandel Coast in India from the early 1600s until the demise of the country's control in the early 1800s. Popular writing in the form of travelogues has also been a central discursive site for the production and exploration of the wild and the primitive, the colonial and the imperial, and Norwegian heroic or barbaric exploits, depending on the narrative. Such accounts by Norwegian authors flooded the book market and newspapers in the interwar period (Kjerland 2010: 180ff.), and this literary tradition, steeped in popular culture, has arguably influenced both Norwegian development policies and general discourses about the world outside Europe and North America (Bangstad and Bertelsen 2010; Eide 2010; Tvedt 1990). However, as Landau (2002: 4) argues in an incisive analysis of colonialist fantasies of barbaric Africans and head-hunting savages from Melanesia, the Norwegian literary genre concerned with the production of colony-prone imagery was generally in keeping with contemporary European and American literary and political developments.

This book brings together both the impact of such imaginaries and how Norwegians were practically involved – an involvement that underlines the importance of studying colonialism beyond the established (and sometimes somewhat stale) discourses that pertain to the former colonizing countries. By analysing the noncolonial colonials – mainly through empirical material – this book acknowledges the relevance of both the following somewhat adversely positioned approaches to colonialism.

First, we recognize the need to map the structural elements of colonialism and its imperial infrastructure as established by Wallersteinian approaches. Recognition of systemic dimensions is necessary to make sense of both the crucial shipping component of the Norwegian colonial engagement as well as the scale of business ventures: between 1860 and 1914 world trade quadrupled and the Norwegian tonnage grew almost fivefold, from 298,000 tons in 1850 to 1,526,000 tons in 1880 (Nygaard, chapter 1). As early as 1879 some 544 Norwegian ships freighted 30 per cent of all North American wheat to ports across the world (Vigeland 1943: 99–100, 140ff.). What these figures indicate is that Norwegian colonialism was integral to the country's significant role in the global shipping systems and maritime trade upon which colonial orders were premised.

Second, and based on Norwegians' diverse navigation within, without and on the fringes of such orders, this book also recognizes colonialism's cracks, ambiguities, negotiations and multisemics as they have been developed especially forcefully in Stolerian and Cooperian approaches. As Stoler (2006: 137–38) notes, empire and, by extension, colonial orders as imperial systems may also be seen as unsteady and as 'supremely mobile polities of dislocation, dependent not on stable populations so much as on highly moveable ones, on systemic recruitments and "transfers" of colonial agents, on native military, on a redistribution of peoples and resources, on relocations and dispersions, on contiguous and overseas territories'.[12] Noncolonial colonials were often ambiguous figures who negotiated between adversely positioned colonial orders, as well as directly fomenting (or being integral to) imperial or colonial politics. This is evident in Rio's chapter 10 on Hawai'i, Jonassen's chapter 9 on the Cook Islands and Eidsvik's chapter 3 on South Africa, where in all of these contexts identity politics and strategic self-representation were integral to Norwegian entrepreneurs' navigation across the political, social and cultural colonial (and postcolonial) landscape.

While recognizing the salience of both these positions, the problem remains of how to properly represent and analyse such a Norwegian presence within flows and formations, flux and system. The question of representation, of course, is not unique to analyses of Norwegian colonialism, but points to enduring concerns about colonial and imperial historiography and its politics.

Visual Economy, Imperial Nostalgia and the Problem of Colonial Representation

The representation of the colonial era remains, perhaps unsurprisingly, a contentious issue – and not only in academic circles. An example is the reception of Niall Ferguson's *Civilization: The West and the Rest* (2011a). Ferguson claims that he attempts to explain the ascendancy of 'Western civilization', which is 'quite simply, the pre-eminent historical phenomenon of the second half of the second millennium after Christ' (2011a: 18). Further, and with much rhetorical pomp, Ferguson asserts that Western civilization (and our continued faith in it) provides the global and universal recipe for the continued dominance of the West against impeding and emergent sovereign powers.

Advocating such a staunchly Churchill-quoting position in 2011 is provocative, and Pankaj Mishra (2011) in a scathing critique in the *London Review of Books* demonstrates the links between Ferguson's position and a long line of imperial apologists and racialized analyses, from Stoddard's *The Rising Tide of Color against White World Supremacy* ([1920]

1924) to Huntington's only slightly less alarmist *The Clash of Civiliza-tions and the Remaking of World Order* (1996). Mishra perceived Ferguson's book as being not only neoimperialist in its call for a continuation of Western dominance but also bordering dangerously close to revisionism through a highly selective representation of colonial exploits and violence. This critique engendered a heated exchange between the two, including Ferguson's call (2011b) for a public apology from both Mishra and the *London Review of Books*.

The Mishra-Ferguson skirmish exemplifies the tensions internal to colonial and imperial studies and its inescapable politics of representation. It also elucidates a more general feature of colonial studies, namely, the opposition between those who approach it as an unearthing of the past largely devoid of a politics of representation bearing upon the present, and those who address colonialism as necessarily unended, in that struggles to renegotiate, undo and redress the effects and orders of colonialism are internal to any understanding of the phenomenon (see also Dirks 1992; Knauft 1999; Stoler 2013; Thomas 1994). Mishra's critique of Ferguson's book further points to disciplinary connections with colonialism transcending disagreements over a politics of representation: as Pels (1997) has asserted, both history and anthropology may be framed within and seen as inseparable from (the study of) colonialism. Indeed, one may argue, as Pels does, that particularly anthropology was not merely born within the context of colonialism – that is, by producing ethnographies of colonized subjects ('natives') – it was also directly involved in statecraft by comprising/producing a form of governmentality as 'an academic offshoot of a set of universal technologies of domination ... that developed in a dialectic between colonial and European states' (Pels 1997: 165; see also Stocking 1991).[13]

An example of this is the way in which Australian anthropology was complicit in producing imaginaries serving colonial purposes, which ultimately comprised a colonial form of science. In a thorough analysis of the anthropological journal *South Pacific*'s volumes from 1946 to 1959, Westermark argues that it 'served as a vehicle for formulating and promoting a science of colonialism, a set of concepts and examples that would enable the Australians to provide a rational and, hopefully, humane system that could be defended against its critics abroad' (2001: 160). Thus, although often exhibiting an ambiguous attitude towards the colonial enterprise, anthropology's input into the journal was part of the discipline's wider contribution to the translocal development of 'a coherent body of colonial studies from Africa to Papua New Guinea' (Westermark 2001: 175). Such general arguments about the colonially complicit nature of anthropological knowledge may easily be expanded to encompass terminologies for and categories of colonized people. This is, of course, a main concern in some postcolonial studies by, for instance, Chakrabarty (2000), Prakash (1995) and Spivak (1999) – as well being the main thrust of Said's *Orientalism* (1978).[14]

Representational history is not confined to the textual domain, however; in a recent study (Landau and Kaspin 2002) of the complex relations between imagery and empire in colonial and postcolonial Africa, Kaspin (2002) usefully draws on Roland Barthes's work on visual myths to analyse the circulation of colonial imagery – the traffic of postcards, the production of colonial photographic memorabilia, or the postcolonial reproduction and reenactment of colonial-style photographic fashion (see also Allina 1997). Kaspin draws a key insight from Barthes regarding how such circulation produced visual myths that 'naturalize[d] imperial interests in the consciousness of the masses' (Kaspin 2002: 321). Similarly, and borrowing Poole's term 'visual economies', Banks and Vokes (2010: 338ff.) see photographs of Melanesians and Polynesians, Africans and Aboriginals as comprising a visual currency in which single or multiple images move in and out of archival, mass media or research contexts.

Entanglements between a broader politics of representation and colonial rule have been consistently argued for in the cases of both Oceania and Africa. For example, Thomas has shown that in colonial Fiji and other Oceania locations photographs and visual imagery were fundamental to the production of the colonial order and its politics of subjugation (1994: 33–65). Keesing (1986: 167), on the other hand, demonstrates how the intensification of labour recruitment for the emerging plantation economy in Melanesia from the 1860s onwards drew on and produced specific ethnic categories (e.g., Man Tanna and Malaita Man) that were imbued with particular capacities and, thereby, afforded certain roles and spaces within the wider colonial order (see also Reinhard 2011: 185–86). For the sub-Saharan African context, Vail ([1989] 1991) has also shown how 'tribes', visually typologized in photographs, were construed to differently embody particular weaknesses and strengths that needed to be recognized in order to optimize changing and diverse colonial economic needs.

Mirroring the sites of production and the networks of labour extraction – as Keesing (1986) shows – there were also other loci for the generation of image, namely, popular literature. As Douglas (1999) demonstrates for the imagery of the South Seas, the media of literature and photography were crucial to the creation, perpetuation and distribution of racialized stereotypes that served imperial educational purposes during the colonial era. Importantly, the presence of such imagery *beyond* formal colonial domains – as the photographs reproduced in this anthology illustrate – testify to the slippage and instability of the visual tropes and myths of colonial photography (Vokes 2010, 2012).

The critique above implies that this anthology's exploration of the Norwegian colonial encounter needs to be sensitive to the vast colonial and imperial history of hierarchical and, often, racialized representation. For us, this has meant that while many chapters follow personal biographies of traders, entrepreneurs, sailors, plantation owners and jacks-of-all-trades, the contributions strive to contextualize the use of contemporary sources and imagery in terms of their origins and visual-political economies of representation. The contributors to this anthology have chosen to do so by reframing rather than reproducing these images and the contexts of their generation in order both to underscore the trans-European visual economy of colonial desire and memory and to highlight the somewhat ambiguous, in-between role of the Norwegian entrepreneurs we depict (see also Stoler [2002] 2010: 162–203). Thus, rather than including photographs as a retreat from oral history, as one could argue (see Allina 1997: 9), or narratively extending the colonially derived rhetoric of othering, we have chosen to include carefully selected photographs as well as maps in attempting to situate Norwegian colonial entrepreneurship within broader imperial and colonial political desires (for a similar argument about Denmark, Sweden and Finland, see Naum and Nordin 2013).[15] However, two clarifications are in order.

First, adding complexity to the histories of the colonial orders that Norwegians navigated should by no means be interpreted as somehow apologetic towards the (enduring) violence of the colonial legacy. Instead, accounts of Norwegian entrepreneurship in Africa and Oceania in the period investigated here (and, in some contributions, beyond) point to the brute, open-ended and multisemic reality of colonial orders in which, as has been argued (Bertelsen, chapter 12; Hansen and Stepputat 2001, 2005), colonial sovereignty and imperial control were a mirage, or intensely contested (Benton 2010; Boone 2003; Butlin 2009; Stoler 2006; Young 1994).[16] Further, studies such as those by Ittmann, Cordell and Maddo (2011) and Stoler (2009) show how cadastral and demographic knowledge in colonial settings failed to correspond, or only partially corresponded, to sociological reality, thereby testifying to the limits, paradoxes and epistemic disorientations of colonial power. Endorsing the general thrust of such perspectives, we assert that any analysis of the nascent or formative era of the colonial orders in question must nevertheless take into account the scrambles of other imperial forces, such as those of capitalist companies and minor countries.

Second, the biographical sketches are not to be taken as simplistic celebrations of individual achievement, but should be read as shedding light on the intricacies and heterogeneity of colonial formations. Neither should such individual accounts of entrepreneurship, trade and adventure within the wider colonial framework be seen as what Rosaldo (1989) calls 'imperialist nostalgia' – the particular (and paradoxical) form of remembrance that characterizes the colonial venture in which the colonizer longs for and is nostalgic towards that which is destroyed by the colonial system itself.[17] For Oceania, the diverse instances in which colonial realities are invoked, recreated, referred to and longed for are integral to current politics and popular imaginaries (see Eriksen 2013; Neumann 1993). As Edmond (1997) has established – based on extensive studies of representations of the South Pacific from the 1700s well into the 1900s – the rich tradition in imagining and representing this part of the world in differing (and differentiating) terms has itself rich, multifaceted and largely colonial origins (see also Borofsky 2000; Hviding, chapters 7 and 8; Lamb, Smith and Thomas 2000). For Africa, nostalgia's discursive force as well as its impact on political developments and national and collective memory has long been recognized (Werbner 1998: 1; see also Bissell 2005; Englund 1996; Mazrui 2000; McNeil 2011).

Integral to Africa's and Oceania's memoropolitical developments, there is also an increasing rhetoric of ruination, disintegration and collapse relating to a proposed decline of the West – a tendency that lends itself to colonial and imperial nostalgia (Stoler 2008, 2013); arguably, Ferguson's work is part of this trend. The focus on ruination and on nostalgia for orders past is often tied to what amounts to a fetishization of the physical, desolate and disintegrated places of the ancien régime (Hell and Schönle 2010). Cooper (2002) rightly cautions against nostalgia for the physical remnants, as well as the thrust of some postcolonial studies, which tend to flatten or compress colonial time-space and thereby to 'unmoor' the relations among colonial policy and administration and postcolonial realities.

By pursuing individual biographies, focusing on sites and flows and, generally, framing these within specific colonial orders, we attempt in this book to distance ourselves from imperial nostalgia, the romance of ruination or the undue 'unmooring' of some postcolonial approaches. Following Cooper, we aim to 'remoor' the Norwegian colonial presence rather than navigating into problematic representational backwaters of imperial nostalgia or colonial visuals.

Nationalizing and Denationalizing Colonial History

The title of this anthology could easily lend itself to the criticism of it being yet another retreat into methodological nationalism. Indeed, the pitfalls of a national framework are several. As Ebert (2008) points out, for example, to designate the various European traders in West and Central Africa in the 1500s and 1600s as 'Portuguese' or 'Dutch', or to subsume them under national economies, is a historical misconstruction made post hoc: '[T]his reading back of a national maritime tradition does not accurately describe the nature of merchant networks in the sixteenth century and their involvement on the West African coast' (Ebert 2008: 55). Ebert is undoubtedly correct in underlining the broader methodological, historiographic, analytic and ideological problems inherent in retrospectively allocating national characteristics to merchants and their network – a challenge identified in European imperial and colonial history writing generally (see Wolf [1982] 1997).[18]

However, once we move into the middle of the 1800s and the 1900s, and given the consolidation of the Nordic nation-states, to these editors it makes sense at least initially to designate different traders by the broad national terms presented in this introduction. The problems inherent in assuming Norwegian-ness, however, and whether the lives and biographies dealt with in this anthology may be categorized as 'Norwegian', are issues that several of the contributions address explicitly. An obvious empirical reason is the predominantly transnational character of business and trade within colonial orders, where long stays or journeys often meant ties with Norway were weakened or transfigured. Several of those whose lives are pursued here – as well as their family members and offspring – left Norway never to return: while they became more or less fully integrated into the colonial (and later, postcolonial) settings, the Norwegian aspects receded to become mere parts of identity projects or their politics. Chapters 3, 8 and 9, by Eidsvik, Hviding and Jonassen, respectively, are cases in point here. Our choice, nevertheless, to retain the nationalist gloss of 'Norwegian' must be read as another analytic tool, neither reflecting a celebratory rhetoric of newfound Norwegian colonialists in Africa and Oceania nor being a recourse to a simplified methodological nationalism. Thus, the contributors pursue this motley group of Norwegians in order to shed light on a category of colonial actors who are often excluded from colonial history writing – often produced in the colonial and imperial metropoles of old – as well as to complicate Norwegian historiography.

There is an additional problem, however: as Hansen and Stepputat (2001), Ong (2006) and others have noted, the colonies were diverse, changing and contested domains with shifting borders, ephemeral governance structures and practices characterized by flexibility in terms of personnel and resources – past realities that produce a present multipolar postcolonial order (see also Grosfoguel 2002). Given this complexity, Stoler points out that terms such as 'colonial legacy' and 'colonial vestige' work as 'placeholders for processes that unite disparate forces under one term and gloss too easily over dispersed effects' (2008: 196). Furthermore, Stoler argues, 'terms like *metropole* and *colony, core* and *periphery* presume to make clear what is not' (Stoler 2008: 200), in a clear reference to Andre Gunder Frank's terms 'metropole' and 'satellite' (Frank 1966; Frank and Gills 2000), and to Wallerstein's notions of 'core' and 'periphery' (Wallerstein 2004).

As noted above, the book's chapters often seek a middle road between Wallersteinian systemic approaches to colonialism and the muddled landscape of contestation, negotiation and multiplicity opened up by Stoler and associates. Our approach reflects to some degree Thomas's (2010: 297; see also 1991) view of imperial formation in Oceania, which, using what Stoler would call 'colonial heterogenics', made the case for rethinking colonialism and empire: 'Empire involved, and involves, straightforward matters that we know – the appropriation of lands, the command of labour, the killings of those who resist. But it was always, at the same time, and equally profound, something other than what we know, a more elusive matter of imagination, and activity inspired by imagination.' In charting this middle ground between imagination and entrepreneurship, structure and empire, our anthology does not invoke the sense that the colonial era somehow constitutes a progressive alternative frame of mind when confronting postcolonial presences. Rather, the focus on Norwegians negotiating colonial orders subscribes to the importance of different forms of entrepreneurship and negotiation – 'imagination' in Thomas's parlance – in colonial orders.

This book's examination of colonial entrepreneurship and capital through a Norwegian lens seems curiously timely on a planet that is not only multipolar but where the very character of statehood is arguably changing towards a more neoliberal or corporate form that valorizes and empowers venture capital, entrepreneurship and large-scale companies (Kapferer and Bertelsen 2009). Nowhere are these emerging twenty-first-century world order challenges to Westphalian notions of the nation-state more evident than in postcolonial orders such as Oceania and Africa. Here, postcolonial processes articulate key traits of past colonial orders, which include the impact of transnational social and religious movements (Eriksen 2013), the political reconfiguring of national sovereignty faced with Chinese intervention in both Africa

(Raine 2009) and Oceania (Wesley-Smith and Porter 2010) and, lastly, an increase of illegal, paralegal and covert/shadowy economic, territorial and political interventions in relation to illegal drugs, weapons and terrorism (see Nordstrom 2004; Roitman 2006). While Africa has been cast as a laboratory of the future pointing towards postnational and, perhaps, postsovereign possibilities (Comaroff and Comaroff 2012; see also Santos and Meneses 2010) – and a similar argument has been made for postcolonial Oceanic contexts (Hviding and Rio 2011) – there is a considerable amount to be learnt from the formative and late colonial period in terms of nonmainstream colonial engagements – the Norwegian noncolonial colonials being a case in point. Specifically, this concerns how these agents navigated the historical moment of flux, violence and political and social upheaval that characterized colonialism.

Across a postcolonial landscape dominated by current political and economic investments in and territorialization of land and resources by Asian, European and American interests, there is an argument to be made for unearthing Norwegian colonial microhistories (and some mesohistories) from the archives. Stoler argues that archives are 're-cords of uncertainty and doubt in how people imagined they could and might make the rubrics of rule correspond to a changing imperial world' (2009: 4). This resonates with two key aspects of this volume. The first is the argument that is expounded in some detail above about the unfinished, emergent and continually contested nature of colonial rule in all the locations – as well as the sea and river routes between them – presented in this volume. Second, however, attention is given to precisely such archival material, which often discloses the personal, the intimate and the desperate in letters and other texts. While one may argue that these microhistories reflect moments of epistemic murk, they nevertheless reveal traces of the opportunities afforded by the encompassing, structural and infrastructural dynamics of colonial rule.

The editors maintain that the histories and complexities of Norwegian enterprises and entrepreneurs constitute a novel take on current debates and understandings of colonial orders and their agents and navigators. Works such as this anthology aim to counter simplifying (and imperialist) tendencies in global history writing: the writing of microhistories of nonconventional colonialists helps make the national histories more complex and, thereby, lend themselves less to the arc of grand narratives. As Falola points out in defence of the continued developing and teaching of national history in African contexts, 'National histories of Africa represent one of the powerful counters to the attempt to provincialize history. The very first task of writing and teaching national history in Africa is to understand the agenda of global history'

(2006: 169). Such a call for a reconnection, reframing and reconceptualization of national and global history resonates with analysing general Norwegian aspects of the colonial era and understanding Norwegians as noncolonial colonials.[19] In a minor way, then, this anthology contributes to such a reframing by also asserting the role of Norwegians as navigating across Oceanic and African colonial orders – sometimes while also being minor and major agents in establishing such orders. This means, as Stoler and McGranahan (2007: 2–3) remind us, in a reflection on *who* the colonial was, that 'different notions of a colony and who its members were coexisted, were contested, and were actively compared'. If their analysis is right, and we believe it is, then looking at the noncolonial colonials as people that entered, frequently thrived and sometimes also succumbed to the dangers in these settings presents an alternative view of these diverse colonial orders. So, more concretely, what did the Norwegian agents do?

The Anthology and Its Chapters

In this anthology, different forms of transactions assume importance for understanding very different forms of Norwegian colonial intervention in Oceania: trading around the Solomon Islands (Hviding, chapter 7 and 8), the establishment of a plantation on Hawai'i (Rio, chapter 10) and the long-term effects of a Norwegian presence in terms of complex and productive identity dynamics (Jonassen, chapter 9). Rio's exploration of the emergence of the role of Valdemar Knudsen (1820–98) and the construction of a sugar plantation on Hawai'i is, of course, part of a broader history of plantation economies in Melanesia and Oceania more generally. As Keesing has argued (1986: 164), the 'waterborne' establishment of varieties of pidgin – through seafaring, trade and, eventually, plantations – had diffused a number of people across the Pacific who spoke pidgin and who 'acted as crucial agents and brokers of language and culture when plantation recruiters began in the 1860s'. When the plantation system developed from the 1860s onwards, the competition intensified for recruitment among German, French and British colonial powers (see also Butlin 2009: 543–56). It is also within this budding colonial development that the emergence of trade may be framed – a *formation* in the making into which Norwegian entrepreneurs also entered and became engaged.

Thomas asserts in a reassessment of history writing about the Pacific that 'colonial transactions and representations, conceived in the broadest sense, pervade the subject matter of Pacific history' (1990: 141; see

also 1997: 36ff.). He goes on to note that '[e]arly "traffic" between Islanders and European vessels, and the later, more regularised trade in
such things as axes, tobacco and muskets for sandalwood and bêche-
de-mer, constitute significant phases in the economic history of the
region', and that a key task for historians and anthropologists is to
understand what both objects and traders became in indigenous understandings (1990: 147; see also Thomas 1991). A somewhat different
context – characterized by the ephemerality and negotiation of flow – is
the maritime landscape across which Edvard Hviding's motley crew of
traders navigated. Exploiting the absence of a clear sovereign power
and skilfully navigating complex social and political local orders, the
Norwegian entrepreneurs in Hviding's two chapters demonstrate the
spaces opened up to such noncolonial colonials and their unique histories in, especially, the Solomon Islands. Similarly, Jonassen explores
his own Norwegian ancestry through the recounting of the history of
Norwegian captain Reinert G. Jonassen and his entrepreneurship in
terms of trade, copra and orange plantations in the Cook Islands. The
author intriguingly weaves together his personal biography with that
of the Norwegian seafaring trader, entrepreneur, musician and local
diplomat – providing a colonial and postcolonial Norwegian and Cook
Island microhistory.

African historiography on colonialism is largely covered in numerous broader historical works than is the case for Oceania. This includes
tomes of history (see, e.g., UNESCO 1981–1993), biographies of its key
historical actors (see Gates and Akyeampong 2012), overviews of studies of Africa (see Zeleza 2006, 2007) and vast numbers of country-based
colonial histories. Although there is thus less need to detail these developments, this is not to say that the contributions here fail to relate
to debates on colonialism in Africa. In particular, this refers to the research on what one may see as colonialism of minor countries, as well
as the entrepreneurship of noncolonial colonials. A case in point here is
the work cataloguing the quite numerous Swiss colonial presences in
Mozambique (Linder 2001). By providing an overview of the important
roles and functions that the Swiss undertook during different phases of
colonialism (and under the first decades of Mozambican independence
after 1975), the work provides a corrective to more general works on
colonialism in Mozambique that focus mainly on the major colonizing powers (cf. Newitt 1995). More generally, Linder's approach to the
colonial era in Africa, as an open space that afforded opportunities, is
in line with the present argument about the colonial order's flow and
formation. Similarly, the African contributions in our anthology are directed towards carving out and delineating these spaces through an

examination of business networks, personal biographies and analyses of colonial systems.

An illuminating case here is Kjerland's chapter 13 about Norwegian investments and, particularly, managers settling on Norwegian-owned farms in Kenya, following in the footsteps of other European farmers. Through the letters they wrote, we learn of the everyday life, hardships and challenges faced – including those encountered on a personal level. Coupled with an analysis of one Norwegian company (Azania Ltd, later Krag Estates Ltd), this chapter illustrates key aspects of entrepreneurship in colonial Africa. Kjerland's work is in some ways mirrored by Bang's account (chapter 4) of the Norway-East Africa Trading Company (NEAT) in Zanzibar between 1895 and 1920 – a company that mainly imported timber and wood directly from Norway. Bang shows that one of the main agents in NEAT, a Norwegian entrepreneur nicknamed Zanzibar-Olsen, was integral to European colonial expansion in East Africa and, significantly, to the telecommunications revolution in telegrams and railways.

A contrastive account of entrepreneurship is presented by Eidsvik (chapter 3), who focuses on the emergence and growth of a Norwegian-origin family dynasty in Knysna, South Africa. Being involved in a number of trades, as well as politics and governance in South Africa in general, the Thesen family is a key reference point for any history of the timber trade, as well as in relation to the broader history of the Knysna region. Mirroring, to some extent, the grandeur and scale of the Knysna enterprise, chapters 11 and 12 by Reiersen and Bertelsen, respectively, in different ways explore the vast plantation of Madal in colonial Mozambique from the early 1900s onwards. Reiersen provides a detailed analysis of the entrepreneurship of Norwegian businessman, international strategist and architect Christian Thams, focusing on his African investments in general and the dynamics of how Madal came to be in Norwegian hands. Bertelsen, meanwhile, seeks to show how Norwegian investments in and control over Madal were integral to Portuguese colonial politics. He argues that it was a form of business in which near-sovereign control was exercised on the part of companies like Madal; its extraction of monetary and other resources through taxation (in money or goods) from African subjects, for instance, assumed great proportions – and these resources were freighted out of colonial Africa on Norwegian ships.

The anthology provides two starkly contrasting snapshots of Norwegian maritime history in Oceania and South Africa – in Hviding's chapter 7 on Norwegian shipping in Oceania and in Nygaard's chapter 1 on the emergence of the Norwegian sailing ship business, with a particular focus on South Africa. Both chapters offer relatively short introductions to key (but divergent) aspects of the Norwegian navigation of colonial waters in Africa and Oceania. Hviding, in his introductory chapter to Norwegian seafaring in Oceania (chapter 7), highlights the copra trade and its rogue character. Building his introduction to Norwegian shipping, seafaring and trade around the histories of a range of ships – from the 1840s until well into the twentieth century – his account revolves around the adaptability and practical nature of the relatively numerous Norwegians (compared to similarly sized shipping states) that chose to settle in the area. Contrasting Oceania with other parts of the world with a Norwegian maritime presence, shipping activities in Oceania, as Hviding shows us, was in the main small-scale and was often comprised of the individually based enterprises that followed in colonialism's wake. Contrary to what one might assume, Norwegians adapted very well to an early colonial (and in some cases nearly pre-colonial) island context, where warfare between groups and violence against merchants was not unknown.

Nygaard, on the other hand, provides an analysis of a key maritime contrast between the systems of liner shipping and that of the tramp trade by comparing Swedish and Norwegian shipping to South Africa from around 1850 until World War I (chapter 1). Mainly concerned with the economic and structural aspects of such shipping, as well as its sheer volume, he demonstrates how Norwegian shipping in the period was able to exploit an economic niche in the market of sailing ships – based on their knowledge of ports and conditions in colonial southern and South Africa. Moreover, both texts exemplify the maritime aspect of Norwegian colonial entrepreneurship – a dimension clearly supported by, for instance, Børresen's and Sætra's chapters 5 and 2, respectively. The former is concerned with the extraction of resources in the form of whaling, and focuses on whaling stations and the use of African labourers on African soil, offshore and in Antarctic or near-Antarctic waters. Børresen shows – perhaps surprisingly – how dependent Norwegian whaling was on nonwhite labour in Africa and at Grytviken on the British sub-Antarctic island of South Georgia. Effectively showing the links among different aspects of colonialism – migration, pacification, missionary activities and whaling – he brings forth novel and interesting aspects of Norwegian whaling, international labour history and colonialism.

Sætra's chapter 2 follows up the maritime aspect and analyses and charts the global waters of the long-haul tramp trade by following the movements of Captain Haave, who came from a southern Norwegian town. Sætra shows how such tramp trade was dependent on a global system of ship chandlers, agents and other economic and structural aspects of shipping. By detailing the biography of Captain Haave and those close to him, Sætra, by way of empirical example, examines the key maritime aspect of Norwegian ventures in the colonial era.

While also concerned with Norwegian seamanship, Wæhle's chapter 14 takes the reader to the colonization of the vast area of the Congo and situates a few Norwegian traders of collections of ethnographic items (ethnographica) within this myth-ridden area of the colonial world. Through relating the story of King Leopold II's aspirations for expansion towards the Nile, and demonstrating anthropological and historical knowledge of the Congo, Wæhle relates the collection of ethnographica that his main characters – Norwegian sea captains Andersen, Martini and Schønberg, as well as engineers Scharffenberg and Johannesen – to both Leopold's plans and to the present-day existence of ethnographic collections in Norway and elsewhere.

As the individual chapters show, the ebbs and tides of the possibilities of colonial navigation varied greatly across time and space and, of course, in relation to particular areas in Africa and Oceania. These possibilities were also conditioned by political, social and economic developments in Norway. In chapter 6 Angell provides a minute analysis of Norway's political developments in relation to the 'consular question' during the last decades leading up to full Norwegian independence, showing a global business orientation towards the colonial world that was part of the political aspirations of this emerging nation-state, which gained full sovereignty from Sweden in 1905. By analysing key sources, documents and actors, Angell demonstrates that the process leading up to that year was part of a period of great expansionist and nationalist orientation – and one in which the separation issue had both a colonial and a commercial side.

The various chapters that now follow may be read as separate entities, as each is concerned with a particular aspect of Norwegian colonial entrepreneurship. The contributors explore specific situations from the point of view of a variety of disciplines, such as history, geography and anthropology. However, while each provides a unique narrative – as tentatively outlined in the sections above – the chapters also exemplify what has been argued in this introduction as characterizing the colonial order: diverse aspects of flow and formation. Seen from this perspective, each author has made a contribution here towards making more complex Norwegian understandings of their past, as well as adding to the important and ever-changing field of colonial studies and history in Africa and Oceania more generally.

Notes

In writing an overview of Nordic colonial history, the author has received valuable bibliographic and other input from coeditor Kirsten Alsaker Kjerland, as well as a number of colleagues, including Michael Barrett, Markku Hokkanen, Henrik Vigh, Timo Särkkä, Espen Wæhle and Erlend Eidsvik. Thanks are extended to all of these. This text also draws, in part, on Kjerland and Rio's (2009a) introductory chapter of an earlier Norwegian edition on the same theme (Kjerland and Rio 2009b).

 1. In one version of the world systems approach, Giovanni Arrighi sees imperialism and colonialism as integral to a globalized history of industrialization and capitalist transformation. In Arrighi's view, historical lineages of both the twentieth and the twenty-first century need to be firmly and systematically rooted in analyses of such historical forces of expansion and transformation (Arrighi 1978, 1994, 2007; see also Graeber 2011).
 2. Perhaps such openings for navigation, and aspects that point to the colonial order's fracture and 'in-betweenness', have also been recognized in the Marxian tradition. As Eric Wolf ([1982] 1997: xiii) notes, reflecting on the historical global impact of capitalism, 'the capitalist mode may thus be propelled forward by a unitary logic and yet simultaneously produce differentiation and heterogeneity through the great variability of its operations'. As capitalist expansion is integral to the colonial era examined in this volume, the case studies presented here may, following Wolf, illustrate the heterogeneity of colonial encounters, agents and dynamics.
 3. Translation by author.
 4. Translation by author.
 5. The Nordic desire for, relation to and vision of the colonial order has aptly been dubbed 'the Nordic colonial mind' (Palmberg 2009; see also Palmberg 2001 for a previous exploration of Nordic-African encounters).
 6. Cissé and Falahat (2011) provide an important alternative exploration of Africans in Norway; they tie their four hundred years of documented presence to broader European politics and the slave trade.
 7. Some scholarly work not covered here deals with what has been called the colonization by Norway, Sweden and Finland of their northern territories and the Saami and Finn indigenous peoples. See, for instance, Zorgdrager's (1997) analysis of Saami resistance against Norwegian colonialism in the far north in the mid-1800s, or Homme's anthology (1969), inspired by contemporary civil rights movements, which approaches Swedish, Norwegian and Finnish governmental politics as instances of neocolonial repression. More recently, Fur (2006; see also Kent 2008: 80–81; Naum and Nordin 2013) compares Swedish colonial activities in New Sweden, Delaware, from the 1660s onwards with the Swedish state's engagements in Lapland. These debates also frame the scant literature on Icelandic colonial ambitions as well as connectivities (but see Loftsdóttir 2010; Loftsdóttir and Pálsson 2013; Lucas and Parigoris 2013). However, going into these debates as well as postcolonial studies (see, e.g., Keskinen et al. 2009 or

Jensen 2010) remains outside the geographical and thematic scope of this anthology and its introduction.

8. Interestingly, a detailed work on archival sources for, among other ventures, Danish enterprises on the Gold Coast between 1671 and 1755 (Bro-Jørgensen and Rasch 1969: 187ff.) show that the Norwegian port of Bergen was a hub for the resources, letters and ships flowing between Africa, Europe and the Americas. For example, the Bergen-based Norwegian merchant Jørgen Thormølen participated in the slave trade with his ship *Cornelia,* which brought 103 slaves to Saint Thomas in 1673 (Nørregaard 1968: 87–88) – Thormølen also being the administrator of Saint Thomas in the period 1690–95 (Bro-Jørgensen 1966; see also Hernæs 1995). Further, Nørregaard notes (1969: 40; see also Gøbel 2011; P.H. Jensen 1983) that a substantial number of the sailors involved in the triangular slave trade between the Danish Gold Coast and the West Indies were Norwegian, and also Danish and Swedish.

9. Jónsson asserts (2009: 23; see also Jørgensen 2011) that Tranquebar (also spelt Trankebar) was the sole place where the Kingdom of Denmark (and Denmark-Norway, before that) had a colonial presence with some permanence – beyond Africa, that is, as seen in the kingdom's possessions and physical presence on the Gold Coast.

10. This contrasts with some of the older Danish history writing – especially the eight-volume series *Vore gamle tropekolonier* (Our Old Colonies in the Tropics), edited by Johannes Brøndsted ([1952–53] 1966–68), which smacks of imperial history writing. In the same vein, we could mention Rasch's 1967 book, *Dansk Ostindien, 1777–1945: Storhedstid og hensygnen* (Danish East India, 1777–1945: Era of Greatness and of Enfeeblement).

11. Thomasson (2013); see also Fur (2013) for an argument about Swedish colonial complicity in general.

12. In emphasizing the multisemic nature of colonialism, however, we refrain from engaging in the recurring colonial and imperial nostalgia that has been a feature of, for instance, French academic approaches to colonial history (see Cooper 2002). As Stoler (2011: 125) argues, there has been a tendency in recent French academic writing 'of endowing the colonial past with a politically active and progressive voice in the present'. This is not to say that there is no record of critical approaches to colonial studies in French academia and among public intellectuals – as Stoler recognizes. The immediate concerns of such postcolonial analysis were, however, forcefully prefigured by such early critical intellectuals and scholars as Frantz Fanon ([1961] 2004), Albert Memmi ([1957] 1991) and Aimé Césaire (1955) and, again, in the work of Georges Balandier ([1951] 1966; see also [1967] 1970: 158–85).

13. Wallerstein (2004: 8) identifies anthropology as being 'useful to colonial rulers by offering information that could make the governors more cognizant of what they could and could not do (or should not do) in their administration'.

14. Postcolonial scholars' concerns with the discursive formations of categories of 'natives' and their 'culture' have also been amply expressed in anthropo-

logical works such as Fabian's *Time and the Other* (1983), which scrutinizes temporal tropes in anthropological analysis and how, in a representational economy, the Other is allocated a temporal position outside or beyond Western time. See Asad (1973), Devisch and Nyamnjoh (2011), L'Estoile, Neiburg and Sigaud (2005), Tilley and Gordon (2007) and Trouillot (1991) for other relevant interventions.

15. The argument made here for photographs could easily be extended to material dimensions: while strong in the ethnography and history of colonial encounters – and, indeed, in the contemporary anthropology of Oceania, as Knauft (1999) or Lattas (2010) testify to – the material dimensions of colonialism and its encounters often remain not analysed or underrepresented. In this volume, Wæhle in particular attempts to bring out some of this materiality for the African cases (see also Rio 1999).

16. Interestingly, a questioning of sovereign coherence and unity may be turned on the colonial powers and their metropoles – an exercise Cooper (2007; see also 2002 and 2005) undertakes in an analysis of the French polity as well as Mbembe (2010) more recently.

17. In anthropology, such imperial nostalgia, with its implicit longing for and construction of 'traditional society', has engendered debates about the nature of representation and encounters among different cultural, historical and social orders (Obeyesekere 1992; Rosaldo 1989; Sahlins 1995).

18. Another relevant scholarly trend looks at how colonial agents are in some current literature seen as acting predominantly out of self-interest and less out of a sense of civic duty or necessarily due to a shared sense of colonial or imperial ethos. See, for example, Sunderland's (2004) study of the 'Crown agents' employed by the British Empire.

19. The other two main areas Falola (2006) identifies are, first, decolonization and nationalism and, second, the postcolonial state and society.

References

Allina, E. 1997. 'Fallacious Mirrors: Colonial Anxiety and Images of African Labor in Mozambique, ca. 1929', *History in Africa* 24: 9–52.

Ardener, S. and K. Knutson. 2002. *Swedish Ventures in Cameroon, 1883–1923: Trade and Travel, People and Politics*. Oxford: Berghahn Books.

Arrighi, G. 1978. *The Geometry of Imperialism: The Limits of Hobson's Paradigm*. London: NLB.

———. 1994. *The Long Twentieth Century: Money, Power, and the Origins of Our Times*. London: Verso.

———. 2007. *Adam Smith in Beijing: Lineages of the Twenty-First Century*. London and New York: Verso.

Asad, T. (ed.). 1973. *Anthropology and the Colonial Encounter*. London: Ithaca Press.

Balandier, G. (1951) 1966. 'The Colonial Situation: A Theoretical Approach', in I. Wallerstein (ed.), *Social Change: The Colonial Situation*. New York: John Wiley, pp. 34–61.

————. (1967) 1970. *Political Anthropology*. London: Allen Lane.

Bangstad, S. and B.E. Bertelsen. 2010. 'Heart of Darkness Re-invented? A Tale of Norwegian Ex-soldiers in the Democratic Republic of Congo', *Anthropology Today* 26(1): 8–12.

Banks, M. and R. Vokes. 2010. 'Introduction: Anthropology, Photography and the Archive', *History and Anthropology* 21(4): 337–49.

Benton, L. 2010. *A Search for Sovereignty: Law and Geography in European Empires, 1400–1900*. Cambridge: Cambridge University Press.

Bissell, W.C. 2005. 'Engaging Colonial Nostalgia', *Cultural Anthropology* 20(2): 215–48.

Bomann-Larsen, T. 2008. *Makten: Haakon og Maud*. Oslo: Cappelen Damm.

Boone, C. 2003. *Political Topographies of the African State: Territorial Authority and Institutional Choice*. Cambridge: Cambridge University Press.

Borofsky, R. 2000. 'An Invitation', in R. Borofsky (ed.), *Remembrance of Pacific Pasts: An Invitation to Remake History*. Honolulu: University of Hawai'i Press, pp. 1–30.

Braudel, F. (1987) 1995. *A History of Civilizations*. London: Penguin Books.

Brautaset, C. and S. Tenold. 2008. 'Globalisation and Norwegian Shipping Policy, 1850–2000', *Business History* 50(5): 565–82.

Bro-Jørgensen, J.O. 1966. *Dansk vestindien indtil 1755: Kolonisation og kompagnistyre*. Copenhagen: Fremad.

Bro-Jørgensen, J.O. and A. Rasch. 1969. *Asiatiske, vestindiske og guinesiske handelskompagnier*. Copenhagen: Rigsarkivet.

Brøndsted, J. (1952–53) 1966–68. *Vore gamle tropekolonier*, vols 1–8. Copenhagen: Fremad.

Brundenius, C., K. Hermele and M. Palmberg. 1980. *Gränslösa affärer: Om svenska företag i tredje världen*. Stockholm: Liber Förlag.

Butlin, R.A. 2009. *Geographies of Empire: European Empires and Colonies, c.1880–1960*. Cambridge: Cambridge University Press.

Césaire, A. 1955. *Discours sur le colonialisme*. Paris: Présence Africaine.

Chakrabarty, D. 2000. *Provincializing Europe: Postcolonial Thought and Historical Difference*. Princeton, N.J.: Princeton University Press.

Chaturvedi, S. 1996. *The Polar Regions: A Political Geography*. New York: Wiley.

Cissé, Y. and A. Falahat (eds). 2011. *Afrikanere i Norge gjennom 400 år*. Oslo: Afrikanere i Norge.

Comaroff, J. and J.L. Comaroff. 2012. *Theory from the South: Or, How Euro-America is Evolving towards Africa*. Boulder, C.O.: Paradigm Publishers.

Cooper, F. 2002. 'Decolonizing Situations: The Rise, Fall, and Rise of Colonial Studies, 1951–2001', *French Politics, Culture, and Society* 20(2): 47–76.

————. 2005. *Colonialism in Question: Theory, Knowledge, History*. Berkeley: University of California Press.

————. 2007. 'Provincializing France', in A.L. Stoler, C. McGranahan and P.C. Perdue (eds), *Imperial Formations*. Santa Fe, N.M.: SAR Press and James Currey, pp. 341–77.

DeCorse, C.R. 1993. 'The Danes on the Gold Coast: Culture Change and the European Presence', *African Archaeological Review* 11(1): 149–73.

DeLanda, M. 1997. *A Thousand Years of Nonlinear History*. New York: Zone Books.

Det statistiske centralbureau. 1887. *International Skibsfartsstatistik: Tabeller vedkommende Handelsflaaderne i aarene, 1850–86.* Kristiania: Aschehoug.

Devisch, R. and F.B. Nyamnjoh (eds). 2011. *The Postcolonial Turn: Re-imagining Anthropology and Africa.* Bamenda: Langaa RPIG; Leiden: African Studies Centre.

Dirks, N. 1992. *Colonialism and Culture.* Ann Arbor: University of Michigan Press.

Douglas, B. 1999. 'Science and the Art of Representing "Savages": Reading "Race" in Text and Image in South Seas Voyage Literature', *History and Anthropology* 11(2–3): 157–201.

Ebert, C.C. 2008. 'European Competition and Cooperation in Pre-modern Globalization: "Portuguese" West and Central Africa, 1500–1600', *African Economic History* 36: 53–78.

Edmond, R. 1997. *Representing the South Pacific: Colonial Discourse from Cook to Gauguin.* Cambridge: Cambridge University Press.

Eide, E. 2010. *Down There and Up Here: Orientalism and Othering in Feature Stories.* New York: Hampton Press.

Englund, H. 1996. 'Waiting for the Portuguese: Nostalgia, Exploitation and the Meaning of Land in the Malawi-Mozambique Borderland', *Journal of Contemporary African Studies* 14(2): 157–72.

Eriksen, A. 2013. 'Christian Politics in Vanuatu: Lay Priests and New State Forms', in M. Tomlinson and D. MacDougall (eds), *Christian Politics in Oceania.* Oxford: Berghahn Books, pp. 103–21.

Fabian, J. 1983. *Time and the Other: How Anthropology Makes Its Objects.* New York: Columbia University Press.

Falola, T. 2006. 'Writing and Teaching National History in Africa in an Era of Global History', in P.T. Zeleza (ed.), *The Study of Africa,* vol. 1, *Disciplinary and Interdisciplinary Encounters.* Dakar: CODESRIA, pp. 168–86.

Fanon, F. (1961) 2004. *The Wretched of the Earth.* New York: Grove Press.

Feldbaek, O. 1978. 'Danish East India trade, 1772–1807: Statistics and Structure', *Scandinavian Economic History Review* 26(2): 128–44.

Ferguson, N. 2011a. *Civilization: The West and the Rest.* London: Allen Lane.

———. 2011b. 'Watch This Man', *London Review of Books* 33(17). Retrieved 23 October 2013 from http://www.lrb.co.uk/v33/n22/letters.

Frank, A.G. 1966. 'The Development of Underdevelopment', *Monthly Review* 18(4): 17–30.

Frank, A.G. and B.K. Gills. 2000. 'The Five Thousand Year World System in Theory and Praxis', in R.A. Denemark et al. (eds), *World System Theory: The Social Science of Long-term Change.* London: Routledge, pp. 3–23.

Fur, G. 2006. *Colonialism in the Margins: Cultural Encounters in New Sweden and Lapland.* Leiden: Brill.

———. 2013. 'Colonialism and Swedish History: Unthinkable Connections?', in M. Naum and J.M. Nordin (eds), *Scandinavian Colonialism and the Rise of Modernity. Small Time Agents in a Global Arena.* New York: Springer, pp. 17–36.

Gates Jr, H.L. and E. Akyeampong (eds). 2012. *Dictionary of African Biography,* vols 1–3. New York: Oxford University Press.

Gjerde, J. 2001. 'Transatlantic Linkages: The Interaction between the Norwegian American and Norwegian "Nations" during the Century of Migration, 1825–1920', *Immigrants & Minorities* 20(1): 19–34.

Gøbel, E. 2011. 'Danish Shipping along the Triangular Route, 1671–1802: Voyages and Conditions on Board', *Scandinavian Journal of History* 36(2): 135–55.

Godøy, B.A. 2010. *Solskinn og død: Nordmenn i kong Leopolds Kongo.* Oslo: Spartacus.

Graeber, D. 2011. *Debt: The First 5,000 Years.* New York: Melville House.

Grosfoguel, R. 2002. 'Colonial Difference, Geopolitics of Knowledge, and Global Coloniality in the Modern/Colonial Capitalist World-System', *Review (Fernand Braudel Center)* 25(3): 203–24.

Hansen, T.B. and F. Stepputat. 2001. 'Introduction: States of Imagination', in T.B. Hansen and F. Stepputat (eds), *States of Imagination: Ethnographic Explorations of the Postcolonial State.* Durham, N.C.: Duke University Press, pp. 1–38.

———. 2005. 'Introduction', in T.B. Hansen and F. Stepputat (eds), *Sovereign Bodies: Citizens, Migrants and States in the Postcolonial World.* Princeton, N.J.: Princeton University Press, pp. 1–36.

Hell, J. and A. Schönle (eds). 2010. *Ruins of Modernity.* Durham, N.C.: Duke University Press.

Hernæs, P. 1995. *Slaves, Danes, and African Coast Society: The Danish Slave Trade from West Africa and Afro-Danish Relations on the Eighteenth-century Gold Coast.* Trondheim: University of Trondheim.

Hokkanen, M. and T. Särkkä. 2008. 'Puheenvuoroja kolonialistisen vallan ja väkivallan tutkimuksesta', *Historiallinen Aikakauskirja* 106(2): 189–97.

Homme, K. (ed.). 1969. *Nordisk nykolonialisme: Samiske problem i dag.* Oslo: Samlaget.

Huntington, S.P. 1996. *The Clash of Civilizations and the Remaking of World Order.* New York: Simon & Schuster.

Hviding, E. and K.M. Rio (eds). 2011. *Made in Oceania: Social Movements, Cultural Heritage and the State in the Pacific.* Wantage, U.K.: Sean Kingston.

Ittmann, K., D.D. Cordell and G.H. Maddox (eds). 2011. *The Demographics of Empire: The Colonial Order and the Creation of Knowledge.* Athens: Ohio University Press.

Jensen, L. 2010. 'Provincializing Scandinavia', *Kult* 7: 7–21.

Jensen, P.H. (ed.). 1983. *Dansk kolonihistorie: Indføring og studier.* Aarhus: Forlaget Historia.

Jónsson, M. 2009. 'Denmark-Norway as a Potential World Power in the Early Seventeenth Century', *Itinerario* 33(2): 17–27.

Jørgensen, H. 2011. 'Remoteness and Development: Transnational Constructions of Heritage in a Former Danish Trading Colony in South India', *History and Anthropology* 22(2): 169–86.

Kapferer, B. and B.E. Bertelsen. 2009. 'Introduction: The Crisis of Power and Reformations of the State in Globalizing Realities', in B. Kapferer and B.E. Bertelsen (eds), *Crisis of the State: War and Social Upheaval.* New York: Berghahn Books, pp. 1–26.

Kaspin, D. 2002. 'Signifying Power in Africa', in P.S. Landau and D.D. Kaspin (eds), *Images and Empires: Visuality in Colonial and Postcolonial Africa.* Berkeley: University of California Press, pp. 320–35.

Keesing, R.M. 1986. 'Plantation Networks, Plantation Culture: The Hidden Side of Colonial Melanesia', *Journal de la Société des océanistes* 42(82–83): 163–70.

Kent, N. 2008. *A Concise History of Sweden*. Cambridge: Cambridge University Press.

Keskinen, S., et al. (eds). 2009. *Complying with Colonialism: Gender, Race and Ethnicity in the Nordic Region*. Surrey, U.K.: Ashgate.

Kjerland, K.A. 2010. *Nordmenn i det koloniale Kenya*. Oslo: Scandinavian Academic Press.

Kjerland, K.A. and A.K. Bang (eds). 2002. *Nordmenn i Afrika – afrikanere i Norge*. Bergen: Vigmostad Bjørke.

Kjerland, K.A. and K.M. Rio. 2009a. 'Introduksjon', in K.A. Kjerland and K.M. Rio (eds), *Kolonitid: Nordmenn på eventyr og big business i Afrika og Stillehavet*. Oslo: Scandinavian Academic Press, pp. 5–11.

——— (eds). 2009b. *Kolonitid: Nordmenn på eventyr og big business i Afrika og Stillehavet*. Oslo: Scandinavian Academic Press.

Knauft, B. 1999. *From Primitive to Postcolonial in Melanesia and Anthropology*. Ann Arbor: University of Michigan Press.

Koponen, J. and H. Heinonen. 2002. 'Africa in Finnish Policy: Deepening Involvement', in Lennart Wohlgemut (ed.), *The Nordic Countries and Africa: Old and New Relations*. Uppsala: Nordic Africa Institute, pp. 15–28.

Krautwurst, U. 2010. 'What Is Settler Colonialism? An Anthropological Meditation on Frantz Fanon's "Concerning Violence"', *History and Anthropology* 14(1): 55–72.

Kuparinen, E. 1991. *An African Alternative: Nordic Migration to South Africa, 1815–1914*. Helsinki: Finnish Historical Society.

Lamb, J., V. Smith and N. Thomas (eds). 2000. *Exploration and Exchange: A South Seas Anthology, 1680–1900*. Chicago: University of Chicago Press.

Landau, P.S. 2002. 'An Amazing Distance: Pictures and People in Africa', in P.S. Landau and D.D. Kaspin (eds), *Images and Empires: Visuality in Colonial and Postcolonial Africa*. Berkeley: University of California Press, pp. 1–40.

Landau, P.S. and D.D. Kaspin (eds). 2002. *Images and Empires: Visuality in Colonial and Postcolonial Africa*. Berkeley: University of California Press.

Lattas, A. 2010. *Dreams, Madness, and Fairy Tales in New Britain*. Durham, N.C.: Carolina Academic Press.

L'Estoile, B., F. Neiburg and L. Sigaud (eds). 2005. *Empires, Nations, and Natives: Anthropology and State-Making*. Durham, N.C., and London: Duke University Press.

Linder, A. 2001. *Os Suíços em Moçambique*. Maputo: Arquivo Histórico de Moçambique.

Loftsdóttir, K. 2010. 'Becoming Civilized: Iceland and the Colonial Project During the 19th Century', *Kult* 7: 41–68.

Loftsdóttir, K. and G. Pálsson. 2013. 'Black on White: Danish Colonialism, Iceland and the Caribbean', in M. Naum and J.M. Nordin (eds), *Scandinavian Colonialism and the Rise of Modernity: Small Time Agents in a Global Arena*. New York: Springer, pp. 37–52.

Lucas, G. and A. Parigoris. 2013. 'Icelandic Archaeology and the Ambiguities of Colonialism', in M. Naum and J.M. Nordin (eds), *Scandinavian Colonial-*

ism and the Rise of Modernity: Small Time Agents in a Global Arena. New York: Springer, pp. 89–104.

Mazrui, A.A. 2000. 'Cultural Amnesia, Cultural Nostalgia and False Memory: Africa's Identity Crisis Revisited', *African Philosophy* 13(2): 87–98.

Mbembe, A. 2010. 'Provincializing France?', *Public Culture* 23(1): 85–119.

McNeil, D. 2011. '"The Rivers of Zimbabwe Will Run Red with Blood": Enoch Powell and the Post-Imperial Nostalgia of the Monday Club', *Journal of Southern African Studies* 37(4): 731–45.

Memmi, A. (1957) 1991. *The Colonizer and the Colonized.* Boston: Beacon Press.

Mishra, P. 2011. 'Watch This Man: Review of "Civilization: The West and the Rest" by Niall Ferguson', *London Review of Books* 33(21): 10–12.

Møller, A. 1986. *Australiafarere: Nordmenn som tok en annen vei.* Oslo: Cappelen.

Naum, M. and J.M. Nordin (eds). 2013. *Scandinavian Colonialism and the Rise of Modernity: Small Time Agents in a Global Arena.* New York: Springer.

Neumann, K. 1993. 'Nostalgia for Rabaul', *Oceania* 67(3): 177–93.

Newitt, M.D.D. 1995. *A History of Mozambique.* London: Hurst.

Norman, H. and H. Runblom. 1988. *Transatlantic Connections: Nordic Migration to the New World after 1800.* Oslo: Norwegian University Press.

Nordstrom, C. 2004. *Shadows of War: Violence, Power, and International Profiteering in the Twenty-first Century.* Berkeley: University of California Press.

Nørregaard, G. 1968. *Guldkysten: De danske etablissementer i Guinea.* Copenhagen: Fremad.

———. 1969. *Farefulde danske sørejser: Togter til Afrika i det 18. århundrede.* Copenhagen: Fremad.

Nováky, G. 1999. *Handelskompanier och kompanihandel: Svenska Afrikakompaniet, 1649–1663.* Uppsala: Uppsala University.

Obeyesekere, G. 1992. *The Apotheosis of Captain Cook: European Mythmaking in the Pacific.* Princeton, N.J.: Princeton University Press.

Ong, A. 2006. *Neoliberalism as Exception: Mutations in Citizenship and Sovereignty.* Durham, N.C.: Duke University Press.

Palmberg, M. (ed.). 2001. *Encounter Images in the Meetings between Africa and Europe.* Uppsala: Nordiska Afrikainstitutet.

———. 2009. 'The Nordic Colonial Mind', in S. Keskinen et al. (eds), *Complying with Colonialism: Gender, Race and Ethnicity in the Nordic Region.* Surrey, U.K.: Ashgate, pp. 35–50.

Pels, P. 1997. 'The Anthropology of Colonialism: Culture, History, and the Emergence of Western Governmentality', *Annual Review of Anthropology* 26: 163–83.

Prakash, G. (ed.). 1995. *After Colonialism: Imperial Histories and Postcolonial Displacements.* Princeton, N.J.: Princeton University Press.

Rasch, A. 1967. *Dansk Ostindien, 1777–1845: Storhedstid og hensygnen.* Copenhagen: Fremad.

Raine, S. 2009. *China's African Challenges.* London: International Institute for Strategic Studies.

Reinhard, W. 2011. *A Short History of Colonialism.* Manchester: Manchester University Press.

Rio, K. 1999. *Oceania gjenoppdaget i Bergen: Reiser i Bergen museums samlinger fra Stillehavet.* Bergen: Bergen Museum.

Roitman, J. 2006. 'The Ethics of Illegality in the Chad Basin', in J. Comaroff and J.L. Comaroff (eds), *Law and Disorder in the Postcolony.* Chicago: University of Chicago Press, pp. 247–72.

Rosaldo, R. 1989. 'Imperialist nostalgia', *Representations* 26: 107–22.

Runblom, H. 1987. 'Nordic Immigrants in the New World', in H. Norman and H. Runblom (eds), *Transatlantic Connection: Nordic Migration to the New World after 1800.* Oslo: Norwegian University Press, pp. 139–276.

Ruud, A.E. and K.A. Kjerland. 2003. *1975–1989: Vekst, velvilje og utfordringer,* Norsk utviklingshjelps historie 2. Bergen: Fagbokforlaget.

Sahlins, M. 1995. *How 'Natives' Think: About Captain Cook, For Example.* Chicago: University of Chicago Press.

Said, E. 1978. *Orientalism.* London: Kegan Paul.

Santos, B. de S. and M.P. Meneses (eds). 2010. *Epistemologias do sul.* Coimbra: Almedina.

Särkkä, T. 2007. 'Näkökulmia kolonialismin kulttuurihistoriaan: Suomi, suomalaiset ja eteläisen Afrikan imperiuminrakennus, 1895–1939', *Historiatieteellinen aikakauskirja 2007.* Lähde, pp. 91–103.

―――. 2012. 'A Perspective on Nordic Colonialism: Finns as Empire-Builders in Southern Africa', paper presented at the ninth European Social Science History Conference, Glasgow, 11–14 April.

Schmitt, C. (1932) 1996. *The Concept of the Political.* Chicago: University of Chicago Press.

Schnakenbourg, E. 2013. 'Sweden and the Atlantic: The Dynamism of Sweden's Colonial Projects in the Eighteenth Century', in M. Naum and J.M. Nordin (eds), *Scandinavian Colonialism and the Rise of Modernity: Small Time Agents in a Global Arena.* New York: Springer, pp. 229–42.

Simensen, J. 2003. *1952–1975: Norge møter den tredje verden,* Norsk utviklingshjelps historie 1. Bergen: Fagbokforlaget.

Simonsen, A.H. 2010. 'Fantasies and Experiences: The Norwegian Press Coverage of Africa, 1900–2002', *Kult* 7: 22–40.

Smith-Simonsen, C. 2011. 'Mythbusting: Looking for Norwegians in the Colonies', *Deshima* 5: 11–26.

Spivak, G.C. 1999. *A Critique of Postcolonial Reason: Toward a History of the Vanishing Present.* Cambridge, M.A.: Harvard University Press.

Stocking Jr, G.W. (ed.). 1991. *Colonial Situations: Essays in the Contextualization of Ethnographic Knowledge.* Madison: University of Wisconsin Press.

Stoddard, T.L. (1920) 1924. *The Rising Tide of Color against White World-Supremacy.* New York: Charles Scribner's Sons.

Stoler, A.L. 1989. 'Rethinking Colonial Categories: European Communities and the Boundaries of Rule', *Comparative Studies in Society and History* 31(1): 134–61.

―――. (2002) 2010. *Carnal Knowledge and Imperial Power: Race and the Intimate in Colonial Rule.* Berkeley: University of California Press.

―――. 2006. 'On Degrees of Imperial Sovereignty', *Public Culture* 18(1): 125–46.

―――. 2008. 'Imperial Debris: Reflections on Ruins and Ruination', *Cultural Anthropology* 23(2): 191–219.

―――. 2009. *Along the Archival Grain: Epistemic Anxieties and Colonial Common Sense.* Princeton, N.J.: Princeton University Press.

————. 2011. 'Colonial Aphasia: Race and Disabled Histories in France', *Public Culture* 23(1): 121–56.

———— (ed.). 2013. *Imperial Debris: On Ruins and Ruination*. Durham, N.C.: Duke University Press.

Stoler, A.L. and F. Cooper. 1997. 'Between Metropole and Colony: Rethinking a Research Agenda', in A.L. Stoler and F. Cooper (eds), *Tensions of Empire: Colonial Cultures in a Bourgeois World*. Berkeley: University of California Press, pp. 1–56.

Stoler, A.L. and C. McGranahan. 2007. 'Introduction: Refiguring Imperial Terrains', in A.L. Stoler, C. McGranahan and P.C. Perdue (eds), *Imperial Formations*. Santa Fe, N.M.: SAR Press and James Currey, pp. 3–42.

Sunderland, D. 2004. *Managing the British Empire: The Crown Agents, 1833–1814*. Suffolk, U.K.: Boydell Press.

Thomas, N. 1990. 'Partial Texts: Representation, Colonialism and Agency in Pacific History', *Journal of Pacific History* 25(2): 139–58.

————. 1991. *Entangled Objects: Exchange, Material Culture, and Colonialism in the Pacific*. Cambridge, M.A.: Harvard University Press.

————. 1994. *Colonialism's Culture: Anthropology, Travel and Government*. London: Polity Press.

————. 1997. *In Oceania: Visions, Artifacts, Histories*. Durham, N.C.: Duke University Press.

————. 2010. *Islanders: The Pacific in the Age of Empire*. New Haven, C.T.: Yale University Press.

Thomasson, F. 2013. '32 piskrapp vid Quatre Piquets: Svensk rättvisa och slavlager på Saint Barthélemy', in B. Nilson (ed.), *Historielärarnas årsskrift 2013*. Historielärarnas årsskrift: Bromma, pp. 7–29.

————. 2014. 'Raynal and Sweden: Royal Propaganda and Colonial Aspirations', in J. Mander et al. (eds), *Raynal's Histoire philosophique des deux Indes*. Oxford: Voltaire Foundation, pp. 32–46.

Tilley, H. and R.J. Gordon (eds). 2007. *Ordering Africa: Anthropology, European Imperialism, and the Politics of Knowledge*. Manchester: Manchester University Press.

Trouillot, M.-R. 1991. 'Anthropology and the Savage Slot: The Poetics and Politics of Otherness', in R.G. Fox (ed.), *Recapturing Anthropology in the Present*. Santa Fe, N.M.: SAR Press, pp. 17–44.

Tvedt, T. 1990. *Bilder av 'de andre': Om utviklingslandene i bistandsepoken*. Oslo: Universitetsforlaget.

Tygesen, P. and E. Wæhle. 2007. *Kongospor: Norden i Kongo – Kongo i Norden*. Stockholm.

UNESCO. 1981–93. *General History of Africa*, vols 1–8. London: Heinemann.

Ustvedt, Y. 2001. *Trankebar: Nordmenn i de gamle tropekolonier*. Oslo: Cappelen.

Vail, L. (ed.). (1989) 1991. *The Creation of Tribalism in Southern Africa*. Berkeley: University of California Press.

Vigeland, N.P. 1943. *Norsk seilskipsfart erobrer verdenshavene*. Brun: Trondheim.

Vokes, R. 2010. 'Reflections on a Complex (and Cosmopolitan) Archive: Postcards and Photography in Early Colonial Uganda, c. 1904–1928', *History and Anthropology* 21(4): 375–409.

—— (ed.). 2012. *Photography in Africa: Ethnographic Perspectives*. Woodbridge, U.K.: James Currey.

Wadström, C.B. (1794–95) 1968. *An Essay on Colonization Particularly Applied to the Western Coast of Africa with Some Free Thoughts on Cultivation and Commerce*. London: Darton and Harvey.

Wallerstein, I. 2004. *World-Systems Analysis: An Introduction*. Durham, N.C.: Duke University Press.

Wedel Jarlsberg, F. 1932. *Reisen gjennem livet*. Oslo: Gyldendal.

Weiss, H. 2013. 'The Danish Gold Coast as a Multinational and Entangled Space, c. 1700–1850', in M. Naum and J.M. Nordin (eds), *Scandinavian Colonialism and the Rise of Modernity: Small Time Agents in a Global Arena*. New York: Springer, pp. 243–60.

Werbner, R.P. 1998. 'Introduction: Beyond Oblivion – Confronting Memory Crisis', in R.P. Werbner (ed.), *Memory and the Postcolony: African Anthropology and the Critique of Power*. London: Zed Books, pp. 1–17.

Wesley-Smith, T. and E.A. Porter (eds) 2010. *China in Oceania: Reshaping the Pacific?* Oxford: Berghahn Books.

Wesseling, H.L. 2004. *The European Colonial Empires, 1815–1919*. Harlow, U.K.: Pearson and Longman.

Westermark, G.D. 2001. 'Reading *South Pacific*: Colonialism and Anthropology in An Australian Journal', *History and Anthropology* 12(2): 159–78.

Winquist, A.H. 1978. *Scandinavians and South Africa: Their Impact on the Cultural, Social and Economic Development of Pre-1902 South Africa*. Cape Town: Balkema.

Wohlgemut, L. (ed.). 2002. *The Nordic Countries and Africa: Old and New Relations*. Uppsala: Nordic Africa Institute.

Wolf, E. (1982) 1997. *Europe and the People without History*. Berkeley: University of California Press.

Woolf, D. 2011. *A Global History of History*. Cambridge: Cambridge University Press.

Young, C. 1994. *The African Colonial State in Perspective*. New Haven, C.T.: Yale University Press.

Zeleza, P.T. (ed.). 2006. *The Study of Africa*, vol. 1, *Disciplinary and Interdisciplinary Encounters*. Dakar: CODESRIA.

—— (ed.). 2007. *The Study of Africa*, vol. 2, *Global and Transnational Engagements*. Dakar: CODESRIA.

Zorgdrager, N. 1997. *De rettferdiges strid: Kautokeino 1852 – Samisk motstand mot norsk kolonialisme*. Oslo: Vett og viten.

1

INTERCONNECTING THE BRITISH EMPIRE
Swedish and Norwegian Shipping to South Africa, 1850–1914

Knut M. Nygaard

According to economic historian John Forbes Munro, the southern tip of Africa – the area around the Cape of Good Hope, with Cape Town as the focal point – was the area in sub-Saharan Africa that was most thoroughly integrated into the international economy in the 1800s (Munro 1976: 14). Trade routes passed the Cape of Good Hope, and ships coming from Europe, Asia and Oceania called at Cape Town to refill fresh water, food and – after the 1830s – coal for fuel (Munro 1976: 56; see also Feinstein 2005: 23). This chapter focuses on the experiences Swedish and Norwegian shipowners had with shipping to this globally integrated part of Africa from the 1850s until the beginning of the First World War. Emphasis is put on aspects of the development of the two countries shipping to, in particular, what became South Africa.

By comparing the two countries' sailing ship industries, differing developments are explained. Type of cargo will also be touched upon, as this is an important – sometimes decisively so – factor in analysis of this particular trade. Moreover, the market conditions in South Africa caused by the Anglo-Boer War will be mentioned in brief. However, priority is first given to the context within which the Swedish and Norwegian shipping trade with South Africa emerged and operated, focusing upon some elements of the economic development in South Africa, as well as the characteristics of Swedish and Norwegian shipping in the nineteenth century.

South African Development and Swedish and Norwegian Shipping in the 1800s

At the beginning of the 1800s the southern part of the African continent was the only substantial African area with notable European immigration. The first settlement, a Dutch colony in the Cape area in 1652, was taken over some 150 years later by the British when a colony was established in 1806. As British rule limited the Boers' traditional way of living and English was made the official language of the colony, a steady movement of Boers left the Cape, and between 1836 and 1846 some ten thousand Boers established independent republics (the Orange Free State and Transvaal) on the plateaus farther inland: a movement known as the Great Trek (Munro 1976: 58). When, half a century later, diamonds and later gold were discovered, political and social tensions between the two groups of people intensified, fuelled by the subterranean riches.

The first diamonds were discovered in 1867 near Hope Town in the northern part of the Cape Colony – strongly associated with the town of Kimberley, established in 1873, which soon became the centre of the industry (Beinart 2001: 27; Goodfellow 1931: 96). Gold was discovered in the 1880s in the Witwatersrand area in the Transvaal, and a gold mining industry developed with Johannesburg as the administrative and economic centre (Goodfellow 1931: 96; Feinstein 2005: 2). These industries caused a tremendous boom in South Africa's economy and export and import businesses increased sharply, attracting foreign capital, manpower and numerous shipping companies.

A crucial backdrop for their subsequent involvement was the upturn around 1825 of the Swedish and Norwegian shipping industries following the signing of a trade agreement between the two countries and Great Britain, further boosted after changes in the protectionist British trade policy in the 1840s. The most important was the repeal of the British Navigation Act in 1850. These changes in British commercial policy led to the 'golden age of sail' for Norwegian (in particular) and Swedish shipping (Nordvik 1985: 121). In 1866 Norway was the most dominant foreign nation in the shipping trade with Great Britain (Hodne 1981: 145). Some 443,000 tons of Norwegian tonnage was annually engaged in this trade between 1861 and 1865, increasing to about 2,200,000 tons annually in the period from 1876 to 1880 (Nordvik 1985: 142).

The total registered Norwegian tonnage increased 5.4 times from 1850 to 1880, from 301,000 tons in 1850 to 1,620,000 tons in 1880 (Det statistiske centralbureau 1887: table 9).[1] In the same period Swedish tonnage increased 3.4 times, from 214,000 to 728,000 tons. In 1850 the total world tonnage was 8,588,000 tons, and in 1880 it had grown 3.3 times to 28,257,000 tons. The Norwegian tonnage, which accounted for 3.5 per cent of the world tonnage in 1850, had increased to 5.7 per cent in 1880. Swedish tonnage accounted for 2.5 per cent of the world tonnage in 1850, with a minimal increase to 2.6 per cent thirty years later.

In 1880 Norway was the third-largest shipping nation in the world in terms of tonnage; only the United States and Great Britain had larger tonnage (Det statistiske centralbureau 1887: table 9). In other words, Norway, a sparsely populated country with limited financial resources, became one of the major actors on the world shipping scene.[2] In figure 1.1, Norwegian and Swedish growth from 1850 to 1914 is illustrated.

The export of timber provided the platform for the Norwegian expansion, but the shipping industries soon outgrew the limitations imposed by the export sector. After 1860 the Norwegian and, to a lesser degree, Swedish vessels became engaged in cross-trade as a part of the international shipping industry (Nordvik 1985: 146). In 1880 almost 70 per cent of the Norwegian tonnage was engaged in such trade, accounting for almost 80 per cent of the gross revenue earned (Worm-Müller 1950: 175). The fast-growing Norwegian tonnage indicates a fairly high profit level, a fact confirmed by several studies.[3] This was not exceptional to Norwegian tonnage, as high net profit and relatively stable expenses characterized the sector more generally during this period. The growth was made possible due to a strong increase in world trade from the 1840s: between 1840 and 1870 world trade increased by 53 per cent per ten years, whereas from 1800 to 1914 it increased by an average of 33 per cent per decade (Hodne 1981: 135).

In contrast to Norway, Swedish participation in international trade contributed to the development of commercial shipping. This led to Swedish sailing vessels becoming heavily involved in transoceanic trade from the middle of the nineteenth century (Fritz 1980: 156) – for instance, through considerable trading involvement in South America and the Dutch East Indies. The import of coffee and sugar to Sweden

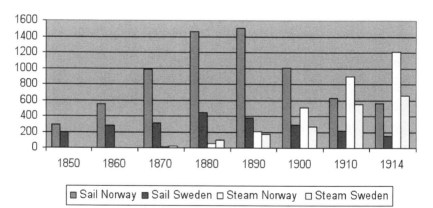

Figure 1.1. The Swedish and Norwegian tonnage development from 1850 to 1914 (per thousand tons). *Source:* Based on Nordic shipping statistics, SSB.

was combined with the export of iron or timber or carriage of cargoes from Europe. Coal and piece goods from England, Germany or Belgium and salt and wine from Portugal and the Mediterranean was carried on Swedish vessels, for instance, to Brazil, Sweden's main trading partner in South America (Nordvik 1985: 129).[4]

When the Swedish direct trade with overseas markets fell away during the 1860s, there was little interest in maintaining the shipping connections with the overseas countries (Fritz 1980: 156). This led to only 2 per cent of Swedish tonnage being involved in intercontinental shipping from 1896 to 1900 (Fritz 1980: 159). It was not until the start of overseas liner trade in 1904 that Sweden again became heavily engaged in intercontinental shipping (Fritz 1980: 160).

Significantly, it is recognized that the Norwegians during this period (and later) sailed at a lower cost than the Swedes – despite the fact that wages were about the same in Sweden and Norway. Crucial to the Norwegian success was the purchase of inexpensive secondhand vessels on which they subsequently reduced the number of sails to save on crew. The speed was naturally reduced, but in the European bulk trade travel time was of less importance. Put differently, the disadvantage of longer travel time was more than offset by lower manning costs (Hanisch 1983: 110). This strategy characterized the Norwegian shipowners during the nineteenth century (Hodne 1981: 142). The poor quality of the Norwegian ships, however, meant they were unable to manage the strains of intercontinental trade and resulted in a high loss percentage (Worm-Müller 1935: 389; Hodne 1981: 142).[5]

As a consequence, Norwegian foreign shipping was, for a long period, largely confined to European trade.[6] By 1855 only 2.7 per cent of the Norwegian foreign fleet was engaged in intercontinental trade. Five years later, in 1860, the proportion had increased to 9 per cent (Worm-Müller 1935: 327). When the Norwegians eventually became engaged in intercontinental shipping, the trade with timber was still of special importance, and 53.2 per cent of the gross revenue from Norwegian sailing ships was earned in this trade in 1879 (Hodne 1981: 144; Worm-Müller 1950: 173). Now the ships were carrying timber all over the globe – lumber from Canada and the American West Coast, redwood and logwood from Central America and the West Indies, and teak from Burma and the East Indies (Worm-Müller 1950: 173). The ships mainly went to Great Britain and to the British Empire more generally, but also, to a lesser degree, to other European nations. Figure 1.2. shows unloading of timber in Durban. Other important overseas trades in 1879 were grain, representing 8.7 per cent of the gross revenue, petroleum, 8.1 per cent, coal, 6.4 per cent, and cotton, 3.5 per cent. Cross-trade amounted

Figure 1.2. Unloading timber in Durban. *Source:* Local History Museum, Durban; reproduced with permission.

to 14.7 per cent and included, among others, guano, saltpetre, iron, sugar, coffee and piece goods (Worm-Müller 1950: 173).

The Swedes were experienced in overseas trades in the 1850s and tended to dominate in those trades in the 1850s and 1860s. The Swedish vessels were also of better quality than the Norwegian vessels and could therefore withstand the strains of longer trips. This can help explain why Swedish sailing ships dominated the South African trade from the very start. Illustrative of the quality of Norwegian ships of this period was that the limited export of Norwegian timber to South Africa that actually occurred went through England and was transported on English ships (Worm-Müller 1935: 389).

A Differentiated Development: Norwegian and Swedish Strategies

As indicated in figure 1.3, the Swedes were present on the southern tip of the African continent significantly earlier than the Norwegians. In 1857, thirty-three Swedish sailing ships arrived in South Africa, fifteen of which held cargo from the Nordic countries. Only three Norwegian vessels arrived in the same year, and none with Nordic cargo. This pattern continued in 1862, when forty-one Swedish ships arrived – twenty-one with Nordic cargo. In the same year four Norwegian vessels arrived, all carrying such cargo, however (Worm-Müller 1935: 389–90). This exemplifies that South Africa was largely unimportant for Norwegian shipping until the 1860s. Only Cape Town played a certain role, but primarily as a bunkering station for ships heading towards Asia or Australia (Worm-Müller 1950: 274).

Twenty-five years later, by 1885, Norwegian sailing ships exceeded the number of Swedish ships, and by 1895 the Norwegians dominated this market. This happened because of changes in Swedish trading pat-

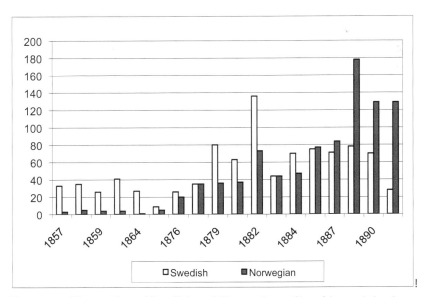

Figure 1.3. The number of Swedish and Norwegian sailing ships arriving in South Africa, 1857–95. *Source*: Based on Norwegian shipping history, consular reports from Cape Town, shipping tables, SSB.

terns and a fall in the market for sailing vessels. Steamships had become increasingly more efficient and took over the traditional sailing ship markets.[7] Sailing ships were first pushed out of European trade, followed by the Atlantic trade and gradually other trades across the globe.

Given this general global pattern, it is perhaps surprising that the Norwegian sailing ship fleet continued to grow, but the major reason for this was the fact that the Norwegian sailing ship trade was still profitable. Therefore, Norwegian shipowners continued to invest in a segment of the market that rapidly became smaller, one that shipowners from most other nations left to move into steam. In line with this development, the trade with South Africa in 1889 was characterized as one of the last great trades for sailing ships.[8] For Norwegian shipowners, who still invested in sailing vessels, this trade was important. They bought a considerable number of used sailing vessels from abroad, mainly with hulls of iron or steel well suited for the trade with South Africa – ships that the predominantly foreign owners now sold as they ventured into the rapidly emerging international steamship business. For Norway, however, these secondhand iron and steel sailing ships continued to dominate shipping to distant locations for the next three decades.

As illustrated by figure 1.1, the Swedish sailing ship fleet did not grow at the same rate as the Norwegian fleet. By the 1890s the Swedes were rapidly moving into the steam age, and by 1899 the Swedish steamship tonnage was greater than the sailing ship tonnage (Larsson 2000: 26). In Norway this change did not occur before 1907 (Hanisch 1983: 121). In that same year the steamship tonnage in Sweden was twice as big as the sailing ship tonnage (Larsson 2000: 26).

By comparing the Swedish and Norwegian shipping developments, it becomes clear that Norwegian shipowners were comparative latecomers in the overseas sailing ship trade. It may be argued that while the Norwegians focused on low wages and low-quality and slow-going vessels in European trade, the Swedes focused on quality in overseas trade. Historian Tore Hanisch claims that the Norwegians almost outdid the Swedes in the timber trade. His argument is that among the Swedish shipowners there was a widespread belief that shipping, especially with lumber, was unprofitable (Hanisch 1983: 110). Hanisch moreover argues that a number of Swedish ships were sold to Norway.

These assertions may be correct for the European timber trade, where the Swedes sold their older timber vessels to Norwegian owners. However, the analysis above suggests that the Swedes neither gave up shipping nor the timber trade – Swedish companies simply focused on quality and long-distance intercontinental shipping as part of a strategy for participation in international trade.

Sailing Ship Cargo

Although the Cape area was closely integrated into the international economy, agriculture remained the most important livelihood for the European population in South Africa until the discovery of diamonds and gold towards the end of the 1800s (Goodfellow 1931: 96; Feinstein 2005: 2). The colony was practically self-sufficient, with an economy almost totally dependent on agriculture. Furthermore, South Africa was a part of the British Empire, which historian Sarah Palmer describes as not only British-dominated, but also extremely difficult and risky to gain access to. She emphasizes that the wheels of nineteenth-century commerce were oiled by personal contacts, forming a network of business relationships that favoured Britain as the imperial power, and also favoured the first comer (Palmer 1985: 111). This meant that up to the 1880s there was a limited volume of import to South Africa, with a strong preference for imports from the British Empire.

Reflecting this overall British dominance and the peculiarities of the South African market, the Swedish and Norwegian sailing vessels established their niche by transporting cargo mainly from the British Empire and from the Nordic countries: Nordic timber and British coal (Worm-Müller 1950: 276). The vessels could also call at South Africa on voyages from other continents, such as with timber from Canada or grain from Australia. Another important (but dangerous) cargo was petroleum in tin cans, tin boxes or wooden barrels loaded in the United States and unloaded in South Africa (Worm-Müller 1950: 223). Common for all these cargoes was that the duration of the voyage was not crucial. In fact, a long voyage could be advantageous, because the cargo owner thus saved on storage costs ashore (Sargent 1930).

A major challenge to South African trade was that of getting cargo for the return journey to Europe. Unlike other colonies such as Canada (timber) and Australia (wool and wheat), there was no European market for South African raw materials and goods at the time: the country's primary export commodity after 1880 was gold, which was transported on steamships. After unloading in South Africa the ships continued elsewhere in ballast to find return cargo.[9] However, South Africa's geographical location meant that the distance to the Americas, Asia and Australia was relatively short, and this is often from where return cargo had to be attained. This trade is also known as 'triangular trade' in the sense that a voyage starting and ending in Europe consisted of three legs, two with cargo and one in ballast. A vessel could, for example, load a cargo of timber in the Baltic Sea or coal in the U.K. and then sail to South Africa and unload there. Then the ship sailed in ballast to the

Figure 1.4. Sailing vessels in the Alfred Basin, Cape Town, ca. 1880. *Source*:
Ship Society of South Africa; reproduced with permission.

Americas, Asia or Australia and loaded for Europe (Worm-Müller 1950:
183 and 276). Figure 1.4. shows sailing ships in the busy port of Cape
Town.

The Anglo-Boer War (1899–1902) and Norwegian Shipping

The Anglo-Boer War began because of conflicting interests between the
British ambitions in South Africa and the independent Boer republics,
the Orange Free State and Transvaal. As gold was found in the independent Boer republic of Transvaal, according to historian William Beinart,
'Transvaal's new wealth seemed to threaten British interests in the region as a whole' (2001: 64). The British initiated the war by attacking in
1899, and in the spring of 1902 the Boers finally had to capitulate due to
overwhelming British superiority. For shipping, this war created novel
opportunities. Figure 1.5 demonstrates the increase in revenue per ton
from 1897 until the outbreak of war in 1899, a levelling out and even a
small decrease in profit in the war's second year (1900), followed by a
boom in 1901. But by 1903 it was all over, and revenues per ton were
again on par with the year preceding the war.

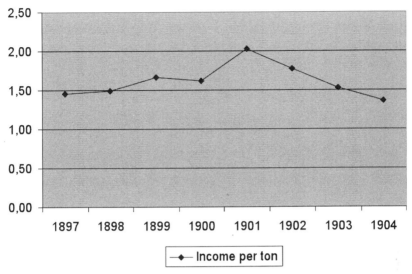

Figure 1.5. Income per ton of loaded Norwegian sailing ships arriving in South Africa, 1897–1904 (in GBP). *Source:* Based on Tønnesen (1951), Sir Karl Knudsen's letter to Jacob Worm-Müller.

The Steamers Take Over

In the years before the Anglo-Boer War, ship traffic to South Africa increased significantly and, as seen in figure 1.5 for sailing ships, the war itself boosted this development. The traffic continued to grow after the war. The already-mentioned discovery of diamonds and gold led to an acceleration of the economic development in South Africa, and in the 1890s imports rose sharply as demand for both raw materials and finished goods for the mining industry grew. Increasing amounts of goods were exported to South Africa from a number of European countries, the United States and Australia (Goodfellow 1931: 100–1). From the United States, which had its own gold mines with conditions similar to those in the Transvaal, both mining engineers and mining equipment were acquired – the American engineers favoured equipment they knew (Goodfellow 1931: 100–1). Similar dynamics structured South Africa's emerging agricultural sector, because American equipment suited South African conditions very well. Almost all fabrics, on the other hand, came from the United Kingdom. Most foodstuffs came from the British Empire, while Australia and Canada were major export countries for wheat (Goodfellow 1931: 100–1). These countries were also prominent in South Africa's national trade revenue (see table 1.1).

Table 1.1. Total imports to South Africa, 1904–14, by exporting countries (in per cent; in GBP)

Import from	1904	1908	1912	1914
Great Britain	62	56	58	55
United States	11	8	9	9
The British Empire	10	14	10	12
Germany	5	8	9	7
The Nordic Countries	2	2	3	3
The Netherlands with colonies	1	2	2	2
Other	9	9	9	12
Total	100	100	100	100

Source: Based on Statistics Norway: Annual Statements of the Trade and Shipping of the Union of South Africa in £.

This economic development is reflected in a sharp increase in the steamship traffic to South Africa. Despite this, the Norwegian-Swedish consul in Cape Town reported that times were also quite favourable for the Norwegian sailing ships largely transporting timber from Scandinavia (Worm-Müller 1950: 276). This may be illustrated by the fact that only a single Norwegian steamer called in 1875 – generally regarded as the first Norwegian steamship arriving in South Africa (Ytreberg 1951: 286). In 1905 forty-six Norwegian steamships had called at South African ports. The very same year, a total of 161 Norwegian sailing ships arrived in southeastern Africa (Ytreberg 1951: 492–93).

The era of sailing ships was now nonetheless undeniably declining. As mentioned above, increased profitability of steamships due to technological improvements meant that steamers gradually gained larger portions of trade previously carried by sailing ships. In regard to trade with South Africa, the general trend was now one where tramp steamers[10] fully loaded with cargo for the mining industry arrived from Europe. A new opportunity that opened up with the arrival of steam was liner trade – steamships in regular service to specific ports (De Kerchove 1961: 459).

Three Nordic shipping companies were among those seizing this opportunity to start liner trade with South Africa: the East Asiatic Company (Denmark), the Transatlantic Shipping Company (Sweden) and the Norwegian Africa and Australia Line (Norway). The Danish and Swedish lines operated from 1903 and 1904, respectively, while the Norwegian line joined in 1910. South Africa's economic boom may help to explain why this happened just at the turn of the century: timber had been exported from the Nordic countries to South Africa since the 1850s, and after the boom the Nordic countries continued to hold a position among the countries exporting to South Africa. In the period between 1904 and 1914, as shown in table 1.1, Nordic exports comprised about 2 per cent of South Africa's total imports.[11]

In the period before the First World War, Sweden was the largest Nordic exporter to South Africa, followed by Norway and Finland. Denmark, which did not export timber, had the lowest export figures.[12] The main cargo of the liner trade in this period was timber, complemented by general cargo.[13] The latter was more profitable than lumber, and the liner companies therefore aimed to increase this percentage.[14] The value of timber totalled 99.8 per cent of total export value in 1903, when the first Scandinavian line was started.[15] In 1914, however, general cargo value had grown to 47.7 per cent of total export value.

The increase in exports of general cargo from the Nordic countries coincides with the start of direct steamship connections, a relationship emphasized in consular reports.[16] These unanimously underlined how the initiation of regular direct steamship lines was of crucial importance for exports to South Africa. Earlier, when the carriage was by sailing vessels, only large consignments were shipped from the Nordic countries to South Africa. The new lines brought smaller consignments, meaning that Nordic goods were available for smaller importers and for consumers in South Africa.[17]

For all three direct steamship lines between the Nordic countries and South Africa started in this period, the combination of timber and general cargo was important. The three lines dominated the trade through a close transnational cooperation, and carried a large part of both timber and other raw materials, as well as finished goods, exported to South Africa from the Nordic countries throughout the 1900s. Similarly, steamship lines were established from other countries and continents to South Africa. Both liner and tramp steamers took market shares from sailing ships.

In 1913 the number of Norwegian sailing ships calling at the southeast African ports had dropped to a mere fifty-one ships, while there were forty-three steamers (Ytreberg 1951: 494–95). It was evidently only a matter of time before the sailing ships' days were permanently over, and by 1925 only a single Norwegian sailing ship arrived in South Africa (Ytreberg 1951: 496–97).

Conclusion

This chapter indicates that Swedish and Norwegian shipowners (and seafarers) were well acquainted with South African waters based on the sailing ship trade. This trade was boosted by policies of free trade and by the repeal of the British 'Navigating Act' in 1850. In 1880 Norway was the third-largest shipping nation in the world. At the same time, almost 80 percent of the gross revenue of the Norwegian shipping industry was made in cross-trade, as 'the freights men of the world' interconnecting the colonies and the colonizing nations in Europe.

As documented above, the history of Norwegian and Swedish shipping varies considerably, and the two countries' shipping industries therefore adopted distinctly different strategies – a conclusion that challenges earlier notions that the Norwegians ousted the Swedes. The Swedes sent sailing ships regularly to South Africa in the 1850s, while it was only in the 1870s that the Norwegians changed strategy and followed the Swedes to South Africa, because steamships were increasingly taking over the European trade. Towards the middle of the 1890s the Norwegians dominated what remained of the sailing ship trade. At the beginning of the 1900s the trade with South Africa was gradually taken over by steamships – a development prompting liner shipping and giving birth to three steamship lines between the Nordic countries and South Africa. Similarly, steamship lines were established from other countries and continents. The steamships rapidly gained large market shares from sailing ships, and the market for sailing ships eventually dried out completely. In 1925 the last Norwegian sailing ship called in South Africa, and an era was over.

Notes

1. The figures are 'estimated tonnage' following the method introduced by A.N. Kjær, former director of Statistics Norway (SSB). The tonnage is adjusted for increased importance and efficiency of steam tonnage by multiplying the steam tonnage by three .
2. In 1880 the Norwegian population was about two million people.
3. In an investigation carried out in 1871 by SSB for the years from 1867 to 1869, the net profit varies between 18.3 per cent and 15.6 per cent, about three times the rate of return from bank savings (Nordvik 1985: 145; see also Hodne 1983: 141). In a study of the Stavanger shipping industry during the mid-1870s, the return on capital invested varied between 11.5 per cent and 22 per cent, depending on the type of vessel (Nordvik 1985: 144).
4. Brazilian ports were opened for foreign vessels in 1808, and the Swedish consulate in Rio de Janeiro opened the following year (Bjørklund and Jensen 1989: 299).
5. For a review of quality and measurement of quality of Norwegian sailing vessels, see Nygaard (1999: 34–35).

6. In the context of this chapter, vessels in 'foreign trade' are ships sailing between Scandinavia and abroad or between foreign ports. In contrast, 'European trade' is defined as voyages between Scandinavia and ports in Europe, or between foreign ports in Europe.

7. The steamships' gradual development made them increasingly effective and thus economical in ever-longer journeys. The steamship also had an advantage over sailing ships in being able to take cargo on the deck and load more per ton. Another major advantage was regular speed, as they were not dependent on wind propulsion.

8. South Africa – the eastern coast in particular – is exposed to strong southeast onshore wind. This wind caused major problems for sailing ships in South African waters in the 1800s and made conditions in the harbours risky, with the great danger being that the ships could come loose from their moorings or lose anchorage. The result was often that the vessel ran ashore and became wrecked. There were, however, differences between the conditions in the various ports. From a report in 1895 it is evident that Mossel Bay on the southeastern coast was considered the best harbour in the Cape Colony, but that port was also exposed to the weather and precautions were necessary. For ships at anchor in this harbour, it was advised to use strong chains and exercise caution when navigating. Furthermore, the ship's captain was advised to be on board as much as possible during the stay (Worm-Müller 1950: 278–79). Another important port was Port Elizabeth in Algoa Bay farther east. This port was well protected from all winds, except from the south, which caused waves that made the ships roll and made loading and unloading difficult. In this port, a particular fear was that a southeasterly storm would blow up – a weather condition that had wrecked many ships over the years. East London was another dangerous port severely exposed to the sea (Worm-Müller 1950: 278–79). The best natural harbour in southern African waters was Delagoa Bay in what is now Mozambique (Worm-Müller 1950: 278–79). By deploying two anchors the ships here could even ride out a storm from the southeast. Delagoa Bay was also the nearest port for the gold fields in the Transvaal and the new great city of Johannesburg. In 1894, a railway from Delagoa Bay to Johannesburg was built and caused an increase in the amount of cargo handled in this port (Beinart 2001: 62–69).

9. The expression to sail 'in ballast' means the ship is sailing without revenue-earning cargo. Ballast is heavy, often valueless material (even water) intended to securing a 'cargoless' ship by counterbalancing the weight of superstructure and sail if keel and rudder are not enough.

10. 'Tramp trade' is defined as transporting cargo to any port, and it is organized by the shipping company renting out the vessel for a specific journey.

11. Annual Statements of the Trade and Shipping of the Union of South Africa, SSB.

12. National trade statistics for Norway, Sweden, Denmark and Finland, SSB.

13. General cargo is considered for convenience all the goods that are weighed in tons, including typical bulk commodities such as grain, coal and cement, or pulp and paper products. Lumber is processed timber, and common

units of measure are standard cubic feet or cubic meters (De Kerchove 1961: 775).

14. Annual Report/Board of Directors' Report, 1907, for Rederiaktiebolaget Transatlantic, A1C1, GLA.
15. Nordic trade statistics, SSB.
16. H1-F Consular reports, Ugesutgaven No. 44, 3 November 1906, report to the Norwegian Ministry of Foreign Affairs from Consul General N.P. Thesen in Cape Town, RA UD; TAA press clippings, report to the Swedish Ministry of Foreign Affairs from the Consulate General in Cape Town from October 1907, quoted in the Swedish press, 10 August 1907, RA UD; report to the Swedish Ministry of Foreign Affairs from the Swedish Consul in Lourenco Marques, quoted in the Swedish press, 29 January 1908, RA UD (which newspapers are not indicated).
17. H1-F Consular reports, Ugesutgaven No. 44, 3 November 1906, report to the Norwegian Ministry of Foreign Affairs from Consul General N.P. Thesen in Cape Town, RA UD.

Archives and Sources Consulted

Annual Statements of the Trade and Shipping of the Union of South Africa, Nordic shipping statistics and Nordic trade statistics, Statistics Norway (Statistisk Sentralbyrå, SSB), Oslo.

The archive of the Transatlantic Shipping Company, Swedish National Archives (Landsarkivet Göteborg, GLA), Gothenburg.

The Norwegian Foreign Ministry's archive, National Archives of Norway (Riksarkivet, RA UD), Oslo.

References

Beinart, W. 2001. *Twentieth-Century South Africa*. Cambridge: Cambridge University Press.

Bjørklund, J.G. and I. Jensen. 1989. 'Norsk sjøfart 1814-1900, del 1', in B. Berggren, A.E. Christensen and B. Kolltveit (eds), *Norsk sjøfart bind 1*. Oslo: Dreyer, pp. 260–328.

De Kerchove, R. 1961. *International Maritime Dictionary*. New York: D. Van Nostrand Company.

Det statistiske centralbureau. 1887. *International Skibsfartsstatistik: Tabeller vedkommende Handelsflaaderne i aarene 1850–86*. Kristiania: Aschehoug.

Feinstein, C.H. 2005. *An Economic History of South Africa: Conquest, Discrimination and Development*. Cambridge: Cambridge University Press.

Fritz, M. 1980. 'Shipping in Sweden, 1850–1913', *The Scandinavian Economic History Review* 28(1–2): 147–60.

Goodfellow, D.M. 1931. *A Modern Economic History of South Africa*. London.

Hanisch, T. 1983. 'Fire transformasjoner i skipsfarten', in T. Bergh et al. (eds), *Norge fra u-land til i-land: Vekst og utviklingslinjer 1830–1980*. Oslo: Gyldendal.

Hodne, F. 1981. *Norges økonomiske historie 1815–1970*. Oslo: Cappelen.

Larsson, B. 2000. 'Svenska varor på svenska kölar: Staten, industrialiseringen och linjesjöfartens framväxt i Sverige 1890–1925', PhD dissertation. Gothenburg: Gothenburg University.

Munro, J.F. 1976. *Africa and the International Economy 1800–1960: An Introduction to the Modern Economic History of Africa South of the Sahara*. London: J.M. Dent.

Nordvik, H.W. 1985. 'The Shipping Industries of the Scandinavian Countries 1850–1914', in L.R. Fischer and G.E. Panting (eds), *Change and Adaption in Maritime History The North Atlantic Fleets in the Nineteenth Century*. St. John's: Memorial University of Newfoundland, pp. 117–48.

Nygaard, K.M. 1999. 'Fra seilskip av tre til dampskip i linjefart Fred: Olsens rederivirksomhet 1886–1914', master's thesis. Oslo: University of Oslo.

———. 2011. 'The Scandinavian Lines og Sør-Afrika-konferanse: Linjefart mellom Europa og Sør-Afrika 1900–1940', PhD dissertation. Bergen: University of Bergen.

Palmer, S. 1985. 'The British Shipping Industry 1850–1914', in L.R. Fischer and G.E. Panting (eds), *Change and Adaption in Maritime History: The North Atlantic Fleets in the Nineteenth Century*. St. John's: Memorial University of Newfoundland, pp. 89–116.

Sargent, A.J. 1930. *Seaways of the Empire: Notes on the Geography of Transport*. Black: London.

Tønnesen, J.N. 1951. 'Jern- og stålseilskuter', in J.S. Worm-Müller (ed.), *Den norske sjøfarts historie*, vol. 2,3. Oslo: Cappelen, pp. 1–97.

Worm-Müller, J.S. 1935. 'Fra klipperen til motorskibet: Verdenskrigen', in J.S. Worm-Müller (ed.), *Den norske sjøfarts historie*, vol. 2,1. Oslo: Steenske forlag, pp. 235–705.

———. 1950. 'Skibsfartsbevegelsen og farvann 1860–80', in J.S. Worm-Müller (ed.), *Den norske sjøfarts historie*, vol. 2,2. Oslo: Cappelen, pp. 151–344.

Ytreberg, N.A. 1951. 'De første farvann erobres', in J.S. Worm-Müller (ed.), *Den norske sjøfarts historie*, vol. 2,3. Oslo: Cappelen, pp. 271–86.

2

Long-Haul Tramp Trade and Norwegian Sailing Ships in Africa, Australia and the Pacific, 1850–1920

Captain Haave's Voyages

Gustav Sætra

A lot has been published on the Norwegian sailing ships involved in the long-haul tramp trade, but little has been written about the agents involved and its organization. In this chapter priority is given to a general introduction to the traits, organization, agents and overall context for the trade, illuminated by accompanying Captain Jørgen Haave – a sea captain from the Norwegian southern coastal town of Grimstad – on three ships during the period 1902–14.

The tramp trade implied that ships traded on the spot; a charter party was negotiated for each individual voyage. Thus, ships' captains played a central role and were in charge of the day-to-day running of the vessels. This gradually changed at the beginning of the 1900s, when the corresponding shipowner at home began to actively use brokers in Africa, Australia and New Zealand for charter party contracts with European merchants. The captains now turned to such agents in connection with all matters relating to cargo, in particular everything to do with the loading and unloading of the ships. To an increasing degree captains and shipowners became a part of the global trade system and brokers became an integral part of the colonial system.

Building Wooden Ships and the Local Community

Long-haul voyages involving Norwegian sailing vessels started before the 1800s. However, the latter half of the nineteenth century represents the final period during which they were competing against steamships (see Nygaard's chapter and Hviding's chapters, this volume). Norwegian sailing ships entered this arena as a result of the liberalization of trade and shipping around 1850. The long-haul runs to the colonies by sailing vessels, from the 1880s until the First World War, were particularly important for such ships due to increasingly losing out to steamships in European waters. In particular, this applied to the southern coastal Grimstad area, where the leading shipyards in Norway had specialized in the building of wooden-hulled sailing vessels. Since the local community was dependent on the income generated from shipbuilding and shipping, these shipyards continued building sailing ships until the 1880s and 1890s. Although fully aware that the old order was doomed, this continuation postponed the inevitable transfer to steam (Sætra 2008: 13–70).

Steamships and Foreign Vessels

Sailing ships were operating in a relentlessly shrinking market where from 1866 to 1880 steamships increasingly took over the European cargo market, by far the biggest and most lucrative. From the 1870s onwards, steamships gradually entered the overseas markets, particularly the North American market, whereas tramp shipping had to compete with regular freight liners from about 1900. Here, too, the competition first arose in Europe, and then on the North Atlantic runs. From 1911 the competition was extended to southern and eastern Africa and then to Madagascar, Mauritius and Réunion; by 1914, it had reached Australia (Worm-Müller 1950: 152–53.). The prime reason why these sail ships were able to compete with foreign vessels was primarily the fact that the Norwegian wage level was comparatively low and the shipping companies had very little debt. Thus, running costs were low. In other words, the Norwegians managed to compete successfully with foreign shipping by keeping cost levels down and providing the shipping companies with freight assignments on behalf of European trading companies.[1]

The Tønnevold Company

After the shipyards in Arendal and Grimstad in the Agder area had ceased building wooden sailing ships, several shipowners gradually made the change to steam. However, until the end of the First World War many of them also opted for another solution, that is, the purchase of cheap iron-and-steel sailing vessels from abroad, mainly Great Britain (see Nygaard's contribution, this volume). In the short term this was a viable business: the large steel-and-iron sailing ships were on average three to four times larger than the previously used wooden sailing ships. Profitability depended on the size of the ships and on the overseas trade. A number of shipping companies in the Agder area were given a final lease on life thanks to the steel-and-iron sailing vessels – particularly those that kept going throughout the First World War.

One of the largest companies was O.T. Tønnevold in Grimstad, named after its owner, Ole Thomassen Tønnevold. From 1904 to 1912 Tønnevold acquired nine vessels of this type, effectively meaning that from 1907 to 1917 he managed about half of Grimstad's tonnage of this category of vessel. Tønnevold was the majority shareholder, except for three ships that he controlled in partnership with the captain. Within Norwegian shipping at that time, the shipowner and the captain were the two major shareholders. However, British shipbrokers also had ownership interests in the iron-and-steel sailing ships. The vast majority of Tønnevold's ships, if not all, were purchased through the shipbrokers Andorsen, Becker & Co. Ltd in London. The close links with the firm were emphasized by the fact that the shipowner's son Olaf Tønnevold was employed by the London brokers from 1909 to 1911.

Andorsen, Becker & Co. and the Salvesen Family

The reason Tønnevold forged links with this shipbroking company was probably because Anderson, Becker & Co. was controlled by the intermarried families Salvesen and Andorsen, who originated from the southern coastal town of Mandal, also in the Agder area. They both established themselves as merchants, shipbrokers and shipowners in several towns in Great Britain. From 1862 Harald Andorsen managed the company's London office. Later, J. Herman Becker became a partner. He married into the Salvesen family, hence the name Andorsen, Becker & Co. From the very beginning the company attracted business from clients in the Agder area – a success largely based on its family network being located there.

The brokers' income from the ships in which they had an ownership interest came from commissions on purchases and sales, commissions on freight, and income from being a shareholder of the ship. The small Norwegian shipowners were totally dependent on their shipbrokers being centrally located in London, with access to the international sales and freight markets, banks and other sources of credit, and important players in Europe and the colonies. The Salvesen family was one such player, with substantial capital assets and worldwide commercial activities.

The Shipbroking Connections

A number of charter parties relating to Tønnevold's ships provide evidence that the transition from wooden to iron-and-steel vessels led to a change of shipbrokers. While the Norwegians Gerhard Smith Petersen and Carsten S. Due were used as the main brokers for wooden sailing ships,[2] Andorsen, Becker & Co. in London was the main shipbroker for iron-and-steel ships. After 1900 overseas shipbrokers were also used for Tønnevold's wooden ships, but they usually acted as intermediaries between the overseas buyer and the Norwegian broker. Moreover, the overseas brokers visited Norwegian shipping companies in summer in order to stay in touch and maintain their contacts. Such visits resulted in the circulation of information on available cargoes and the current rates, information that Norwegians also received when visiting overseas ports.[3]

Some of the overseas brokers who acted as intermediaries for Tønnevold were originally Norwegian, such as Andorsen in London and Thorvald Salvesen in Liverpool.[4] For these companies and their clients it was essential that some of their employees had a command of written and spoken Norwegian. Over the years sons of Norwegian shipowners and brokers worked overseas as part of their training and education. This resulted in close ties between the business partners and an extension of global networks (Aalholm 1983: 62–63; Sætra 2008: 57–60).

The Overseas Cargo Trade

The sailing ships dealt with in this chapter operated within the tramp shipping trade: for each individual voyage, a charter agreement was made. The voyages were from Europe to Africa, the Far East and the Americas and then back to Europe. Some ships sailed from Europe to the Americas, mainly South America, and then on to Africa and the Far East. On these long runs the iron-and-steel sailing vessels were competitive with the steamships because the time taken and the regularity of the runs were not that decisive (see Nygaard's chapter, this volume, for a similar argument for the trade in South Africa). The sailing ships also had another competitive advantage: they did not have the expenses the steamships were subject to, such as coal and costs in connection with the transit fees charged for ships to pass (after 1869) through the Suez Canal. They sailed from Norway, Sweden and the Baltic ports with timber for Africa, Australia, New Zealand and the many islands throughout the Pacific. They also carried timber and wood products to other

European countries and continued from there with part of the original timber cargo plus additional cargo for other overseas countries. The wood products mainly consisted of planed planks and boards. From Norway in the 1860s whole shiploads of building materials left the country for foreign destinations. Not surprisingly, the southeast of the country – 'timber Norway', as it was called – emerged to lead this trade. In the 1870s exports increased significantly, particularly to Australia. A great many Norwegian vessels entered the cargo trade in this area and also the west and east coasts of Africa. Numerous Norwegian ships also carried coal to the Cape Verde Islands from England (Worm-Müller 1950: 274–81; Ytreberg 1951: 284–86).

The Captain as Owner

Because the captains owned shares of the ships, they were shipowners in their own right. They furthermore were in command of the ship and crew on a daily basis and responsible for the ship's correspondence and the accounts. This was the basis on which many sea captains at the end of the 1800s were categorized as 'corresponding shipowners' in the registry of the Norwegian classification company (Norsk Veritas). Often they were 'professional' shipowners, merchants and timber traders who submitted their annual accounts to the other part owners or shareholders. This change as well as the fact that the telegraph and telephone made it easier for shipping companies to be in touch with brokers worldwide led to a transfer of power from small local communities to shipowners, shipbrokers and shipyards in larger towns in Norway and abroad.

This development was reinforced by the decline in local shipbuilding and in the 'farmer shipping companies' (small, local companies consisting of farmers who had invested in wooden sailing ships and whose role had also been to deliver timber to the yards) when the iron-and-steel ships had taken over. However, this transfer of power was not manifested equally everywhere. For instance, the change took place somewhat later in the case of shipping companies run from rural areas and those engaged in overseas trade over long distances – as opposed to steamship companies that operated in European waters (Sætra 2008: 4–57). Originally it was the captains who entered into charter parties for their ships, and even the advent of the ship's telegraph did not undermine their authority. In 1873 the captain of *Ceres* demonstrated this in a written statement to the shipowner in Grimstad: 'You also note that I am to send a cable stating the freight tariffs. But if, in my capacity as co-owner, I might not care to do so, it would not be of any importance.

As far as I am concerned, I would gladly inform you of my arrival at any port, and I do not believe the Company would be worse off for it.'[5]

To understand how the tramp trade was organized, we shall look at the three sailing ships Jørgen Haave captained during the period 1902–14: the wooden barks *Freidig* and *Sirrah,* as well as the steel bark *Socotra.* Captain Haave left copybooks and cargo contracts covering the years 1901–14, and these documents provide insights into the relationships between the shipowner, the captain, the merchants who exported the goods, the brokers and the agents.[6]

Captain Haave originated from Eide near Grimstad, but settled in Lillesand after marrying. O.T. Tønnevold, also in Grimstad, was the corresponding shipowner for all three vessels. Tønnevold headed a part ownership shipping company that bought the four-year-old *Sirrah* in 1895 in a depressed market for half its initial construction costs. In 1897, in his capacity as shipyard owner, Tønnevold was able to build *Freidig* at an exceptionally low cost, in a final attempt to build wooden sailing vessels in the Grimstad area. *Freidig* also took advantage of a relatively favourable freight market for a couple of years from 1897 onwards.[7] In 1909 the steel bark *Socotra* was purchased from England at a third of the cost for which *Freidig* had been built, on a cost-per-ton basis. The low price of *Socotra* was due to the fact that British shipowners at the time were getting rid of their sailing ships at scrap price.[8]

Regarding *Freidig, Sirrah* and *Socotra,* the shareholders opted for what might be termed the 'next best technology', that is, sailing vessels rather than steamships. This gave them lower capital costs than was the case for the steamship companies, making them competitive with steam over long distances at sea. Haave was twenty-five when he became a captain with Tønnevold in 1902: he had just obtained his captain's certificate. The copybooks show that he was familiar with the skippers and their agents in the various ports abroad, and this gave him an advantage the shipowner did not enjoy. Haave expressed his views clearly regarding those of the shippers and agents he had confidence in and those he did not.[9] Telegraphing home was expensive, and on many occasions Haave cited this as a reason for making decisions on his own without consultation. For instance, in a letter from Cape Haiti in 1903, he states that 'I can see little point in telegraphing, since it is quite expensive'.[10]

The Captain as Manager

It was the captain who met the merchants' agents in the numerous ports and through them that he secured new charter parties. From Padang

(Telek Bayur) in Indonesia, Haave reported that 'the merchant was so satisfied with *Freidig* that he very much wanted to charter the ship again'.[11] Many contracts stated that they had been entered into with the owners of *Freidig, Sirrah* and *Socotra,* meaning all the part owners or shareholders, although other contracts specified that they had been entered into with Tønnevold. But sometimes a foregone conclusion meant that the captain was responsible for procuring freight contracts. One such instance was when Haave obtained an assignment for freight in Valparaiso when timber from a foundered Norwegian vessel was transferred to *Socotra.*[12] Even in Europe, Haave visited brokers to discuss possible freight contracts and then informed Tønnevold afterwards.[13] In other words, Captain Haave at that time had functions and responsibilities that today lie with the shipowner himself.

However, in some cases he admitted that it was convenient when the company at home entered into cargo contracts: in 1905 at Barbados, for instance. On that particular occasion it proved impossible for him to obtain cargoes.[14] During his early years as captain, he visited those ship chandlers who had been used by captains before him. For instance, after Tønnevold had secured a fixed agreement with Gourock in Glasgow (for the supply of rope and canvas), Haave was instructed to use this new supplier. Of his own accord Haave then adopted two alternatives: he made some purchases from Gourock and some from the 'old' ship chandlers, claiming that the latter supplied better goods at lower prices. Haave's objections were to no avail, and in the long term the ship chandlers appointed by the company took over deliveries.[15]

Haave was by no means satisfied with 'the new shipbrokers' in Europe. This was due to the fact that they were shipowners and acted as agents for the established shipping lines. He claimed they knew nothing about sailing ships, and in their offices no one spoke any of the Scandinavian languages any longer.[16] Thus, it was not only in the colonies that the captain was still in charge; sometimes this was the case also in the heart of Europe.

The charter party was forwarded to the captain from the merchant with whom the cargo contract had been entered into. Haave was given advance payments for the freight revenues from the European merchant, or from the latter's agents in the colonies. He required such payments in order to cover the running costs relating to the ship and its crew, including his own wages.[17] In addition, he was paid commission.[18] Haave was also paid an additional sum (*kalpak*) by the merchant, equivalent to a commission of 5 per cent of the freight payment. In practice, the two latter payments were what might now be called an administrative surcharge – even 'perks'. At the end of the voyage Haave shared the commission with Andorsen, Becker & Co. and Tønnevold.

The 'tug-of-war' between the captain and the shipowner was thus a negotiation involving authority, prestige and power, and ultimately a battle to secure income. Such income had a variety of designations: wages, fees, commissions, remunerations or perks. The captain as well as the shipowners had access to an additional source of income known as *føring:* that is, the right to carry their own goods aboard the ships.[19] All this never caused any trouble between Haave and Tønnevold; both were determined to cooperate with a view to securing the shareholders' interests. The value of Haave's invested share capital in Tønnevold's ships amounted to NOK 10,000. This meant that he owned one-sixth of *Socotra,* the company's largest vessel.

The Captain's Wife

In maritime literature women are largely ignored. However, Haave's wife deserves mentioning. She was called Anna and was on board his ships on several occasions. She accompanied him on visits to brokers, ship chandlers and agents. Moreover, she invested her own means in her husband's business: Haave's copybook shows that he represented a company that produced oil skins and a firm that sold cigars and cigarettes. Both companies were located in Cardiff, South Wales. He also sold insurance policies on behalf of a working clothes company in Grimstad. Anna came from a wealthy family, and Haave therefore not only had to deal with Tønnevold; he also had to consult with his wife, whose wealth constituted the basis for a substantial part of the family's investments. He sought her advice in financial matters[20] and wrote many letters to Tønnevold and others asking them to get in touch with Anna so that she could take care of various matters concerning shares, agencies and incoming and outgoing payments. He also asked his business connections to deposit money in an account held by Anna.[21] She even purchased a house while he was at sea.

Haave was keen for Anna to accompany him on his voyages, though he was aware that Tønnevold did not want women on board his ships. On the longest voyage, to Rio de Janeiro, she also brought along their eldest child (see figure 2.1).[22]

Desertions and Wages

On the whole the Europeans were left with a surplus from the trade with the colonies. Cargo contracts were entered into between the ship and traders and merchants in the major European ports, with brokers

Figure 2.1. Captain Jørgen Haave with his wife, Anna, and his son on his lap, together with the crew of *Socotra* in Rio de Janeiro in 1912. *Source:* Photo in possession of the author; reproduced with permission.

in Europe and the United States acting as intermediaries.[23] The many activities in the colonies, including the building of railways, mining, whaling and the plantations, provided ample opportunities for Norwegian shipping companies to be involved in transporting cargoes.[24]

Norway was part of Europe, but was nevertheless on the periphery of the continent, exhibiting at the time some of the characteristic features of a developing nation. The many desertions by Norwegian crews testify to the lower wage levels on Norwegian ships as compared with British and American vessels. On several occasions Haave's correspondence copybook mentions that his seamen had deserted to British and American ships because of higher wages, or they had deserted and gone ashore in order to work or settle elsewhere. Such desertions also happened in African and Australian ports of call. Haave, therefore, had to adjust the wages he paid in accordance with the circumstances in which he found himself. In 1912–13, when it was quite hard to recruit crew in overseas ports, Haave offered wages on a par with those offered on British and American ships so as to keep his crew. When they still deserted, he concluded that they had left the ship in order to settle ashore temporarily or permanently. Also, it frequently happened that whole crews were signed off after each completed voyage, not only in Europe, but also in the Americas, Africa and Australia. It is evident that a good many sought work on board merely as a means to emigrate or to rove the world. Indeed, Haave and other skippers hired several individuals who had deserted other vessels and transported them from one destination to another, such as from South America to Australia, or from Africa to Australia.[25]

Round the World with *Freidig*

The account of Captain Haave's voyages will focus on the African and Australian ports, and mention of the other ports will only serve to trace the whole route of the ship's voyage from the European port of departure and back again.

The first voyage takes as its point of departure a charter party entered into by the shipbroker Gerhard Smith Petersen in Grimstad in February 1902 on behalf of the owners of the bark *Freidig* and the merchant Gustave Doz in Marseilles, via the shipbroker D. & E. Salles, Marseilles. *Freidig* was to load merchandise in Marseilles and go to the two ports Tamatave (Toamasina) and Mananjari on the east coast of Madagascar. The Norwegians were familiar with the shipping routes to Madagascar: as early as 1873, a report from the Norwegian consul in Marseilles stated that for some years a number of Norwegian ships had sailed from Marseilles and entered ports on the island's east coast (Worm-Müller 1950: 274).

In September 1901 Jørgen Haave went on board *Freidig* as first mate (later on the voyage becoming captain), with a crew totalling eleven. A cargo of 280 tons of merchandise was loaded in Marseilles, of which some tons were unloaded in Tamatave at the end of July and the beginning of August. The remaining cargo, most of it salt, was unloaded in Mananjari at the end of August. In a letter to Tønnevold, Haave explained that for various reasons the unloading had been very protracted. One was that it had been necessary to transfer the cargo to be unloaded onto barges off the coast in the open sea. A second was that the local harbour workers started work in the late morning and finished early in the evening. Furthermore, the work was slowed down by rain, and the steamships were dealt with first.[26] However, Haave later mentioned that it was far safer to use barges for loading and unloading off the coast of South Africa, Madagascar and Réunion than off the coast of South America.[27]

Freidig was not the only ship to call at Madagascar. *Spero* of Lillesand had, 'some time ago', taken aboard cargo on behalf of Norway's consul Christian Bang and had continued to Réunion in order to take aboard a full load.[28] According to Haave it was possible to purchase parts from wrecked ships from Bang. In Madagascar ballast was purchased for *Freidig,* as well as provisions for the stay and the onwards voyage to Padang in Indonesia.

Freidig arrived in Indonesia in early October 1902. In Batavia (Dja-karta) the ship loaded 14,478 sacks of coffee destined for New York. She had sailed in this trade for some years and made good profits. Discern-ing merchants preferred wooden ships to iron ships because the aroma of the coffee was better preserved on board the former (Dannevig 1977: 27). The merchant in Batavia told Haave that most of the coffee was old and light and that it actually came from Madagascar, but that they would be getting heavier coffee from Padang when they arrived there to take aboard the last third of the coffee cargo and 1,010 bundles of rat-tan stalks. *Freidig* left Padang in the middle of November loaded with 21,717 sacks of coffee and the bundles of rattan. En route to New York it called at Saint Helena on the southwest coast of Africa in order to report and take aboard provisions.[29] At the beginning of January 1903 *Freidig* spent a few hours at Saint Helena and at the beginning of March arrived at the port of New York, where the coffee was unloaded. From there the ship carried ballast to Haiti and returned to Staten Island with wood products or so-called Haiti parts or wooden boards. The next voyage also included Haiti, but this time the ship carried Haiti parts for Le Havre in France, where it arrived at the beginning of June. Haave left Le Havre at the end of July and went home to marry Anna in Sep-tember the same year, 1903.

On Board *Sirrah* from the Pacific to Africa

In September 1903 Haave became captain of *Sirrah.* Until 1900 the ves-sel had carried copra, and partly also guano, from the Pacific Islands to Europe. Many Grimstad-registered vessels were involved in such trade, and the majority called at the oil-processing mills in Marseilles. As a rule the sailing vessels would carry timber from Scandinavia to Africa or Australia and continue to the Pacific to collect cargoes for Eu-rope. After the turn of the century they would carry their copra cargoes to Australia, where they would be transferred to liners bound for Eu-rope (Dannevig 1971: 264–83, 1977: 29, 37).

It was generally claimed that wooden ships were best suited for spe-cific cargoes such as copra or coffee, but after the turn of the century *Sirrah* carried timber to Senegal, where loading, unloading and formal-ities were carried on off the coast. As late as in the 1860s Africa was insignificant in the context of European shipping – apart from North

Africa, which was in fact part of the Mediterranean trade and not part of the overseas trade. It was only with the partition of the African continent by the major colonial powers in the 1880s that the opportunities for Scandinavian shipping opened up in earnest. Numerous vessels arrived mainly with local timber, and with coal cargoes from British ports destined for such ports as Cape Town, Port Elizabeth and East London in South Africa.

The 1870s saw the beginnings of the growth of the oil seed trade from the west coast of Africa. An increasing number of ships carried coconuts and nuts from Sierra Leone and Nigeria. In the 1880s Norwegian ships began sailing up the Congo River and to Liberia. The Norwegian African Trading Co. started trade with Liberia involving general goods, such as gunpowder from the Norwegian manufacturer Nitedals Krudtverk. Payment was in the form of coffee, coco products, palm oil, rubber, piassava, mahogany and leopard and snake skins, which were carried back to Europe (Worm-Müller 1950: 274–81; Ytreberg 1951: 284–86, 440–41). For instance, Tønnevold's iron bark *Oakhurst* sailed several voyages from Newport in the Bristol Channel with coal for San Paul de Luanda in the Portuguese Congo (now Luanda in present-day Angola). From there it carried ballast to Grand Conetable Island on the coast of French Guinea, near the French penal colony of Devil's Island. From Grand Conetable Island it carried guano back to Newport.[30]

Figure 2.2. The wooden bark *Freidig* was built at Tønnevold's yard in Vikkilen, east of Grimstad in 1897. *Source:* Photo in possession of the author; reproduced with permission.

When Haave first took command of *Sirrah* he obtained charter parties for voyages to Africa that the vessel had made earlier. The shipbroker Gerhard Smith Petersen in Grimstad had entered into all of these agreements on behalf of *Sirrah*. The first charter party was from October 1901 and dealt with a cargo of coal from Hull to Saint Helena for the merchant Chas. G. Wise in London. The second was from May 1902. It had been entered into by Petersen, who acted as an agent for the shipbroker Charles Scholl in Bordeaux on behalf of the merchant L.A. Videau & fils in Bordeaux to carry timber and wood products from Härnes in Sweden to Rufisque and Dakar in Senegal. The third charter party, from the end of October 1902, was concluded with the merchant Neumann, Epp & Co. in London via an English shipbroker whereby the vessel would continue from Senegal to Santos in South America, where it would load coffee for London. A fourth charter party, which Petersen had concluded on behalf of the above-mentioned businesses in Bordeaux in September 1903, covered the freight of standard wood beams and planks from Härnes and Gävle in Sweden to Rufisque and Dakar.

Before Haave left Le Havre and *Freidig* he wrote Tønnevold that he would endeavour to conclude a charter party for Rufisque in Senegal. At the end of November he arrived in Rufisque with his cargo of wood after encountering strong winds and heavy weather in the North Sea. They were able to unload quickly and went on to Dakar to unload the remaining cargo. Haave wrote that he had been there the previous year, that is, the spring of 1902, when he was first officer of *Freidig*. He observed that the ship was not unloaded by the same stevedores as the year before. The unloading was completed by mid-December, and it seems strange that *Sirrah* did not leave Senegal with a cargo of groundnuts for Marseilles, since that trade had started in earnest around 1900. From 1901 the shipbroker Ludvig Aadnesen (originally from the Agder area and who later established himself as a shipbroker in Cardiff) arranged for steamships from the Agder area (as well as Sweden) to transport groundnuts from Senegal to the oil mills in Bordeaux and Marseilles. Similarly, the shipbroker Carl O. Lie, with the shipping company Fearnley & Eger, provided steamships that combined freight for the whaling companies headed for South Africa with the transport of groundnuts from Senegal to France (Ytreberg 1951: 440–41).

However, *Sirrah* did not return to Europe, but left Senegal and headed for Santiago de Cuba, arriving there in January 1904 before sailing for Bremen. From there *Sirrah* went on to Progreso on the Yucatán Peninsula in Mexico and then on to Jobos in Puerto Rico. In both places it loaded various types of cargo before going on to Hull and Goole in

England. At the beginning of December 1904 Haave returned home to Grimstad to celebrate Christmas.

Back as Captain of *Freidig*

Jørgen Haave remained at home until August 1905, when he went to Copenhagen to board *Freidig* once more. The ship was ready to carry ballast to Karlskrona in Sweden, where it loaded planed wood products for Rufisque and Dakar. On that occasion Gerhard Smith Petersen had concluded a charter party for Humbert Balguerie in Bordeaux on behalf of Tønnevold and the merchant Maurel Frères in Bordeaux. *Freidig* called at Grimstad to take aboard provisions and to load various goods, most likely goods from Tønnevold. The vessel remained in Grimstad for one week before embarking on its voyage to Rufisque at the end of October 1905, where its wood cargo was unloaded. Then it proceeded to Dakar to unload the remaining cargo, and by the beginning of November the unloading had been completed. *Freidig* then carried ballast from Dakar to Barbados, where instructions were given to proceed to Port de Paix in Haiti to load hardwood for England.

At the New Year in 1906 Haave arrived home after unloading in England. He had felt unwell for some time and went straight to Lovisenberg Hospital in Christiania (now Oslo). He came back to Grimstad from Kristiania[31] in April 1906 and left Grimstad again on *Freidig* in May. Gerhard Smith Petersen had acted as agent for the shipbrokers Henriksen & Roll in London and had concluded a charter party for the ship involving a cargo of timber on behalf of the merchant William Dunn & Co. in London. The cargo was to be sent from Gothenburg to Cape Town, East London, Port Natal (Durban) or Delagoa Bay (Maputo) in Portuguese East Africa (Mozambique). *Freidig* carried the timber to Cape Town. While Dunn's timber was being unloaded Haave tried to sell those goods that had been taken aboard for Tønnevold and goods that remained on board from earlier voyages. The latter was a batch of coffee that he did not succeed in selling. He did, however, managed to sell some small rowing boats for three pounds each. It seems likely that the boats came from Tønnevold's father-in-law and brothers-in-law, who built small rowing boats in Landvik and Fjære, or from other boatbuilders in the Grimstad or Arendal area. Haave also managed to sell stripwood to a Swedish bark and props to a Cape Town ship chandler.

At the end of April *Freidig* left Cape Town for the Far East carrying ballast and called at Saint Helena for provisions and to report back home. On an earlier occasion Haave had experienced the crippling symptoms of beriberi in the Far East. He therefore purchased potatoes and vegetables in Saint Helena as a preventative measure.

Freidig sailed to Bangkok and loaded planks and large teak beams for Newcastle. After unloading, Haave and Tønnevold had difficulty finding charter parties from Great Britain. Finally, through Chr. Salvesen & Co., they succeeded in securing a cargo of coal from Leith to Rio Grande (Tramandai) in Brazil. *Freidig* left Rio Grande at the end of January 1908 and sailed in ballast bound for Batavia and Padang, where coffee was loaded for New York. From New York the ship sailed to Reykjavik and Eskefjord in Iceland with paraffin and firewood, and then on to Liverpool in ballast, where the vessel went into dry dock for repairs and maintenance. Haave returned home to Grimstad just before Christmas 1908. He stayed at home until the summer of 1909, when he went to Newcastle to inspect the steel bark *Socotra*.

Socotra: A Moneymaker

On the basis of Captain Haave's favourable comments, Tønnevold purchased the steel bark *Socotra* through Andorsen, Becker & Co. The ship was taken over in Newcastle in the middle of September 1909. As for all the sailing ships Tønnevold bought through this shipbroker, it was on the express condition that all the charter parties should go through Andorsen, Becker & Co. The crew of nineteen, including the captain, was signed on in Grimstad and sent to Newcastle. This was twice as many as on the two wooden barks, but then *Socotra* was three times bigger.[32]

One of the junior seamen who signed on for the first time on this journey was Harald Tønnesen from near Grimstad. He kept a written account of the experiences he had on his voyages on board *Socotra* until he signed off in June 1911. His accounts are a useful supplement to Haave's records.[33] In mid-October 1910 *Socotra* left Newcastle bound for Valparaiso in Chile with a cargo of coke and water ballast. In Valparaiso the coke was transferred to barges while the ship was at anchor outside the harbour. Afterwards the ship loaded general cargo and bales of hay for Iquique, a little farther north along the coast. In Iquique they loaded sacks containing Chile saltpetre, or sodium nitrate, from barges off the coast. Then they sailed even farther north to Caleta Buena and took aboard a full load of saltpetre in the same way for Cape Town, Port Natal in South Africa or possibly Delagoa Bay. The cargoes for Chile were transported for the merchant Andrew West & Co. in London, and the agent in Chile was J. Carrat.

Eventually *Socotra* unloaded in Delagoa Bay in October. A considerable number of Norwegian ships carried cargoes to harbours on the east coast of Africa, and many carried timber from Norway or Sweden. Other vessels transported coal from England. The demand was due to diamond finds in Kimberley about 1870 as well as gold finds in the Transvaal in the late 1880s, which resulted in a tremendous influx of people. The discovery of gold created the mining town of Johannesburg, which, in turn, gave rise to the Delagoa Bay railway line (Worm-Müller 1950: 274–81; Ytreberg 1951: 284–86).

Instead of carrying Norwegian timber, *Socotra* brought saltpetre from Chile, which was unloaded onto railway wagons and transported to Johannesburg. The junior seaman saw a whole gang of African labourers toiling in the boiling heat under the supervision of white foremen.[34] When *Freidig* had finished unloading, one of the crew signed off, and in the night two others deserted to an English ship. Haave turned for help to the Norwegian consul, who advised him to get in touch with the merchant and ship chandler N. Meyer in Durban, since it was much easier to recruit seamen there. Meyer and the consul Jakob Egeland in Durban (born in Farsund near Grimstad), were amongst the two most prominent Norwegians in South Africa. Meyer supplied Norwegians both on land and on the ships with Norwegian food, such as fish balls, anchovies, Norwegian *mysost* (whey cheese) and *gammelost* (pungent Norwegian cheese). Meyer would invite up to twenty Norwegian skippers to attend his Christmas parties (Saxe 1914: 88–89). This high number of skippers is indicative of the volume of the trade in South Africa on Norwegian ships at the time. While the unloading took place in Delagoa Bay, Andorsen, Becker & Co. concluded a charter party with the merchant John Darling & Son in Adelaide. The agreement covered a consignment of wheat from Australia to Great Britain. In November *Socotra* took on ballast in Delagoa Bay before sailing to Australia.

The Grimstad Colony in Delagoa Bay

In Delagoa Bay (in present-day Mozambique) junior seaman Harald Tønnesen met a number of people from his own area at home. He noted that the ballast was supplied by Mathias Jørgensen, who originally came from Hesnes near Grimstad and who was known to most of the crew. Jørgensen ran a firm in Delagoa Bay. In 1912 a Norwegian journalist, Ludvig Saxe, arrived in Delagoa Bay, stating that among the many Norwegians who had returned to Norway pleased with their stay there were the Abrahamsen brothers, M. Jørgensen and others, all from Grimstad. According to Saxe, half the population of Grimstad had been to Delagoa Bay. As soon as Saxe arrived there by steamer he met a fair-haired man followed by a whole company of what they called 'caffers' (Africans). The person in question was Anders Woxholt, from near Grimstad. He was employed by an English stevedore company, which would be responsible for unloading the ship. On the next ship was G. Guttormsen from Grimstad, and on the third one was N. Bjønnes from Tønsberg, close to Grimstad.

The three men (Woxholt, Guttormsen and Bjønnes) were all employed by the English stevedore company and gave orders to the dock workers in what they called the 'caffer language', while the African workers rushed back and forth carrying sacks of coal, boxes and crates. A few years earlier there had been far more Norwegians in the area, but a great many of them had left during the hard times after the Anglo-Boer War. H. Rosholt, also from near Grimstad, was head of a freight and transport company in Delagoa Bay.[35] After the war there could be as many as twenty-five Norwegian ships at any one time in the port of Durban, but during Saxe's visit in 1912 there were only six or seven ships at any time. Most of them carried cargoes for foreign clients. After hearing this account from Woxholt, Saxe went to a large timber storage site outside the city, where he met the manager, Alf Solberg, the son of the owner of a large estate north of Christiania (now Oslo). Most of his store consisted of planed planks from Norway (Saxe 1914: 62–63). Whereas neither Captain Haave nor junior seaman Harald Jørgensen mentioned that Woxholt was in charge of the unloading of *Socotra*, it is likely that it was he. On the other hand, Jørgensen does point out that he himself and the rest of the crew worked together with the black workers in order to get the ballast down into the hold. In a letter Haave mentioned that he conducted business with Woxholt without going into further detail.[36]

Onwards to Australia and New Zealand – and Beyond

The tug pulled *Socotra* out of the harbour at Delagoa Bay so that the voyage could begin. It arrived at Port Jackson, Sydney, just before Christmas 1910. Junior seaman Jørgensen had to agree with the older members of the crew that the Sydney harbour was one of the most scenic harbours in the world, but found it nevertheless strange to be celebrating Christmas in the middle of summer. In Port Jackson the ship loaded sacks of wheat for Dalgety & Co. in London. The sacks were fetched from large storage buildings and transferred to the ship by means of what the ju-

nior seaman called a 'roller coaster', a transport system which originally carried coal from mines. The sacks disappeared elegantly into the
hold without being damaged. Stevedores from ashore stowed the cargo
in the hold.

The background for the trade involving the carriage of cargo by
Norwegian sailing ships to Australia and New Zealand was in many
respects similar to the corresponding African shipping trade. From
1870 the Australian and New Zealand trade showed a marked increase,
partly because of the discovery of gold in Australia in 1851. This trig-
gered a tremendous population growth, creating a demand for Scandinavian building materials. An estimated one thousand Norwegians
were engaged in gold-digging activities in the country. In addition, the
Australian authorities offered the temptation of free travel from Europe
to anyone who wanted to settle there as a farmer. Many Norwegians
took advantage of this opportunity (Worm-Müller 1950: 162–63; Møller
1986: 58–83, 90–98, 111–13).

The Norwegian consul general, Christophersen, in Buenos Aires was
sent to Australia in 1872 by the Norwegian government to look into
the potential market for Norwegian goods and Norwegian shipping.
He concluded that, due to the considerable building activity, there
would be a demand for timber, particularly in Australia and partly also
in New Zealand and the small islands in the Pacific. Moreover, there
would be opportunities for the freight of timber from New Zealand to
Australia and the freight of coal from one part of Australia to another.
Also, it was essential to take advantage of the opportunity for freight
from Australia, in case that should turn out to be a lucrative business.

There were three major categories of cargo available from Australia:
wool, wheat and coal. While coal and wheat were the most usual cargoes from Australia, Christophersen recommended that the Norwegians go in for the freight of wool to the United States (Worm-Müller
1950: 152–53, 162–63). And here the consul general was making an important point: the sailing ships engaged in long-distance trade did not
have as their primary destinations Africa, Australia, New Zealand and
the Pacific Islands. Their voyages there were frequently only part of a
longer voyage to the Far East and the Americas. This meant that such
vessels might be away from Norway for several years before returning
home. One such example was the newly built bark *Atlantic,* which left
Grimstad in 1866 and did not return to a Norwegian harbour until thirteen years later (Dannevig 1971: 146).

Socotra sailed for Europe from Australia at the end of January 1911.
Its planned voyage would take it round Cape Horn, the southernmost
point of South America. The ship first had to sail southwards in order

to take advantage of the westerlies that can almost always be relied on by sailing ships. After passing New Zealand the sailing became rough and *Socotra* encountered heavy seas in waters known by sailors as the Roaring Forties. There was nothing but open sea ahead, and there was no sign of any steamships. At times a solitary sailing ship was observed, as well as icebergs, whales and albatross. When the vessel had rounded the Horn, *Socotra* sailed to Falmouth for further orders. Nearly all the sailing ships called at Falmouth in England and Queenstown (a harbour town near Cork) in Ireland to await further instructions, because the final destination and recipient of the cargo had not as yet been determined. In Falmouth, Haave was instructed to unload in the French port of Dieppe, to which *Socotra* was towed. When she had been unloaded *Socotra* took aboard ballast and sailed for Newport in the Bristol Channel, where she went into dry dock for maintenance and repairs. The crew, including the junior seaman Harald Jørgensen, signed off.

In July the ship left the dock in Newport, ready to load coal. At the end of July *Socotra* left Newport, bound for Montevideo in Uruguay with its cargo of coal for the Central Railway Co. The ship sailed onwards to Australia in ballast from Montevideo, because Andorsen, Becker & Co. had arranged for another cargo of wheat for Europe on behalf of the merchant and grain exporter John Darling. In early November *Socotra* dropped anchor in Port Lincoln in Australia to await further instructions. The steel bark *Bølgen,* which Tønnevold had recently acquired through Andorsen, Becker & Co., was also waiting for cargo in Port Lincoln. Naturally enough, Haave went aboard *Bølgen* to greet its skipper and crew. At the beginning of January *Socotra* received orders to proceed to Port Victoria, between Port Lincoln and Adelaide, to load a cargo of wheat for Europe. The agent warned Haave that they would have to put up with many days' delay before a cargo became available, as John Darling & Co. normally paid a higher price for wheat than the other merchants were willing to offer. They therefore obtained many cargoes and thus had to charter more ships in order to handle the cargoes. At the end of January 1912 *Socotra* had completed loading its cargo of 33,694 sacks of wheat. When *Socotra* sailed from the harbour Captain Haave saw *Bølgen* at anchor off the coast, waiting for its cargo of wheat.

At the beginning of June 1912 *Socotra* had arrived safely in Falmouth, where it awaited further instructions regarding the unloading of the cargo. Within the space of a few hours another ten ships dropped anchor outside the harbour. They had all arrived from Australia, but *Bølgen* had not yet appeared. Haave was told to unload his ship at Penarth in the Bristol Channel, and when the unloading had been completed *Socotra* went to one of the coal tips at Penarth to load coal for Rio de Janeiro, and at the end of September 1912 the unloading started in Rio. While there they observed Tønnevold's iron bark *Natuna* arriving with coal. The vessel had just been bought through Andorsen, Becker & Co. Soon afterwards *Bølgen* also arrived there with a cargo of coal. Unloading coal from *Socotra* went slowly, and taking aboard ballast for Australia was an equally protracted affair. The other two Tønnevold ships also loaded ballast for Australia. Once there, they loaded wheat for Europe.

In mid-January 1913 *Socotra* arrived in Freemantle, Australia. There it got rid of its ballast and took aboard wheat before sailing to Falmouth to await further instructions. Before long orders were received to continue to Cardiff to unload. The charter party covering the cargo of wheat from Australia included one of the most profitable freight rates paid from Australia. The net profit from that single voyage almost corresponded to the purchase price of *Socotra* (Dannevig 1977: 70). Having unloaded the wheat, *Socotra* entered dry dock for maintenance and repairs before loading coal for Buenos Aires.

Socotra reached Buenos Aires towards the end of September 1913. Here the coal was unloaded and ballast loaded for Geraldton, a port in Western Australia, north of Perth. There it took aboard 33,846 sacks of wheat for the merchant James Bell & Co. in Melbourne. At the beginning of February 1914 the vessel had been fully loaded and set sail for Port Elizabeth in South Africa, where it arrived at the beginning of March. Some of the cargo was transferred to the British Union-Castle Line's large iron cargo ships, which were moored offshore because *Socotra* had a draft that was too large for it to dock alongside the quay. After unloading 370 tons of cargo the vessel was able to go alongside the quay to unload the remaining cargo. It then took aboard ballast to sail for Halifax, Nova Scotia. There it entered dry dock for the usual maintenance and repairs. Haave's last letter to Tønnevold was dated 9 June 1914, Halifax. The letter was inserted into the last page of the copybook. Haave probably returned to Europe with *Socotra* and signed off on arrival.

Haave sailed as master for thirteen years, from 1902 to 1914. From then on he spent time at sea only for a couple of voyages, as first mate. During the time Haave was at sea his wife Anna and their children lived in a rented house in Lillesand, but when he came ashore for good they bought a magnificent house in Kristiansand, where he ran his own business. The couple was very well-off and always had a healthy bank balance.[37]

The Profitable Overseas Tramp Trade

There was a sevenfold increase in the nominal value of Ole Tønnevold's assets over the period 1901–13, mainly due to his ownership of shares in ships. During the same period his income rose by 300 per cent, and as much as 77 per cent of his income derived from ships. Most of this was profit, while a small part was accounted for by directorship fees. In 1910 the profit from the sailing ships averaged 10 per cent, rising to 20–30 per cent in 1914. During the First World War profits rose to astronomical heights. A single ship could produce a profit of up to 550 per cent, which meant that more than 500 per cent of its initial cost was recouped within a single year. *Socotra*'s profits were among the best. Thus, they shot up from 17 per cent in 1910 to as much as 500 per cent in 1916. As captain of the three vessels *Freidig, Sirrah* and *Socotra* during the thirteen years from 1902 to 1914, Haave received wages totalling almost NOK 40,000. If Haave had been a shareholder in *Socotra* during the seven years from 1910 to 1916 he would, with an ownership of 10 per cent of the vessel, have received more than NOK 52,000 in profit. He was not paid that amount because he retired from his post as captain in 1914 and therefore only received a total of NOK 15,000 as captain's commission for all five years. During the years 1873–84, a captain in the Grimstad area was paid more in *kaplak* (gratuities) than in wages.[38] It is not unreasonable to assume that much the same was true of Haave. Also, both Haave and Tønnevold made additional profits from their agencies, commissions and fees. In other words, both of them made large sums from sailing vessels in the overseas trade. The same was undoubtedly true for the merchants they carried cargoes for and the shipbrokers that concluded the charter parties.

Captain Haave's personal logs on the three sailing ships from 1902 to 1914 provide some insight into how this long-haul tramp trade was organized. By means of such sources as charter parties, letter copybooks and personal papers we have seen how the owner and captain cooperated in order to secure cargoes for their sailing vessels, even though there were occasional rivalries between the captain and the corresponding shipowner for influence in running the company and its ships. We have seen how the sailing vessels were easily able to compete with steamships when it came to overseas voyages, thanks to modest capital expenditures and long sailing distances. The local shipbrokers in Grimstad cooperated with British and French brokers to negotiate the charter parties for the two wooden sailing ships with British and French merchants. These vessels were built in Grimstad and financed locally. The steel bark had been bought secondhand in Newcastle. The shipbroking firm Andorsen, Becker & Co. in London was responsible for the transfer of the ship to the Norwegian owners and bought shares in the vessel on the condition that all charter parties for the ship be concluded by the firm.

The charter parties for the wooden sailing ships were initially for timber exports from Sweden to Africa, but also merchandise from French ports and coal from British ports. However, the wooden sailing ships to a great extent carried cargoes from one overseas harbour to another – from the Americas to Australia, the Pacific Islands, Africa and the Far East. This situation was reinforced with the introduction of the steel bark, which contributed strongly to the Australian wheat trade that brought grain from Australia to Europe, and where sailing ships could compete with powered vessels. In the case of Tønnevold's ships this meant that they carried freight for merchants in Europe to and from Europe and the colonies, as well as between the colonies themselves. Yet they did not carry one single cargo to Norway.

Both Tønnevold and Haave were dependent on their network of contacts with shipbrokers in Grimstad and abroad. But Haave also had personal contacts, particularly among ship chandlers overseas. It has not always been equally easy to trace and map all of these connections, but there is no doubt that in Delagoa Bay he had a number of local contacts who worked in the harbour areas. It may very well be assumed that he had such networks in other ports as well, because in the era of sailing ships, as well as in the latter part of the twentieth century, one could meet shipbrokers, ship chandlers and agents with Norwegian names in a great many ports worldwide, and many of them could still speak Norwegian.

Notes

1. For further details, see also Fischer and Nordvik (1988) and Sætra (1997: 184–88, 2008: 14–43).
2. Petersen established a shipbroking company in Grimstad after working in England and France in 1884. He arranged charter parties for European and overseas destinations, facilitated the purchase and sale of ships and also ran a timber company. Due lived in Sydney for three years before returning home to take over his father's business, which comprised a steamship agency, a business dealing with the sale of boats and coal, and shipbroking. Both joined the consular corps; Pettersen was appointed French vice-consul in 1892, while Due was appointed Swedish vice-consul in 1909 (Gundersen 1927: 748, 752–53).
3. Tønnevold used the shipbroking firm Bahr, Behrend & Co. in Liverpool, while French shipbrokers were involved when goods were sent from French ports or to French colonies.

4. Gerhard Smith Petersen in commission for the shipbroker Thorvald Salvesen in Liverpool, charter party for *Sirrah*, 27 April 1904, OTT 8.015B.
5. Captain J. Gundersen, New Orleans, 7 November 1873. Quote from Stein Tveite's transcript of captains' letters, manuscript collection, NMM.
6. The originals of the documents were made available by Haave's grandson Jørgen Egil Haave in Kristiansand, together with copies of other material dealing with details of the lives of other family members. All of these documents are deposited in Tønnevold's archives, OTT 8.015B. References to Haave's copybook from here on will only give the location and date.
7. *Sirrah* had been built in Vikkilen in 1891 for NOK 76,000, and Tønnevold acquired the vessel in 1895 for NOK 38,000. *Freidig* was built for NOK 60,000, corresponding to NOK 120 per net ton. In the 1880s a corresponding vessel had a cost of NOK 150–200 per ton (Dannevig 1977: 21–27).
8. *Socotra* was three times the size of *Freidig*, yet its price was the same (Sætra 2009: chap. 3).
9. Cape Town, 24 September 1906: Haave expresses dissatisfaction that Tønnevold has entered into a charter party involving a run to Bangkok, which meant a long voyage and meagre profit.
10. Cape Haiti, 10 April 1903.
11. Padang, 12 March 1908.
12. Valparaiso, 12 and 20 March and 2 April 1904.
13. Among others, shipbrokers in Bremen, 21 April 1904; the shipbrokers Hoskins, Mears & Co., London, and Gjemre & Company in Jarrow (Stoke on Tyne) and Newcastle, 14, 18, 24, 25, 27 June and 4 July 1907; Padang, 12 March 1908; the shipbrokers Hoskins, Mears & Co. and Bahr, Berend & Co. in Liverpool 28 and 13 November and 22 December 1908.
14. Barbados, 22 November 1905.
15. Leith, 25 July 1907; Tyne, 25 September 1909.
16. Cape Town, 30 September 1906; Tyne, 1 October 1909.
17. Accounts, Padang, 7 October 1902; Haiti, 18 April 1903; Jarrow (Stoke on Tyne), 14 June 1907.
18. Jarrow (Stoke on Tyne), 18 June 1907.
19. Tyne, 8 October 1909.
20. Interview with Jørgen Haave's son-in-law Jørgen Egil Haave. His account is partly based on information provided by his aunt, Jørgen Haave's daughter, 160A 0-136, OTT 8.024.
21. Tyne, 21 September 1909.
22. Gothenburg, 3 June 1906; Jarrow (Stoke on Tyne), 18 June 1907; Buenos Aires, 22 September to 2 November 1913; picture of Anna, Jørgen and their son in Buenos Aires.
23. Tyne, 8 October 1909.
24. See, e.g., Reiersen's analysis of Christian Thams, this volume, for an elaboration of this argument.
25. Captain Haave's copybook contains a number of references to desertions: Santiago de Cuba 3 and 8 February 1904; Bremen, 12 April 1904; Newcastle, 16 and 25 June and 4 July 1907; Leith, 12 July 1907; Rio Grande, 25 October and 13 November 1907; New York, 7 August 1908; Valparaiso, 7 May 1910;

Delagoa Bay, 13, 18 and 29 October 1910; Sydney, 13 January 1911; Montevideo, 3 and 18 October 1911 and 5 January 1912; Dieppe, 4 July 1912; Rio de Janeiro, 20 and 30 September and 5 and 7 November 1912; Freemantle, 15 January and 2 February 1913; Cardiff, 9 July 1913; Geraldton, 9 January and 3 February 1914.
26. Tamatave, 26 July to 8 August 1902; Mananjari, 19 to 22 August 1902.
27. Rio Grande, 8 October 1907.
28. The consul's duty was to help Norwegian ships abroad on behalf of the Norwegian government. However, he was frequently personally involved in business as well. Consul Bang in Tamatave in Madagascar was such a businessman. In addition, he also served as British consul and probably also acted as agent for the merchant Gustave Doz in Marseilles. Jørgen Haave had known Bang previously. The latter arrived in Madagascar together with his parents in 1876 and remained there until his death in 1931. He was born in Bergen, settled in Tamatave and became a highly successful businessman there. In 1899 Bang was appointed both Swedish and Norwegian consul, and he continued as Norwegian consul after Norwegian independence from Sweden in 1905.
29. The British had colonized Saint Helena already in the 1600s. The island was of great importance to shipping, as ships took on water and provisions there on their voyages to and from the Far East.
30. Paul Woxholt's manuscript from his voyages with *Oakhurst*, 1911–14, OTT 8.023.
31. The name for Oslo between 1624 and 1925. In the period 1877 to 1897, the name was also spelt 'Christiania'.
32. *Sirrah* was 451 net tons and *Freidig* 496 net tons; *Socotra* had a gross tonnage of 1,704 tons.
33. Haave's accounts as given by Halvdan I. Drevdal in the local newspaper *Grimstad Adressetidende* and later reproduced in Dannevig (1977: 54–63).
34. Letter from Haave, 20 October 1910, in Haaves copy-book in OTT.
35. Before and after the Second World War Tønnevold used the ship chandler Martin Rosholt in Durban for his company's steam- and engine-propelled ships. Tønnevold's brother-in-law, Captain Jørgen Tellefsen, was then invited to Rosholt's home. This information was provided by the shipowner Johan Tønnevold, Ole Tønnevold's grandson. K.M. Rosholt acted as treasurer of the Norwegian War Relief Fund (Lear 1980: 38).
36. Rio de Janeiro, 14 November 1912; Cardiff, 26 June 1913.
37. Interview with Jørgen Egil Haave, 160A 0-48, OTT 8.024.
38. Captain, and later shipowner, Jørgen Halvorsen Ugland, the father of the founder of the large-scale international shipping company Uglands Rederi (Sætra 2008: 49–50).

Archives and Sources Consulted

Archives of O.T. Tønnevold (OTT), Grimstad, Norway.
Norwegian Maritime Museum (Norsk Maritimt Museum, NMM), Oslo.

References

Aalholm, O.A. 1983. *Handelshuset Thommesen Smith, Smith & Thommesen A/S.* Arendal.

Dannevig, B. 1971. *Grimstads sjøfarts historie.* Grimstad.

———. 1977. *Tønnevolds Rederi/Olaf Tønnevold & Sønner.* Grimstad: Tønnevolds Rederi.

Fischer, L.R. and H. Nordvik. 1988. 'The Norwegian Maritime Sector 1850–1914: A Reinterpretation', in L.R. Fischer, H. Nordvik and W.E. Minchinton (eds), *Shipping and Trade in the Northern Seas.* Bergen, pp. 9–12.

Gundersen, H. 1927. 'Hundrede Borgere i Hundredeaaret', in *Grimstad bys historie.* Grimstad, pp. 682–755.

Lear, M.F. 1980. *The St. Olaf Lutheran Church 1880–1980: Its Origins and History over One Hundred Years.* Durban: Unity Publications.

Møller, A. 1986. *Australia-farere: Nordmenn som tok en annen vei.* Oslo: Cappelen.

Sætra, G. 1997. 'International Labour Market for Seamen 1600–1900: Norway and Norwegian Participation', in P. van Royen, J. Bruijn J. and T. Lucassen (eds), *Those Emblems of Hell,* Research in Maritime History 13. St. John's: Maritime Studies Research Unit, Memorial University of Newfoundland, pp. 173–210.

———. 2008. *Aust-Agder og sjøfarten: Rederens rolle.* Arendal: Aust-Agder rederiforening.

Saxe, L. 1914. *Nordmænd jorden rundt.* Kristiania: Aschehoug.

Tønnessen, J.N. 1951. *Jern- og stålseilskuter: Siste treseilskutetid.* Oslo: Steenske forlag.

Worm-Müller, J.S. 1935. 'Fra klipperen til motorskibet: Verdenskrigen', in J.S. Worm-Müller (ed.), *Den norske sjøfarts historie,* vol. 1. Oslo: Steenske forlag.

——— (ed.). 1950. *Den norske sjøfarts historie,* vol. 2. Oslo: Steenske forlag.

☯) 3

LIMINAL BUT OMNIPOTENT

Thesen & Co. – Norwegian Migrants in the Cape Colony

Erlend Eidsvik

This chapter is concerned with how Thesen & Co., a company founded by Norwegian migrants in Knysna in the Cape Colony in 1870, expanded from its modest beginnings to become a powerful and influential force in the economic sphere of the Cape region.[1] Thesen & Co. embarked upon a variety of commercial ventures throughout its century-long existence. In a memorandum from 1905, the objectives for which the company was established are summarized in sixty specific points. These objectives comprise a kaleidoscope of commercial activities envisioning a ubiquitous economic presence, including shipping and passenger services, forestry and lumber milling, mining, whaling, shipbuilding, trading and merchandising, property, and garage and motor services, to mention the most significant branches.[2] Some of these objectives also encompassed political strategies in order to secure political conditions under which the company could thrive.[3] Nevertheless, throughout the company's century-long existence, many of its subenterprises and branches were subsequently abandoned. When the company was sold in 1974 the core activities included forestry and timber processing, merchandising, wholesale and retail trading stores, and property investment.[4]

How, then, was it possible for a group of Norwegian migrants to succeed economically in a British colony, and how was it possible to gain a position of such a ubiquitous nature? These questions are addressed here by analysing how the company was embedded in collaborative relations – networks – and by investigating the nature of these at different levels. The dynamics and characteristics of networks – in terms of strength, weakness and embeddedness (Granovetter 1973, 1985) – are necessarily different in local networks as compared to networks with national and international ramifications.

Notwithstanding its economic expansion, the history of Thesen & Co. is also one of controversies and performance of power. Involvement in networks is seen in correspondence to being an *omnipotent entrepreneur*. This omnipotence, I would argue, is propelled by involvement in multiple networks and is conditioned by a state of liminality, as the entrepreneurs of Thesen & Co. gained advantages through manoeuvring into a position wedged between the dominant white groups – British and Boer. Liminality is a useful concept within postcolonial thought and refers to a spatial notion of in-betweenness, an interstitial space of continuous interchanges and processes of movements (Bhabha [1994] 2004: 5). A colonized subject, for example, might dwell in a liminal space between colonial discourse and the idea of a new 'noncolonial' identity. Yet a constant process of engagement, contestation and appropriation can blur transformation between these identities (Ashcroft, Griffiths and Tiffin 2007: 117). However, this in-between space also blurs the identity of 'colonizers'. In this particular case, the interstitial passage between fixed identifications, for example, between being a migrant oneself (from a 'noncolonial' country) and being a partaker in colonial discourse, can add impetus to how identities are forged and fashioned.

The concept of colonial discourse is derived from a Foucauldian tradition and refined by Bhabha ([1994] 2004), and is understood here as a system of statements through which the world can be known regarding how knowledge and beliefs constitute the relation between colonizers and the colonized (Ashcroft, Griffiths and Tiffin 2007: 37). The state of liminality in colonial discourse is therefore also seen as a potential for economic achievements and political influence.

The chapter begins by presenting the establishment and expansion of Thesen & Co., followed by an empirically and theoretically informed analysis of the entrepreneurship, social networks and discursive networks, where notions of liminality, power and omnipotence are also addressed. The chapter emphasizes the early phase of the business establishment until the Second World War – concurrent with the management period (1875–1940) of the major entrepreneur in the enterprise, Charles Wilhelm Thesen (1856–1940).

Shipping and Exodus

In 1845, more than two decades before migrating to South Africa, the brothers Arent Leonard (A.L.) and Frederik Thesen established A.L. Thesen & Co. in Stavanger, Norway. Following more than twenty years of relative economic success in the shipping and grain trade in the Baltic and the North Sea area, the company suffered bankruptcy when an economic slump hit Stavanger at the end of the 1860s. The economic prospects in the domestic arena seemed gloomy, and A.L. Thesen planned to restart his career on foreign shores. His brother Frederik chose to stay in Stavanger. The majority of economic migrants leaving Norway in the latter part of the nineteenth century, as from many other European countries, sought new opportunities in North America.[5] The Thesens, however, aimed for New Zealand. Experience from three decades of European trade had provided them with a network of British agents and merchants, and a fresh start in one of the British colonies seemed plausible. To facilitate such a scheme, the British consul in Stavanger, a close acquaintance of A.L. Thesen, issued a letter of recommendation for the Thesens to settle in a British colony.[6] However, they never reached their planned destination, instead ending halfway through their journey in the Cape Colony, where they established a business empire that would last for a century.

Together with his wife, Ane Kathrine, and his brother Mathias, A.L. Thesen repurchased the schooner *Albatros* from the liquidated property of their company.[7] Before leaving Norway in 1869, a cargo of timber was provided as saleable capital upon arrival. After nearly three months at sea, *Albatros* arrived in Cape Town in November 1869, carrying twenty people, thirteen from the Thesen family and seven others who wished to be part of a common venture for new opportunities. The ship needed maintenance, and provisions were taken on board. The voyage continued towards New Zealand, but a storm at Cape Agulhas caused severe damage and *Albatros* was forced to return to Cape Town. The timber cargo was sold to pay for the repairs. Halfway to their intended destination, and without sufficient means, the stranded Norwegians sought assistance from the Swedish-Norwegian consul in Cape Town, Carl Gustav Åkerberg, a merchant in shipping and trade. At the time, increased tensions between Prussia and France and political instability in Europe had caused a shortage in vessels that even affected South Africa.[8] Hence, the demand for freighters along the coast was considerable, and the consul accommodated through his extensive business network freight charters to and from Knysna, which is situated between Cape Town and Port Elizabeth.

At the time of *Albatros*'s arrival, Knysna was a small and remote settlement that housed a few hundred people, with around three thousand people living in the extended Knysna region.[9] However, being one of the few sheltered ports on the rugged coast between the Cape and Natal, the town was strategically important, as well as being surrounded by vast forest resources – which were already scarce at that time. A major part of the supplies to the region, from George in the west to the scattered settlements in the Tsitsikamma region in the east (figure 3.1),

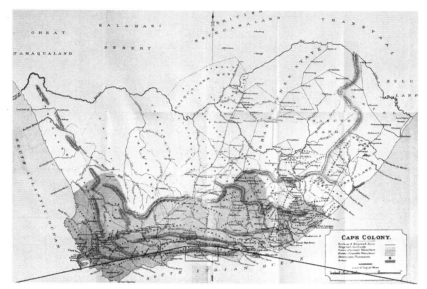

Figure 3.1. The Cape Colony, 1886 (adapted from Noble 1886). *Source:* Erlend Eidsvik; reproduced with permission.

arrived by ship in Knysna or Mossel Bay and then transported by ox-wagons to the settlements in the region. Knysna and the surrounding mountain ranges of Outeniqua and Tsitsikamma constituted a fertile region where forestry and agriculture was, and still is, economically significant.

Establishment in the Cape Colony

Hans Thesen, the nephew of A.L. Thesen, was appointed to take *Albatros* to Knysna with a chartered cargo on a mission from Consul Åkerberg and his business partners. Over the next three months in early 1870, *Albatros* shuttled supplies to Knysna and then loaded timber to return to Cape Town, where the family temporarily resided. Hans, the young skipper, was enthusiastic about Knysna, and fondly depicted the afforested hills surrounding the village and the sheltered fjord-like estuary.[10] In April 1870, the *Albatros* moored in Knysna, as the family had decided to settle permanently and restart their livelihood there. A few weeks before their arrival in Knysna, one of two local merchants had died, leaving a combined living compound and shop facilities behind.[11] The Thesens bought the house with financial assistance from Consul Åkerberg and commenced retail business immediately.[12]

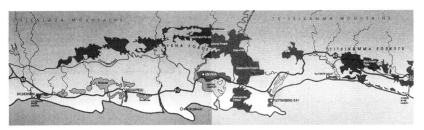

Figure 3.2. Knysna and its surrounding regions at present. Forests marked in dark grey (van der Merwe 2002). *Source:* Erlend Eidsvik; reproduced with permission.

A.L. Thesen died in 1875. Two of his sons, Nils Peter and Charles Wilhelm (C.W.), had undertaken four and two years of mercantile training, respectively, at the shipping agent William Anderson & Co. in Port Elizabeth. Both returned to Knysna, and C.W., who was only seventeen, assumed responsibility, together with his brothers Rolf and Hjalmar. Supported by his brothers, C.W. became the leading entrepreneur in the company until he died at age eighty-three in 1940. He led the company's development from a minor enterprise in a small village to a large-scale business with national and southern African ramifications and global connections. Nils Peter left for Cape Town to head the Thesen & Co. branch office there, where the shipping section was managed.[13] He also became the first general consul for Norway in Cape Town upon the establishment of the Norwegian consulate in 1905, when Norway achieved independence from Sweden, a position he held until 1915, when his nephew Mathias Thesen succeeded him.[14]

Forest and Timber

The decisive factors involved in settling down in Knysna were the sheltered harbour and its vast forested hinterland. Timber was a long-standing scarce resource in the region, as the Cape Peninsula was depleted of its forests only a few decades after the establishment of the Dutch East India Company (Vereenigde Oostindische Compagnie, or VOC) in Table Bay (later to become Cape Town) in 1652 (van der Merwe 2002). The demand for wood increased proportionally with the growing population of European migrants in the Cape region. Settlers of mainly Dutch, French and German origin migrated eastwards into the forests of Outeniqua and Tsitsikamma during the mid-eighteenth century. The Swedish botanists Carl Peter Thunberg and Anders Sparrmann surveyed the region in the 1770s and concluded that commercial exploitation of timber from the forests was viable, on the condition that a port could be established in the region. The VOC initiated forest stations in George and Plettenberg (van der Merwe 2002: 24).

When the Thesens arrived in Knysna, the forest resources had already been exploited for a century, but on a moderate scale. Both the VOC and the British colonial administration, from 1795 onwards, enforced regulations to limit the volume of material and species that could be extracted from the forest. Only woodcutters holding a license were allowed to cut timber for sale to the colonial administration. The first governmental forest conservator for Knysna was appointed in 1874 as a consequence of concerns expressed by a governmental commission. The woodcutters did not comply with the regulations, the commission concluded, and the endogen species were being cut at such a pace that the aftergrowth could not be sustained. Tapson confirms this narrative and states that 'of all the enemies, the forest ever had – the fires, berg winds, storms disease and wild animals – the greatest of them all he [the forest conservator] found to be the woodcutter' (1961: 117–18). The official handbook for the Cape Colony prepared by the colonial government in 1886 estimated the forest areas in Knysna and Tsitsikamma to be approximately one hundred thousand acres, equivalent to four hundred square kilometres. As much as 75 per cent of the forest was already 'considerably exhausted by reckless and indiscriminate felling', the colonial administration stated (Noble 1886: 141).

The most valuable species was the endogen species stinkwood (*Ocotea bullata*) and Outeniqua yellowwood (*Podocarpus falcatus*).[15] 'I can not imagine why a pleasanter name than stinkwood has not been found for a wood which people take so eagerly in their homes', the traveller and writer Morton rhetorically stated (1948: 127). Stinkwood was, and still is, a highly appreciated hardwood for processing furniture. Yellowwood was, to a greater extent, processed into sleepers, telephone poles, handles, fences, doors and furniture.

To ensure aftergrowth, the forest conservator introduced the sectioning of the forest to allow grids to be fallow while others were harvested. Following a retrenchment in management the governmental forest was opened for commercial operation in 1876 (Phillips 1963). In the same year, Thesen & Co. bought two thousand acres (eight square kilometres) of forest and promptly informed interested parties that they could supply buyers with stinkwood and yellowwood logs and planks.[16] Subsequently, the company continued to purchase forest properties, and by 1926 Thesen & Co. owned one-sixth of the land in the Knysna region.[17]

European species, such as pine and oak, were introduced into the Cape region during the nineteenth century (Nimmo 1976: 106). Pine was imported mainly for economic reasons, while oak brought European (and particularly British) aesthetics to the colonies (Nash 2000; Wynn 1997).[18] Thesen & Co. imported pine to secure fast-growing wood and a viable future within forestry, and consequently contributed to reconfirming the existing colonial discourse on ecological adjustments and adapting the natural landscape of the colony into a familiar economic and ecological sphere reminiscent of Europe. Knowledge and experiences from forestry enterprises were sought in the Nordic countries in particular. Potential innovations and developments in forestry were also carried out in correspondence with the colonial authorities, and later with the agricultural and forestry authorities in the Union of South Africa.[19] The timber products were mainly aimed at the domestic market, in addition to the export of high-end stinkwood furniture to Europe.

Shipping and Railway

After forestry, shipping constituted the other main business branch in the early history of Thesen & Co. *Albatros* shuttled between Knysna, Cape Town and Port Elizabeth until 1874, when she was wrecked at Cape Agulhas. After the loss of the mother ship, the Thesens, together with Åkerberg, bought the brig *Ambulant*, which sailed for ten years. Towards the turn of the century, Thesen & Co. had accumulated sufficient funds to invest in a steamship. Hjalmar, one of C.W.'s eight siblings, travelled to Norway to purchase a vessel that could serve Knysna and the coastal towns along the southern tip of the African continent. The steamer *Agnar* was purchased in Stavanger in 1895, and later *Ingerid*, built in Glasgow, was purchased in 1901, followed by the German-built *Karatara* in 1913 and *Outeniqua*, constructed in Porsgrund, Norway, in 1915. All these purchases were undertaken through a network of family and business relationships in the Cape region combined with a network of business connections in northern Europe, in particular Norway. These connections were carefully maintained during regular trips to Norway by several of the leading members of the firm.

In general, the economy of shipping enterprises boomed during the First World War, as the shortage of ships caused an increase in freight rates. Thesen & Co. was encouraged by the government of the young Union of South Africa[20] to acquire more ships and establish a steamship company. Thesen's Steamship Ltd was subsequently founded in 1916 and held a shareholders' equity of GBP 100,000.

A recession in the regional economy in the 1920s caused a deficit for the new shipping line, and most shares were sold in 1921 to the Liverpool-based Houston Line. Yet the new owners continued to operate between Knysna, Cape Town and Port Elizabeth, now sailing as Thesen & Co. Steamship, 'in order to preserve the valuable goodwill'.[21]

C.W. Thesen turned his interest towards the railway and became an ardent advocate in public and political forums of connecting Knysna to the provincial capital George and to the national railway network. Already in 1888, the *George and Knysna Herald* reported enthusiastically on the planned railway between Knysna and George.[22] Forty years later, in 1928, the railway was inaugurated with daily connections between the two towns. Throughout this period, C.W. Thesen was involved in a series of political and economic alliances on regional as well as national levels to put pressure on decision makers and to seek economic support among private enterprises that would benefit from the opportunities a railway could offer. For a region hampered by infrequent shipping connections and cart roads, a railway connection improved the infrastructure significantly. Ships called upon Knysna less frequently after the railway opened, and the port was officially closed in 1954, when South African Railways and Harbours announced the juridical repeal of Knysna as a commercial port.[23]

Expansion, Growth and Networks

Towards the 1880s Thesen & Co. invested in steam engines for sawmilling. Wood was needed for wagon manufacturing, and there was a considerable demand for railway sleepers serving the construction of railways throughout the colonies in South Africa.[24] Hundreds of thousands of creosote-treated sleepers were shipped from Knysna. The production process from raw material to final product serves to illustrate how networks on local, regional, national and international scales were intertwined. Tenders for sleepers were called for by the colonial government. The timber was procured through a local network of woodcutters on contract with Thesen & Co., and processed locally on machinery acquired mainly in northern Europe through business partners. The creosote, used for impregnation, was loaded in Yorkshire, England, and mainly freighted on Norwegian sailing ships, which offered cheap freight until early in the twentieth century.[25]

Thesen & Co. established branches in Cape Town in 1888, in Paarl in 1898 and in Durban in 1908. Later, offices were also opened in Umtali in 1950 (present-day Mutare in Zimbabwe) and in Johannesburg in 1959.

The Paarl branch serves as an example of how the company saw opportunities in new economic niches. Situated sixty kilometres northeast of
Cape Town, Paarl became an industrial centre in the Cape Colony in
the early nineteenth century when hydro resources were utilized for
industrial purposes such as wagon manufacturing. The demand for
wagon wood was substantial, and Thesen & Co. supplied the factories
with hardwood from the Outeniqua forests, transported on their own
vessels to Cape Town and farther on to Paarl on wagons, and later by
railway. In 1898 Thesen & Co. invested in a flour mill that had already
been in operation for nearly two decades. In addition to milling wheat
from South Africa, different sorts of grain were imported from South
America, North America and Australia. Their brand, White Star flour,
was exported to southern Africa south of the Zambezi. Also, in search
of new markets, coffee from Kenya was imported to be ground at the
mill. The management of the mill was not headed by family members,
but was instead in the charge of a business acquaintance from Stavanger.[26] The Thesens withdrew from the flour milling business in 1935
when competition from cooperatives became insurmountable.[27]

In 1974, after 104 years of continuous operation, Thesen & Co. was
sold to the Johannesburg-based Rand Mines Properties Ltd and Barlow
Rand Ltd.[28] The board of Thesen & Co. accepted the offer after considering three main financial and operational facets. First, the valuable
assets in the company could not be realized without the injection of a
considerable amount of capital. Second, the liquidity of the company
had been adversely affected by losses incurred over recent years. Third,
the structure as a private family company – and its recent negative
profit history – would not merit it being listed at the stock exchange in
Johannesburg.[29] Thesen & Co. was sold the same year. The new owners
continued in wood processing until 2001, when the factory, employing
six hundred people, was closed down. The industrial area at Thesen
Island (originally Paarden Island), a small island in the Knysna estuary
where timber processing plants were located, has since been converted
into real estate development and an upmarket gated waterfront village
upon the initiative of the Thesen Island Development Company.[30]

Strong Ties, Weak Ties: Questioning
Entrepreneurship and Networks

Throughout its century-long existence, timber and the processing of
timber constituted the backbone of Thesen & Co. More than forty subsidiaries were established, evincing strong entrepreneurial momen-

tum. In addition to the branches already mentioned, the company was involved in whaling, fisheries, oyster breeding, boatbuilding, real estate, mining and transport companies. A fundamental factor for these enterprises was involvement and participation in networks. Theoretically, this calls for an investigation of the connection between entrepreneurship and social networks.

Studies of entrepreneurship have rather bifurcated trajectories, with either an emphasis on individual levels or structural levels (see, e.g., Thornton and Flynn 2003). For instance, Alvarez, Agarwal and Sorenson (2005) address what they see as an overemphasis on the individual(s) in entrepreneurship research, and thus strive to focus on the structural levels – on macroeconomic measures, social and kinship ties, and the interaction between institutions and entrepreneurship. Yet the last decade has seen a renaissance of studies pursuing the characteristics of the individual, such as social cognition, attitudes and effectuation (Sarasvathy 2001; Shaver 2003). Bridging these levels, Aldrich and Zimmer, for one, connected entrepreneurs and networks in an understanding whereby entrepreneurship is seen as being 'embedded in networks of continuing social relations. Within complex networks of relationships, entrepreneurship is facilitated or constrained by linkages between aspiring entrepreneurs, resources and opportunities' (1986: 8). Lately, studies on networks and social relations have emphasized the consequences and implications of networks in entrepreneurship and contributed to forge these different theoretical footholds (Uhlaner 2002; Jack, Rose and Johnston 2009). Entrepreneurship is here seen processually to consist of distinctive activities, herein opportunity identification, resource mobilization and the creation of an organization (Shane and Venkataraman 2000). Hence, it is the connected processes of entrepreneurship, and how these processes are conditioned by networks, that are under scrutiny.

Social networks, in the understanding of 'the sets of ties linking several actors' (Nelson 1988: 40), enables access to privileged information, opportunities and resources and serve as a stimulant for entrepreneurial activities (Brüderl and Preisendörfer 1998; Jack 2005). Studies of networks include the application and analysis of concepts such as weak (heterogeneous) and strong (homogenous) ties (Granovetter 1973); embeddedness – how actors are embroiled in ongoing systems of social relations (Uzzi 1997); and social capital – the set of trust (Gambetta 1988), norms and networks people are involved in to gain access to power (Putnam 1993).

A social network approach often aims to focus on the behaviour of network elements and the interaction between the elements, or nodes, as they are often called (Grabher 2006, 2009). These nodes consist of social actors, in the form of individuals, groups or organizations. Here, such nodes are also seen in reference to how networks on local, regional and international levels are constituted, interconnected and maintained, and how these networks enabled strategies in economic performance for Thesen & Co.

Networks with strong ties, as first introduced by Granovetter (1973), are characterized by frequent interactions among network members, and information gained through networks with strong ties offer a multitude of benefits: it is inexpensive, reliable and trustworthy, since it is rich in information and hence accurate and detailed, and the information usually emanates from continuing relations, which account for reliability (Granovetter 1985: 490). However, strong ties are in many cases perceived as being less beneficial than weak ties, as participants are likely to circulate in the same social arenas, providing redundant information, and this may lead to fragmentation (Burt 1992). Weak ties, characterized by infrequent contact between the participants (Granovetter 1973), are seen as being instrumental in business, as they enable information to flow across and into other social clusters. Hence, the strength of weak ties is conditioned by the potential to connect to other and contingent social systems (Ibarra 1993), and to include actors who might be described as marginal, as such actors can provide crucial information, particularly in the establishment phase of a firm (Grabher 2009).

The many subsidiaries established by Thesen & Co. were furnished by networks typically characterized by strong ties, where family members and business associates were instrumental in entrepreneurial processes and management of the enterprises. These strong ties were consolidated and institutionalized through alteration of the position of board chair among several members of the Thesen family. Also, the directorship was shared among several Thesens.[31] The board institutionalized power and responsibility to the members – in the capacity of the director – to carry out specific businesses and transactions on behalf of the company.[32] Additionally, to maintain these strong ties and remain in control, measures were also taken to minimize the amount of members (shareholders) in the enterprise(s), to be verified through resolutions endorsed by the board.[33]

The variety of agencies of southern African and European firms in which Thesen & Co. were involved can be characterized as a web of networks of weak ties, with rather infrequent contact and divided by long physical distances. Still, these ties were often formalized and confirmed through economic contracts. An overview from 1936 shows that Thesen & Co. served as agents for twenty-nine whaling companies (mostly Norwegian, but also English, Scottish, Danish and French), thirty-seven shipping companies (mainly Norwegian, in addition to a few English, Danish and Finnish) and thirty-one Norwegian and Danish shipping insurance companies.[34] Typically, the company bought shares in the firm they served as agent, so as to formalize their involvement and ensure mutual commitment. What seems to gain currency in this case is how these weak ties provided information, advice and resources (Katrishen, Sandberg and Logan 1993) as well as knowledge, opportunities and responsibilities (Bloodgood, Sapienza and Carsrud 1995).

When combined, these networks composed of strong and weak ties constitute what can be perceived as discursive networks. Such discursive networks refer to how both metropolitan and colonial societies and places can be configured simultaneously through an extensive (transnational) exchange of materiality, ideas and practices (Lester 2002). Local, national and transnational networks of discursive connections fashioned and formed the patterns of practice that constituted Thesen & Co. Furthermore, this concept provides perspectives that contests, or even disrupts, the traditional binaries of centre/periphery and metropole/colony (Lester 2002: 44–45) – as also discussed in the introduction to this volume.

Power, Omnipotence, Monopoly – and Liminality

The history of Thesen & Co. is a history of economic expansion – yet also one of controversies, allegations of abuses of its near monopoly and performance of power. For instance, as early as the 1890s fellow merchants in Knysna expressed discontent about the competitive situation and accused Thesen & Co. of monopolizing the economic sphere in Knysna. The Thesen steamers *Ingerid* and *Agnar* operated between Knysna, Cape Town and Durban, and for competing merchants it proved difficult to export their goods, as the Thesen & Co. freighters gave priority to their own products, not to mention the limited cargo capacity of their vessels. In addition to Thesen & Co., two other companies (Parkes & Co. and Tempelman & Co.) were also involved in the timber business, and were dependent on access to the markets in Cape Town, Port Elizabeth and Durban and the growing mining towns on the Witwatersrand (Johannesburg) and in Pretoria. A syndicate of business enterprises in Knysna and merchants in Cape Town established the Cape of Good Hope Steamship Syndicate in 1901 as a counter-move to contest the shipping monopoly. However, the syndicate only operated a steamer for a few months, as shipping services proved not worthwhile following a pronounced slump in the demand for timber (Parkes and Williams 1988: 153–54). Yet the number of disgruntled merchants in the region increased at the beginning of the twentieth century. In 1913, all merchants in Knysna signed a letter addressed to Thesen & Co., claiming that the leading company in town monopolized the entire mercantile arena:

> We the undersigned Merchants and Storekeepers are entirely dissatisfied with the present unheard of unique conditions existing in Knysna, under which business is being conducted; and with the unfair in fact we might say suicidal competition in almost every branch of Mercantile business and Trade generally, due solely to your firm being Storekeepers as well as Ship owners, the latter being practically a monopoly, at present.[35]

The merchants complained, in particular, about the ubiquitous presence of the Thesens, as they operated as both wholesalers and retailers, in addition to handling agencies for other companies. The freight rates set by Thesen & Co. for their competitors were too high, the merchants alleged, hampering the conditions for trade and business. In conclusion, the accusers demanded Thesen & Co. of abandoning retail business to secure fair conditions for other merchants. The company responded by offering reduced freight rates. All other allegations were discarded as being incorrect.[36]

In addition to maintaining a strong presence in the economic sphere, the Thesens were also conspicuously present in political and administrative fields. C.W. Thesen held electoral positions in the Knysna Divisional Council from 1880 at the young age of twenty-three, and as divisional councillor and later municipal councillor and mayor. In addition, he was chairman of the local chamber of commerce from 1922 to 1938,[37] and involved in the telephone service, the telegram service, the hospital, the harbour, the yacht club and welfare institutions.[38] He was also elected as a member of the Cape Provincial Council between 1911 and 1913. The centennial jubilee publication for the Knysna Divisional Council reports: 'His resignation from the Divisional Council in October 1928, brought a sense of shock. After nearly fifty years of public service in every facet of life, he had become an institution' (Tapson 1962: 30). Other members of the Thesen family were also involved in electoral positions for shorter periods in the Knysna Division Council,[39] and C.W.'s brother Rolf was chief constable of the Knysna police at the end of the 1870s.[40]

Figure 3.3a, b. Manifestations of power and capital: Thesen residence, 'The Hill', 1899 (above), and Knysna, 1910 (below). The top image shows the Thesen residence towering over the townscape. Long Street, which we can see in the bottom image, commenced at the residence and terminated at the port. The timber processing factories, the warehouse and offices were located between the port and the residence. *Source:* Western Cape Archives and Record Service; reproduced with permission.

Between British and Boers

This seeming state of omnipresence, or even omnipotence, needs to be nuanced: the position of the Thesens suggests a degree of liminality, which becomes particularly apparent during and in the aftermath of the Anglo-Boer War (1899–1902).

Knysna, like other places in the Cape Colony, was racially and socially stratified, with the British at the high end, followed by Boers, Coloureds[41] and Bantu linguistic groups categorized at the lowest level. This form of stratification was introduced as a set of official categories during the nineteenth century under British colonial rule (Keegan 1996; Christopher 2002). The British Empire itself was extremely hierarchical, to borrow the phrasing of Kwarteng (2011: 4).

Shortly after their arrival, the Thesen family was assimilated into the British segment in Knysna, yet maintained a balance vis-à-vis the Boers. At the outbreak of the Anglo-Boer War in 1899, the Knysna Division Council declared loyalty to the British Empire. During the last phase of the war, the Thesen residence was requisitioned by the British to prevent the advancing Boer troops from taking possession of the house and gaining control of Knysna (Parkes and Williams 1999). At least, that was the official explanation given to the family, which had to leave the house with two hours' notice.[42] Most likely, the British suspected the Thesens of supporting the Boers. C.W. Thesen became a naturalized citizen of the Cape Colony in 1884,[43] having explicitly expressed his support for the British. However, his brothers Sigurd and Theodor, who lived in the Orange Free State,[44] were burghers[45] and supported the Boers. Sigurd did not enrol for war service, but Theodor fought for the Boers and participated in the siege of Ladysmith in 1900. Later, when the British took control of Kroonstad, Sigurd's residential town, he surrendered to the British and swore loyalty to the British Crown. Both Sigurd and Theodor were in Knysna when the British requisitioned the Thesen residence in August 1901.

The Thesens' tentative balancing act between Boer and British interests and politics was made additionally delicate when the sister of C.W. Thesen, Blanca Thesen, married into the Boer elite. In 1874 she married the lawyer Francis Wilhelm Reitz, later to become president of the Orange Free State from 1889 to 1895. During the Anglo-Boer War, Reitz was state secretary for President Kruger.[46] Blanca died in 1887, but contact between the Reitz and the Thesen families continued to be close after Blanca's demise. Blanca's sons, Deneys and Hjalmar Reitz, frequently visited the family in Knysna, and both became pronounced voices in South African public opinion.[47]

The vessels owned by Thesen & Co. were searched for weapons, as the British alleged that firearms were being carried to Deneys for distribution to the Boer divisions. However, nothing but food supplies was found. Like many fellow Scandinavians in South Africa (Carlsson 2002; Berg 2003), the Thesen family was divided during the Anglo-Boer War. Sympathies had to be expressed and interpreted towards both British and Boer in a careful balance to secure a neutral position, confirming a position of liminality and operations in interstitial space.

As indicated, the presence of the Thesens as the economic, political and organizational centre of the small town of Knysna also indicates a position of omnipotence. The relationship between the timber merchant Thesen & Co. and the woodcutters may serve to illustrate this position. Woodcutters are ascribed a specific and stigmatized position in South African political and social history as a marginalized, exploited and poor group.[48] Upon the establishment of governmental woodcutter posts in the Outeniqua and Tsitsikamma region in the mid-eighteenth century, woodcutters of Dutch and French descent settled in the forest to supply timber to the colonial government. Following the deregulation of governmental forests and their transformation to private ownership in 1876, the woodcutters supplied timber to the timber merchants, of which Thesen & Co. was the foremost in the region from the 1880s onwards. Addressing the marginal situation of the woodcutters, Grundlingh (1992) argues that the suppressive dependency enforced by the timber merchants trapped the woodcutters in a state of poverty with limited space for social mobility. In many cases, the woodcutters were paid in coupons (*goodfor*) that could be redeemed for various commodities. Such *goodfors* were also issued on credit, which kept the woodcutter indebted, dependent and loyal to the merchants. The government-appointed district forest officer in Knysna, R. Burton, concluded in a 1911 letter that 'the woodcutter has in the past, I regret to say, been exploited for political purposes'.[49] Another forest officer, H. Ryan, complained the same year about the contrast between the accumulation of capital among the timber merchants and the prevailing misery among the woodcutters. These statements were responses to a scheme for the amelioration of the condition of the woodcutters.[50] The scheme was proposed by C.W. Thesen and suggested measures be taken to ensure that the woodcutters were licensed, trained and capable of working the forest in alignment with forest regulations. The forest officer found it somewhat ironic that the scheme was proposed by 'the principal member of a class which, by its absorption of the profits attending the timber industry, has been chiefly responsible for the impoverishment of the woodcutter'.[51] The Forest Department acknowledged the intentions of the scheme but found it impracticable to implement, and argued that forest management cannot be governed by the same principles as a business enterprise.[52]

Even more explicit in their criticism were the members of parliament for George and Humansdorp (A.J. Werth and P.O. Sauer, respectively). In a heated parliamentary debate concerning the Woodcutters Annuities Bill with the minister of agriculture and forestry, Mr Werth complained that the timber companies Parkes & Son and Thesen & Co. intimidated the woodcutters by mixing their roles as timber merchants and agents of the Forest Department.[53] Mr Sauer argued further and alleged: 'The firm of Thesens are people who want to buy the timber as cheaply as possible. They are the people who throughout the whole history have never yet done anything to help these people out of the forest. Their object is to get rich out of timber and they have, as a matter of fact, succeeded.'[54]

From 1776 until 1939, the forests in the Knysna region yielded approximately GBP 50 million, according to a calculation made by von Breitenbach (1974). The woodcutters' share of the yield is questionable. An agreement from 1902 between a woodcutter (NN) and three Thesen brothers – Hjalmar, Nils Peter and C.W. – demonstrates the existence of contractual loyalty between the woodcutter and the Thesens. The agreement stated:

> That whereas the said Thesen and Company have agreed to assist the said [NN] of Knysna with certain advances to the amount on Nine hundred pounds or thereabouts secured by Deed of Hypothecation, for the better enabling the said [NN] to carry on his business of a woodcutter and trader in wood and transport rider and in part consideration thereof the said [NN] has agreed to deliver all timber cut or acquired by him to the said Thesen and Company and to ride transport for the said Thesen and Company and for no one else for the term and upon the terms and conditions following.[55]

The agreement also specified mutual commitments. Two paragraphs concerned the obligation of the said woodcutter to deliver and transport materials for Thesen & Co. only. A third paragraph committed Thesen & Co. to accept and purchase all the timber delivered by the woodcutter.[56] Additionally, the last paragraph underlined that the woodcutter could be released from the contract with three months' notice upon payment of the entire debt.

This contract, as well as the statements from the parliament members and the district forest officers, is part of a larger discourse on the so-called poor white problem. The first conference to improve the situation of the poor white was organized by the Dutch Reformed Church in 1893. However, poverty among the black population was much more severe than white poverty. Terreblanche (2002: 393) has estimated that income per capita among whites was eleven times larger than income among blacks in 1917 and thirteen times larger in 1936. Still, eradicating white poverty, and not black, was prioritized by the government, and by the early 1930s the Carnegie Commission of New York was commissioned to address causes and corrective measures concerning the white poverty issue (Fourie 2007).[57]

Concerning Thesen & Co., the statements from bureaucrats and politicians address a concern over the exploitative relation between the woodcutters and the timber merchants.[58] Adding to the complaints and allegations from competing merchants and woodcutters, an image of performance of power, marginalizing of clients and monopolization of the economic sphere comes to the fore. Thesen & Co. controlled trade for a significant period, along with retailing and the import and export of goods. The company was also the single largest landowner in the region, and the company's multitude of commercial enterprises interconnected their interests with commercial and administrative levels in the town. In addition, the Thesens gained a position of political power through electoral government seats.

Conclusion

Thesen & Co. became intertwined in several economic niches and manoeuvred itself into a space in which its entrepreneurial activities had considerable value, yet at the expense of competitors and labourers by an omnipresent performance of power (see also Eidsvik 2012, 2013). Indeed, it can even be argued that the specific entrepreneurship displayed in this case can be described as omnipotent entrepreneurship, referring to conditionalities of monopoly and control and to the company's decisive influence at all levels in the economic sphere.

This position of omnipotence was conditioned by participation in networks constituted by strong and weak ties, and the utilization of the advantages these networks could offer. An enterprise with networks consisting of both strong and weak ties is more likely to succeed, at least according to the scholarly tradition of Granovetter. In the case of Thesen & Co., strong ties – consolidated by family and business associates and institutionalized by the board – as well as a diverse range of weak ties seem to have supported a variety of businesses that indisputably created a considerable volume of jobs and assets. Still, networks alone, although carefully composed of strong and weak ties, are not sufficient to understand how a position of omnipotence can be achieved – and performed.

Within postcolonial thought, liminality helps to illustrate the relation between colonizer and colonized, in terms of being a spatial notion of in-betweenness (Bhabha [1994] 2004). As newcomers in the colonial arena in the Cape Colony, the Thesens found themselves in a liminal space of in-betweenness, navigating between both groups of colonizers, British and Boer. However, such liminality conditions a potential for exploitation and utilization of economic spaces. Instead of taking part in antagonizing relations, as the relationship between British and Boers is often portrayed, the Thesens were in a position, partly through marital and political bonds, to establish and manage networks within both parts of the white community.

Furthermore, participation in networks with European and mainly Norwegian business partners were vital in the process of expanding and augmenting the business and enterprising activities. Without these connections, the range of enterprises and branches would have been less significant, and their presence in sundry economic arenas would have been correspondingly lower. Instead, the networks allowed Thesen & Co. to become an omnipotent partaker in the economic sphere, and thus contributed to reconfirming and developing the prevailing colonial discourse in the region.

Finally, these networks can be construed as discursive networks. In this case, place and practices are configured through extensive exchanges of ideas, capital and materiality. Consequently, these connections constituted the position of Thesen & Co. within the colonial discourse: products, ideas and capital were exchanged through local, national and transnational networks. These networks conditioned the space for entrepreneurial activities and the performance of power, and simultaneously configured the colonial discourse of which they were an active part.

Notes

Thanks to Ragnhild Overå, Kirsten Alsaker Kjerland, Bjørn Enge Bertelsen, Heidi Bjønnes Larsen, Anne K. Bang and three anonymous reviewers for constructive comments.
   1. The original name from 1870 was 'Thesen and Co'. In 1905, the company was registered as a private company with limited liability under the name 'Thesen and Co. (Proprietary) Limited', provisioned under the Cape Colony Companies Act of 1892. In 'Minutes of Meetings of Directors held at Knysna 28 October 1905', A 2605 Vol. 2/1, KAB. 'Thesen and Co. (Proprie-

tary) Limited' was renamed 'Thesen Industries (Proprietary) Ltd' in 1955. In 'Minutes of Meetings', A 2605 Vol. 3/1, KAB. For convenience, the abbreviated 'Thesen & Co.' is applied in this chapter, which also corresponds to the general phrasing in letters, minutes and correspondence in the archival sources.

2. The objectives are far too voluminous to be included in this chapter, but an illustrative selection displaying the range of activities are: (2) 'To carry on business as Timber Merchants, Sawmill proprietors and timber Growers, and to buy, sell, grow, prepare for market, manipulate, import, export and deal in Timber and Wood of all kinds'; (4) 'To carry on business as Bankers, Capitalists, Financiers'; (9) 'To carry on business of Importers of Horses, Mules, Donkeys, Meat, Live Cattle and Sheep'; (12) 'To carry on Fisheries and Whale Fisheries, Salt, Dry, Can and Preserve Fish'; (14) 'To carry on all or any of the businesses of Hotel, Restaurant, Café, Refreshment Room and Lodging-House Keepers, Licensed Victuallers, Wine, Beer and Spirit Merchants, Brewers, Mallsters, Distillers, Importers and Manufacturers of Aërated, Mineral and Artificial Waters and Other Drinks; Purveyors, Caterers for Public Amusements generally; Coach, Car and Carriage Proprietors, Livery Stable Keepers, Job Masters, Importers and Brokers of Colonial and Foreign Produce of all descriptions; Proprietors of Clubs, Baths, Dressing-Rooms, Laundries, Reading, Writing and Newspapers Rooms, Libraries, Grounds and Places of Amusement, Recreation and Sports, Entertainment and Instruction of all kinds; Agents for Insurance, Railway and Shipping Companies and Carriers, Theatrical and Opera Box Office Proprietors, Entrepreneurs and General Agents'. In 'Memorandum of Association of Thesen & Co., Limited', A 2605 Vol. 2/544, KAB.

3. Objective 53: 'To obtain any Provisional Order or Act of Parliament for enabling the Company to carry any of its objects into effect'. In 'Memorandum of Association of Thesen & Co., Limited', A 2605 Vol. 2/544, KAB.

4. In 'Thesen and Co. (Proprietary) Limited. Memorandum' (1974), A 2605 Vol. 2/89, KAB.

5. According to official immigration statistics, 815,000 Norwegians migrated to the United States between 1820 and 1950 (Norman and Runblom 1987: 291).

6. Letter from British consular in Stavanger, Wilh. S. Hansen, issued to A.L. Thesen, 16 June 1869, A 2605 Vol. 1/31, KAB.

7. Mathias held a master mariner certificate and knew the vessel well, as he had recommended purchase of the schooner for his brothers in 1850. In untitled memo written by Harald Thesen, 1923, A 2605 Vol. 1/25, KAB.

8. Eric Rosenthal, 'The Thesen Chronicles', undated historical chronicle of Thesen & Co., probably prepared for the centennial in 1970, A 2605 Ann. 1/3, KAB. See also Winquist (1978: 92).

9. The 1865 census (the first to be carried out by the colonial administration) registered 2,471 people in the Knysna region, of which 54 per cent were of European descent, while the 1875 census counted 3,218 people in the region, now 57 per cent Europeans (*Census of the Colony* 1866; *Results of a Census of the Colony* 1877).

10. The parallel with the northern European landscape features has been recalled by others, among them the Scottish writer H.V. Morton, who enthusiastically saluted Knysna's resemblance to his homeland: 'The Outeniqua Mountains are extraordinarily Scotland ... They are, indeed, Scotland at her best' (1948: 113–14). Travel accounts from the colonial period suffer from descriptions of landscapes described as being unhistoricized and uninhabited, omitting the presence of the indigenous population, as Pratt (1992) argues.

11. The firm was Wm. McPherson. The other merchant in Knysna was Lloyd & Co. In untitled memo written by Harald Thesen, 1923, A 2605 Vol. 1/25, KAB.

12. The partnership with the brother Mathias Theodor only lasted for a consecutive six months. While A.L. was modest and cautious in his business prospects, the brother was described in the correspondence between the family members as a spendthrift. Mathias settled in neighbouring Plettenberg Bay, where he lived until he died in 1885. In letter from Hjalmar Thesen to Nils Peter Thesen, 5 January 1872, A 2605 Vol. 1/1, KAB.

13. In an undated memo titled 'Mr. Nils Peter Thesen', A 2605 Vol. 1/31, KAB.

14. 'Resignation of N. P Thesen. 20 December 1915', GG 1023 20/631, SAB, and in 'Appointment as consul for Norway in Cape Town, Mathias Theodore Thesen', A 2605 Vol. 1/30, KAB. See also Angell's contribution, this volume, on the establishment of Norwegian consular services.

15. Outeniqua is the name of the mountain range from George in the west to Plettenberg Bay in the east between the coast and Little Karoo (see figure 3.1). The name stems from Khoisan and means 'the bearer of honey'.

16. Letter to Holmes & Sons, Port Elizabeth, February 1876, A 2605 Ann. 2/4, KAB.

17. Family history collected by Harald W. Thesen in 1923. Dispatched to Killie Campbell (founder of Killie Campbell Collection in Durban), 26 June 1958, A 2605 Vol. 1/25, KAB.

18. For issues on the ecological impact of invasive alien species in South Africa, see, e.g., Richardson and van Wilgen (2004). For a discussion on colonial and postcolonial terminology of nature in South Africa, see, e.g., Comaroff and Comaroff (2001).

19. Letter from C.W. Thesen to the Agricultural Department, Cape Town, 10 May 1912, concerning cultivation of imported grass for cattle forage; letter to the Ministry for Agriculture, 22 February 1913, enquiring whether the ministry would consider replacing guano with whale manure as fertilizer, inspired by successful and profitable practices in Europe and the United States, A 2605 Vol. 1/10, KAB; 'The Knysna Timber Industry, note on innovations and development of the timber industry in Knysna', undated, probably written in the 1920s, in both A 2605 Vol. 1/13 and A 2605 Vol. 2/98, KAB.

20. The Cape Colony, Natal, Transvaal and the Orange Free State merged into the Union of South Africa in 1910. The union was founded as a dominion under the British Empire. See, e.g., Thompson (2001).

21. Rosenthal, 'The Thesen Chronicles', undated, 143, A 2605 Ann. 1/3, KAB.

22. *George and Knysna Herald: Government Gazette for the districts of George, Knysna and Uniondale,* 27 June 1888. George Museum: George.
23. South African Railways and Harbours was established by the Union of South Africa in 1916 as a joint unit for railways and harbours in the union. In 'Government Gazette', Pretoria, Government Printer. CLXXVIII, NLS-P.
24. Rosenthal, 'The Thesen Chronicles', undated, A 2605 Ann. 1/3, KAB.
25. Norwegian sailing vessels offered low rates compared to the more sophisticated steam fleet in England or Sweden, to mention only a few. See Nygaard's contribution, this volume, for a more detailed account on the role of sailing vessels versus steamships at the end of the nineteenth century.
26. The manager was Mr Wallem. In Harald Thesen, 'Thesen Family History', 1923, A 2605 Vol. 1/25, KAB.
27. Rosenthal, 'The Thesen Chronicles', undated, 230, A 2605 Ann. 1/3, KAB.
28. Offer by Rand Mines Properties Limited and Barlow Rand Limited to all the shareholders of Thesen & Co (Proprietary) Limited, A 2605 Vol. 2/95, KAB. Rand Mines Properties Limited and Barlow Rand Limited merged subsequently into Barloworld.
29. Letter from S.B. Thesen, Managing Director, to shareholders in Thesen & Co. 16 April 1974, A 2605 Vol. 2/95, KAB.
30. The real estate development, dubbed 'Thesen Harbour Town', consists of 605 residential units in addition to a commercial-retail component (Aupiais 2008). The Thesen Island Development Company was established as a private initiative independent of the Thesen family.
31. Between 1905 and 1929 (for which minute books are available), the board chair altered between Charles Wilhelm Thesen, Nils Peter Thesen, Mathias Theodor Thesen, Adolf Frithjof Thesen and Hjalmar Harrison Thesen. However, Charles Wilhelm Thesen held the chair position most of the time.
32. In 'General Power of Attorney. Know all men whom it may concern', letter issued by C.W. Thesen to the board, 15 September 1914, A 2605 Vol. 2/1, KAB.
33. In 'Special Resolution', Thesen & Co – Durban: Amendments in article of association, 16 March 1927: 'The number of members should not exceed fifty.' A 2605 Vol. 2/1, KAB.
34. In 'Memorandum of agreement between Thesen & Co Limited and Mitchell, Cotts & Company', A 2605 Ann. 2/98, KAB.
35. Letter from fifteen merchants in Knysna, dated 19 March 1913, titled 'Complaints re monopoly of Thesen and Co Ltd.', A 2605 Vol. 2/81, KAB.
36. Letter of response signed C.W. Thesen, 10 April 1913, titled 'Complaints re monopoly', A 2605 Vol. 2/81, KAB.
37. In minute books, Knysna Chamber of Commerce, 1922–46, A 2605 Vol. 5/4, KAB.
38. Rosenthal, 'The Thesen Chronicles', undated, 243, A 2605 Ann. 1/3, KAB.
39. Hjalmar and Rolf Thesen, brothers of C.W. Thesen, had brief sojourns in the Knysna Divisional Council, as did Charles Eric Thesen and Stanley B. Thesen, son and grandson of C.W. Thesen.
40. Rosenthal, 'The Thesen Chronicles', undated, 87, A 2605 Ann. 1/3, KAB.
41. The term 'Coloured' is a contested term, and is often perceived as pejorative. It stems from the categorization of people under British colonial rule in the

Cape Colony. In general, it refers to people who were not Bantu-speaking Africans, but to those of Khoi, slave or 'mixed-race' descent, most of whom spoke Afrikaans (Bickford-Smith 2005: 105–6). See also Christopher (2002) for an analysis of the South African demographic classification system from the colonial period until the present.
42. Letter titled 'Re the Hill house', A 2605 Vol. 1/31, KAB.
43. C.W. Thesen became a naturalized citizen of the Cape Colony on 23 April 1884. In A 2605 Vol. 1/1, KAB.
44. The Orange Free State was an independent Boer republic from 1854 until 1902. The Boer republics (the Orange Free State and Transvaal) became subjects of British colonial dominion upon the termination of the Anglo-Boer War (1899–1902), yet with the promise of limited autonomy. See, e.g., Judd and Surridge (2002) for an overview of the Anglo-Boer War.
45. A 'burgher' refers to an enfranchised citizen of the Boer republics of Transvaal and the Orange Free State. The term derives from 'freeburgher', referring to Dutch farmers in the Cape who were released from their contracts with the VOC as early as 1657 (Elphick and Giliomee 1989: 11).
46. Paul Kruger (Stephanus Johannes Paulus Kruger) was president of the South African Republic, aka the Transvaal Republic, not to be confused with the Union of South Africa or the present-day Republic of South Africa.
47. See, e.g., *No Outspan* by Deneys Reitz (1943) and *The Conversion of a South African Nationalist* by Hjalmar Reitz (1946).
48. In 'Woodcutters Grievances. Correspondence from 20 August 1906 to 24 April 1911', FOR 58/56A, SAB. The status and conditions of the woodcutters was discussed on different political levels from the beginning of the twentieth century, yet it was only in the 1930s that the 'poor white issue' was addressed more systematically.
49. Letter issued by the District Forest Officer, Knysna, to the Acting Chief Conservator of Forests, Cape Town: 'Woodcutters in Knysna and adjoining Districts. 6. March 1911', FOR 58/56A, SAB.
50. Letter by C.W. Thesen addressed to Hon. F.S Malan, Cape Town, 'Proposed Scheme for the amelioration of the Condition of the Wood Cutters of the Knysna and adjoining Districts', 6 December 1910, FOR 58/56A, SAB.
51. In 'H. Ryan to Assistant Conservator Forest Knysna. 15. February 1911', FOR 58/56A, SAB.
52. Letter issued by the District Forest Officer, Knysna, to the Acting Chief Conservator of Forests, Cape Town: 'Woodcutters in Knysna and adjoining Districts. 6. March 1911', FOR 58/56A, SAB.
53. In 'Debates of the House of Assembly', 33, 16 February 1939, col. 402, NLS-P.
54. Ibid., cols 410–11.
55. 'Memorandum of agreement between Hjalmar, Charles Wilhelm and Nils Peter Thesen and NN of Knysna', signed 17 March 1902, A 2605 Vol. 2/536, KAB.
56. Ibid.
57. 'The Poor White Problem in South Africa: Report of the Carnegie Commission' (1932) suggested establishing 'employment sanctuaries' where black

workers would be replaced by poor white workers. The report concluded that racial deterioration and miscegenation would be the consequence if the situation with the poor white was allowed to continue (Füredi 1998: 66–67; Johnson and Jacobs 2011: 63). It has also been argued that the report contributed to the rise of the National Party and its victory in the 1948 election, as the suggestions in the report were applied to solidify racial segregation (Golden 2004: 6).

58. The relationship between woodcutters and timber merchants was also given a literate voice through the novel *Circles in the Forest* (*Kringe in'n Bos*) by Dalene Matthee (1984).

Archives Consulted

Western Cape Archives Repository (KAB), Cape Town.
National Archive Repository (SAB), Pretoria.
The National Library of South Africa (NLS-P), Pretoria.
The National Library of South Africa (NLS-CT), Cape Town.
George Museum (GM), George, South Africa.

References

Aldrich, H. and C. Zimmer. 1986. 'Entrepreneurship through Social Networks', in D. Sexton and R. Smiler (eds), *The Art and Science of Entrepreneurship*. New York: Ballinger, pp. 3–23.

Alvarez, S., R. Agarwal and O. Sorenson (eds). 2005. *Handbook of Entrepreneurship Research: Interdisciplinary Perspectives*. New York: Springer.

Ashcroft, B., G. Griffiths and H. Tiffin. 2007. *Post-Colonial Studies: The Key Concepts*. London: Routledge.

Aupiais, L. 2008. *Thesen Islands*. Cape Town: Quivertree Publications.

Berg, R. 2003. 'Norge og England på 1800-tallet: Litt om Følelser og Interesser i Storpolitikken', in S.G. Holtsmark, H.Ø. Pharo and R. Tamnes (eds), *Motstrøms: Olav Riste og norsk internasjonal historieskrivning*. Oslo: Cappelen, pp. 89–109.

Bhabha, H.K. (1994) 2004. *The Location of Culture*. London: Routledge.

Bickford-Smith, V. 2005. 'Coloured: Southern Africa', in P. Poddar and D. Johnson (eds), *A Historical Companion to Postcolonial Thought in English*. New York: Colombia University Press, pp. 105–6.

Bloodgood, J.M, J. Sapienza and A.L. Carsrud. 1995. 'The Dynamics of New Business Start-Ups: Person, Context and Process', in J.A. Katz and S. Brockhaus (eds), *Advances in Entrepreneurship, Firm Emergence and Growth*, vol. 2. Greenwich, C.T.: JAI Press, pp. 123–44.

Breitenbach, F. von. 1974. *Southern Cape Forests and Trees*. Cape Town: Government Printer.

Brüderl, J. and P. Preisendörfer. 1998. 'Network Support and the Success of Newly Founded Businesses', *Small Business Economics* 10: 213–25.

Burt, R.S. 1992. *Structural Holes: The Social Structure of Competition.* Boston: Harvard University Press

Carlsson, A.G. 2002. 'Norge og Boerkrigen', in K.A. Kjerland and A.K. Bang, *Nordmenn i Afrika – afrikanere i Norge.* Bergen: Fagbokforlaget, pp. 107–17.

Census of the Colony of the Cape of Good Hope, 1865. 1866. Cape Town: Saul Solomon.

Christopher, A.J. 2002. '"To Define the Indefinable": Population Classification and the Census in South Africa', *Area* 34(4): 401–8.

Comaroff, J. and J.L. Comaroff. 2001. 'Naturing the Nation: Aliens, Apocaloypse, and the Postcolonial State', *Social Identities* 7(2): 233–65.

Eidsvik, E. 2012. 'Colonial Discourse and Ambivalence: Norwegian Participation on the Colonial Arena in South Africa', in K. Loftsdottir and L. Jensen (eds), *Whiteness and Postcolonialism in the Nordic Region: Exceptionalism, Migrant Others and National Identities.* Surrey: Ashgate, pp. 13–28.

———. 2013. *Spaces of Scandinavian Encounters in Colonial South Africa: Reconfiguring Colonial Discourses.* PhD thesis. Bergen: University of Bergen.

Elphick, R. and H. Giliomee. 1989. *The Shaping of South African Society, 1652–1840.* Middletown, C.T.: Wesleyan University Press.

Fourie, J. 2007. 'The South African Poor White Problem in the Early 20th Century: Lessons for Poverty Today', *Management Decision* 45(8): 1270–96.

Füredi, F. 1998. *The Silent War: Imperialism and the Changing Perception of Race.* New Brunswick, N.J.: Rutgers University Press.

Gambetta, D. 1988. *Trust: Making and Breaking Cooperative Relations.* Oxford: Blackwell.

Golden, M. 2004. 'Carnegie Corporation in South Africa: A Difficult Past Leads to a Commitment to Change', *Carnegie Results,* Winter: 1–16.

Grabher, G. 2006. 'Trading Routes, Bypasses, and Risky Intersections: Mapping the Travels of "Networks" Between Economic Sociology and Economic Geography', *Progress in Human Geography* 30: 163–89.

———. 2009. 'Networks', in N. Thrift and R. Kitchin (eds), *International Encyclopedia of Human Geography.* London: Elsevier, pp. 405–13.

Granovetter, M. 1973. 'The Strength of Weak Ties', *American Journal of Sociology* 78(6): 1360–80.

———. 1985. 'Economic Action and Social Structure: The Problem of Embeddedness', *American Journal of Sociology* 91(3): 481–510.

Grundlingh, A. 1992. '"God Het Ons Arm Mense die Houtjies Gegee": Poor White Woodcutters in the Southern Cape Forest Area, c. 1900–1939', in R. Morell (ed.), *White but Poor: Essays on the History of Poor Whites in Southern Africa 1880–1940.* Pretoria: University of South Africa, pp. 40–56.

Ibarra, H. 1993. 'Personal Networks of Women and Minorities in Management: A Conceptual Framework', *Academy of Management Review* 18: 56–88.

Jack, S. 2005. 'The Role, Use and Activation of Strong and Weak Ties: A Qualitative Analysis', *Journal of Management Studies* 42(6): 1233–59.

Jack, S., M. Rose and L. Johnston. 2009. 'Tracing the Historical Foundations of Social Networks in Entrepreneurship Research', *ISBE 32nd Annual*

Conference, November 2009. Liverpool: Institute for Small Business and Entrepreneurship.

Johnson, K. and S. Jacobs (eds). 2011. *Encyclopedia of South Africa.* London: Lynne Rienner Publishers.

Judd, D. and K. Surridge. 2002. *The Boer War.* London: John Murray.

Katrishen, F.A., W.R. Sandberg and J.E. Logan. 1993. 'Social Networks and Entrepreneurial Performance', in M. Schnake (ed.), *Proceedings of the Annual Meeting of the Southern Management Association.* Atlanta.

Keegan, T. 1996. *Colonial South Africa and the Origins of the Racial Order.* Charlottesville: University Press of Virginia.

Kwarteng, K. 2011. *Ghost of Empire: Britain's Legacies in the Modern World.* London: Bloomsbury.

Lester, A. 2002. 'Constructing Colonial Discourse: Britain, South Africa and the Empire in the Nineteenth Century', in A. Blunt and C. McEwan (eds), *Postcolonial Geographies.* New York: Continuum, pp. 29–45.

Matthee, D. 1984. *Circles in a Forest.* London: Penguin.

Morton, H.V. 1948. *In Search of South Africa.* London: Methuen.

Nash, C. 2000. 'Historical Geographies of Modernity', in B. Graham and C. Nash (eds), *Modern Historical Geographies.* Harlow: Pearson Longman, pp. 13–40.

Nelson, R. 1988. 'Social Network Analysis as an Intervention Tool', *Group and Organization Studies* 13(1): 39–58.

Nimmo, A. 1976. *The Knysna Story.* Cape Town: Juta.

Noble, J. 1886. *Cape of Good Hope: Official Handbook.* Cape Town: Saul Solomon.

Norman, H. and H. Runblom. 1987. *Transatlantic Connections: Nordic Migration to the New World after 1800.* Oslo: Norwegian University Press.

Parkes, M. and V. Williams. 1988. *Knysna the Forgotten Port: The Maritime Story.* Knysna: Emu Publishers.

———. 1999. *Knysna and the Anglo-Boer War: Its Effects on the People of the Town and District.* Knysna: Emu Publishers.

Phillips, J. 1963. *The Forests of George, Knysna and the Zitzikama: A Brief History of Their Management: 1778–1939.* Pretoria: Republic of South Africa.

Pratt, M.L. 1992. *Imperial Eyes: Travel Writing and Transculturation.* London: Routledge.

Putnam, R.D. 1993. *Making Democracy Work.* Princeton, N.J.: Princeton University Press.

Reitz, D. 1943. *No Outspan.* London: Faber and Faber.

Reitz, H. 1946. *The Conversion of a South African Nationalist.* Cape Town: Unievolkspers Beperk.

Results of a Census of the Colony of the Cape of Good Hope, taken on the night of Sunday, the 7th March, 1875. 1877. Cape Town: Saul Solomon.

Richardson, D.M. and B. van Wilgen. 2004. 'Invasive Alien Plants in South Africa: How Well Do We Understand the Ecological Impacts?', *South African Journal of Science* 100: 45–52.

Sarasvathy, S.D. 2001. 'Causation and Effectuation: Toward a Theoretical Shift From Economic Inevitability to Entrepreneurial Contingency', *Academy of Management Review* 26(2): 195–222.

Shane, S. and S. Venkataraman. 2000. 'The Promise of Entrepreneurship as a Field of Research', *Academy of Management Review* 25(1): 217–26.

Shaver, K.G. 2003. 'The Social Psychology of Entrepreneurial Behaviour', in Z.J. Acs and D.B. Audretsch (eds), *Handbook of Entrepreneurship Research*. Dordrecht: Kluwer Academic Publishers, pp. 331–57.

Tapson, W. 1961. *Timber and Tides: The Story of Knysna and Plettenberg Bay*. Johannesburg: General Litho.

———. 1962. *The Knysna Divisional Council: The First Hundred Years, 1862–1962*. Knysna: Knysna Divisional Council.

Terreblanche, S. 2002. *A History of Inequality in South Africa, 1652–2002*. Pietermaritzburg: University of Natal Press.

Thompson, L. 2001. *A History of South Africa*. New Haven, C.T.: Yale Nota Bene.

Thornton, P.H. and K.H. Flynn. 2003. 'Entrepreneurship, Networks and Geographies', in Z.J. Acs and D.B. Audretsch (eds), *Handbook of Entrepreneurship Research*. Kluwer: Academic Publishers, pp. 401–33.

Uhlaner, L. 2002. 'Trends in European Research at the Turn of the Century', *Small Business Economics* 21(4): 321–28.

Union of South Africa. 1939. *Debates of the House of Assembly: Second Session-Eight Parliament,. 3rd February to 31st March 1939*. Cape Town: Nasional Pers, Beperk. 33.

Uzzi, B. 1997. 'Social Structure and Competition: The Paradox of Embeddedness', *Administrative Science Quarterly* 42: 35–67.

van der Merwe, I. 2002. *The Knysna and Tsitsikamma Forests: Their History, Ecology and Management*. Knysna: Forestry Department of Water Affairs and Forestry.

Winquist, A.H. 1978. *Scandinavians and South Africa: Their Impact on Cultural, Social and Economic Development Before 1900*. Cape Town: Balkema.

Wynn, G. 1997. 'Remapping Tutira: Contours in the Environmental History of New Zealand', *Journal of Historical Geography* 23: 418–46.

4

BUSINESS COMMUNICATION IN COLONIAL TIMES

The Norway-East Africa Trading Company in Zanzibar,
1895–1925

Anne K. Bang

The Norway-East Africa Trading Company (NEAT) in Zanzibar operated from 1895 until the late 1920s, importing timber and wood from Scandinavia to the East African colonies. It was a small enterprise, run for long periods by two men. The structure was well tested and simple: the agent, in the colony, would report to his partner in Norway about the demands arising; ships would then be chartered, loaded and eventually offloaded and their cargo sold. The history of NEAT and its timber-laden ships is one of innumerable subplots to the history of the European colonial expansion in late nineteenth-century Africa.[1]

As this chapter shows, the history of NEAT also illustrates the communication revolution taking place during this period, which again served to tie Europe closer to its colonies. Among the most important innovations were telecommunications (cable and wireless telegraphs) and the eventual dominance of steamships over sailing ships. In this perspective, the history of NEAT is the history of forty-six sailing ships calling at the harbours of Zanzibar, Mombasa, Dar-es-Salaam and Tanga, loaded with timber, planks and other goods. The history of the company can be traced in thousands of letters between Zanzibar and Norway,[2] hundreds of telegrams and an unknown number of messages delivered by any means possible. Together, these histories further demonstrate how improved communications offered new promises of profits – even for a small and noncolonial European nation like Norway.

The Origins of NEAT: Three Men,
One Telegram and a Sailing Ship

The ship *Lärkan* was to become the pioneering vessel for Norwegian economic involvement in Zanzibar. It should be noted that *Lärkan* was far from the first Norwegian ship to call at Zanzibar. The Lloyds Ships Register at Zanzibar shows Norwegian ships as far back as the register goes – that is, until 1890, with an average of two ships per year.[3] Zanzibar must, in other words, have been a port of call also long before the register was started, mostly for sailing vessels in the tramp trade.

In 1888, *Lärkan* was sold to a joint venture company in the city of Halden (then known as Fredrikshald) in the southeast of Norway. At that time, Norway and Sweden were still a union – headed by the king of Sweden but with two separate bureaucracies (see Angell, this volume). The company that bought *Lärkan* was led by Wilhelm Klein. In 1883, he had been appointed 'bureau chief' for the firm Saugbrugs-foreningen in Halden.[4] This was an association of forest and sawmill owners, one of Norway's largest producers of timber and wood at the time. From the docks in Halden, timber and cut wood was exported to England, France, Belgium and the Netherlands on a regular basis (Norløff 1935). Ships also sailed to Russia and the Baltic countries to buy wood for further processing.

By 1890, *Lärkan* was plying the route to and from Saint Petersburg and the ports around the Baltic Sea, steadily bringing back timber for the sawmills at the Saugbrugsforeningen. The ship would probably have continued in this trade for years had a telegram not arrived from Zanzibar some time in the summer of 1894, indicating that substantial profits could be made by the right person willing to risk exporting wood and planks to the new British possessions in East Africa.[5] This message reached Mr Klein and changed the fate of *Lärkan* and its captain. It was also to start a new wave of sailing ships from Norway to East Africa lasting well into the twentieth century.

To trace the origin of the fateful telegram, we must move to Zanzibar. On 3 April 1894, a Norwegian by the name of Jens Jørgen Bull Anderssen stepped ashore from the German steamer *Safari*. At that time, the colonial newspaper the *Zanzibar Gazette* did not have much local news to report, and consequently every single European passenger who arrived in the protectorate was certain to get his name in the paper. Some also got their title in print, or a brief account of their reasons for coming to Zanzibar. About Anderssen, however, only the name is given and nothing more.[6] What we do know is that Anderssen was an engineer, educated in England where he, typically for his time,[7] had specialized in the emerging field of telephones and telegraphs.

Still, there is no doubt that Anderssen came to Zanzibar from Madagascar. He had recently left the Norwegian Mission Society in Madagascar, where he had been commissioned to build a school. Anderssen's commitment to the missionary call seems to have been somewhat limited, and he was duly fired. After completing the school, he spent his time installing telephone cables in the royal palace in Antananarivo (Madagascar) before securing a position as 'trade agent' for the Norwegian state. By this time, the Swedish-Norwegian union was becoming an increasingly uneasy one, and the Norwegian government responded to Swedish restrictions on foreign trade policy by appointing a corps of agents paid to seek out new trade opportunities for the expanding Norwegian merchant fleet.

Anderssen took immediate action in Zanzibar. Less than a year after his arrival, a wooden 'chalet' arrived in parts from Norway and was set up at Chwaka on the east coast of Zanzibar – the site chosen by the British colonial administrators A. Hardinge and L. Matthews as the most suitable for a holiday retreat, the 'Brighton of Zanzibar', as the *Zanzibar Gazette* called it.[8] The building came to be known as the Norwegian Bungalow and served until 1964 as a holiday retreat for employees of the colonial administration – originally open to Europeans only, but from 1940 also to non-Europeans.

In addition, Anderssen must have observed the need for building material in the Zanzibar Protectorate, including timber and wood for new institutions like a courthouse, various administrative buildings and housing for colonial officers. Moreover, he must have followed closely the British plans to build a railway in the then East Africa Protectorate . All in all, his conclusion was that Norwegian planks would find a growing market in East Africa.

The connection of East Africa to the global, transcontinental cable lines was a gradual process that paralleled the growing influence of Great Britain in the Indian Ocean. It started in the 1870s, with a cable connected Cape Town, via East Africa, to Aden.[9] By the next decade, Zanzibar, via the telegraph office on Kelele Square in the city centre, was connected to Bombay and Mauritius, and later also to Dar-es-Salaam and Mombasa. As J. Prestholt has argued, the time-space compression introduced by the telegraph – reducing communication time between Europe and Africa from months to minutes – was greater than the advent of the Internet (Prestholt 2008: 173). It was to this technology Anderssen turned to convey his opinion about the market for Norwegian timber. It was also to this technology that NEAT was to turn in the future – however, only when really needed. The telegraph was fast and reliable, but expensive.

Klein cannot have been a man averse to taking risks. Upon receiving Anderssen's telegram, he contacted the captain of *Lärkan*, who was in Russia awaiting cargo for Halden. The captain's name was Oscar

Christian Olsen, later to be known as Zanzibar-Olsen. He was born in Halden in 1857, the son of a sea captain who perished at sea while Olsen was still a boy. As a young man, Olsen took responsibility for his mother and sisters and went to sea himself at around the age of sixteen. In due time he reached the rank of captain and entered the established trading routes between Halden, England and the Baltic Sea. However, the suggestion from Klein was something else entirely.

Klein simply suggested that he, together with Olsen, finance a shipload of various-sized planks and timber to Zanzibar, and that Olsen bring *Lärkan* there. It was a daring move, into waters that were unchartered even for an internationally oriented company like Saugbrugsforeningen.

By October 1894 – a mere six months after Anderssen first arrived in Zanzibar – *Lärkan* was lying fully loaded at the docks in Halden. On board, above and belowdecks, were about 450 cubic metres of various sizes and quality of planks, in addition to four boats intended for sale in

Figure 4.1. The Norway-East Africa Trading Company receives a visit from home: Mr Stang (centre), the director of Saugbrugsforeningen, visited Zanzibar in 1902. Olsen is on the right. *Source:* Olsen family; reproduced with permission.

Zanzibar. Captain Olsen would later in his life describe this pioneering voyage as anything but easy:

> We had storm from the North-East, so forceful we were unable to keep water out of the cabins. I myself was tied to the wheel, wet and cold while all the men were struggling to keep the deck load strapped to the ship. ... When we reached the Canary Islands, the chronometer malfunctioned, which meant that we could no longer navigate properly. However, we managed as best as we could with the watch of the ship's carpenter.[10]

After four months at sea, *Lärkan* anchored off Zanzibar on 9 March 1895 – almost exactly one year after Anderssen's arrival. It had been a long and cumbersome journey, but – as was noted by Olsen – not unusually long for a passage from northern Europe to Zanzibar. All in all, the *Lärkan* initiative must be said to have been very swift, mainly due to the use of telegraph communication and to the ready availability of tonnage in Norway.

In Zanzibar, Olsen was met by Anderssen, who acted as the cargo's agent. In less than a week, the entire shipload was sold to the Indian Zanzibari trader Muhammad Juma Thawar. The price was as good as Anderssen had predicted: 82 rupees per ton. Despite unfavourable rates for pounds sterling, and despite the long transport, the pioneering project of Klein and Captain Olsen resulted in a considerable profit. Olsen wrote that 'an entire army' of 'negroes' was needed to carry all the silver rupees to the bank, where they were exchanged for sterling.

The Communication of a Colonial Business

One year later, in the spring of 1896, Olsen returned to Zanzibar. This time he was not tied to the wheel of *Lärkan*, but travelled comfortably through Suez on board the German steamer *Kaizer*. The 37-year- old captain had become a trader – the Zanzibar agent for the newly founded NEAT. The company comprised Klein as representative of the Saugbrugsforeningen and Olsen. Together, the two financed the transport and carried the risk.

Anderssen, who had set the whole enterprise in motion, had since tired of his role as Norwegian state agent and had joined the British colonial service in Kenya, where he became assistant district commissioner in Lamu. The departure of Anderssen meant that Olsen was now the only Norwegian in Zanzibar. Upon arrival, he was to establish an office for NEAT, storage facilities and not least a home for himself. During the first weeks, Olsen went to see several houses in Shangani, the district most favoured by Europeans, but none seems to have suited his purposes. Eventually he found an all-in-one solution in the Malindi quarter. The building was near, but not directly on, the shore, close to the customs office, and was – according to Olsen's descriptions – a classic 'go-down', with storage area downstairs and office/living quarters upstairs.[11] Olsen took no heed of the warnings from other Europeans, who insisted that Malindi was 'unhealthy' and that Shangani would be a better option. By September 1896 he was well installed in his new home and could express his satisfaction in letters to his partner Klein.

The next step was to learn Swahili, in order to communicate with his subagents and staff. In his letters, Olsen repeatedly stressed the necessity of learning the language, as Swahili was 'the language of trade' and the single common language in a trading community where Arabic, Gujarati, Hindi, English, German, French, Portuguese and Italian were used on a regular basis. In 1902, Olsen gave the following advice to a young Norwegian man who wished to make a life for himself in East Africa: '[Swahili] is a very viable language, and even the British have had to learn it. In public offices and among Europeans, English is most commonly used, failing this, with a Greek or an Italian, Swahili is the language of choice.'[12]

After its first year in Zanzibar, NEAT had become a company fully able to compete in East Africa. The books showed a healthy profit, and Olsen had every reason to be optimistic, despite heavy competition from the established German firms in Zanzibar,[13] notably Oswald & Co. and Hansing & Co., which traded in Swedish planks imported via Gothenburg, and – not least – the French trader Leon Besson.[14]

From Olsen's arrival in 1896 until the outbreak of the First World War, NEAT was operating continuously from its head office in Malindi, Zanzibar. In the same period, a total of forty-six sailing ships were sent from Halden, destined for East Africa. In addition, seven cargo loads were sent by steamer, from 1911 to 1914. Unfortunately, account books and shipment papers are not among the papers remaining from NEAT. Thus, it is difficult to get an overview of exactly how much and what type of wood was sent. However, judging from the many letters that exist concerning the shipments, the average shipload seems to have consisted of approximately 1,380 cubic metres.[15] This would make a total of 63,480 cubic metres of wood during the period 1896–1914, or an average of 3,526 cubic metres per year.[16]

The system operated by NEAT was simple and straightforward. In Zanzibar, Olsen estimated the need for planks and timber according to information from his (mostly Indian) subagents, and according to news about colonial building projects and so forth. This information would be forwarded to Klein by mail, and the latter would then start preparing the relevant dimensions[17] and look for a suitable ship. Once a charter had been made, Klein would then notify Olsen by telegram, specifying the volume of wood to be transported. A second telegram would on some occasions be sent when the vessel had commenced loading in Halden, and finally a third when the vessel departed for Zanzibar. Olsen, who routinely picked up his telegrams at the British Club, could then expect the load three to four months later. The actual charter agreement was sent in copy to Olsen by mail steamer, and would thus arrive before the load itself. When the ship arrived, Olsen would confirm its arrival by letter to Klein, and once the cargo was sold, Olsen would send off a full account – also by letter. In the early years, Olsen only used the telegraph on very few occasions, especially to correct specifications of a particular load of planks.

The ships that were used by NEAT were all, without exception until 1911, sailing vessels of about five hundred to eight hundred registered tons. By the 1890s, Norway had already begun to build a fleet of steam vessels. However, Norway's transition from sail to steam was late compared to other shipping nations; the reasons for this have been a topic for much scholarly debate (see, e.g., Grytten 1991, and Nygaard, this volume). What is certain is that for owners of medium-sized sailing vessels in the tramp trade, there existed little incentive to make the transition to steam, as they made solid profits within the North Sea zone, in Mediterranean waters and even – like *Lärkan* – globally.

The ships chartered by NEAT were chartered without return freight, meaning that the captain of the ship would be responsible for contracting the next charter party – either home or to another destination. This was the typical pattern of the so-called tramp trade, and the typical pattern of Norwegian sail-driven shipping (Sætra, this volume). Olsen himself, on his initial voyage with *Lärkan*, set sail without return freight. He ended up with a cargo of rum from Mauritius to Dahomey in West Africa.

As mentioned above, owners of small or medium-sized ships in the tramp trade could make good profits throughout the 1890s and well into the 1900s. As a consequence of an ever-expanding fleet, the competition between shipowners for tonnage was stiff in Norway. For NEAT, the main problem was that the shipowners, given the choice, preferred to charter their vessels to South African harbours (Cape Town, Port Elizabeth or Durban). Return freight was easier to obtain from South Africa, and the longer journey, around the Cape and along

Figure 4.2. SS *Deka* in Dar-es-Salaam: transhipment of timber from Norway.
Source: Olsen family; reproduced with permission.

the East African coast, was less profitable from the shipowners' point of view. From 1898 to 1900 letters between Olsen and Klein are filled with complaints about greedy owners who demand 'unreasonable' rates, fully aware that they controlled the market. Despite this, Olsen and Klein remained in perfect agreement that sails were preferable to steam.

In 1906 the freight market was particularly difficult, and in a letter to Olsen dated 6 July, Klein noted (with an air of exasperation): 'We may have to consider steam as an option.'[18] Three years and ten sailing ships later, Klein was still reluctant to consider steam transport: 'Sails are much cheaper and not least much more convenient. In general, we have little to gain from steamers in our line of business, as each shipment must be assembled over a long period.'[19]

By using relatively small sailing vessels, NEAT could charter and load according to detailed specifications from Olsen, and thus respond more directly to market demands than they could with prebooked tonnage on board steam liners. Only in late 1909 did Klein condescend to contact Deutsche Ost-Afrika Linie (DOAL) in Hamburg to enquire about prices for the shipment of planks to Zanzibar. However, as table 4.1 shows, the transition was very gradual. In 1912 and 1913, four shipments were sent by steamer from Halden to Zanzibar. In the same years, five sailing ships departed on the same route.

Table 4.1. Overview of chartered ships that departed with timber and wood for NEAT, Zanzibar, 1894–1918

	Chartered	Name of ship	Departure from Halden
1	Juli1894	Schooner *Lärkan*	21 okt 1894
2	?	Barque *Sigrid*	Ca. sept 1896
3	Jan 1897	Barque *Alpha*	Ca. feb 1897
4	Aug 1897	Barque *Victor*	Mar 1898
5	Apr 1898	*Guldregn*	?
6	Oct 1898	*Adela*	?
7	Mar 1889	*Ringhorn*	?
8	Sept 1889	Iron ship *Tana*	?
9	Apr 1900	Barque *Alpha*	?
10	Nov 1900	Barque *Ellen*	21 Apr 1901
11	Mar 1901	Barque *Bjarne*	18 Mai 1901
12	Aug 1901	Iron ship *Warinca*	18 Okt 1901
POSSIBLY ONE OR TWO SHIPS MISSING DUE TO ONE MISSING COPYBOOK			
13	Sept 1902	Steel ship *Turist*	Des 1902
14	Mai 1903	Steel ship *Gartha*	1 Jun 1903
15	Jul 1903	Steek ship *Barden*	?
16	Feb 1904	*HC Richard*	4 Mai 1904
17	Aug 1904	*Viking*	?
18	Des 1904	Steel ship *Sydenhavn*	24 Feb 1905
19	Mai 1905	Iron ship *Fram*	4 Jul 1905
20	Sept 1905	*Bas Rock*	9 Nov 1905
21	Feb 1906	Iron ship *Titania*	7 Apr 1906
22	Aug 1906	Steel ship *Fox*	30 Okt 1906
23	Mar 1907	Iron ship *Hermes*	7 Jun 1906
24	Jun 1907	Iron ship *Collingswood*	27 Jul 1907
25	Des 1907	Iron ship *Fridtjof Bryde*	19 Feb 1908
26	Mar 1908	Iron ship *Saturnus*	25 Mai 1908
27	Jul 1908	Iron ship *Concordia*	20 Sept 1908
28	Okt 1908	Iron ship *Deka*	9 Jan 1909
29	Apr 1909	Eos	Ca Jun 1909
30	Okt 1909	Iron ship *Dorothea*	20 Des 1909
31	Nov 1909	Barque *Barghany*	23 Feb 1910
32	Jun 1910	Iron ship *Lysglimt*	20 Aug 1910

| 33 | Jul 1910 | Steel ship *Erling* | 20 Sept 1910 |
| 34 | Nov 1910 | Steel ship *Anglo Normann* | Ca. Feb 1911 |

May 1911: First shipment by steamer. This consignment was sent by Norwegian liner company *Søndenfjeldske* to Hamburg. From there, it continued by Deutsche Ost-Afrika Linie S/S *Oswald,* departing from Hamburg 15 June 1911.

| 35 | May 1911 | Barque *Alpha* | 3 Jul 1911 |
| 36 | Jun 1911 | *Eos* | 30 Sept 1911 |

Oct 1911: Second shipment by steamer DOAL S/S *Oswald* fra Hamburg 15 Okt. Cargo: Plank for Tanga and Dar es Salaam

37	Okt 1911	Iron ship *Valdivia*	15 Dec 1911
38	Mar 1912	Iron ship *Aktiv*	5 May 1912
39	Apr 1912	Iron ship *Lila*	6 Jul 1912

Apr 1912:DOAL S/S *Rufiji* from Hamburg 15 Juni. Cargo: plank for Tanga and Dar es Salaam

| 40 | Jul 1912 | Iron ship "Sator" | 7 Sept 1912 |

Dec 1912: DOAL S/S *Emin* from Hamburg 15 Feb 1913. Cargo: Plank for Mombasa and Dar es Salaam

Feb 1913: DOAL S/S *Kommodore* from Hamburg 15 April 1913. Cargo: Plank for Mombasa and Tanga.

Feb 1913: DOAL S/S *Emin* from Hamburg 15 May 1913. Cargo: Plank for Mombasa and Dar es Salaam

| 41 | Feb 1913 | Iron ship *Elfeda* | 1 Jul 1913 |

May 1913: First shipment directly from Norway to Zanzibar by Scandinavia East Africa Line (SEAL) steamer *Troldfos* departing Halden 15 June 1913 via Suez. Cargo: Plank for Mombasa and Zanzibar.

42	Jul 1913	Iron ship *Alexandra*	Ca Sept 1913
43	Sept 1913	Iron ship *Aktiv*	10 Jan 1914
44	Okt 1913	Iron ship *Fram*	16 Jan 1914
45	Jan 1914	Iron ship *Titania*	Ca May 191
46	Jul 1914	Iron ship *Fredrikssten*	Outbreak of war. Charter party cancelled.

Sept 1915: SEAL S/S *Ulefos* fra Halden 5 Nov 1915. Cargo: Plank for Mombasa.

Apr 1916: SEAL S/S *Kaggefos* departing Halden 26 July 1916. Cargo: Plank for Mombasa. The ship came under fire in the North Sea and sustained damages but reached Mombasa.

Source: Olsen-Klein correspondence, 1894–1918

The Agent and His Subagents: An East African Network

The first shipment that arrived in Zanzibar via NEAT came on the bark *Sigrid*. The journey took even longer than that of *Lärkan* – almost five months, around the Cape of Good Hope. Despite Olsen's best efforts, the entire load was not sold by the time *Sigrid* arrived on 5 January 1897. The cargo was unloaded to NEAT's go-down and cleared customs there – a special service from the director of customs, who had been given a present of an especially finely carved Norwegian knife.

Sigrid then continued onwards to Mombasa, where the main bulk of its cargo was to be sold to NEAT's most important customer by far in the years 1896–1900: the Uganda Railway. In Mombasa, Olsen had entered into an agency contract with A.K. Jeevanjee, a relative of the famous Alibhai Mulla Jeevanjee, founder of the *East African Standard* newspaper and chief buyer for the Uganda Railway (Patel 2002). According to Olsen's correspondence, the partnership worked very well; the Jeevanjees paid regularly, as Olsen reported to Klein. The cargo delivered to the Uganda Railway consisted mostly of rough planks, so-called scantlings and ceilings to be used for scaffolding, fences, walkways and barracks. In addition, NEAT provided doors and windows, which implies that they were used for barracks and/or stations.

In 1898, the British company Boustead & Ridley replaced the Jeevanjees as agents in Mombasa. A few years later (probably around 1902), the company Smith & MacKenzie became NEAT's agents in Mombasa, the contract including the provision that Smith & MacKenzie would provide storage for the goods. This agreement continued until 1918, albeit with intermittent conflicts concerning the price of storage facilities and so forth. The ships from Norway would unload cargo in Mombasa directly from 1896 onwards. However, on occasion Olsen would charter local dhows to bring cargo destined for the railway from Zanzibar to Mombasa.

In Dar-es-Salaam, NEAT entered into an agency agreement with the Hamburg trader Max Steffens. From 1906, ships were directed to Dar-es-Salaam directly to offload goods on consignment for Max Steffens, who would provide storage himself. Furthermore, NEAT sold wood directly to Tanga, where they at times kept one of their staff employed – at other times, they relied on local agents.

In Zanzibar itself, NEAT depended on the network of Indian traders who bought wholesale directly from storage. They would sell the goods onwards as retail to the locals from their own outlets.

Occasional customers were the various missions, in Zanzibar itself and on the mainland. The Swedish Mission in Bagamoyo was a regular customer, as was the French White Fathers Mission in the same place. In Zanzibar, the Catholic Mission was, for a period, the 'best private customer'. Planks were also sold to ships in harbour, for repair and construction of boxes and other storage vessels.

Finally, goods were sold to the most important purchaser in Zanzibar, the British-Busaidi government. Here, NEAT had trouble getting into the market, delivering offer after offer to government building projects only to be underpriced by others. However, the company gradually worked its way into the list of suppliers to the Zanzibar government.

With his local and regional partners and clients, Olsen would correspond mainly by letters. The correspondence is in English, German and Swahili, with even the occasional outgoing letter in Gujarati. In the latter case, we must assume that Olsen made use of the language skills of one NEAT's Indian staff. Olsen also personally travelled to Mombasa and Dar-es-Salaam on a regular basis, and much of the contact was kept up by direct, face-to-face meetings.

The Management in East Africa

During the first year in Zanzibar, Olsen managed the business himself. He was aided by his Indian ('Hindu', as he writes) clerk, who did 'an excellent job'. The clerk was evidently a Hindu Banya, as Olsen describes him as being completely vegetarian. In addition, he employed a number of 'boys' for the storage room, two servants for his own home and a cook, Mabruki, who was to stay with him for many years. Nevertheless, Olsen was extremely overworked and, according to himself, 'tied to the office like a dog in chain'. More importantly, he was unable to travel to, for example, Mombasa to establish new contacts there and other places. The solution came in 1898, when Olsen brought out his sister Agnes, unmarried, aged thirty-three. She arrived in Zanzibar on 15 June 1898 and was employed as 'assistant' in the office. This left her brother free to travel to set up subagencies along the coast and network for new customers while Agnes managed the firm and sold wood from the store in Zanzibar. She was, according to Olsen, 'the first female secretary employed in British East Africa'.

However, by 1902, Olsen's mother had become old and frail, and Agnes (whose life seems to have been completely tied to that of her family) was sent home to nurse her. In her place, a new assistant was sent out from Norway, Christian Janssen, who was to stay with NEAT until 1920, and who, when the Swedish-Norwegian union was dissolved in 1905, became the first Norwegian consul to Zanzibar.

By 1910, the local trade of NEAT had expanded to include German East Africa. A third man was needed, and Olaf Dahl was sent out. He suffered badly from the climate and was sent home in 1912, and a new man arrived, only to last less than two years. From 1914, there was a third assistant, Kristian Hejer, who eventually was to lead NEAT into the postwar years.

Wartime East Africa: Communication Ruptures

The outbreak of war created serious problems for NEAT. First and foremost, communication between Zanzibar and Norway, which until then had been stable and reliable, albeit at times slow, now became unpredictable. From the copybooks, we can read that several letters never reached their destinations, as postal steamers were sunk. Those that did arrive were often censored. Second, transport of planks became nearly impossible, as tonnage for East Africa became practically unavailable. In addition, all communication between Zanzibar and the German-held ports of Tanga and Dar-es-Salaam was cut off.[20] Last, transport of staff from Norway to Zanzibar became cumbersome, slow and at times dangerous. Given these problems, the war years were first and foremost years of improvisation – especially when it came to communication and transport. The war also made clear that NEAT, like many small companies based in neutral countries, navigated the waters between two colonial giants, England and Germany. In these waters, great fortunes could be made but also lost.

Upon the outbreak of war, the sailing ship *Fredrikssten* was lying almost fully loaded in the harbour in Halden, ready to sail for Dar-es-Salaam and Tanga. But the war meant the blockade of German-held ports, and the entire shipment was eventually cancelled. This singular piece of news was important enough to be transmitted by telegram – a message that heralded difficult years to come. It read, brutally: 'Vessel cancelled.'[21] All in all, a mere two shipments made it from Halden to Zanzibar during the war years.

Undoubtedly, the main problem for NEAT was the interrupted communication between Zanzibar and Halden. A letter from Norway to Zanzibar could now take up to four months, almost twice as long as before the war.[22] Very often they did not arrive at all. Olsen's correspondence from 1916 and 1917 is filled with complaints about mail that never arrives, and repeated enquiries for confirmation that his letters have reached their recipients. Cable communications were restricted and still expensive for regular communication. The near-total isolation clearly had an effect on the personal level, and Olsen felt, as he repeatedly stated, 'quite alone'. To his sister Agnes, he was at his most honest and vulnerable: 'I receive no letters. Do people no longer have the time to write to me, or is the mail lost? I will spend Christmas all by myself.'[23]

The communication ruptures also made the running of NEAT more complicated. First, Olsen and Klein were now forced to communicate in English; otherwise, the letters would simply have been confiscated altogether. Second, every letter had to be sent in duplicate, ideally by two different mail steamers. However, Olsen complained that this precaution was not very helpful, as both original and duplicate would anyway end up on the same ship across the North Sea – the most dangerous stretch on the journey. Finally, many topics were simply off-limits. In February 1915, Klein wrote to Olsen: 'I have received your letter, but only the first and last four lines of it, the rest having been cut by censors. I presume that the middle contained information about Dar-es-Salaam.'[24]

The response from Olsen and Klein was the only one possible. They communicated less, and very few letters passed between them compared to the prewar years. Instead, they relied on brief messages by telegram, but only when it was really necessary.

Another recurring problem during the war years was the transport of staff, which became highly unpredictable. Kristian Hejer was to return home on leave in December 1916, having served a three-year stint in Zanzibar. He made it to London, but there he found the North Sea completely off-limits due to German submarines. He was stuck for four months in London, awaiting passage to Norway. In the company correspondence, Hejer is jokingly referred to as 'our modern Ulysses'.

Olsen himself was stranded in Zanzibar for almost two years. He left Norway in June 1916 for what was originally intended as a tour of inspection, probably to check the state of affairs in Dar-es-Salaam. Shortly after arrival in Zanzibar, his correspondence is filled with plans for his prompt return to Norway. However, the war disrupted his plans. In February 1917, Olsen wrote to Klein, with open disappointment: 'I had hoped to celebrate my sixtieth birthday at home, but if that is not to be, one has to take things as they come.'[25] His next hope was to celebrate his tenth wedding anniversary at home, on 28 August 1917. To his wife, he wrote sadly: 'I do not think I will make it home to our wedding anniversary.'[26] Growing increasingly frustrated, Olsen considered a detour through Asia, envisioning a return to Norway via the Northeast Passage north of Siberia. In this, he was strongly discouraged by Klein.

Olsen had no choice but to stay in Zanzibar until 1918, when he was finally able to return.

Conditions changed in Zanzibar, too, as a consequence of the war. First, all contact with the German-held cities on the coast was forbidden. Second, all Germans in Zanzibar were expelled from the protectorate upon the outbreak of war. Among them were the representatives of the Oswald and Hansing houses, which had been trading on the island since the 1840s. All German properties were confiscated, including a German holiday villa near the Norwegian Bungalow in Chwaka. Third, the Zanzibar War Decree, issued 5 August 1914, placed strict limitations on freedom of trade and movement for representatives of neutral countries. This related especially to the import and export of any cargo that could be remotely viewed as contraband. Norwegian ships were not allowed to call at German ports, and it was illegal to keep on board any cargo that could conceivably be considered war matériel. An example of the latter was two boats that were shipped out on board the Scandinavian East Africa liner *Troldfos* in December 1914. Upon arrival in Zanzibar, the two boats were immediately confiscated, as they could be sold to German ships in open waters. The confiscation was the start of a long and intricate legal process that ended with the two boats finally being relinquished in 1917.

Olsen's main worry was the state of NEAT's substantial storage of planks in both Tanga and Dar-es-Salaam. In 1914, a concerned Klein had written to Olsen: 'The newspapers here report that the British have wrecked Dar-es-Salaam. Is that the case, and if so, do you have any idea about the state of our goods in storage?'[27] Olsen, at that time at home in Norway, could only report that 'no man – British or otherwise' was allowed across the Zanzibar channel, and thus he was in no position to know the fate of the cargo stored on the coast.[28]

In his descriptions of the colonial powers, Olsen is clearly most positive towards the British. To his wife, he noted: 'Here in Zanzibar, the British rulers are no less friendly than they were before the war broke out.'[29] However, he also maintained a close friendship with his agent in Dar-es-Salaam, the German Max Steffens, and during the war years he worried as much about the fate of his friend as about his planks. Regarding Germans in general, however, his tone is markedly negative. Not surprisingly for an old sea captain, he seemed most irritated by the German naval tactics: 'pirates at sea' is a recurring phrase in his correspondence.

In Zanzibar, Olsen made every effort to keep in the good books of the British authorities. Controversies were smoothed over; complaints over import taxes were never raised. In the cases where protest was necessary, it was done in a quiet, roundabout way. One example came just after the outbreak of the war, in August 1914, when the Scandinavian East Africa liner *Troldfos* arrived in Zanzibar with the German vice-consul of Mombasa and his wife aboard. The hapless consul had been placed on the ship by the British authorities of Mombasa, where Germans were being summarily expelled. The captain of *Troldfos* did not want the two Germans on board, fearing that he would not be able to land them in any of his ports of call. However, he had agreed to take them to the nearest neutral port in Mozambique. In Zanzibar, the captain wanted a guarantee from the British authorities that he would be able to 'get rid of' (the captain's own words) the Germans. After some diplomacy, a guarantee was provided, and *Troldfos* was allowed to continue to Mozambique with its unwanted human cargo. In general, it seems that the staff of NEAT did their utmost to keep local Zanzibar authorities, as Olsen put it, 'as forthcoming as is possible under martial law'.[30]

One way of doing this was to contribute generously and frequently to the British Red Cross Relief Fund. The *Zanzibar Gazette* reported regularly on donations to the fund throughout the war. Among the most generous was Major F.B. Pearce, the British Resident from 1914 to 1922. Other British colonial officers were also frequent donors, as were many of Zanzibar's rich Indian families, prominent Arabs and Islamic judges. NEAT, too, appears on the list of benefactors. Besides money, the company donated tables, chairs and planks to the annual Red Cross carnival held to raise money for the relief fund. From November 1916, Olsen even functioned as vice president for the Zanzibar branch of the relief fund, the Resident himself being president.

Olsen seems to have regarded his efforts for the Red Cross Relief Fund as an 'extra tax' – the price to be paid for the sake of maintaining good relations during difficult times. The actual donations were deducted in the accounts as taxes, pure and simple. However, Olsen viewed the carnival with great enthusiasm, describing to his wife the various matinees, cinema shows, lotteries and sport events, as well as the food and drink.

The inevitable result of all these obstacles was that the store was empty. By January 1917, Olsen reported: 'It's a sad sight to stroll around our storage room these days. All you see is a big empty space, for which we, mind you, have to pay rent.'[31] To compensate, Olsen made a few attempts to import 'African wood', amongst others, from the Equator Saw Mill in Kenya. This created some turnover in the company accounts but yielded only limited profit given the stiff competition from Indian traders.

Private Correspondence: Colonial Life Communicated

So far, this chapter has focused on the business communication between the partners of NEAT and the various obstacles they faced. However, it is important to note that Olsen, during his years in Zanzibar,
also communicated stories of everyday, colonial life, of small and big
events, and offered his own opinion about life in Zanzibar. Recipients
of these letters were Klein, his wife, Maiken, and later their sons, his
sister Agnes, his assistant, Janssen, as well as friends and acquaintances
in Halden. In this correspondence, Olsen joined ranks with thousands
of other Europeans who found colonies an arena for upwards mobility,
and who reported back to their homelands about life overseas.

Conversely, Olsen would receive news from home by letter – or by
telegram if the news were important, such as births or deaths. Other
major news also arrived by telegram, such as Roald Amundsen becoming the first to reach the South Pole. 'We hoisted our flags immediately',
Olsen reports in a letter the day after.[32] The news of Amundsen's successful journey reached Zanzibar only a day after Amundsen himself
sent his telegram from Hobart in Australia and the very same day the
news broke in Norway. It is worth noting how fast news could travel
by 1911, but also what type of news was deemed worthy of a telegram
rather than a letter.

Overall, Olsen seems to have been very pleased with his life in
Zanzibar, and this is what he communicated in his letters. Even while
stranded during the war, Olsen had to concede that life in Zanzibar was
'not at all bad' – at least not compared to conditions in Europe, as Olsen
repeatedly emphasized in his letters. He referred to the war in Europe
as a 'witch dance' between parties bent on mutual destruction. In Zanzibar, as Olsen wrote, life was relatively peaceful. Basic goods, although
more expensive, were still available. In January 1918 he made the following observation to Klein: 'If I did not have a family at home, I would
have lived rather nicely here. We have plenty of sunshine, enough food
and rest. Old hands like myself no longer worry about mosquitoes. We
have a club, a library, and an elegant bar where teetotallers are banned
and have no voice whatsoever.'[33]

The Final Years of NEAT

In January 1897, after almost two years of constant work in Zanzibar,
Olsen was optimistic about the future. 'People here are beginning to
take note that a serious competitor has arrived', he wrote, adding: 'I

hear that even the Indians believe I will make good business here.'[34] A better recommendation could hardly be had in Zanzibar around the turn of the century, where Indian traders held a monopoly on most consumer goods entering the protectorate.

On 19 January 1918, Olsen received a message from Klein, this time in the form of a short and simple telegram: 'Sold business. Await letter. Meanwhile conduct business as usual.'[35] Postal communication being slow, Olsen had to 'await letter' until April, when the news finally arrived in written form. There, Olsen could read details about the transaction and the new owners – a Norwegian consortium of large-scale shipping and industry.

The news proved the prediction from 1897 to be correct. When the company was sold in 1918, it was for NOK 240,000. Of this, Olsen received NOK 140,000, with a later additional bonus of NOK 20,000, a total NOK 160,000. This equals more than NOK 2.5 million or about USD 450,000 in 2013 values.[36] Sitting in his inherited family home at Sauøen, an island outside Halden, it was more than enough for 'Zanzibar-Olsen': for the remaining seven years of his life he could title himself a 'rentier'. In his retirement, Olsen corresponded frequently with Hejer, the new manager in Zanzibar. Upon learning about the new harbour being built there, he often expressed a wish to see his 'second home' again, and he even made some tentative plans for a journey. However, he added: 'It may be, by that time, that I have embarked on a much longer journey to a destination we all must reach eventually.'[37]

For 'Zanzibar-Olsen', only two destinations could possibly lure him from his comfortable retirement: Zanzibar or death. It was a fitting observation from a man whose entire fortune was built upon European expansion into Africa, and not least on the improved communications that made this possible – the ships, the postal steamers, the Uganda Railway and the telegraph.

Notes

1. The history of the Norway-East Africa Trading Company has been treated in detail in Bang (2008, 2011).
2. A major source for this study are five volumes of copybooks (approximately one thousand pages each) containing the letters of O. Chr. Olsen from the period 1894–1922, the bulk of which he spent in Zanzibar. The majority of the letters are in Norwegian and addressed to his partner, W. Klein, to his sister and later to his wife, Maiken Olsen, as well as to friends and others in Norway. Some letters are in English, mainly to British personnel in the

colonial administration, or to managers of various firms, including Smith & MacKenzie and the Uganda Railway. Some are in German, addressed to partners in German East Africa. The letters are in the possession of the descendants of O. Chr. Olsen, Wenche Koren, Tore Holm-Olsen and Petter Koren. I am grateful for the generosity they have shown in providing copies for me, and in providing oral information and photographic material.

3. Lloyds Ships Register, kept by Zanzibar agents, ARC4/28, ZNA.
4. Copybooks of outgoing letters from the Saugbrugsforeningen, Halden, from W. Klein (and others in his absence) to NEAT in the period 1896–1918, ANSS.
5. Olsen, outgoing letters, copybook 5, 'A Brief History of NEAT'. The telegram is quoted in Olsen's retrospective account, and it is worth noting that it does not mention any concrete orders. Anderssen simply reports that Norwegian wood will find 'a ready market' in East Africa.
6. The *Zanzibar Gazette*, 5 April 1894.
7. On the East African career of J.J. Bull Anderssen, see Kjerland (2010: 25–41).
8. The *Zanzibar Gazette*, 26 June 1895.
9. On the establishment of communication technology in Zanzibar, see Prestholt (2008) and Bissel (2011).
10. Olsen, outgoing letters, copybook 5, 'A Brief History of NEAT'.
11. Assessment Files 1, ZNA. NEAT's go-down was house no. 976, Malindi. The house was among those demolished for the harbour extensions in the 1920s.
12. Olsen, outgoing letters, copybook 2, letter to Herrene Mestergaard, 20 June 1902.
13. On the history of the German trading firms in Zanzibar, see Schneppen (2003).
14. Leon Besson first established himself in Zanzibar in 1886, trading in everything from building materials (wood, iron, cement) to consumer items like soap, kitchenware and so forth. (see North 2005).
15. Olsen, outgoing letters, copybooks 1–5; outgoing letters, copybooks 91–119, ANSS.
16. It should be mentioned that the total Norwegian wood exports for the same years averaged ca. 1.7 million cubic metres per year. This makes the export to East Africa from the Saugbrugsforeningen about 0.25 per cent of the total Norwegian exports. *Statistical Yearbook of Norway*, 1911–1914. http://www.ssb.no.
17. The preparations included cutting the relevant dimensions according to Olsen's specifications and leaving the planks to dry.
18. Outgoing letters, copybook 107, letter to Olsen, 6 July 1906, ANSS.
19. Ibid.
20. During the First World War, both the storage in Dar-es-Salaam, and all the wood within it, and Steffens himself vanished. NEAT was prepared to write off a very heavy loss when, in 1919, Steffens showed up again in Hamburg, prepared to offer compensation for the loss.
21. Outgoing letters, copybook 130, telegram to Olsen, 12 September 1914, ANSS.

22. Olsen, outgoing letters, copybook 5, letter to Maiken, 22 December 1917, ANSS.
23. Olsen, outgoing letters, copybook 5, letter to Agnes, 21 December 1917, ANSS.
24. Outgoing letters, copybook 131, letter to Olsen, 3 February 1915, ANSS.
25. Olsen, outgoing letters, copybook 5, letter to Klein, 24 February 1917, ANSS.
26. Olsen, outgoing letters, copybook 5, letter to Maiken, 4 May 1917, ANSS.
27. Outgoing letters, copybook 130, letter to NEAT, 23 September 1909, ANSS.
28. Olsen, outgoing letters, copybook 5, letter to Klein, 21 October 1916, ANSS.
29. Olsen, outgoing letters, copybook 5, letter to Maiken, 10 October 1916, ANSS.
30. Letter from Olsen, acting as Norwegian consul, to the Ministry of Foreign Affairs, 26 August 1916, 3615 (K5-E-74/06), RA-UD.
31. Olsen, outgoing letters, copybook 5, letter to Jansen, 1 August 1917, ANSS.
32. Olsen, outgoing letters, copybook 4, letter to Jansen, 8 March 1912, ANSS.
33. Olsen, outgoing letters, copybook 5, letter to Dr Klem in Halden, 31 January 1918, ANSS.
34. Olsen, outgoing letters, copybook 1, letter to Klein, 20 January 1897, ANSS.
35. Outgoing letters, copybook 134, telegram to Olsen, 19 January 1918, ANSS.
36. Norwegian Statistical Bureau, *Wholesale Price Index*; corrected for purchasing power.
37. Olsen, outgoing letters, copybook 6, letter to Hejer, 8 February 1921, ANSS.

Archives and Sources Consulted

Archives of Norske Skog Saugbrugsforeningen (ANSS), Halden, Norway.
The Central Office of the National Archives of Norway (Riksarkivet, RA), Oslo.
Letters of O. Chr. Olsen, in the possession of Wenche Koren, Tore Holm-Olsen and Petter Koren.
Zanzibar National Archives (ZNA), Zanzibar.

References

Bang, A.K. 2008. *Zanzibar-Olsen: Norsk trelasthandel i Øst-Afrika 1895–1925*. Bergen: Fagbokforlaget.
———. 2011. *Zanzibar-Olsen: A Norwegian Timber Trader in Zanzibar, 1895–1925*. Bergen: Eden Olympia.
Bissel, W.C. 2011. *Urban Design, Chaos and Colonial Power in Zanzibar*. Bloomington: Indiana University Press.
Grytten, O.H. 1991. *Krise eller glemt storhetstid? Transformasjonen fra seil til damp i norsk skipsfart, 1880–1910*. Bergen: Norges Handelshøyskole.
Kjerland, K.A. 2010. *Nordmenn i det koloniale Kenya*. Oslo: Scandinavian Academic Press.
Norløff, H.P. 1935. *Saugbrugsforeningen gjennem 75 år, 1859–1934*. Oslo: Aschehoug.

Patel, Z. 2002. *Jeevanjee: Rebel of the Empire*. Nairobi: Sasa Sema.

Prestholt, J. 2008. *Domesticating the World: African Consumerism and the Genealogies of Globalization*. Berkeley: University of California Press.

Schneppen, H. 2003. *Sansibar und die Deutschen: Ein besonderes Verhältnis, 1844–1966*. Munster: LIT Verlag.

❧ 5

'THREE BLACK LABOURERS DID THE JOB OF TWO WHITES'

African Labourers in Modern Norwegian Whaling

Dag Ingemar Børresen

The establishment of whaling stations represented the single largest Norwegian industrial operation outside of Norway in the period 1883–1924. From the inception of the modern whaling industry in the 1860s in the north of Norway, whaling then spread globally, first to the closest catching grounds in the North Atlantic, Newfoundland and Japan and then to the North American Pacific coastline and Alaska. The first modern whaling station in the southern hemisphere was established in Grytviken on the British sub-Antarctic island of South Georgia in 1904. While the station was Argentinian-owned, it was managed and operated by Norwegians. Following South Georgia, land stations were established in South America, South Africa and Australia, north to the Bering Sea and back to Alaska, the span of Norwegian whaling thus encircling the globe (Tønnessen 1967: 11). It took only a few years after whaling commenced in Antarctic waters for Norwegian entrepreneurs and businessmen to establish companies with the purpose of utilizing the whale stocks in African waters.

This chapter analyses a particular aspect of the African element in the expansion of Norwegian global whaling, namely, the usage and representation of African labour. In this way it seeks not only to uncover African elements in Norwegian colonial maritime and whaling history, but also to contribute to labour history more generally. Labour history is a thoroughly under researched area of whaling history – which is often national (and sometimes even nationalistic) in tenor – as well as a key factor in the maritime basis of Norwegian colonial entrepreneurship in the period.

The Whaling Boom in African Waters

In October 1910, the Norwegian captain Alfred Aadnesen sailed from Durban in South Africa to Inhambane in Portuguese East Africa (present-day Mozambique). Captain Aadnesen had been commissioned by a group of businessmen in Durban who planned to build a whaling station at Linga Linga, and he arrived with a concession from the Portuguese colonial authorities already in hand. Captain Aadnesen's task was to observe and report anything potentially significant for establishing a land station. In his conclusions, he found that the harbour was suitable, that there was easy access to fresh water and that there were thousands of whales swimming along the coastline. He also observed: 'There is plenty of black labour to be had, and the pay is about six pence a day. To feed them will not run up to much, as their food consists of rice and fish, the latter can be supplied by bringing a few nets from home, as fish are plentiful.'[1]

The first modern whaling station in African waters had been established by Norwegians two years earlier (1908), when the South African Whaling Company (SAWC) erected a factory on the Bluff Peninsula close to Durban's harbour. SAWC was founded by shipowner and industrialist Johan Bryde, from the small coastal town of Sandefjord, and Jacob J. Egeland and Abraham E. Larsen, from Spind in southern Norway. Egeland and Larsen were cousins and immigrants to South Africa. Egeland was already a successful businessman in South Africa and was appointed Norwegian consul in Durban in 1905.[2] Sandefjord became the headquarters of the SAWC, which was managed by Bryde.

As an experienced businessman in South Africa for nearly thirty years, Egeland easily managed to obtain a licence for whaling in Natal waters from the government of the colony. The combination of money, ships, equipment and knowhow from Norway and an already-established network in South Africa were crucial factors contributing to SAWC's rapid economic success. As Captain Aadnesen had observed in Portuguese East Africa, access to an abundance of inexpensive labour was a great advantage and key to planning the establishment of the company. The SAWC's early years also coincided with an era when the South African mining industry was booming; it was one of the major consumers of whale oil produced in Durban.[3]

Before whaling operations at Durban commenced in 1908, Egeland and Larsen travelled to Zululand with the intention of hiring African workers for the land station (Hale 1986: 569). The two Norwegians regarded African labourers a worthwhile substitute for (the preferred but more expensive) Europeans, who demanded free transport from Europe, higher wages and better food and facilities. Most Africans were regarded as second- or third-rate citizens by the colonists and also ranked at the bottom of the hierarchy at the whaling factories. However, while most Africans worked as unskilled labourers or stevedores at the whaling factories, some were also trained as seal hunters and flensers, work traditionally performed by relatively highly paid, skilled Norwegian workers (Børresen 2006: 153).

The relatively short-lived whaling boom in African waters reached its peak in 1913, when twenty-six whaling companies were active in whaling grounds that stretched from Portuguese East Africa in the east to the French Congo (now Gabon) on the western coastline (Hvalfangernes Assuranceforening 1926: 60-63).[4] One of the main reasons for the decline was the outbreak of the First World War, which made the transport of whaling products, such as whale oil and baleen, to European markets difficult and dangerous. Also, most floating factory ships were converted into freight liners operating in the Atlantic Ocean during the war. More important still was a dramatic decline in the number of humpback whales: the overexploitation was making whaling increasingly unprofitable. However, at the onset of the African whaling boom, unlimited access to cheap African labour was an important precondition for the whaling companies.

African Labour in the Factories

Captain Aadnesen's 1910 report from his visit to Mozambique was full of superlatives concerning the favourable conditions for establishing a whaling station at Linga Linga.[5] While the Durban businessman's plans failed to come to fruition, one year later Johan Bryde nevertheless founded the Mozambique Whaling Company (MWC) in Sandefjord. He planned to utilize the same whaling grounds and built a whaling station at Linga Linga in 1911. For Bryde, an important argument for establishing the Linga Linga station was (as in Durban in 1908) the proliferation of inexpensive African labour, plus the availability of cheap coal. At the newly built factory, the African labourers were commanded by an unnamed Norwegian captain. Reflecting the racialized structure of South African society at the time, the Norwegian expression for the captain's position at Linga Linga was *kafferdriver* (a [slave] driver of kaffirs). It seems there was little or no objection to the term by the Norwegians involved in whaling at the time. In addition to his tasks of organizing African labourers, the captain also served as a local agent for MWC, and later on he became manager of the station.[6]

In order for Norwegian whaling companies to control labourers derogatorily termed 'kaffirs' and to access enough African labour, good
relationships with the local colonial authorities were needed. In the
Portuguese colonies in southern Africa – Portuguese West Africa (now
Angola) and Portuguese East Africa – a system of forced labour called
chibalo gave the colonial power unlimited access to cheap labour for factories, plantations and development of infrastructure (Penvenne 1995:
26–27). With their dealings in Portuguese colonies, Norwegian whaling
companies benefited from the same forced labour system (see also Bertelsen's chapter, this volume).

Reports were also made on the conditions at these stations. A Norwegian sailor visiting the MWC's Linga Linga station in 1923 reported
a factory manned by local African labour. The owner of the Linga Linga
station was now Sophus Pettersen, a successful businessman and chandler from Sandefjord living in Durban.[7] The sailor reported that at this
time, two hundred Africans were employed at the station, that ten Africans worked for the salary of one white man and that the company's expenses for food supplies for the Africans were much lower than
for the Europeans. He further explained to the Norwegian newspaper
Sandefjords Blad on 27 November 1923 that it was important that every
African work gang had a foreman who knew how to push 'the boys'
(as they were often derogatorily called) to work hard: 'You could then
safely say that three black labourers did the job of two whites.' Reflecting this racial stereotype, the Africans at Linga Linga were also in other
sources generally described as 'lazy' and 'childish'. If the foremen were
dissatisfied with the pace of work, the Norwegian sailor is quoted as
saying that they gave the 'big lazy rascals a tender swift lash with a
whip' – underlining the violence with which the Portuguese colonial
order produced labour regimes for international companies.

Mozambique was, however, not the only Portuguese colony in which
Norwegian whalers were operating. Already in 1909, the Viking Whaling Company (VWC) from Sandefjord established a base in the small
town of Porto Alexandre in today's Angola. In 1911, the company hired
thirty 'negroes' (*negre*) as labourers on board the floating factory ship
Ambra. They were paid two pounds a month and received free food.[8]
One year later, another team of twenty Africans was hired to work in
the newly built factory at the land station.

However, even though these Norwegian whaling companies benefited greatly from aspects of the Portuguese colonial system, such as the
forced labour system, the relationship was sometimes difficult between
the local authorities and the Norwegian managers. For instance, VWC
managers repeatedly complained that the Portuguese authorities con-

stantly changed contracts and raised taxes and harbour fees without prior warning. From the Norwegian side it was therefore seen as necessary to use bribes as a means to get access to harbour facilities, docks and so forth. The Norwegian station manager elaborated in detail how he used silver cutlery and hunting rifles purchased in Sandefjord, combined with hard cash, as efficient door openers in this regard. Thus, from a Norwegian point of view and reflecting their inferior position, the African kaffirs were much easier to deal with than the Portuguese. Although Norwegian whalers often repeated that the Africans lived like pigs and ate whale meat from the rotting whale carcasses on the beach, they were not seen to cause trouble, unlike 'the Portuguese devils', as they were frequently called (Børresen 2002: 167–76).

As noted, although the whaling boom in African waters was short-lived and collapsed in 1914–15, some South African companies established and managed by Norwegians nevertheless survived for decades. The largest company, the Union Whaling & Fishing Company Ltd (UWFC), was established in Durban in 1909, when Jacob J. Egeland and Abraham E. Larsen ended their cooperation with Johan Bryde and erected a second whaling factory on a neighbouring site on the Bluff Peninsula. While this station closed down and was dismantled in 1917 as a result of the First World War, the UWFC was reorganized in 1920 when the management decided to purchase an abandoned Norwegian whaling station in Plettenberg Bay at a very favourable price. Under the supervision of Larsen, machinery from the Plettenberg Bay factory was transported to Durban, where it was reassembled in time for the 1921 whaling season. UWFC (renamed the Union Whaling Company Ltd, UWC, in 1920) operated in Durban for more than sixty years.[9]

One of the main reasons for the long-time survival of the industry in South Africa (compared to the rest of Africa) was probably that it was run by well-established companies and experienced local managers. The whale population in South African waters was also relatively stable. The UWFC/UWC is a case in point. It expanded greatly and even became involved in pelagic whaling in Antarctic waters from 1937–40 and 1946–56, and the Bluff Peninsula factory was modernized in the 1960s. Main products such as whale oil, fertilizer and meat extract (a liquid produce used in soups, for instance) were exported to Europe in large quantities. There is no doubt that one of the main preconditions for the success of the industry, especially in the early phase of whaling in Africa, was African labour, and the UWFC/UWC, again as an example, used Africans extensively for the greater part of their workforce until the land station at the Bluff Peninsula closed down as late as 1975.

Zulus Forced into Labour Migration

As previously stated, access to African labourers was an important pre-condition when both the SAWC and the UWFC were founded in 1908–9. The companies' representatives in Durban, Egeland and Larsen, travelled to Zululand and employed what were termed 'Zulus' as labourers, flensers and crew for the land stations.

At the time the majority of the African population in the colony of Natal and Zululand were characterized as 'Zulus' (*amaZulu*). Why did such Zulu men engage in labour migration for employment at the whaling stations? One answer could be colonial politics, as Zululand was incorporated into the colony of Natal in 1897. At the start of the last century, conditions were difficult for Africans in Natal. The South African historian Jeff Guy describes Natal in this period as a 'deeply racist society, characterised by increasing racial antagonism and economic insecurity' (Guy 2006: 21). In Zululand, 40 per cent of the most fertile soil was confiscated from African landowners and sold to private European investors. They were mostly British, but Norwegians (as well as other Europeans) also became landowners in Zululand. The remaining areas were consolidated into reserves for the African population, and many Zulus became tenant farmers for white landowners. However, when taxes and rents were raised, one result was that large numbers of Africans were forced away from the farms, becoming day labourers with no alternative work outside the reserves (Mellemsether 2001: 34). After 1910, with this proletarianzation of the African population, the reserves were being transformed into reservoirs of cheap, unskilled labour for white farmers and industrialists. Increased government taxes also forced young African men into labour migration, breaking up the family and the traditional life of the homestead. (Guy 2006: 21–23) The fact that Zulus travelled from their inland villages to the whaling stations scattered along the South African coastline (and also toiled in the factories on the remote, inhospitable islands of Kerguelen and South Georgia in sub-Antarctic waters) has to be understood in this South African political context (Thompson 2006: 158–60).

A Multifaceted Norwegian Recruitment System

There are many unanswered questions concerning the recruitment of African labourers for whaling purposes. The African labourers at the whaling stations are in general seldom visible in terms of their names or personal information, but there are exceptions. At the Chief Magistrate's Office in Durban several contracts were signed between Norwegian or British whaling companies and African labourers.

For instance, in April 1914, the Norwegian manager of the British Durban Whaling Company, Enok Tobias Olufsen, employed fifty-two 'Natives' to work on board the factory ship *Pentaur* for operations at Walvis Bay, the South African enclave in South West Africa (now Namibia). So-called special passes 'to leave the province by sea' show us that approximately one-third of these workers, for example, 'Mginge Mdhlanya' from the 'Makanya Tribe', resided on 'location' in Durban and the surrounding areas. Almost as many, such as the nineteen-year-old 'Godhlimpi Ndhlela' from the 'Kolwa Tribe', in the 'Magisterial Division' of Eshowe, stayed in 'native reserves', while the rest, such as 'Charlie Gungu', also from the 'Kolwa Tribe' and Eshowe, were based at missionary stations or 'mission reserves'.[10]

South African historian Frederick Hale (1986: 569) claims that many Zulu labourers at the first Norwegian whaling station in Durban 'came from the vicinity of Eshowe' – the colonial capital of Zululand. Through analysis of the contracts mentioned, it is possible to verify this claim about labour recruitment from Eshowe both in the Norwegian and, later on, British companies.

The town of Eshowe, located in a region of Zululand (where Norwegian missionaries had a stronghold in South Africa), was an important recruitment area. The presence of the Norwegian missionaries is significant, as it was probably no coincidence that the whaling companies established, owned and/or managed by Norwegians chose to employ Zulu labourers here. The Norwegian mission station was the first non-Zulu building to be erected in the town (Mellemsether 2001: 97).

Undoubtedly, it was essential for the Norwegian immigrants and businessmen in South Africa to access an established network – as we also saw in the Aadnesen case above. The missionaries were an important part of this network, together with Norwegian consulates, farmers, companies and second-generation immigrants employed in government posts. It was this network that helped reinforce Norwegian business interests and ensure the flow of African workers to the whaling stations both in and outside South Africa.

Both managers of the UWFC/UWC, Egeland and Larsen, were experienced businessmen in this region and often recruited Africans as labourers for their nonwhaling companies as well. For instance, as early as 1889, Egeland asked the secretary for native affairs in Natal for permission to transport two hundred Africans from Zululand through the Natal colony to Johannesburg. These labourers were to work for

Egeland's own company, the Egeland Brothers, and were probably engaged in the mining industry.[11] Twenty years later, Egeland and Larsen
also recruited Zulu men from Eshowe as labourers at the land station at
the Bluff Peninsula in Durban.

A further dimension should be noted: many of the Norwegian missionaries, settlers and businessmen in Natal and Zululand were closely
related. Larsen, who soon became a wealthy whaling magnate in
Durban as manager of the UWFC/UWC, was married to one of Sven
Eriksen's daughters – Eriksen being a well-known missionary and
priest at the Norwegian Seamen's Church in Durban. Both Egeland and
Larsen were deeply religious men. It is said that the Norwegian Missionary Society held regular church services for the African labourers at
the whaling factory at the Bluff Peninsula (Mellemsether 2001: 95–96).
As far as we know this was not a common practice at other African
whaling stations. Moreover, the UWFC/UWC's catchers did not go out
to sea on Sundays, also a rare state of affairs within the whaling industry. These aspects are telling in terms of how the devout Christian attitudes of the Norwegian directors impinged on both whaling practices
and on labour relations (Ommanney 1938: 98).

The Norwegians in Natal created an informal social network that was
useful for the sons of Norwegian missionaries when they were seeking
employment. Knowledge of the Zulu language and culture made them
suitable for positions as magistrates or high-ranking officials in the Native Affairs Department and as interpreters or inspectors of the African
workers in mines or on farms (Mellemsether 2001: 100–2). The result
of this extensive and multifaceted Norwegian recruitment system was
that from 1908 to 1920, teams of African labourers were employed and
shipped out of Durban to work at whaling stations in South Africa, as
well as on the islands of Kerguelen and South Georgia in sub-Antarctic
waters.

However, Norwegians were also more directly involved in the governmental side of these matters. For instance, in 1912, H.P. Braatvedt,
son of a Norwegian missionary, was employed at the Chief Magistrate's Office in Durban. Braatvedt was one of two clerks and worked in
the Native Affairs Department as an interpreter in the criminal courts
and as a mediator in conflicts between African labourers and white employers (Braatvedt 1949: 54–55). He was also involved in drawing up
contracts between whaling companies and Africans, functioning as an
interpreter and as a witness during the signing of the contracts. The
presence of Norwegian connections in the Native Affairs Department
undoubtedly benefited the Norwegian whaling companies.

A Desolate Island in the Indian Ocean

The first transport of South African labourers for whaling purposes left Durban for the uninhabited French archipelago of Kerguelen in the southern Indian Ocean in 1908. The event more or less coincided with the establishment of the first whaling station in Africa at the Bluff Peninsula. The Durban newspaper the *Natal Mercury* received a telegram on 2 February 1908 from Reuters in London:

'The Kerguelen Whaling Company's ship *Jeanne D'Arc* leaves the Tyne to-day with the object of colonising Kerguelen's Island, in view of hunting for whales and sea elephants. The vessel carries sixty Norwegian settlers, a number of ponies, poultry, sheep and pigs. She calls at Durban to take on board thirty blacks to work in the colony.'

The aforementioned whaling company was founded in the Norwegian capital of Kristiania (now Oslo) and managed by Storm, Bull & Co. As noted above, access to African labour was strictly regulated in the Natal colony, and when the Kerguelen Whaling Company (KWC) planned to hire in Durban, their request had to be confirmed by the Chief Native Commissioner for Natal. The next step was to sign a contract at the Chief Magistrate's Office, who also issued special passes for the Africans, after which the local agent and ship chandler could finally start hiring workers on behalf of the Norwegian company.[12]

In October 1908, the KWC signed a contract with a group of twenty-three African labourers from Natal and Zululand at the Chief Magistrate's Office. The labourers were obliged to work on Kerguelen for a period of six months for £2 per month. The main tasks were 'cutting up whales and seals and other animals which may be caught'.[13] The Norwegian Olaf Edwin Olsen was appointed as foreman, as he had lived in Natal for twenty-four years, working as a ferryman, and was fluent in the Zulu language. The contract gave the 'Natives' the right to 'good sufficient food and lodgings' and suitable clothing and blankets 'at fair and reasonable prices'. It was a condition of the agreement, approved by the chief magistrate, that 'no intoxicating liquor' was to be supplied to any of the 'Natives'. The contract included the names of all the Africans, starting with 'Sikukuku Ka Nkayitshana', 'Mnarana Ka Ngini', 'Ngalaza Ka Valela', 'Silshabate Ka Danyela' and 'Dhlamlomo Ka Tekele'. The labourer 'Ali Hassam' was probably of Asian descent, and 'Benedik Mangussen' was the only European in the group and employed under the 'same conditions' as the 'Natives'.[14] The Africans were probably illiterate. Their full names and X-mark signatures seem to have been written in the same handwriting as the signature of Percy Binns, the chief magistrate himself.

The land station and the factory at Kerguelen were both constructed during the first months after arrival, with whaling commencing in January and continuing until July 1909 (Galteland 2013: 27). The Africans worked in the factory, processing the total catch of 232 whales, mostly humpbacks, and producing a total of 7,400 barrels of whale oil. In May 1909, the Africans returned to Durban and the KWC acquired permission to hire 'a further fifteen or twenty boys', with the same conditions as before. The only difference was that the Africans were now expected to work as seal hunters, as well as transporting and processing the animals at the factory (Tønnessen 1967: 407–9).

Whaling failed the following season, but sealing continued. At the end of the 1910–11 season, whaling operations were closed down and the equipment transferred to Africa. Sealing on Kerguelen continued and reached a peak in 1911, yielding 11,000 barrels of oil. In 1914 the KWC had a huge deficit and the Kerguelen station was shut down as a result. Throughout the station's period of operation, the KWC employed African labourers. The groups of Africans hired for one season at the time rarely numbered more than thirty men (Tønnessen 1967: 407–9). Special passes for a group of thirteen African labourers ready to embark on the transport vessel for Kerguelen in August 1911 show that the men were mostly in their twenties and from Natal.

For instance, 'Ndhlazi Zibisi', son of 'Jojweni', was a subordinate to 'Kraalhead Nhlabati' and 'Chief Sikonyana'. Also, 'Muleku Koza' and 'Mansele Gumede' were subordinates of the same 'Chief', but from a different 'Kraal'. Including 'Mvutu Mayeza', son of 'Mangamba', subordinate to 'Chief Bagibile', these men all belonged to the 'Magisterial Division' of Eshowe. Four labourers came from the Umlazi area close to Durban. The oldest participant, 'Sikukuku Mtungwa' (thirty-one years old), was the son of 'Cakijana', from the 'Magisterial Division' of Bergville in the foothills of the Drakensberg Mountains. The only 'outsider' was John Henderick Luhlongwana, from the 'Cape Province'.[15]

By all accounts, there were close bonds between the Norwegian whaling companies operating in South Africa and the areas of Natal and Zululand, with Norwegian connections facilitating the recruitment of African labourers for the factories. Norwegian whaling companies, agents and chandlers operated on several continents and were also involved in the hiring of Africans who worked on the remote British island of South Georgia in the South Atlantic Ocean, described next.

African Labourers at South Georgia

The Africans at South Georgia outnumbered those at Kerguelen. On South Georgia there were Zulu labourers in at least three land stations: the British station at Prince Olav Harbour, the Argentine station in Grytviken and Ocean, the Norwegian station in New Fortuna Bay. A Norwegian stoker employed at the Scottish land station at Leith Harbour (run by Chr. Salvesen & Co.) informed the Norwegian newspaper *Vestfold* on 29 March 1938 that in 1919 there had been three hundred to four hundred Africans working on South Georgia. Also replicating the racialized discourse of the time, he divulged that many of them were 'fullblooded negroes, others of mixed colour and some of them were so white that they could be mistaken for white men'. He also said that many of the Africans arrived on the island as stowaways and lacked suitable clothing; they had to make their own clothes using old sacks.

The 'negroes' on South Georgia were most likely of Zulu origin, recruited in Natal in South Africa on regular contracts and shipped down to South Georgia from Cape Town. The other group of Africans, those of 'mixed colour', probably came mainly from the Cape Verde Islands. It is well documented that many of the Cape Verdeans arrived on South Georgia as stowaways on board transport vessels or floating factory ships (Børresen 2009: 92).

The Southern Whaling & Sealing Company (SWSC) began operations at Prince Olav Harbour in 1911 using a floating factory ship. In 1916, SWSC established the last factory to be built on South Georgia at the same spot (Basberg 2004: 31–35). In August 1913, the company's agent in Cape Town made a request to the Shepstone Whaling Company (SWC) in Durban to see if the SWC could arrange to send to South Georgia 'fifty … Natives about October next for employment on their Floating Whaling Factory *"Restitution"'*.[16] Both companies were owned by the British company Irvin & Johnson Ltd. The floating factory ship *Restitution* operated at Porto Alexandre in Angola, and when the season in Africa ended, they would transfer their expedition to Prince Olav Harbour in South Georgia.[17] The response from the SWC was positive. The whaling season in Natal was over, 'the boys [were] all paid off' and it was seen as 'desirable to keep them together as much as possible for the next season'.

This example of the circulation and re-recruitment of labourers indicates that experienced and skilled Africans rapidly became valuable to the whaling companies. In October 1913, a SWC representative signed

Figure 5.1. The Norwegian factory complex at Porto Alexandre, Angola, 1913–14. The station was operated by the whaling company A/S Viking. *Source:* Commander Chr. Christensen's Whaling Museum, Sandefjord; reproduced with permission.

an agreement with thirty-three 'Native' labourers at the Chief Magistrate's Office in Durban to work on board the floating factory ship *Restitution* for six months for £4 per month. The employer was obliged to supply 'the natives with good and sufficient food and quarters for the period'.[18] The African labourers were transported by sea from Durban to Cape Town, where they embarked on *Restitution*. One month later, the floating factory ship arrived at South Georgia together with two whale catchers.[19]

In May the following year, another team of thirty-four African labourers were hired for the same purpose. This group returned to Durban one year later and was paid off at the Chief Magistrate's Office. In August 1915, a team of African labourers had just returned from Walvis Bay after working for the Durban Whaling Company. The operations at Walvis Bay were shut down due to the First World War. Braatvedt, the Norwegian clerk at the Chief Magistrate's Office in Durban, reported: 'The natives were very well treated, … and satisfied with the exception of a few who had some dispute over wages due for overtime, … the matter was however settled satisfactorily.'[20]

In the autumn of 1916, *Restitution* was shipwrecked off the English coast on its way to South Georgia. The 130 crew and whaling men, most of them Norwegians, were rescued. The SWSC continued whaling on South Georgia, based at the newly erected factory at Prince Olav Harbour. Most of the equipment at the station was brought down from the company's obsolete whaling stations in Angola and Natal.[21]

'The Boys Will Die Like Flies'

In March 1919, South Georgia and the Zulu labourers received unexpected attention from the Department of Native Affairs in Pretoria and the director of native labour in Johannesburg. The South African Chief Censor's Office in Cape Town had confiscated a letter sent from Durban to the Johannesburg communist newspaper *The International*[22] (Visser 2004: 429).

The letter, written by a man calling himself Harry, said that there had recently been signs of industrial unrest at the whaling stations on South Georgia when the Scandinavians on the island went on strike.[23] The letter noted sardonically that in a 'temperature a few degrees below zero even a Scandinavian becomes discontented'. However, the main message was to inform *The International* that the Norwegian floating factory ship, *Perth* of Larvik, had recently arrived at Durban's harbour to load machinery and supplies for the land stations on South Georgia, with the assistance of the Norwegian chandler Norman Meyer. Meyer was for £1 'a head [recruiting] sub-tropical "boys" to go down to South Georgia where labour – on account of the severe climatic conditions – is very scarce and where docility is at the moment urgently required'. Meyer was an influential businessman and a well-known figure in the Norwegian Association in Durban, acting as Norwegian consul there while Egeland was abroad.[24] As part of his business as chandler, he imported traditional Norwegian goods such as goat cheese and fish balls for sale among his fellow countrymen (Saxe 1914: 89). It is well documented that he employed Norwegians as well as Africans to work in his store, but not that he was involved in hiring African labourers for the whaling stations at South Georgia.

Harry wrote that he had spent time down in the Durban docks, spying on the operation. He wrote that the loading of the vessel was supervised by the Norwegian chandler himself, who led 'motley groups of niggers' on board. *Perth* was in reality 'a modern slave ship', Harry concluded, and he expected that 'the boys' would 'die like flies on South Georgia'. He had heard that the temperature often fell below twenty-five degrees centigrade below zero, that it snowed during the summer and that there was no animal life on the island.

It might sound strange that a communist would use racist terminology such as 'boys' and 'niggers' when referring to African labourers.

One explanation for such terminology is that the labour movement in South Africa was racially divided at the time, with one for whites and another for Africans. Most workplaces were organized in a racial hierarchy in which white workers had higher status and wages than blacks. As was generally the case within South African society, the master-servant relationship also made its mark on the labour movement (Krikler 2005: 26).

The Chief Magistrate's Office in Durban denounced the rumours concerning a slave ship and reported that the Norwegian chandler acted as agent for two whaling companies operating on South Georgia. 'Native interests protected every way. Meyer is not a labour agent', the chief magistrate wrote.[25] He probably meant to underline that the recruitment of Zulu men as labourers at South Georgia had been approved by Natal's chief native commissioner and that they were not employed by an illegal labour agent. The chandler had applied for passes for fifty-two Africans from Durban and for permission to employ the same men on South Georgia on behalf of the whaling companies. Half of the group, twenty-six Zulus, were going to work for the Argentine company Compañia Argentina de Pesca in Grytviken, and the rest for the Norwegian company Ocean Whaling Co. in New Fortuna Bay. The contracts and all the formalities were in order, according to the Chief Magistrate's Office.[26]

The *Nativos* at Grytviken

The Africans transported to South Georgia on board *Perth* were paid £5 a month and half a shilling (6 pence) per hour for overtime at the land stations.[27] These wages were 25 per cent higher than those of African dockworkers or stevedores in Durban. In the 1920s, an average week's wages for African labourers amounted to 18 shillings (approximately £3.90 a month) (Hemson 1977: 91).

The Zulu labourers in Grytviken were registered by their names in the account for Compañia Argentina de Pesca, but also as *nativos* (natives) with numbers from one to twenty-six. *Nativo* no. 1, 'Alfred Dunu', was probably hired as foreman of the group. 'Josiah Pepu', *nativo* no. 2, 'Gadelana Magwaza', no. 5, 'Philip Makaye', no. 24, and the rest of the group were all signed on for one year and paid one and a half month's wages in advance prior to their departure from Durban.[28]

As leader of the African labourers, Alfred Dunu earned £50 more per year of the other Africans at Grytviken. The average income was £70 for one year's work, but the amounts received when signing off at the Chief

Magistrate's Office in Durban were considerably lower because of a number of deductions. Most Zulu labourers had to buy suitable clothes and necessary equipment from the slop chest at the station because of the harsh climate on South Georgia. While it was common for European workers to bring their own work clothes, bed linen and cutlery, it is unlikely that the Africans were equally well equipped when signing on. Several Zulus spent more than £20 in the slop chest. For instance, 'Pilemon Mlangu', *nativo* no. 13, earned £70 for the whole year, but received only £42 in cash in Durban.

It was only in the 1919–20 season that *nativo* labourers were listed in the account books at Grytviken and probably the only time they comprised part of its regular workforce. The African labourers at New Fortuna Bay during the same season are hardly evident in the existing source material, but the wages account indicates that the average annual pay for the 'native labourers' was £65. This was similar to what the African labourers received at Grytviken, where the numbers of Zulu labourers was exactly the same.[29]

It is difficult to accurately compare the Africans' wages to those of other workers. The crew lists in the account book from Grytviken were written alphabetically, and there was no mention of rank or occupation. The frequency of Spanish names such as Torrés, Martinez and Lopez underlines that Grytviken was run by a Buenos Aires–based company. For the majority of Norwegians at Grytviken, the fixed wages were between approximately £7–11 per month, but they received an additional bonus depending on the volume of whale oil produced during the catching season. The final wages could probably be a lot higher than the fixed salary. This indicates that most Argentines and Norwegians actually earned twice (or more) as much as the African labourers.[30]

Unfulfilled Expectations

In the 1919–20 season there were frequent strikes and unrest among the crews at all the whaling stations on South Georgia, with the exception of Stromness. Most disturbances occurred at Leith Harbour, where many Europeans and a large group of Cape Verdeans were involved in the strikes.[31] There is no evidence that the African labourers at Grytviken and New Fortuna Bay took part, and when returning to South Africa these were signed off in Durban in March 1920 without any complications.

However, conditions worsened when the South African labourers employed by the SWSC at Prince Olav Harbour arrived in Cape Town in May and were denied the salary they expected. The group of labourers consisted of one hundred men, both 'Cape Coloured' and 'South African Natives'.[32] The group were denied the expected payment in Cape Town because a new work contract had been agreed upon at South Georgia, outside of the agent's jurisdiction. These men were employed at a rate of two and a half pounds, 'with bonus privileges', this monthly rate being half of the fixed monthly salary for the Zulu labourers at Grytviken and New Fortuna Bay. The difference was that the Africans at Prince Olav Harbour were promised a bonus related to production results, while those at Grytviken and New Fortuna Bay received only a fixed salary plus overtime.

Any expectations of increased earnings due to bonuses were obviously unfulfilled at Prince Olav Harbour. At some point, the Africans' contracts must have been renegotiated. It is hard to believe that this could occur without a serious conflict arising between the labourers and the company. The archives show that the British magistrate on South Georgia, Edward Binnie, found it necessary to travel from Gryt-

Figure 5.2. Spermacet whale on the flensing platform at Grytviken, South Georgia (1920s). The land station was established by the Argentine company Compañia Argentina de Pesca Sociedad Anónima in 1904. In 1919–20, a group of twenty-six Zulu labourers worked at the factory for a year. *Source:* E. B. Binnie. Commander Chr. Christensen's Whaling Museum, Sandefjord; reproduced with permission.

viken to Prince Olav Harbour to mediate between the manager and the labourers. There the magistrate witnessed the signing of a new work contract.[33]

The South African Native Affairs Department intervened in the conflict in Cape Town and put considerable pressure on the SWSC's agent before the dispute ended in a compromise. The African labourers received a 20 per cent raise in wages and 'recognition of additional pay for special work'.[34]

Sixty-Six Years of Whaling in Durban

The employment of African labourers on Kerguelen and South Georgia was a short-lived phenomenon compared to the extensive period of labour at the UWC's land station in Durban, where they comprised the majority of labourers from the station's start in 1909 until it closed down in 1975. A whaler from Sandefjord reported to the local newspaper *Vestfold* on 11 February 1935 that the UWC workforce at the station in Durban consisted of thirty whites, Norwegians, British and Boers (Afrikaners), and 'about 500 kaffirs, zulunegroes, who came down from the countryside to work at the station during the season'.

Zulus were not the only Africans employed at the station. It was also common to employ 'Coloureds' and 'Asiatics' – the latter a contemporary term for workers of mainly Indian descent. The South African government's racial policies during the apartheid era, which began in 1948, strengthened the already-established divisions and inequality between the ethnic groups. Categorized as 'Blacks', the Zulu labourers were regarded as third-rate citizens. When the UWC station shut down in 1975, 80 Zulu labourers worked on the flensing deck as flensers and winchmen and 170 were ordinary workers and helpers. Approximately 100 labourers labelled 'Asiatics', 'uneducated, though skilled workers', carried out the same work tasks as the 'Black' labourers. While the 'Black' labourers earned from 80 to 250 South African rand a month, the 'Asiatics' received between 100 and 350 rand. The twenty to twenty-five 'Coloureds', regarded within the apartheid-era framework as both second-class citizens and more intelligent than the 'Blacks' because of their lighter skin colour, worked as 'skilled artisans, e.g. welders'. Their monthly pay was 400 rand or more, depending on overtime and so forth. At the top of the hierarchy were the 'Whites': European foremen, laboratory technicians, administrative workers and managers. As privileged first-class citizens, their wages were considerably higher than those of the 'Blacks' and 'Asiatics'. The lowest-paid 'White' clerk earned more than 350 rand a month. The managing director was at the top of the pay list, earning more than 15,000 rand a year.[35]

One Season's Work and No Pay

As mentioned earlier, in addition to Zulu labourers from South Africa, there were also a significant number of men from the Cape Verde Islands working at several land stations on South Georgia. While the largest groups of Zulus were employed by SWSC at Prince Olav Harbour, most Cape Verdeans, or 'Portuguese', as the British magistrate called them, worked for Chr. Salvesen & Co. at Leith Harbour (for Salvesen's businesses, see also the chapters by Sætra and Reiersen, this volume). This was because Salvesen's vessels used Mindelo, a small port on the island of Saint Vincent in Cape Verde, as a coal-bunkering harbour on their way to and from Leith in Scotland and South Georgia.

During the First World War, the workforce at Leith Harbour was mixed. A Norwegian whaling man reported that there were twenty-two different nationalities at the station at one time.[36] The number of Cape Verdeans probably reached a peak in 1919–20, when more than seventy worked at Leith Harbour. There were also smaller groups at the other land stations and on board the floating factory ship *Thor I* at Godthul. While the Zulu labourers were signed on in South Africa, a large number of the Cape Verdeans arrived on the island as stowaways.

At the end of the First World War, it became difficult to recruit skilled Scandinavian whalers, and Salvesen began signing on Cape Verdeans on the island of Saint Vincent with contracts. At the same time, with the company's silent approval, large numbers of stowaways boarded the transport vessels at night. Many of the stowaways worked one season or longer as regular labourers on South Georgia, but they were stripped of any labour rights or benefits. It was not uncommon for their salary to consist of their board and bed. When they disembarked at Saint Vincent during the transport vessel's journey back to Europe, they received no pay or gratitude for their efforts.[37] In many ways, the Cape Verdeans' conditions and experiences on South Georgia during the First World War were reminiscent of the conditions of slavery, similar to those suffered by the African labourers arriving on the island on board the Norwegian transport ship from Durban. In the postwar years, most of the African stowaways did probably receive a minimal salary for their efforts in the factories at South Georgia.

Several conflicts arose between Cape Verdean labourers and Scandinavian crew and labourers at Leith Harbour. The most serious conflict began as a quarrel between the men during Christmas 1919 about the right to a field used for sports. The Cape Verdeans wanted to play cricket and a group of Norwegians wanted to play football at the same time. What began as a petty quarrel intensified rapidly and produced a spontaneous strike full of racial antagonism, and the factory at the land station temporarily shut down. The Cape Verdean José dos Reis Almeida became a spokesman for the 'Portuguese' in the conflict. He was employed by Salvesen as a foreman for the Cape Verdeans and was also assisting the company in signing on labourers at Saint Vincent.[38] During the conflict, Almeida and another 'Portuguese', Pedro Emanuel Silva, became so unpopular among the Scandinavian workers that they demanded they be sent away from the island.

The Cape Verdeans' argument for striking was that they had been offended by the Norwegians calling them 'niggers'. The British *magistrate*, Edward Binnie, intervened in the conflict as a negotiator, but concluded that the Scandinavians' 'aggressive attitude adopted towards the Portuguese are as much in fault as the latter'. There was no charge and no one to arrest in the case.[39] The Norwegian manager at Leith Harbour wanted to solve the conflict as quickly as possible and took the whale catcher *Subra* out of operation just before New Year's Eve, sending it to Buenos Aires with forty-two Cape Verdeans on board who wanted to leave the island. The list of forty-two 'Portuguese' labourers, starting with 'stowaway' João Antonio Coronel, registered as employee no. 17, and ending with 'stowaway' Laurence Manuel Zego, no. 468, also included both Almeida, no. 342, and Silva, no. 343. Approximately thirty Cape Verdeans chose to stay and continue their work at the station.[40]

There is no doubt that the Norwegian station manager was concerned about the conflicts between the groups of workers. It also meant a huge loss of income for the company to take a whale catcher out of operation for several weeks during the high season, but the manager had few alternatives. When the vessel arrived at the harbour in Buenos Aires, the company was even fined for landing the Cape Verdeans, who lacked personal identification papers. The labourers were rapidly replaced with a team of forty-two Russian emigrants hired under six-month contracts for USD 150 in wages and no bonuses. A few days later, the ship departed for South Georgia.[41]

José dos Reis Almeida returned to Leith Harbour six months later (when the Russians left) as foreman of a new team of thirty 'Portuguese', but the conflict had obviously not been forgotten. After a few days of loud protests from the Scandinavians, the station manager was forced to return Almeida to Buenos Aires on board the transport ship

Albuera. The relationship between Scandinavians and Cape Verdeans was also strained at the land station at Husvik Harbour, not far from Leith Harbour. Three weeks earlier the Scandinavians at Husvik went on strike and demanded all 'Portuguese' labourers at the station be sacked. The station manager expressed that he had no alternative but to put the 'Portuguese' on a transport ship back to Saint Vincent.[42]

'Degos', 'Blacks' and 'Slant Eyed'

The accentuation of cultural differences at the land stations was commonplace, and racial prejudices and discrimination were a part of everyday life. Norwegian seamen and whalers imported their own preconceived ideas about racial hierarchies from Norway. The Norwegian historian Knut Kjeldstadli provides numerous examples of how 'yellows' and 'blacks' were thought to be inferior races in Norway at the beginning of the twentieth century. This attitude to racial issues represented the worldview at the time and 'was part of a semi-conscious deep mental structure, which was a view shared by literature professors and seamen, revolutionary socialists and conservatives. ... This view of race issues was put forward by the future class and intellectual elite. This was entirely in line with the thinking of the Western world' (Niemi, Myhre and Kjeldstadli 2003: 324).

Among Norwegian seamen, ethnic and racial prejudices towards foreign seamen were common until quite recently. 'Degos', 'blacks' and 'slant eyed' were not unusual terms – often also used as degrading wisecracks aimed at foreign colleagues. The resentment expressed by Norwegian seamen was strongest towards Africans, people from the Caribbean of African ancestry and Asians, but also towards the Spanish and other southern Europeans. There is no evidence to suggest that whalers' views were any different (Halvorsen 2007: 76–79).

During the early 1920s, Chr. Salvesen & Co. continued to sign on Cape Verdeans for the land station at South Georgia, but how many and for how long is not known. In 1922, on their way north, transport ships docked at Mindelo on Saint Vincent as usual to load coal and put ashore local workers. The captain increased the security on board to avoid any stowaways to the port of Leith in Scotland, where Africans were not allowed to disembark and where the shipping companies were required to transport them back to Cape Verde.[43] As far as we know, Chr. Salvesen & Co. was most likely the last whaling company operating on South Georgia to hire (or to exploit as unpaid) Africans as labourers. It is difficult to estimate precisely how many Africans worked at the whaling stations on South Georgia in total, but it seems that numbers never exceeded three hundred men per season, including both Zulus and Cape Verdeans.

The Flow of Labour across National Borders

The workforce employed in modern whaling during the period from the first establishment of a land station in the Southern Hemisphere (South Georgia in 1904) until the land-based whaling factories were displaced by floating factory ships and pelagic whaling in the late 1920s was surely multinational. This flow of labour crossing oceans and national borders deserves attention and merits further research. The extended Norwegian use and often exploitation of African labour within a framework of colonialism as described in this chapter is one example, but there are still many stories to uncover and narrate. As this case indicates, it may also be time to broaden research perspectives on labour within the whaling industry. The employment of local or imported labour in whaling was a global phenomenon, particularly before the outbreak of the First World War.

I suggest that it is possible to characterize many whaling stations around the world, during limited periods of time, as multicultural, employing people of different origins, occupations and national, ethnic and cultural backgrounds. As in the case of the whaling factories in Africa and with similar parallels on other continents, multicultural workforces at the whaling stations were often organized in a hierarchical and strongly racialized manner.

I further suggest that the concept of transnational labour history could be a suitable tool for broadening perspectives and further research into the subject of modern whaling and labour. Transnational labour history aims to transcend the confines of national borders and abandon the nation-state as the necessary framework for historical analysis. It suggests focusing on 'flows of people, commodities, ideas and organisations across national boundaries. ... It argues for approaches that examine connections across countries, continents and cultures, for comparative studies, for transnational perspectives' (Bonner, Hyslop and Van Der Walt 2007: 144).

The flow of labour across national borders and oceans on a global scale is truly an underresearched aspect of the history of modern Norwegian whaling. As shown above, modern Norwegian whaling is also a tale of frictions and accommodations in terms of cultural orders and stereotypes on a global scale, in this case between Norwegian and European capitalists and the colonial administrations in several African countries, and between European whalers and labourers and local labourers and populations. The history of whaling is also integral to a history of emigration and settlement, with whaling contributing to the dissemination of cultural influences and ideas from abroad being taken back to the home countries of the whalers. These and other underresearched subjects deserve further attention and will hopefully broaden our understanding of modern whaling as a global, transnational and cultural phenomenon.

The histories of modern Norwegian whaling in colonial Africa and beyond, as described here, leave no doubt that the Norwegian businessmen and shipowners who ran the whaling companies were part of the contemporary global capitalist order and were continuously searching for new resources, in this case for new whaling and sealing grounds to exploit. Crucially, however, most whaling companies operating in African waters benefited greatly from easy access to cheap African labour afforded by the existing colonial system of controlling African workers. In this context, the African labourers had few or no rights; they were paid comparatively low wages and most worked under harsh conditions. Norwegian whaling businesses in Africa operated firmly within colonial structures, cooperated closely with local colonial administrations and, as in the case of South Africa, benefited greatly from an already-established Norwegian network of missionaries, farmers, businessmen, consuls and chandlers.

Notes

1. A/S Capella, diverse pakkesaker (a Norwegian archivist term corresponding more or less to miscellaneous), A, E, letter from Viggo Borch, Christiana, to Herr O. R. Sagfører P. Bogen, Sandefjord, dated Christiania 6 November 1911, KCCH; Linga Linga, Inhambane, Captain A. Aadnesen's report, 24 October 1910, KCCH.
2. *Fram*, May 1920, p. 1.
3. A/S Sydhavet, diverse pakkesaker, box 1, letter from Thesen & Co., Cape Town, to Peder Bogen, Sandefjord, 16 November 1910, KCCH.
4. *Norsk Hvalfangst-Tidende*, May 1923, p. 56; Eleven floating factory ships and seventeen land stations were supplied with whales caught by ninety catchers. Eighteen of the companies, all the floating factories and nine land stations were Norwegian-owned. One company was German (German South West Africa, today's Namibia), one Portuguese (Angola), one British (Angola) and five South African.
5. A/S Capella, diverse pakkesaker, A, E, letter from Viggo Borch, Christiana, to Herr O. R. Sagfører P. Bogen, Sandefjord, dated Christiania 6 November

1911, KCCH; Linga Linga, Inhambane, Captain A. Aadnesen's report, 24 October 1910, KCCH.

6. The Mozambique Whaling Company, Ltd, diverse pakkesaker, box 1, A, E, Aktieinnbydelse, 1 November 1911, KCCH; forhandlingsprotokoll, referat fra direksjonsmøte, 4 November 1911, KCCH.

7. *Norsk Hvalfangst-Tidende,* April 1923, p. 41.

8. A/S Viking, brev og telegrammer fra fangstbestyrere, box 1, 1909–15, letter from M. A. Ingebrigtsen, Porto Alexandre, to Peder Bogen, Sandefjord, 5 July 1911, KCCH.

9. Union Whaling Company, box 3, Director's Annual Report, December 1916, Cornelis de Jong Collection, UNISA; box 21, Director's Report, April 1921, Cornelis de Jong Collection, UNISA; Chairman's Notes, Annual Meeting, April 1921, Cornelis de Jong Collection, UNISA.

10. Chief Native Commissioner (CNC) 167 (1914-557), Union of South Africa, Department of Native Affairs, Schedule 'E', 'Pass to leave the province by sea', PAR; Office of CNC, Pietermaritzburg, Natal, 'Particulars regarding the person to whom this Certificate is issued' (fifty-two passes). PAR.

11. Secretary of Native Affairs (SNA) I-1-114 (1889-456), letter from Egeland Bros., Inyoni Store, Zululand, to Resident Magistrate, Stanger, 6 May 1889, PAR.

12. CNC 23 (CNC 1058-1911), letter from CNC, Province of Natal, Pietermaritzburg, to W. Cotts & Co., Durban, 29 July 1911, PAR.

13. SNA I-1-410 (1908-2765), 'Ratification of Surety Bond', Magistrate, Cape Town, 3 December 1908, PAR.

14. SNA I-1-410 (1908-2765), 'Contract of Service Between Kerguelen Whaling Company and Certain Natives of Natal and Zululand and one European', Durban, 17 October 1908, PAR.

15. CNC 23 (1058-1911), letter from CNC, Province of Natal, Pietermaritzburg, to W. Cotts & Co., Durban, 29 July 1911, PAR; Schedule 'E', 'Special Pass to leave the Colony by Sea' (thirteen passes), PAR.

16. CNC 135 (1913-1472), letter from the Shepstone Whaling & Fishing Company Ltd, Durban, to Secretary, Provincial Council, Pietermaritzburg, 22 August 1913, PAR.

17. *Norsk Hvalfangst-Tidende,* January 1914, p. 12.

18. CNC 135 (1913-1472), letter from Chief Magistrate, Durban (CMD), to CNC, Pietermaritzburg, Contract, 25 October 1913, PAR.

19. *Norsk Hvalfangst-Tidende,* January 1914, p. 12.

20. CNC 167 (1914-557), letter from CNC, Pietermaritzburg, to CMD, 27 May 1914, PAR; letter from Chief Magistrates Office, Durban, via Clerk of Court Durban, H.P. Braatvedt, to CMD, 3 September 1915, PAR.

21. *Norsk Hvalfangst-Tidende,* November 1916, p. 249.

22. TAB (Public Records of former Transvaal Province and its predecessors as well as of magistrates and local authorities), GNLB, 202/15, 219, copy of letter from Chief Censor's Office, Cape Town, to SNA, 10 March 1919, NASA.

23. TAB, GNLB, 202/15, 219, copy of letter from 'Harry', Durban, to the Editor, *The International,* Johannesburg, undated, NASA.

24. *Fram,* July 1920, p. 2.

25. TAB, GNLB, 202/15, 219, copy of telegram from CMD to Department of Native Affairs, Pretoria, undated (March 1919), NASA.
26. CNC 369 B (1919-2457), letter from CMD to CNC, Pietermaritzburg, 10 March 1919, PAR.
27. CNC 369 B (1919-2457), letter from CMD to CNC, Pietermaritzburg, 8 October 1919, PAR.
28. Compania Argentina de Pesca (Pesca), Account book no. 17, 1919–20, pp. 530–38, KCCH.
29. A/S Ocean, Account book no. 2, p. 174, KCCH. GBP 1 = NOK 22.
30. Pesca, Account book no. 17, 1919–20, KCCH.
31. Sandefjord Hvalfangerselskab, brev og telegrammer fra fangstbestyrere, box 2, letter from station manager Sørlle, Stromnes, to Firma P. Bogen, Sandefjord, 26 March 1920, KCCH.
32. Office of the Governor-General of South Africa (GG), 151, 50/847, minute no. 440, signed F.S. Malan, 7 May 1920, NASA.
33. GG, 151, 50/847, minute no. 440, signed F.S. Malan, 7 May 1920, NASA.
34. GG, 151, 50/847, Prime Minister's Office, Cape Town, minute no. 463, 12 May 1920, NASA.
35. Union Whaling Company, uncatalogued material, file: Briefwisseling van C. de Jong over walvisvangst van Natal, 1910–90, Cornelis de Jong Collection, UNISA; letter from P.C.N. van der Bryl, Congella, Durban, to Cornelis de Jong, 29 February 1980, UNISA.
36. *Norsk Hvalfangst-Tidende,* June 1919, p. 119.
37. Special Collections, Chr. Salvesen & Co. South Georgia Co. (SC, CS & Co. SGC), Leith Harbour Whaling Station (LHWS) records, 1909–45, box 2 (A-127), correspondence, 1918–25, B, letter from CS & Co., Leith, to the South Georgia Company Limited (SGCL), Leith Harbour, South Georgia, 1 September 1920, EUL; copy letters, 1911–25 (A-145), 1918–20, vol. 5, letter from manager Ant. S. Andersen, LHWS, to CS & Co., Leith, Scotland, 6 March 1920, EUL; LHWS records, 1909–45, box 2 (A-127), correspondence, 1918–25, A, letter from CS & Co., Leith, to SGCL, 8 April 1920, EUL.
38. SC, CS & Co. SGC, copy letters, 1918–20 (A-145), vol. 5, letter to CS & Co., Leith, from manager Ant. S. Andersen, LHWS, 13 June 1919, EUL.
39. SC, CS & Co. SGC, copy letters, 1911–25 (A-145), 1918–20, vol. 5, letter from Magistrates Office, South Georgia, to the Manager, SGCL, 30 December 1920, EUL.
40. SC, CS & Co. SGC, copy letters, 1911–25 (A-145), 1918–20, vol. 5, passenger, LHWS, 30 December 1919, EUL.
41. SC, CS & Co. SGC, LHWS records, 1909–45, box 2 (A-127), correspondence, 1918–25, B, letter from CS & Co., Leith, to SGCL, 1 September 1920, EUL; copy letters, 1911–25 (A-145), 1918–20, vol. 5, letter from manager Ant. S. Andersen, LHWS, to CS & Co., Leith, Scotland, 6 March 1920, EUL; LHWS records, 1909–45, box 2 (A-127), correspondence, 1918–25, A, letter from CS & Co., Leith, to SGCL, 8 April 1920, EUL.
42. SC, CS & Co. SGC, copy letters, 1911–25 (A-144), 1917–24, vol. 4, letter to CS & Co., Leith, from manager L.H. Hansen, 1 August 1920, EUL.

43. SC, CS & Co. SGC, LHWS records, 1909–45, box 3 (A-128), correspondence, 1918–28, C, letter from CS & Co., Leith, to SGCL, 16 March 1922, EUL.

Archives Consulted

Commander Chr. Christensen's Whaling Museum (Kommandør Chr. Christensens Hvalfangstmuseum, KCCI I), Sandefjord, Norway.
Edinburgh University Library (EUL), Edinburgh, Scotland
National Archives of South Africa (NASA), Pretoria, South Africa.
Pietermaritzburg Archives Repository (PAR), Pietermaritzburg, South Africa.
University of South Africa (UNISA), multiple campuses, South Africa.

References

Basberg, B.L. 2004. *The Shore Whaling Stations at South Georgia: A Study in Antarctic Industrial Archaeology.* Oslo: Novus forlag.
Braatvedt, H.P. 1949. *Roaming Zululand with a Native Commissioner.* Pietermaritzburg: Shuter and Shooter.
Bonner, P., J. Hyslop and L. Van Der Walt. 2007. 'Rethinking Worlds of Labour: Southern African Labour History in International Context', *African Studies* 66(2): 137–67.
Børresen, D.I. 2002. '"Her er kjeltringer fra guvernøren til den sorteste slave": Om det norske hvalfangstselskapet A/S Viking og virksomheten i Angola, 1909–1914', in K.A. Kjerland and A.K. Bang (eds), *Nordmenn i Afrika – afrikanere i Norge.* Bergen: Fagbokforlaget Vigmostad & Bjørke, pp. 161–79.
———. 2006. 'Hvalfangere på alle hav … : Arbeidskonflikter, organisering og svartelisting i hvalfangsten 1904–1914', in *Arbeiderhistorie: Årbok for arbeiderbevegelsens arkiv og bibliotek.* Oslo: Forlaget Aktuell, pp. 136–63.
———. 2009. '"The boys will die like flies": Afrikanere på hvalfangst i Antarktis 1908–1920', in K.A. Kjerland and K.M. Rio (eds), *Kolonitid: Nordmenn på eventyr og big business i Afrika og Stillehavet.* Oslo: Scandinavian Academic Press, pp. 77–110.
Galteland, Odd. 2013. *A/S Kerguelen 1908–1921: The Optimism, the Dreams – and the Dull Working Day.* Sandefjord: Kommandør Chr. Christensens Hvalfangstmuseum.
Guy, J. 2006. *Remembering the Rebellion: The Zulu Uprising of 1906.* Pietermaritzburg: University of KwaZulu-Natal Press.
Hale, F. 1986. 'The History of Norwegian Missionaires and Immigrants in South Africa', PhD dissertation. Pretoria: University of South Africa.
Halvorsen, T. 2007. *Vi seiler for velstand og lykke. Norsk Sjømannsforbunds historie.* Bind 2. Oslo. Pax.
Hemson, D. 1977. 'Dock Workers, Labour Circulation, and Class Struggles in Durban, 1940–59', *Journal of Southern African Studies* 4(1): 88–124.

Hvalfangernes Assuranceforening 1926: Register over Hvalfangerflaaten. Sandefjord: Hvalfangernes Assuranceforening.

Krikler, J. 2005. *The Rand Revolt: The 1922 Insurrection and Racial Killings in South Africa*. Johannesburg and Cape Town: Jonathan Bull Publishers.

Mellemsether, H. 2001. 'Misjonærer, settlersamfunn og afrikansk opposisjon: Striden om selvstendiggjøring i den norske Zulukirken, Sør-Afrika ca. 1920–1930', PhD dissertation. Norwegian University of Science and Technology. Trondheim.

Niemi, E., J.E. Myhre and K. Kjeldstadli. 2003. *Norsk innvandringshistorie,* vol. 3, *I nasjonalstatens tid, 1814–1940*. Oslo: Pax forlag.

Ommanney, F.D. 1938. *South Latitude*. London: Longmans.

Penvenne, J.M. 1995. *African Workers and Colonial Racism. Mozambican Strategies and Struggles in Lourenco Marques, 1877-1962*. Portsmouth, NH/ London: Heinemann/Currey.

Saxe, L. 1914. *Nordmænd jorden rundt*. Kristiania: Aschehoug.

Thompson, L. 2006. *A History of South Africa*. Johannesburg: Jonathan Bull Publishers.

Tønnessen, J.N. 1967. *Den moderne hvalfangsts historie,* vol. 2. Sandefjord: Kommandør Chr. Christensens Hvalfangstmuseum.

Visser, W.P. 2004. '"To Fight the Battles of the Workers": The Emergence of Pro-strike Publications in Early Twentieth-Century South Africa', *International Review of Social History* 49: 401–34.

❧ 6

THE CONSULAR AFFAIRS ISSUE AND COLONIALISM

Svein Ivar Angell

> Four years ago, there were about forty or fifty timber merchants in Johannesburg, importing full cargos of wood, while presently there are only five companies left. The other traders have liquidated and sold their stock far below cost.[1]

In a report in 1907 the Norwegian consul to British South Africa, F. Sandberg, indicated that exports to the British colony had been reduced substantially. In 1903 and 1904 Norwegian building materials had sold well in British South Africa. According to the consul, the construction industry was 'very considerable indeed' due to 'the expectation that gold production and the mining industry will grow rapidly in the near future … and thus positively affect trade'. When these expectations failed, he believed this to be a consequence of 'the market being flooded with all kinds of building materials, especially wood'.[2]

Sandberg meticulously registered sales of Norwegian as well as imported products from other colonial states in his region. In addition to building materials, products like salted and dried fish, matches, paper, butter and margarine, condensed milk, beer, calcium carbide and explosives like dynamite were registered. Some represented potential for increased Norwegian export to British South Africa, while Norwegian companies were ousted by other countries or local enterprises where other products were concerned. Similar assessments were also made by others: the very same year that Sandberg wrote his report, the Foreign Ministry received reports of the same tenor from Norwegian consuls in Asia, Caribbean, North Africa, North America and several European countries.

Issues relating to consular services are significant to Norwegian historical research, and certain factors stemming from such issues were at play during the dissolution of the Swedish-Norwegian union in 1905. After the dissolution of the Danish-Norwegian union in 1814, Norway participated in a so-called personal union with its neighbour Sweden. Norway remained an independent state within this union, however, both retaining and developing autonomous government institutions. The union was primarily upheld by the royal person – the king (Danielsen 2002: 247).

However, this construction created a common foreign policy under Swedish governance, as the Swedish constitution set the overall premises for Norwegian foreign policy. A joint committee for foreign affairs, which included diplomatic relations and consular services, emerged as the chief bilateral arrangement of the two countries. With time, this arrangement became a problem, in particular in relation to what the Norwegian side saw as a lack of influence over consular services. Norway's dissatisfaction was mainly related to the fact that the consuls were trade representatives and thus important to the shipping industry – a significant factor in Norwegian trade (see also Nygaard, this volume). Towards the end of the nineteenth century, a demand for a separate Norwegian consular service was made, a claim initiating the process that lead to the dissolution of the Swedish-Norwegian union in 1905 (Kaartvedt 1995: 237, 346). The shared consular services and its role in the dissolution of the union is a recurring theme in Norwegian historical research (Kaartvedt 1995: 327–55). However, there are no historians who have reviewed the public debate on the consular services issue during the decades around 1900 from a colonial perspective. This is the theme of this chapter.

In late nineteenth century consular representation became an important factor for several countries in establishing national interests around the world as well as an instrument in colonial expansionism (Kirk-Greene 2000: 77). For small noncolonial powers like Sweden and Norway, the consular service was largely seen as an instrument to participate in and take advantage of the economic development taking place in the international arena. For Norway, with its open economy and shipping interests, and with its opportunity to express its foreign interests constrained by the union, consular representation was considered *particularly* significant for international participation.[3] Because export from and import to Norway went via other European ports, the activity of Norwegian business interests in European colonies in Africa and other continents is difficult to discern from official statistics.[4] But some statistics are available: in 1908, for instance, 73 Norwegian vessels docked at South African ports, followed by 83 in 1909 and 111 in 1910. The total net weight was 105,386 registered tons. In Algeria 80 Norwegian vessels docked in 1910, with a net weight of 85,721 registered

Figure 6.1. The Norwegian consulate in Zanzibar resided in the headquarters of the Norway-East Africa Trading Company. The Norwegian consul, and manager of the company, O. Chr. Olsen, took this photo during the First World War. *Source:* Anne K. Bang; reproduced with permission.

tons (Norges Offisielle Statistikk 1908–10). In some of the British and French settlements in Asia the Norwegian shipping activity was even higher: in British East India 281 Norwegian vessels docked in 1908; the net weight was nearly 250,000 tons. In French East India 131 Norwegian vessels docked that year, with a total net weight of 128,788 tons (Norges Offisielle Statistikk 1908–10).

The Norwegian consul's report from South Africa in 1907, and a number of similar reports during the same period, proves the significance of the consular services issue in Norwegian politics and society in the decades around 1900 and its relation to colonialism. The same must be said about official public records and parliamentary debates dealing with this issue in the same period. This chapter will take a closer look at the Norwegian debate on the consular services issue in the period from about 1890 until 1920. The focus will particularly be on to what extent, and in which ways, Norwegian motives and interests regarding the colonies were expressed in this debate during this period.

Sweden-Norway and a New Colonial Order

The asymmetrical political and economic relationship between the West and what used to be referred to as the Third World was fundamentally shaped during the nineteenth century. Arrighi (1994: 53), for one, points out that European powers controlled 35 per cent of the earth's surface at the onset of this period, increasing to 67 per cent in 1878 and totalling 85 per cent at the onset of the First World War in 1914. The various forms of control were diverse and complex, but a key factor in the international arrangement at the turn of the nineteenth century was how European countries established new colonies, or tightened their grip on those already under their control. The race for the colonies entered a new phase in the 1890s: according to Mommsen (1988), this was mainly caused by public opinion in several European countries advocating further expansion in overseas territories. When Germany emerged as a new European empire, this happened alongside rapid industrial development, causing a change to the European power balance that pushed colonial expansion even farther (Mommsen 1988: 185).

One consequence was the institutionalization of colonial expansion in novel ways. Whereas business interests had mostly driven European expansion in other parts of the world, as competition among the powers increased, commerce, shipping, entrepreneurs and so forth demanded stronger business protection from their own governments in order to pursue their diverse colonial ventures. Meanwhile, it became progressively more important for the European powers to protect their existing territories and to clarify how they envisioned further expansion and consolidation. This development furthermore implied that protection of economic interests became a new aspect of foreign policy (Robinson 1988: 3).

As the massive African continent became the focus of the European powers' ambitions, this formed the basis of the Berlin conference in 1884–85, intended to create an international agreement on issues of free trade, maritime activities and the appropriation of land in the Congo and Niger territories – as well as setting the standards for these activities in the rest of Africa (de Courcel 1988: 249). The Berlin conference comprised both an expression of and catalyst for the process of merging economy and foreign policy that characterized the Western world at that time.

Significantly, despite their peripheral role as independent actors in colonial expansion, Sweden-Norway was invited to the conference. Thus, the invitation itself indicates that the countries were perceived as relevant agents in the economic system regulated by the conference.

This was also the official Swedish-Norwegian justification for participation, at least for Sweden. Gillis Bildt, the Swedish minister who represented the two countries, had been especially instructed to secure
Sweden's equal advantage with other European powers for trade, shipping and the Congo. It was expected that Sweden should – and would
– be optimally engaged in trade between Europe and Africa, although
such trade was economically rather insignificant at the time (Yngfalk
2005: 21–22; Nilsson 2013).

Bildt's mandate and expectations as to the outcome of the Berlin conference are particularly instructive in relation to the themes that characterized the Norwegian debate about the consular system after 1890.
The dominant opinion was that the consular union did not sufficiently
protect Norwegian financial interests abroad. Differences between
Norwegian and Swedish production systems were often referred to as
a key factor, and rightly so, because shipping was far more important
to the Norwegian economy. Sweden, on the other hand, experienced
industrial expansion after 1880 that far exceeded the same Norwegian
sector. These differences were expressed in customs policies: in 1888
Sweden joined the German protectionist system of treaties, while Norway remained with the British system, practising free trade, primarily because this system benefited the shipping industry (Angell 2002:
31). The two countries chose different international financial strategies
(Nilsson 2000: 282; Leira and Neumann 2006: 37). However, Norwegian
politicians were unable to influence the union's foreign policies, as unified and single foreign policy under Swedish management was, after
all, the union's raison d'être. From the Norwegian perspective, the situation therefore justified distrust towards whether the Swedish representative would pursue Norwegian interests in Berlin. Bildt's mandate
in Berlin – which above all protected Sweden's interests – could itself
provide justification for such Norwegian mistrust.

His mandate was built on the premise that Sweden aspired to play
a greater role in the financial activities of the colonial world. There are
reasons to suggest that the underlying premise in the Norwegian controversy on the consular issue in the following years was related to
Norway's larger (and predominantly untapped) potential, especially as
shipping was concerned, a potential effectively obstructed in the consular union. These perspectives are crucial for comprehending how the
consular issue was debated among Norwegian politicians from 1890 to
1920.

This debate entered a new and hectic phase as European powers so-
lidified their economic and political grip on the colonies, an issue hardly
discussed in the Norwegian historical canon. There has been no men-

tion in this literature of the fact that the parliamentary investigation of the late 1880s on this particular issue was written only a few years after the Berlin conference. This is an obvious paradox, considering that the articles referring to the consular issue principally were based on these documents.

The Consular Committee of 1891

The year 1884 is a watershed in Norwegian political history. Since Norwegian independence from Denmark and the signing of the Norwegian Constitution in 1814, a dominant group of civil servants had been in political control. The government was recruited from this cohort of civil servants for seventy years. In 1884 the representative parliamentary system was implemented, and this initiated an era in which the government was recruited on the basis of the composition of the Norwegian parliament. It also initiated the emergence of a modern party system. The forces behind the parliamentary system joined the middle-class, radical party, the Liberals (Venstre). The defenders of the old regime joined the conservative party, the Conservatives (Høgre) (Angell 2002: 65).

The political manifesto from the Liberals' national assembly in 1891 stated that the party would direct its foreign policy towards '[a] separate consular service office and a separate consular service fund' (Danielsen 2002: 247; NSD/ISF 2001). It seems fair to conclude that this decision initiated the emergent Norwegian demand for separate consular services that eventually resulted in dissolving the union in 1905. This issue divided the Norwegian political stratum from right to left during most of this period. When dissolution finally happened in 1905, it was due to support from the Conservatives for the demand for separate Norwegian consular services, at which time the political parties stood united at last (Danielsen 2002: 247).

During the politically turbulent 1880s and 1890s, the Liberals made it part of their strategy to demand a separate consular service in order to confront the Conservatives on the union issue (Mjeldheim 1984: 218). All parties agreed, however, that the existing consular service needed renewal, since the financial interests of the union's partners differed. In the budget debate in 1889, the Norwegian parliament criticized the extensive, but sorely outdated, network of Swedish-Norwegian consulates in Europe, and several representatives suggested establishing more consulates overseas, manned by professional Norwegian staff (Kaartvedt 1995: 346).[5] In 1891 a unanimous parliament asked the Norwegian government to investigate whether, and to what extent, it would be necessary for Norway to employ its own consuls within the existing consular service system, or whether Norway should establish its own consular service at its own cost (Kaartvedt 1995: 364).

A committee was appointed to investigate these issues (St. prp. nr. 49 1892: 1); Christian Michelsen, who later became Norwegian prime minister, was one of the commission members. The fact that Michelsen was a member of the committee reflects how public office and private enterprise shared interests: Michelsen was in the process of establishing one of Norway's leading shipping companies at the time. He also shared political views with the Liberals, and during this phase of the debate that party dominated Norwegian politics. Therefore, in order to promote their own interests, many important shipping magnates and industrialists became party members (Slagstad 1998: 135). The shipping industry considered the consular issue vital, and another future prime minister and prominent shipping magnate and industrialist, Gunnar Knudsen, also involved himself strongly in the issue.

The proposition from the consular committee was submitted in the autumn of 1891, emphasizing Norway's and Sweden's different financial positions, especially regarding shipping. The committee maintained that 'economic principles for shipping' differed so greatly that 'the conditions abroad, which are absolutely contrary to Norwegian interests, according to Swedish opinion seem neither unreasonable nor significant' (*Indstilling fra Konsulatkomiteen* 1891: 11). The committee shared the parliament's perspective that the existing consular services resulted in 'maintaining consular offices in regions with little or no relevance to Norwegian interests' (*Indstilling fra Konsulatkomiteen* 1891: 13). By pointing out the weaknesses of shared consular services, the committee also launched a theme that would come to characterize the debate even after the dissolution of the union: which regions would need strengthening of consular representation. In terms of Norwegian shipping's worldwide trade routes, it was concluded that shipping was 'significant in distant seas, especially to South America, the United States of North America and British North America, but also Africa, South and East Asia, the West Indies, Mexico and Central America' (*Indstilling fra Konsulatkomiteen* 1891: 16). From this perspective, then, there was a need to strengthen the Norwegian presence in the colonial parts of the world.

Existing research also states that the shipping industry relied on an expansion of consular services catering to their interests (see, e.g., Berg 1995: 45; Neumann and Leira 2005b). The proposition from the consular committee, however, emphasized a need to promote Norwegian economic interests in general through the consular services. It was pointed out that the debate on reforms of consular services had ignored that 'a Norwegian consul's most significant objective … is to promote our country's trade', emphasizing the consuls' ability to 'provide guidance and support to our national, and often young, industry's efforts to find foreign markets'. As a consequence, the committee decided that it would not be acceptable 'to award the most significant of these positions to men who presumably are lacking in insight in our trades and also obeying a competing nation in significant areas' (*Indstilling fra Konsulatkomiteen* 1891: 18; Kaartvedt 1995: 348).

Appearing only a few years after the Berlin conference, the proposition from the consular committee provides perspectives on how Norway's economic position in the world was perceived and how this position was related to Norway's economic interests in the colonies during the same period. One premise in the suggestion from the committee and in the subsequent proposition was that the consular union prevented Norway from participating in the growth in international economics on equal terms with other European nations, claiming that 'leading industrial nations' implemented structures to promote export and trade on other continents, like 'commercial trainees, establishment of associations for export … trade councils … among traders and industrialists and in the colonies; participation in local [exhibitions] and World Expositions etc.' (*Indstilling fra Konsulatkomiteen* 1891: 20). It was further argued that Sweden and Norway also became 'exposed to the increasingly stronger international competition' as a result of this development. Sweden had recently established an export council to promote Swedish trade overseas to which Norway sent commercial trainees. According to the committee, such structures were supported by a national consular system in other countries. Additionally, honorary consuls were generally replaced by regular ones recruited among 'men who are especially familiar with their nation's industries'. This reasoning led to the following rhetorical question, coloured by the developing conflict within the union: '[I]t would be out of the question for British, German, Belgian, French or Austrian consular officials, on fixed salaries, to satisfy the demand from their nation's exporters while simultaneously promoting a competing nation's products. What is our position on this question?' (*Indstilling fra Konsulatkomiteen* 1891: 20).

But if we study how strategies to expand Norwegian consular services materialized, it is evident that the need to expand on new continents was considered important independent of this issue: the committee advocated an expansion of the consular services in the United States and Canada as a primary objective. Simultaneously, the consular services were seen as a means to expand Norwegian interests in Latin America and Africa. The committee's explicit support for the establishment of a Norwegian consulate in Havana, Cuba, is a case in point, a proposition that came before the West Indies were liberated from Spain. However, these nations' status as economic clients of the United States was about to solidify (Kapcia 2000: 49), a situation allowing American goods toll-free export to the West Indian market. The committee claimed that this could negatively influence the position of Norwegian fish products: Canadian stockfish, which was Norway's main competitor on this market, could be exported to the West Indies under cover of being American. The committee also emphasized that Norwegian ships were significant in the freight industry between the United States and the Spanish West Indian colonies. A Norwegian consulate in Havana would have a particular responsibility to survey this freight industry and to ensure that 'all which may serve to promote its development immediately be brought to the attention of the interested parties' (*Indstilling fra Konsulatkomiteen* 1891: 43).

It was not only in Latin America that the report was explicit, however. In Africa and Asia 'our interests are … still relatively insignificant', according to the committee. When, in spite of this fact, larger consular representation on these continents was advocated, 'its purpose is more to establish a movement than to satisfy the demands of those interests who are already established' (*Indstilling fra Konsulatkomiteen* 1891: 44). In the committee's perspective, it was vital to allow Norwegian industry to take part in the expansion of the European colonies in Africa and Asia. The committee thus supported the establishment of an employed consul general in Singapore: 'In British East India, Siam and the Dutch, French and Spanish territories in Asia there is ample opportunity for distribution of several of our products, but above all to promote these territories as large open territories for our shipping industry' (*Indstilling fra Konsulatkomiteen* 1891: 46).

In Africa they saw the Cape Colony as significant. Based on shipping and in view of the strong development experienced by the region, it seemed desirable to have effective consular representation, fully capable of support and leadership of established structures as well as promotion of new relations between Norway and the British colonies on Africa's southern coast (*Indstilling fra Konsulatkomiteen* 1891: 47).

The Consular Affairs Issue towards 1905

The consular committee of 1891's report emphasized finding an arrangement serving Norway's economic interests better, and it resulted in a recommendation to establish a separate Norwegian consular affairs division. The following year the parliament allocated funds to prepare for the dissolution of the existing consular union, and the government was asked to request negotiations with Sweden. However, the current king, Oscar II, denied the request and refused to sign the Norwegian parliament's proposition (Omang 1955: 94).

The Liberals chose to continue a confrontational approach, and in 1894 the parliament forced the establishment of a special committee to discuss the consular budget. This was a parliamentary commission, with the previously mentioned shipping magnate Gunnar Knudsen as one of its most prominent members. They agreed with the decisions of the committee from 1891, emphasizing that the consular division should be a 'lever' for Norwegian trade, shipping and industry in areas where it was not yet established, further claiming that businesses were not protected by high customs fees in Norway and advocating that the authorities needed to take action to facilitate conditions for shipping and industry, with the help of 'support from the public sector in order to create new and more profitable markets, especially in remote regions':

> Countries like India, China, Japan, Indochina and the East Indian Islands etc. with their hundreds of millions of inhabitants have not been explored by Norwegian enterprises. If any of our products find their way to these areas it will be via British or German intermediaries who sift off more than their fair share of the profits, which would otherwise have benefited our businessmen. (Indst. S. XX B., 1894: 61–62)

Another characteristic of the 1894 committee's proposition was its references to the experiences of different union consuls around the world, in order to justify the establishment of more consular offices in the colonies. In accordance with the committee of 1891, this committee also strongly supported the establishment of an employed consul general in Singapore. A statement made by the consul in Shanghai was used to support the recommendation:

> Singapore is, similarly to Hong Kong, a British colony and one of Asia's largest trade emporiums for transit. Its key geographical position allows frequent steamship connections with large export harbours in British East India, the Dutch, Spanish and French territories as well as Siam, harbours like Penang, Batavia, Manila, Rangoon, Saigon and Bangkok. These harbours provide major import and export business to the large trading houses in Singapore. (Indst. S. XX B., 1894: 65)

However, this committee went further in its advocacy for Norwegian consulates in colonial areas than the committee of 1891 by suggesting, amongst other things, an employed consul general both in Bombay and in Cape Town and honorary consuls general or consuls in Siam (Thailand), British, Dutch and French colonies in Asia, and in several African countries, including Morocco, Tripoli (Libya), Egypt, the Belgian Congo and Transvaal (South Africa) (Indst. S. XX B., 1894: 69–70).

The expansion of the consular division suggested by the committee from 1894 has been referred to as overblown, unrealistic and heavily influenced by the political situation at the time (Omang 1955: 135), and the effort failed. In 1895 the Liberals argued for a decision to establish separate Norwegian consular services, but as intervention from the Swedish government was a realistic prospect, the Norwegian parliament decided to renegotiate the consular affairs issue on new terms. This decision formed the basis of a bilateral committee established in 1902, equipped with a mandate to reevaluate the issue. Eventually, this committee recommended that Norway be given independent consuls (Kaartvedt 1995: 349). In 1904 a new committee, chaired by Helmer Bryn, was formed to establish a proposal for a plan and budget for a separate Norwegian consular services division (Ot. prp. nr. 3 1905–6). Bryn was a lawyer and diplomat and belonged to the minority in the committees of 1891 and 1894. The 1904 committee's perspectives were somewhat less confrontational than those expressed by the committees of the 1890s, claiming that Norway could not compare its consular services with those of colonial powers. Instead, an independent consular service should primarily service the country's shipping industry (Ot. prp. nr. 3 1905–6: 32–33).

The Bryn committee was also sceptical towards establishing hired consular services in regions it considered too remote for Norwegian economic expansion. It did, as with the former committees, however, support the establishment of consular services in some of the colonial areas, as in the Congo, with reference to a letter received by the Swedish Ministry of Foreign Affairs in 1901 on behalf of 'several Norwegians and Swedes, who have been and to a certain extent still are in the service of the Congolese state, regarding the establishment of a Norwegian and Swedish consular office in Brazzaville'. Approximately one hundred Scandinavians worked in the Belgian Congo at the time (see also Wæhle, this volume). However, Norwegian and Swedish products were not marketed in the region. Now that opportunities seemed to be opening up in the French Congo, it would be suitable to employ a consul who was familiar with the trade conditions at home and who could report back on which products the market was open to receive. It is also important to point out that the majority of the 'Scandinavians were almost helpless since they didn't understand the official language, French'. The committee pointed out that the Swedish Ministry of Domestic Affairs in Stockholm in 1901 had stated that Norwegian trade and shipping interests were minimal in the Congo:

> [B]ut the rapid development this region already seems to have undergone, and to a much larger extent seemingly will come to undergo in the future, it seems significant to have a person employed, who is familiar with local conditions and who could provide guidance to those who seek to establish trade relations with these countries. (Ot. prp. nr. 3 1905–6: 177–78)

The committee agreed to establish hired consular services in Brazzaville in the French Congo, and recommended that a first-class consular office also be established in Leopoldville to serve the Belgian Congo (Ot. prp. nr. 3 1905–6: 177–78).

The committee's view on Norwegian consular representation in the Congo is particularly interesting and reveals some of the key trade ambitions in colonial Africa. During the decades following the Berlin conference – and as is generally known – the Congo became the focus of major European exploitation. In the Belgian Congo, personally controlled by the Belgian king Leopold II, the local workforce was mercilessly exploited to produce natural rubber for the large European

Figure 6.2. The Norwegian Congo officer Martin Engh (on the right) relaxing with unknown companions in 1909. Engh served in several areas in the Congo, among them in the northeast. *Source:* Espen Wæhle; reproduced with permission.

and American markets. The trade was organized through preferential treatment of certain privileged companies awarded concessions. The fact that Nordic businessmen were largely unable to gain access to this system was pointed to by the consular committee of 1904. But at the turn of the century the tables had turned, and the Congo had become a 'miniature job market' for the Nordic countries: sailors operated small steamboats on the Congo River; Nordic captains, guides and craftsmen supported the region's transport system; Nordic citizens were involved in state bureaucracy; and Nordic missionaries were represented in the region. Additionally, many Norwegians, Swedes and Danes worked for companies with concessions to produce rubber and in the mining and mineral industries. According to Wæhle (2007), only a few in the Nordic countries were aware of the brutality of the colonial administration in the Belgian Congo. This brutality was not an issue for the recommendations given by the Norwegian consular committee of 1904 and was never mentioned in parliamentary debates on the consular affairs issue after 1905.[6]

Based on a report from the committee secretary, Halvard Bachke, who previously had been consular trainee in Cape Town, the consular committee chaired by Bryn also recommended representation by a Norwegian consul general in South Africa. In accordance with Bachke's report, it was suggested that 'the opportunity for increased export of Norwegian products to South Africa was obvious' and that the market was open to products other than timber. Moreover, there were potential markets beyond the Cape Colony: 'It seems reasonable that the district of the consul general should include all of South Africa, including the Portuguese, German and British colonies.'[7] The recommendations of the Bryn committee were in this respect also significant expressions of Norwegian motives concerning colonialism.

The Consular System after the Dissolution of the Union

The consular affairs conflict between Sweden and Norway ended with the dissolution of the union in 1905, a move that made Norway an independent agent in foreign policy. But in Norway the conflict regarding the consulates' role was not brought to an end with the dissolution of the union; it soon became a debate about the establishment of an independent Norwegian diplomatic service (Berg 1995: 54). Underneath the nationalist rhetoric the conflict revolved around which competence should be emphasized in future representations – commercial or diplomatic-political.

The Liberals again raised the consular debate in the parliament early in 1906. In a lengthy interpellation, one of the party's members of parliament (MP) argued for a strengthening of Norwegian overseas representation and a reduced activity in Europe. The role of the consular services must be to conquer new markets for Norwegian industry and shipping, he claimed (Omang 1995: 192–93). A political committee was established the same year to evaluate the amount of consular versus diplomatic representation in the Foreign Service.

Although the consular affairs issue was no longer a question for the union, it remained a factor energizing the political struggle between the Norwegian political left and right. The idea that diplomatic services needed to be minimized was an echo from the fight against the civil servant regime before 1884, which the political left claimed the political right had inherited. During the debate on the budget for the Department for Foreign Affairs in 1906, one of the MPs, Johan Castberg, claimed that it was no longer in Norway's interest to be represented by 'these men out there who are seen at parties prancing in their glory … while they actually should be developing our trade, industry and shipping' (Stortingsforhandlinger 1905–6: 996). But Castberg also raised the question of the significance of Norwegian consular representation outside Europe: 'It is difficult for our shipping industry and exporters there to establish business relations with well-known and trustworthy men, and in this respect the consular service has a different and quite significant role' (Stortingsforhandlinger 1905–6: 9).

Public opinion was also concerned with foreign policies during the period after 1905. For instance, consul to Uruguay and whaling industrialist Ole Johannes Storm wrote several articles for the press strongly advocating Norwegian representation abroad through consuls rather than ambassadors. He also claimed that the consuls themselves should be businessmen, preferably with experience overseas, 'where individuality develops faster than at home'. He supported a system of consular representation with business skills and with diplomatic status: Storm wanted individuals with practical or theoretical mercantile or technical training. According to Reidar Omang, who wrote a history of the Norwegian Foreign Service during the 1950s, these were typical business attitudes at the time (Omang 1955: 251–52). However, these views were not only cherished in business circles. When diplomat Johannes Irgens became the minister of foreign affairs in the conservative coalition government in 1910, he emphasized the importance of close relations between diplomacy and business and the importance of involving business in foreign policy. His political program provided clear associations with the way colonial powers conducted their foreign services:

'It was appropriate to create strong ties between the Norwegian "colonies" and the mother country and thereby create "a larger Norway"' (Omang 1955: 292).

Such visions first and foremost must be seen in relation to a recurrent theme in Norwegian public debate during this period – on the one hand, the desire to uphold strong ties between Norwegian emigrants overseas and the mother country, and on the other hand, that emigration implied that Norwegian national culture was being spread to other parts of the world (Angell 2002: 113). However, it must also be seen in relation to Norwegian motives to expand its territory in the Arctic, which reached a temporary peak in 1923, when Spitsbergen became Norwegian territory (Berg 1995: 265).

Despite the vigorous debate in the political and public sphere, no final decisions were made regarding the evaluation of consular versus diplomatic representation in the Foreign Service in these years. However, political public opinion gradually seemed to favour restructuring diplomacy towards serving business. Nor is there any doubt that Norway established stronger consular representation worldwide: the number of Norwegian consular offices rose to total more than six hundred prior to the First World War (Omang 1959: 120; Berg 1995: 57). In 1919, after the war, yet another committee was established to evaluate the Norwegian Foreign Service, emphasizing the political aspect of foreign representation to a much larger extent than those before. This relates to the development during the war, which exposed the Foreign Service to new demands.[8] The commission, however, established that it was important that the representation promoted Norwegian trade in 'remote countries … as commissions before them had done' (Organisasjon av utenriksdepartement og utenriksetat 1920: 19). Yet again, the business interests of shipping were heavily emphasized, but this time it was signalled that it was important to secure the delivery of raw materials for Norwegian industry from remote countries. Diplomats abroad needed to be made aware of this in addition to the potential access to foreign markets for Norwegian industrial goods (Organisasjon av utenriksdepartement og utenriksetat 1920: 19). Norway had experienced a tremendous expansion in the hydropower-based electrometallurgical industry since 1905, and several of the new factories established were dependent on raw materials from colonial areas (Kjeldstadli 1994: 47).

As in the former committees, the 1919 committee also referred to reports by Norwegian representatives in the colonies to support existing Norwegian interests as well as creating new ventures and opportunities, arguing, for one, that the consulate general in Egypt should be responsible for Norwegian interests in Syria and Palestine: 'According to available information it must be assumed that opportunities will open up in this region for Norwegian trade and that this eventually will lead to increased economic activity in the countries at the eastern end of the Mediterranean' (Organisasjon av utenriksdepartement og utenriksetat 1920: 148–49).

Furthermore, the committee suggested a conversion of the honorary consulate in Bangkok to a consulate general, which implied an upgrade: the consul would be an employee of the Ministry of Foreign Affairs, receiving a regular salary. The shipping industry was large and increasing in this region, and the commission felt that 'with regards to our trading interests significant opportunities are at hand in this country'. As for the islands in Dutch East India – 'this large and affluent colony' – the committee pointed to Norwegian exports and imports on the rise, therefore suggesting the establishment of a consulate general in Batavia (Jakarta). This consular district was suggested to include 'all Dutch areas of East India, and the station should have authority of our consular representation in the Straits Settlements and in the Philippines' (Organisasjon av utenriksdepartement og utenriksetat 1920: 210–13).

The committee also presented interesting perspectives on the function of the Norwegian consulate general in Melbourne, responsible for Australia and New Zealand. In this instance the committee referred to the Norwegian consul general's suggestion that the hitherto honorary consulate for the British 'Crown colonies' in the Pacific be subject to the authority of the consul general in Melbourne, whose district would then include all of 'British Australia' (Organisasjon av utenriksdepartement og utenriksetat 1920: 217).

Conclusions

The consular affairs case is entangled with other key political issues in Norwegian politics during the period from 1890 to circa 1920: until 1905 it was inextricably linked to the union with Sweden. Post-1905 the debate more explicitly revolved around the direction of Norway's new position as an independent agent in foreign policies. Yet – as this chapter demonstrates – the debate on objectives and functions of an independent Norwegian consular service also involves motives related to Norway's need to develop and make use of the opportunities presented in the colonies. Shipping interests were of particular importance in this respect, but motives also derived from a desire that Norwegian entrepreneurs should have the opportunity to establish and expand in colonial areas. The viewpoints expressed concerning the Congo in the years around 1900 are particularly interesting. At this stage the resources in this region remained at the centre of European expansionism. Norwegian public records from the time illustrate how Norwegian politicians and civil servants were eager to make arrangements so that Norwegian business could take advantage of this.

The consular system branched into Norwegian business and society. The persons who worked as Norwegian consuls around the world often had strong ties to and represented Norwegian groups, individuals and businesses in the colonies. Several prominent Norwegian entrepreneurs functioned as Norwegian consuls in the colonial world (Reiersen 2006; Bang 2011). A significant example of this can be found in the journalist Ludvig Saxe's book from 1914, published after having visited Norwegian environments around the world. During his journey to what today is South Africa, he visited the Norwegian consul, Jacob Egeland, in Durban, a town housing approximately seven hundred Norwegians at the time, mainly craftsmen. Egeland himself arrived in Zululand in 1880 and set up business there. He was able to inform Saxe that he, during the 'Dinizulu riots in '89 accepted ... delivery to the British army'. When the Zulus were defeated by the British army, Egeland moved to Durban and established business with deepwater fisheries. After a trip to Norway in 1907 he established a whaling company together with Johan Bryde from Sandefjord; he later also established Union Whaling & Fishing Company Ltd. (Saxe 1914: 84–85; see also Tønnessen 1967: 436, 445; Børresen, this volume).

Saxe's story indicates strong ties between different environments in Norway and the colonies. More research is needed to describe these ties more closely; this would provide important additions to the knowledge we already possess on Norway's role in the developing colonial system during the late 1800s and onwards. Such research may very well challenge our perception of Norway as an agent in the international arena in general.

Notes

I would like to express my gratitude to Anne K. Bang, Roald Berg, Bjørn Enge Bertelsen, Kirsten Alsaker Kjerland and Espen Wæhle for reviews of and comments on this article. I would also like to express my gratitude to the participants of the Bjørnson seminar at the Institute of Archeology, History, Cultural and Religious Sciences at the University of Bergen, to whom a preview of this text was submitted. All translations into English were undertaken by the author.
  1. Annual consular reports, MFA (Ministry of Foreign Affairs) archives, box 1003, RA.

2. Ibid.
3. Espen Storli (2001: 122) has demonstrated that the same applies to Norway's efforts to establish separate trade treaties, which went into effect in 1892, when Norway agreed to a treaty with Spain.
4. See, e.g., the report from the Norwegian consul to Dutch East India from 1908, annual consular reports, MFA archives, box 1003, RA.
5. Similar attitudes to consular representation surfaced in Sweden. It was claimed that businesses were quite familiar with European conditions and that the current extent of consular representation was not required. It was also emphasized that customs barriers within Europe had become so high that it would serve Sweden's interests better to expand overseas (Håkansson 1989: 65).
6. See Stortingsforhandlinger (1905–6: 933ff.).
7. The proposal is printed as an addendum to Ot. prp. nr. 3 (1905–6: 171).
8. The proposition pointed out that the First World War had demonstrated Norway's need for a separate foreign policy regarding 'our freedom and independence and our nation's dignity and standing among nations' (Organisasjon av utenriksdepartement og utenriksetat 1920: 18).

Archives Consulted

The Central Office of the National Archives of Norway (Riksarkivet, RA), Oslo.

References

Angell, S.I. 2002. *Den svenske modellen og det norske systemet: Tilhøvet mellom modernisering og identitetsdanning i Sverige og Noreg ved overgangen til det 20. hundreåret.* Oslo: Det norske Samlaget.

Arrighi, G. 1994. *The Long Twentieth Century.* London: Verso.

Bang, A.K. 2011. *'Zanzibar-Olsen': A Norwegian Timber Trader in Zanzibar, 1895–1925.* Bergen: Eden-Olympia.

Berg, R. 1995. *Norge på egen hånd: 1905–1920,* Norsk utenrikspolitikks historie, Volume II. Oslo: Universitetsforlaget.

de Courcel, G. 1988. 'The Berlin Act of 26 February 1885', in S. Förster, W.J. Mommsen and R. Robinson (eds), *Bismarck, Europe, and Africa: The Berlin Africa Conference 1884–1885 and the Onset of Partition.* London: Oxford University Press.

Danielsen, R. 2002. 'På moderationens grund: Några rättsliga och konstitutionella betraktelser över unionsupplösningen', in T. Nilsson and Ø. Sørensen (eds), *1905 – unionsupplösningens år: Nya perspektiv på ett svensk-norskt drama.* Stockholm: Carlssons Bokförlag.

Håkansson, S. 1989. *Konsulerna och exporten: Ett 'Government failure'?* Bibliotheca Historica Lundensis 64. Lund: Lund University Press.

Indstilling fra Konsulatkomiteen [Proposal from the Consular Committee]. 1891. Kristiania. Published in Stortingsforhandlinger. 1892. *St. prp. nr. 49 (1892): Meddelelse til Storthinget angaaende forskjellige Spørgsmaal vedkommende Konsulatvæsenet.*

Indst. S. XX B. 1894. Indstilling fra den til Behandling af Konsulatbudgettet for 1894– 1895 nedsatte Specialkomité. Stortingsforhandlinger. 1894.

Kaartvedt, A. 1995. 'Del III, 1814–1905: Unionen med Sverige', in N. Bjørgo, Ø. Rian and A. Kaartvedt, *Selvstendighet og union: Fra middelalderen til 1905*, Norsk utenrikspolitikks historie. Volume I, pp. 231–365, Oslo: Universitetsforlaget.

Kapcia, A. 2000. *Cuba: Island of Dreams.* Oxford: Berg.

Kirk-Greene, A. 2000. *Britain's Imperial Administrators 1858–1966.* Oxford: Macmillan.

Kjeldstadli, K. 1994. 'Et splittet samfunn 1905–1935', in K. Helle et al. (eds), *Aschehougs Norgeshistorie.* Oslo: Aschehoug.

Leira, H. and I.B. Neumann. 2006. 'Fremmede konsuler i Norge ca. 1660–1905', *Historisk Tidsskrift* 106(2): 449–87.

Mjeldheim, L. 1984. *Folkerørsla som vart parti: Venstre frå 1880-åra til 1905.* Oslo: Universitetsforlaget.

Mommsen, W.J. 1988. 'Bismarck, the Concert of Europe, and the Future of West Africa 1883–1885', in S. Förster, W.J. Mommsen and R. Robinson (eds), *Bismarck, Europe, and Africa: The Berlin Africa Conference 1884–1885 and the Onset of Partition.* London: Oxford University Press.

Neumann, I.B. and H. Leira. 2005. *Unionsoppløsning 1905: Konsulatsaken og rederne.* Oslo: Norges Rederiforbund.

Nilsson, D. 2013. 'Sweden-Norway at the Berlin Conference 1884-85. History, National Identity-Making and Sweden's Relations with Africa', *Current African Issues*, 53. Uppsala: Nordiska Afrikainstitutet.

Nilsson, T. 2000. 'Striden om konsulerna: Unionspolitik och modernisering 1870–1905', in K. Zetterberg and G. Åselius (eds), *Historia, krig och statskonst: En vänbok till Klaus-Richard Böhme.* Stockholm: Probus.

Norges Offisielle Statistikk: Norges skipsfart (Norwegian Official Statistics: Norwegian Shipping). 1908–10. Oslo: Statistisk Sentralbyrå.

Norsk samfunnsvitenskapeleg datatjeneste/Institutt for samfunnsforskning (NSD/ISF). 2001. *Vi vil … ! Norske partiprogrammer 1884–2001* [Norwegian political party programs 1884–2001]. CD-ROM. Available at http://www .nsd.uib.no/polsys/index.cfm?aktuelt=5.

Organisasjon av utenriksdepartement og utenriksetat. 1920. *Innstilling I: Fra Utenrikskommisjonen av 1919–1920* [Proposition from the Foreign Affairs Commission of 1919–1920]. Kristiania: Grøndahl and Sons.

Omang, R. 1955. *Norsk utenrikstjeneste I – Grunnleggende år.* Oslo: Gyldendal.

———. 1959. *Norsk utenrikstjeneste II – Stormfulle tider 1913–1928.* Oslo: Gyldendal.

Reiersen, E.M. 2006. *Fenomenet Thams.* Oslo: Aschehoug.

Robinson, R. 1988. 'The Conference in Berlin and the Future in Africa, 1884– 1885', in S. Förster, W.J. Mommsen and R. Robinson (eds), *Bismarck, Europe, and Africa: The Berlin Africa Conference 1884–1885 and the Onset of Partition.* London: Oxford University Press.

Saxe, L. 1914. *Nordmænd jorden rundt.* Kristiania: H. Aschehoug, W. Nygaard.

Slagstad, R. 1998. *De nasjonale strateger.* Oslo: Pax Forlag.

Storli, E. 2001. '"Det första steget på en för unionen förderflig väg": Norge, Sverige og handelstraktatene med Spania 1892', PhD dissertation. Trondheim: Norwegian University of Science and Technology.

Stortingsforhandlinger. 1892. *St. prp. nr. 49 (1892): Meddelelse til Storthinget angaaende forskjellige Spørgsmaal vedkommende Konsulatvæsenet.*

Stortingsforhandlinger. 1894. *Indst. S. XX B. (1894): Indstilling fra den til Behandling af Konsulatbudgettet for 1894–1895 nedsatte Specialkomité.*

Stortingsforhandlinger. 1905–6. Parliamentary debates. Volume VII.

Stortingsforhandlinger. 1905–6. *Ot. prp. nr. 3. 1905–6. Ang. udfærdigelse af en lov om den konsulære retspleie* (Parliamentary debates). Retrieved 1 August 2014 from https://stortinget.no/no/Saker-og-publikasjoner/Stortingsforhandlinger/Lesevisning/?p=1905-06&paid=3&wid=a&psid=DIVL68&pgid=a_0027&s=True.

Tønnessen, J. 1967. *Verdensfangsten 1883–1924.* Volume I, *1883–1914.* Sandefjord: Norges Hvalfangstsforbund.

Wæhle, E. 2007. 'Kolonialisme i Congo: Norden som medspiller', *Historie-nu.* Retrieved 26 November 2013 from http://www.historienu.dk/site/index.php?option=com_content&task=view&id=494&Itemid=31.

Yngfalk, C. 2005. 'Sverige och den europeiska kolonialpolitiken i Afrika', PhD dissertation. Stockholm: Stockholm University.

Norwegian Shipping and Landfall in the South Sea in the Age of Sail

Edvard Hviding

'Islands of Paradise'

From an assessment of popular folklore and family recollections, it is reasonable to assume that quite a few Norwegian seamen chose to settle in the islands of the tropical Pacific during the latter part of the nineteenth century.[1] The cases of Norwegian settlers in the Solomon Islands are particularly complex, but have the good fortune of being at least partly documented (see chapter 8, this volume). However, most documentation of such exotic instances of permanent nineteenth-century migration reaches no further than the private traditions of families in which an uncle or other relative was remembered to have settled in the distant South Sea (which in Norwegian usage remains the old singular form 'Sydhavet'), never to be heard from again.

How, then, did a number of seamen from such a small and distant country become settlers in the Pacific Islands? It is self-evident that the single most important background for, and context of, the little known and often strange Norwegian presences in the colonial Pacific Islands is that of seafaring in the age of sail. As one of the world's largest shipping nations towards the end of the nineteenth century, the small country of Norway developed a remarkably high level of maritime activity across the Pacific, particularly since its shipowners were slow to abandon large sailing ships when steam became the order of the day (see Nygaard, this volume). Capacious sailing cargo vessels were in demand for the timber trade to Australia and for the copra trade from the Pacific, both of which were economic operations that relied on low transportation costs, with actual time spent at sea not a major issue. In this chapter I present some glimpses of this particular era, during which Norwegian shipping in the Pacific 'navigated colonial orders' in the most literal sense. This was also a time when it became an option for Norwegian seamen to linger on among the tropical islands of the Pacific, and even settle there for life.

In a small, unassuming but very informative book whose title can be translated as *The South Sea in Sun and Storm*, Norwegian maritime historian Birger Dannevig (1976) presents a popularized history of Norwegian seafaring in the Pacific in the age of sail. He explains how by 1875, the southern Pacific Ocean had been well established in Norway's folklore as a region where 'islands of paradise' could be encountered and visited. That particular realm of rapidly developing folklore, Dannevig reminds us, was experience-based. It derived from seamen's accounts, accumulated as 'Norwegian ships through the last decades of the 1800s called at an increasing number of the islands of the South Sea' (1976: 9).[2] Dannevig elaborates on the romance and reality of the Pacific 'paradise':

> If attempts are made to study the background for the light-hearted reflections [of seamen], to find the truth in it all, it appears that the 'South Sea paradise' was far from just a phrase, but could seem real enough.
>
> However, the paradise was only one aspect of the accounts from the South Sea trade. Not a few Norwegian ships were lost there; human tragedies unfolded. Charts, navigational directions, marking of shoals and reefs, and beacons were rather poorly developed in the pioneer era of Norwegian shipping in the Pacific. Then as now, tropical hurricanes could arise in certain areas.
>
> When the various circumstances surrounding the South Sea voyages are considered, accounts of paradise and shipwreck do not take centre stage. The main impression is one of perseverance and effort to create new markets for Norwegian shipping, and of great seamanship. Today it is almost unfathomable how the navigators found their way, how with primitive means cargoes were loaded at innumerable islands with no harbour, even without safe anchorage. Equally impressive is the seamanship demonstrated after shipwreck, so that crews were in most cases saved. (Dannevig 1976: 9–10)

Norwegian Sails in the Pacific: Some Geographies

In the late nineteenth century the tropical Pacific remained something of a last frontier of European seafaring, with considerable parts still uncharted. Not much more than a hundred years had passed since British navigator James Cook had carried out his three famous journeys of Pacific exploration. Cook's travels vastly expanded the fragmentary knowledge of the ocean and its islands, which had previously been obtained by a limited number of Spanish, French and British navigators. They had sailed into the Pacific since the sixteenth century and had made more or less precarious landfalls at various central and eastern Pacific islands, including Tahiti, and further to the west at some of the high islands of Melanesia and coral atolls of Micronesia (for materials on Cook and his predecessors, see, e.g., Dunmore 1991; Smith 1985; Thomas 2003).

Dannevig notes that the first documented journey by a Norwegian vessel around Cape Horn into the Pacific Ocean was by the brig *Preciosa* of the eastern port of Drammen (1976: 17). Bound for Valparaiso in Chile, that ship rounded Cape Horn in 1841. The *Preciosa* may have been the first Norwegian presence in the Pacific Ocean itself, although it is quite possible that Norwegian whalers had ventured into the cold southern waters of the Pacific even earlier. Soon after the journey of the *Preciosa,* the whaling bark *17de Mai* of the southern port of Arendal embarked on a longer and more dedicated expedition deep into the South Sea (sailing the vast distance from far southern to far northern waters and reaching Kamchatka) in 1843–46. Several Norwegian sailing ships plied their trade in the Pacific in the years to come, sailing repeatedly across the ocean between Californian and Chinese ports, mainly San Francisco and Hong Kong. A driving force of this trade was the transport of Norwegian emigrants eager to participate in the Californian gold rush from 1848 onwards. Once gold-hungry Norwegians had disembarked after crossing the Atlantic and rounding Cape Horn, these ships could seek cargo for the trans-Pacific trade. One interesting case is that of the *Amerika Paket* of Christiania (Oslo), which sailed from Norway in December 1850 and arrived at San Francisco in September 1851 after a strenuous journey. The *Amerika Paket* continued to Hong Kong in ballast and returned to San Francisco with Chinese labourers, then for two years sailed with diverse types of cargo between ports in Chile, China, the Philippines and Indonesia, and in December 1853 became the first Norwegian ship to arrive at Sydney.

Such were the beginnings, according to Dannevig's account. He explains how, from the 1850s and well into the twentieth century, many more Norwegian sailing ships navigated the westerly routes around Cape Horn to America's Pacific coasts as well as the easterly routes of the East India trade, around the Cape of Good Hope. From the East Indies and the American Pacific a good proportion of these ships continued into and across the tropical southern Pacific, to reach ports in Australia as well as destinations across the myriad of 'South Sea' archipelagos. Of particular importance was an expanding Australia route on which Norwegian sailing ships transported Scandinavian, Russian and Baltic timber to the rapidly growing colonial economies of Australia and New Zealand, then taking on whatever was available as cargo for

the return journey. The journeys back to Europe were likely to be long
and complex and could include long ocean travel in ballast, or with cargoes of coal for America or Hawai'i, or sequences of shorter sailing with
copra freight among ports in the island Pacific and Australia.

The long eastbound sailing routes from southern Australia took advantage of the steady westerly winds of the far southern Pacific and
would continue across to Pacific ports in North and South America.
Some routes closer to or traversing the equator were also in use. The archipelago of Hawai'i, the emergent American island colony in eastern
Polynesia that had such appeal for people of the cold north, became a
routine port of call for Norwegian ships sailing between Australia or
China and North American ports. Having unloaded their cargo in North
American Pacific ports, ships might sail in ballast to South American
ports to load guano from Chile and then continue around Cape Horn
back to Europe. Such circumnavigations, or in some cases return journeys around Cape Horn or the Cape of Good Hope, made the Pacific
Ocean and its islands and reefs familiar to crew members on the many
Norwegian ships engaged in this trade and to the numerous Norwegian
sailors who worked on American, British or other European ships. As
the years passed towards the turn of the century, many Norwegian seamen became well acquainted with exotic island groups like Fiji, Tonga,
Samoa and Tahiti, and more than a few Norwegian sailing ships carried
copra directly from Pacific island ports all the way to Europe.

Whereas journeys from the west (via the Cape of Good Hope) or
the east (via Cape Horn) with cargoes destined for the east coast of
Australia followed the wide open seas of southern latitudes, onwards
journeys with cargoes for ports in the Americas or in China or Japan involved routes through and between still poorly charted island groups.
Sailing in the open southern latitudes entailed risks from wind and sea
– for example, in 1902 the full-rigged steel ship *Vildanden* of Drammen
disappeared without a trace somewhere in the far south en route from
Florida to South Australia with phosphate. Navigating among the archipelagos of the South Pacific posed additional hazards of uncharted
reefs and islands. For sailing ships travelling directly from Australia
to the Americas, the South Pacific's long season of stable trade winds
blowing from the southeast was especially convenient. However, sudden storms can appear out of nowhere in this area, at any time of the
year, and the period between December and February is dominated
by rainy monsoons from the northwest, sometimes interrupted by cyclones and other extreme weather. The conventional sailing routes
across the southern Pacific Ocean could therefore easily involve sudden detours to ports of refuge in remote islands more or less described

in the navigational directories of the time. On such occasions, seamen were brought into close encounters with islanders who, in the latter part of the nineteenth century, had just started to grasp the radical changes in their lives caused by the combined onslaught of colonialism, Christianity and the cash economy. Some Norwegian seamen were particularly adventurous or, alternatively, unwilling to continue working under demanding and tyrannical captains, and decided to remain in the islands when the ship continued its journey in good weather after repairs had been made.

Towards the end of the 1800s, as Norwegian sailing ships became more regularly involved in the long-distance transport of copra from the Polynesian islands to Europe, remote islands became more than ports of emergency refuge. Norwegian seamen's encounters with the islands and islanders of the tropical Pacific became more regular. The copra trade often involved small and remote ports of call, and encounters and extended contact between Pacific Islanders and Norwegian seamen increased in frequency and diversity. There was an increasing 'risk' for them to succumb to the temptations of the Pacific Islands, rather than return to a cold climate while enduring harsh working conditions on board. Instances of defection and settlement may have become numerous also through the large number of Norwegians who worked on ships of other nationalities engaged in the Pacific Islands trade. However, it would be a simplification to assume that Norwegian seamen only settled in the Pacific out of adventure or free will. Shipwreck, a prominent scenario for Pacific seafaring in the age of sail, was a strong contributing factor as well. Losses of Norwegian ships in the Pacific led to a mixture of voluntary, permanent settlement and unintended, temporary island visits.

Tales of Shipwreck and Island Life

The most thoroughly documented – and best-known – example of Norwegian residence in the Pacific Islands during the early colonial days is that of master mariner Reinert Godtfred Jonassen (1866–1915), from the small port of Korshavn near Farsund on Norway's southern tip. From 1893 Jonassen was the master of the Arendal-built bark *Gyda* of Farsund. In 1897, as *Gyda* was carrying a cargo of copra from Vava'u, Tonga, bound for Europe, she sailed into a cyclone and had to seek emergency harbour at Pape'ete, Tahiti, arriving there with extensive storm damage. *Gyda* was condemned by the insurance agents. The crew members found passage back to Norway, but Captain Jonassen remained at Pape'ete to handle the final formalities. While in Tahiti, he received notice that his wife had died in childbirth at home in Korshavn. Under those sad circumstances, Jonassen decided to remain in Tahiti, where he met and fell in love with an aristocratic woman from the Cook Islands, further west in Polynesia. Jonassen married her and settled at her home island of Aitutaki, where he built up a significant business of interisland trade and shipping. He never returned to Norway, and through the generations the Jonassen family has become prominent and influential in the Cook Islands. This fascinating story has been featured on Norwegian national television and is described in chapter 9 by Captain Jonassen's grandson, Professor Jon Tikivanotau Michael Jonassen.

Gyda's demise, caused by the volatile forces of the tropical Pacific climate, was not an isolated case involving Norwegian seafaring in the region. Stormy weather, poor charts and undermanned, overloaded or simply unseaworthy sailing vessels led to many shipwrecks in the Pacific, caused by storms or by rough encounters with unfamiliar reefs and low-lying islands. The large, hard-driven and often old Norwegian sailing ships were no exception. The best-known Norwegian shipwreck in the tropical Pacific was that of the large bark *Seladon* of Stavanger, a major port on Norway's southwest coast. *Seladon* was carrying coal to Honolulu from the Australian mining town of Newcastle when on the night of 7 August 1896 she sailed right onto the jagged coral reefs surrounding Starbuck Island, a low limestone island located just south of the equator and exactly in the middle of the Pacific. The wreck of *Seladon* and the strange incidents that followed have been thoroughly documented – at first in contemporary accounts in regional dailies like the *Evening Post* of Wellington and the *Stavanger Aftenblad* (the daily of *Seladon*'s home port), and more recently in a novel that dramatized the story (*Evening Post* 1897; Oftedal 1897; Pedersen 1981).

After hitting Starbuck head-on, the large, beautiful ship was soon shattered against the reef by heavy surf, and her crew of sixteen set out in two boats in search of any island more welcoming than dry, barren Starbuck. They had several known islands in mind but found none and drifted for thirty days, during which one boat capsized and two men, including the captain, died. Finally they reached land at the small, uninhabited atoll of Niulakita in Tuvalu (at that time referred to as the Ellice Islands). They were to spend '10 months amongst savages' there, for luckily Niulakita (called Sofia Island on the charts of the time) was temporarily inhabited by ten Polynesians who were there to capture turtles and collect coconuts for copra. The Polynesians took the castaways into their care, and a diet of turtles, seabirds and coconuts soon restored the weakened men of Stavanger, only one of whom died on the island. On 17 July 1897, the thirteen survivors from *Seladon* were picked up by a New Zealand steamer on a voyage of inspection among the atolls. On their homecoming to Stavanger on 25 October that year, they were celebrated and acclaimed as 'faithful and persistent toilers on the deep waters' to be 'welcomed back from the ocean's abyss' (Oftedal 1897: 76). The story of *Seladon's* shipwreck and the fate and 'miraculous rescue' of the crew became widely known at the time and even featured in the *New York Times*. Obviously, the kind of harrowing experience that the men of *Seladon* had was more conducive for longing to get back home to Norway than for developing desires to settle in the islands. At any rate, tiny Niulakita was far from the much-idealized 'paradise island'.

Dannevig's history of Norwegian seafaring in the nineteenth-century Pacific draws on contemporary accounts and maritime enquiries and on the archives of insurance companies to paint a broad and diverse picture of shipwrecks in those distant waters. Evidently, the Pacific trade involved considerable risk, a fact that was also reflected in increasingly high insurance rates. Some Norwegian owners therefore chose to send their ships to the Pacific uninsured, which in turn led to several bankruptcies after shipwreck. I summarize Dannevig's accounts of shipwreck here, and add some detail to them from online materials now available from the Norwegian Maritime Museum.

In 1889 the bark *Atlet* of Kristiansand was destroyed by fire while loading copra at the Micronesian island of Yap. Five years later the iron bark *Dalerne* of Egersund, with a copra cargo on board and bound for Lisbon, ran aground at Yap and was lost. The crews of both ships are reported to have lived for a couple of months at Yap, then still a very exotic and remote island, before being taken on board ships bound for Europe. In July 1894 the bark *Ephialtes* of Grimstad sailed for the Tonga islands from Brisbane, Australia, having there unloaded miscellaneous cargo from New York. With a cargo of coal, iron, cement and mixed goods for Tonga, the plan was for the ship to load a cargo of copra there for Europe. *Ephialtes* never reached Tonga and was wrecked on the Astrolabe Reef of southern Fiji, in foggy weather and with a malfunctioning lighthouse. The crew managed to get into boats and spent twelve days on the tiny island of Solo with scant supplies before being taken to Suva by a government steamer. In January 1896 the bark *West Australia* of Drammen was driven ashore by a tropical cyclone (prevalent in that season) and wrecked while loading copra in the Tonga islands; five crewmen lost their lives.

As Norwegian involvement in the global freight of copra from the Pacific and coal from Australia climaxed around the turn of the century, so did the loss of increasingly old sailing ships. A number of ships were lost on the coast of Australia, the most notable incident being the tragic shipwreck in 1909 of the full-rigged iron ship *Errol* of Mandal at Middleton Reef in the open ocean east of Brisbane. Of the twenty-two people on board only five survived a twenty-four-day ordeal of thirst, hunger, shark attack and sickness, and among those who perished were the captain and his family of five. The incident, regarded as the worst tragedy in Norwegian shipping's age of sail, was reported in Australian, New Zealand and Norwegian newspapers and must have played its part in conveying the dangers of the Pacific trade to the wider public. This tragedy notwithstanding, it is remarkable that in a large number of Norwegian shipwrecks in the Pacific during 1900–10, caused either through fire at sea (a constant danger from both coal and copra cargoes), by sudden cyclones or from running onto reefs (usually at night when even a good lookout might not spot the danger), very few lives were lost. Dannevig attributes this to a particular ability among Norwegian seamen, most of whom had handled small open boats in bad weather since childhood, to handle ships' boats in emergencies and in any kind of weather: 'Often … the crew managed to rescue themselves in lifeboats, even when ships stranded on coral reefs during tropical hurricanes. Today there is every reason to ask how this could be possible' (Dannevig 1976: 123). Losses of ships at or near Tonga, Samoa, Fiji and the guano-rich islands of the central Pacific invariably resulted in some residence by the shipwrecked among islanders or, in the case of the guano islands, among the temporary labourers employed ashore. Although records of most such Norwegian/Pacific encounters are hard to find, there is every reason to believe that shipwreck, as well as the voluntary (but often illegal) departure from ships in port, resulted in some more or less long-term residence in the islands.

The Dark Islands of the Western Pacific

While Dannevig's popular history is focused mainly on the contexts and events of the engagement by Norwegian sailing ships in the copra, coal and guano trades of the southern and central Pacific and the long routes between Australia and the Americas, Norwegian nineteenth-century navigation of the large tropical archipelagos of the western Pacific is only scantily documented. However, for ships heading north from eastern Australia towards China and Japan, where Australian coal was also needed, voyages went along western Pacific routes through the chains of large, forested volcanic islands that stretch in an almost continuous axis from southeast to northwest. This is the region of Melanesia, a part of the tropical Pacific not regarded as very hospitable for European ocean travellers until well into the twentieth century. It may be something of a surprise to learn that the largest numbers of Norwegians visible in the colonial history of the Pacific Islands actually were settlers in Melanesia, especially in the Solomon Islands. That is the story I tell in chapter 8 of this volume, but I devote some space here to describing the geographical and historical backdrop to this little-known scene for nineteenth-century Norwegian navigation and, indirectly, settlement. It is a scene from which some truly extraordinary stories can be extracted.

The archipelagos of the southwestern Pacific have been collectively known as Melanesia – the 'black islands' – since British and French explorers sailed through the islands in the late eighteenth and early nineteenth centuries (see Spriggs 1997: chap. 8 for a summary). It is assumed that the name alludes to the dark skin characteristic of the islanders of the region, but the islands themselves also appear 'black' (or at least dark and gloomy) for those who approach them from the sea, being mountainous and covered in rainforest, usually with dark clouds hovering over steep hills and mountain peaks. Initially, the islands of Melanesia may thus look less welcoming to visitors than the sun-drenched smaller islands and atolls of the southern and central Pacific, but this is deceptive, since Melanesia's natural resource wealth far surpasses any other islands in the Pacific. As is dealt with in detail in chapter 8, it was this resource wealth and its potential for trade and export that created the main incentives for nineteenth-century European settlement.

Throughout the nineteenth century Melanesia was a dangerous area for European visitors. The islanders paddled or sailed between the islands in large ocean-going canoes on expeditions of warfare, headhunting and slave raiding, and, as different islands possessed different repertoires of natural resources and craft specialities, more peaceful sea expeditions for trading purposes also occurred. Initial Spanish explorations were made in the 1500s, but further European visits were rare until the ships of major British and French exploratory expeditions skirted the islands and made infrequent landfall from 1779 onwards. From the late 1700s American whaling ships started calling at some of Melanesia's many good natural harbours for water, wood and other supplies, and considerable knowledge about the geography and populations of the islands was collected by observant ships' masters. From around the 1830s an increasing number of British and Australian small ships sailed to Melanesian coasts in search of exclusive trading goods such as turtle shells, mother-of-pearl and bêche-de-mer. These commodities were desirable in Asian markets, where they could be traded for silk, tea and other luxury goods as well as cotton, and the modest European trade in Melanesia in the latter part of the nineteenth century was therefore a part of the global economic system that developed alongside the Industrial Revolution.

Gradually, more ships arrived to recruit Melanesian islanders for hard labour in the large sugar plantations that were being established in Queensland in northeastern Australia and in Fiji (see also Rio, this volume). This trade became known as 'blackbirding' and was viewed as a ruthless trade in which islanders were tricked into signing contracts of slavery. Blackbirding was also an important factor in the depopulation that took place in Melanesia throughout the nineteenth century, a process that started when visiting ships introduced diseases, including sexually transmitted diseases. From the mid-nineteenth century the European presence in Melanesia expanded, with an increasing number of missionaries from Great Britain, Australia and New Zealand. After converting most of the populations of Polynesia, Anglicans, Catholics, Methodists and other church communities looked to the 'black islands' as a last mission field in dire need, where islanders on the one hand still lived heathen lives of ancestral worship, warfare and cannibalism, and on the other hand suffered under introduced diseases and the assault from ruthless white adventurers and slave traders.

In the latter half of the nineteenth century Melanesia was thus a complex island universe in which old and new worlds met and opposed each other. The Bismarck Archipelago and the Solomon Islands had a particularly bad reputation among European navigators. A significant number of whaling ships and traders' vessels were attacked by islanders, and in several cases crews were murdered and ships plundered and burned. These islands' image of warlike islanders and fearsome diseases was helped neither by a hot, humid and uninviting tropical climate nor by innumerable dangers along the shipping routes in the form of coral reefs, shoals and active underwater volcanoes not shown on charts.

All this notwithstanding, as early as 1839 it was reported in Royal Navy correspondence that European and American 'seasmen' were 'domiciled' in New Georgia, a particularly dangerous part of the western Solomon Islands.[3] We can safely assume that these early 'residents', probably so-called beachcombers (sailors who had run from whalers and other ships to try their luck on an island in the South Sea), lived rather insecure lives in New Georgia, where the islanders were intrepid ocean travellers primarily for purposes of raiding and head-hunting and secondarily for trade. Apart from the unique case of Scotsman John Renton, who lived as a castaway on the island of Malaita between 1868 and 1875, nothing is known about the fate of the earliest European adventurers anywhere in the Solomons. Perhaps the 'seasmen' who lived on New Georgia came to regret ever going ashore there. Several logs of whaling ships that visited the Solomons until well after 1850 mention cases of destitute white men coming near in small canoes and begging to be taken on board for employment. When, about 1875, Lars Nielsen, the first Norwegian known to have settled in the Solomons, arrived there as a shipwrecked seaman, the situation had not improved much. Remarkably, Nielsen lived in the islands until 1908 and succeeded in building a trading empire.

Sailing in the Dark Islands

From the 1850s onwards the first detailed navigation guides were published for Pacific locations deep within lagoons and along dangerous coastlines (e.g., Cheyne 1852; Findlay 1877). They were written either by seasoned Pacific navigators or based on the accumulated information left by pioneering captains of whaling ships and trading vessels. The guides gave detailed (but not always trustworthy) information about local conditions for navigation and trade, and encouraged growth in commerce even in Melanesia's most remote parts (see Hviding 1996: 104–6 for an example based on Findlay's guide). A general increase in long-distance voyages between Australia and eastern Asia also brought ships of many different nationalities through and past these infamous islands.

Some of the locations through which any ship travelling between Australia and China had to pass were considered particularly dangerous. This applied not least to the Bougainville Strait that separates the large island of Bougainville in the northern Solomons from smaller islands in the south – exemplified by the logbooks of American whaling ships that sailed in and around the Solomon Islands from around 1800. The 1860 log of Captain Wood of the whaling bark *Superior* of New Bedford ends abruptly with a peaceful note on practical business while the ship is in 'Treasury Harbour' in the Bougainville Strait: 'Friday sept the 14th to weather fine to work cutting Wood took in 100 bls of water loaded some for vegatibls Loosned the sails to dry' (spelling as in original). A couple of years after working through Captain Wood's mysteriously interrupted log on microfilm at the University of Hawai'i library, I found myself on a cold winter's day in a small library in the old whaling port of Salem, Massachusetts. There I discovered the reason for the interruption of the *Superior*'s log. In an old book I read a short but chilling description of the ship's fate: 'Sailed June 24, 1857, no return. Burned by natives of Solomon Islands, and all but 6 of the crew massacred, September 1860' (Starbuck 1878: 550). At least the log managed to find its way home.

Concrete information on Norwegian nineteenth-century navigation in these dangerous waters is scarce. The records of how the earliest Norwegian settlers in the Solomon Islands came to be there give little information except indicating, quite expectedly, that they were seamen, and that they were not necessarily on Norwegian ships. However, museum collections provide solid evidence of Norwegian ships and seamen not only passing by, but also visiting the 'black islands'. The University Museum of Bergen has a fine collection of spears and other weapons from the Bismarck Archipelago and New Britain, brought home and donated in 1893 by Captains A.M. Rasmussen and F.G. Thorstensen from Borøya, near the southern port of Tvedestrand (Rio 1999: 108–9). Both captains obviously had spent time ashore in those islands. A very special artefact in the Bergen collection (object Bme 160) is a carefully made spear in the style of the island of Bougainville from 'the Kentukka tribe of the Solomon Islands'. Museum accession records note that the spear was 'brought home from the Solomon Islands in 1885 by Captain J.H. Holmen, who with his first mate was held prisoner here for three months' (Rio 1999: 120). Of Captain Holmen's imprisonment by the 'Kentukka tribe' and, indeed, of the 'Kentukka' themselves, nothing is known. But it is well-known that shipwrecks on reefs and attacks on passing ships by islanders (who could paddle faster than a European ship could sail) were far from uncommon in the Solomon Islands at that time, and Captain Holmen and his first mate should be considered lucky to have survived their interactions with the islanders in order to bring exotic artefacts home with them to Norway. We do not know whether Captain Holmen would have been encouraged or disturbed had he known that a countryman by the name of Lars Nielsen was already a well-established trader and businessman in those inhospitable islands, whose 'natives' were prone to 'imprisoning' seamen who were shipwrecked or otherwise destitute.

I have reached a conclusion by way of an observation on the contradictory relationship between the patterns of nineteenth-century Norwegian seafaring in the Pacific and the patterns of permanent Norwegian settlement in the islands. Relatively few Norwegians settled in the (Polynesian) islands most frequently visited by Norwegian sailing ships; and conversely, not many Norwegian ships sailed to or among the (Melanesian) islands, where the most Norwegians settled as increasingly shrewd traders and operators within the emergent colonial economy. As I discuss in detail in chapter 8, this contradiction is founded in the ways in which the islands of Melanesia, and in particular the Solomon Islands group, represented a frontier for late nineteenth-century entrepreneurship, attractive to independent, practically oriented men with an appetite for adventure and, in the case of the Norwegians, not necessarily with imperial connections.

Notes

I am grateful to Bjørn Enge Bertelsen and the anonymous readers for insightful comments on this chapter.

1. An internationally well-known example is found in the Pippi Longstocking tales by Swedish author Astrid Lindgren concerning Pippi's buccaneering father, who sailed from Sweden long ago and established himself as king of an island in the 'South Seas'. More recent media stories in Scandinavia have connected Lindstrom's fiction about Pippi's father with examples of actual Swedes who settled in the Pacific Islands. The view taken in Lindgren's books of the 'South Seas natives' over which Pippi's father reigns is derogatory, but the tales aptly illustrate the Scandinavian genre of romantic stories about family members resident in the Pacific Islands.
2. All translations are my own unless otherwise noted.
3. Grünnadier Blahe to Admiral Maitland, 1839, 'European and American seasmen are domiciled on [New Georgia]', Despatches – A 1282, p. 825, SLNSW.

Archives Consulted

State Library of New South Wales (SLNSW), Sydney.

References

Cheyne, A. 1852. *A Description of Islands in the Western Pacific Ocean, North and South of the Equator: With Sailing Directions: Together with their Productions, Manners and Customs of the Natives, and, Vocabularies of their Various Languages.* London: J.D. Potter.

Dannevig, B. 1976. *Sydhavet i Sol og Storm: Fra norsk skipsfarts pionértid i Stillehavet.* Oslo: Bibliografisk Forlag.

Dunmore, J. 1991. *Who's Who in Pacific Navigation.* Honolulu: University of Hawai'i Press.

Evening Post (Wellington). 1897. 'The Seladon Disaster: Further Particulars. Two Thousand Miles in an Open Boat. By Telegraph from Auckland, 21 August'. 23 August.

Findlay, A.G. 1877. *A Directory for the Navigations of the Pacific Ocean: With Description of Its Coasts, Islands, Etc., from the Strait of Magalhaens to the Arctic Sea, and Those of Asia and Australia: Its Winds, Currents and Other Phenomena.* London: Published for Richard Holmes Laurie.

Hviding, E. 1996. *Guardians of Marovo Lagoon: Practice, Place, and Politics in Maritime Melanesia.* Honolulu: University of Hawai'i Press.

Oftedal, L. (ed.). 1897. *Beretningen om 'Seladon''s sørgelige forlis samt mandskabets redning og ophold paa Sofiaøen i Det Stille Ocean: Uddrag af 'Stavanger Aftenblad''s artikler og breve fra mandskaberne.* Stavanger: 'Aftenbladet''s Forlag. Reprinted 1935, new facsimile edition 1997.

Pedersen, H. 1981. *Seladon og hennes menn.* Stavanger: Dreyer.

Rio, K.M. 1999. *Oceania gjenoppdaget i Bergen: Reiser i Bergen Museums samlinger fra Stillehavet.* Bergen: Bergen University Museum.

Smith, B. 1985. *European Vision and the South Pacific, 1768–1850: A Study in the History of Art and Ideas.* New Haven, C.T.: Yale University Press.

Spriggs, M. 1997. *The Island Melanesians.* Oxford: Blackwell.

Starbuck, A. 1878. *History of the American Whale Fishery from Its Earliest Inception to the Year 1876.* Washington, D.C.: Commission of Fish and Fisheries.

Thomas, N. 2003. *Cook: The Extraordinary Voyages of Captain James Cook.* New York: Walker.

◉⟫ 8

Adventurous Adaptability in the South Sea

Norwegians in 'the Terrible Solomons', ca. 1870–1930

Edvard Hviding

Numerous Norwegians in Remote Islands

I shall recount stories about the diverse activities and remarkable survival abilities of a handful of Norwegians who settled long ago in a
certain Pacific archipelago, well-known to me through anthropological
fieldwork over more than twenty-five years.[1] This is the Solomon Islands, a group of large, volcanic, mountainous islands covered in rainforest and fringed by coral reef lagoons and mangrove swamps, located
in the tropical southwestern Pacific in the cultural and geographical
region referred to as Melanesia or the 'Black Islands'.

In 1897, the first resident representative of imperial rule in the British
Solomon Islands Protectorate, natural scientist Charles M. Woodford,
provided in his report for the preceding year a 'census' of the protectorate's 'foreign population'. That census is noteworthy not for its numbers but for its demography. The British Empire's new colonial outpost
in the Pacific had about fifty largely 'white' foreign residents, only men:
'33 British subjects, including … two natives of Rotuma, and [a] Fijian
half-caste, seven Norwegians, seven French, two Swedes, one each German and Portuguese, and one doubtful' (Woodford 1897: 5–6). About
half were commodity traders who had lived there since before British
imperial interests arrived in 1893. Only four were missionaries, and the
rest were listed as seamen and employees of traders. That as many as
seven Norwegians resided and engaged in trade, shipping, plantation
development and other business in the Solomon Islands as early as
1896 is remarkable and little known in Norwegian history.

In fact, there is little written documentation at all about these early
Norwegian settlers in the Solomons. The only exception among the
individuals whose biographies are examined here is a famous man
named Oscar Svensen, whose career has been described by historian

Judith Bennett (1981) and whose descendants in Brisbane have deposited letters and other materials in Australian university libraries.[2] In Norway it has been difficult to find information, probably since few of the men in question were signed on to Norwegian ships. A particularly important source of information about expatriate residents of the colonial Solomon Islands is *The Early European Settlers of the Solomon Islands,* a 466-page illustrated book by Australian independent scholar Graeme Golden (1993). This work combines diverse (and often obscure) materials and is the best source also for the Norwegian settlers. Additional bits of information are found in Bennett's colonial history *Wealth of the Solomons* (1987), and scattered notes occur in the news magazine *Pacific Islands Monthly,* which, prior to the Second World War, ran columns about the European settlers in the islands, including obituaries. Beyond these varied but scarce sources, unravelling the life stories of Norwegians in the colonial Solomon Islands has involved many conversations with up to three generations of descendants in the islands and with village elders who remembered individual Norwegians and, in some cases, had worked for them.

The stories that follow about Woodford's seven Norwegians (and some more) are fragmented narratives of diversity and surprise, steeped in images of the mystical 'South Sea' that grew familiar in nineteenth-century Norway. Norwegian seamen who had experienced that exotic maritime world returned home and told their families, friends and less worldly colleagues stories about oceans, islands and islanders, dangerous and desirable (for details, see chapter 7, this volume). But some never returned, instead becoming island residents of what Norwegians referred to as *i Sydhavet* ('in the South Sea'). Some arrived precariously as shipwrecked castaways among potentially hostile tribal islanders, others voluntarily left their ships in island ports or in the harbours of Australia and New Zealand, from which many paths led to the islands. In the late nineteenth century it would have been easy to be hooked by romantic tales told in those major ports about adventures waiting in the South Sea. Few places were more mysterious, and more attractive to serious adventurers, than the Solomon Islands.

Tales of the Solomons

After some short-lived fame in the sixteenth century, the Solomon Islands received scant attention in the minds, charts and logbooks of European seafarers until the late eighteenth century. The islands were first visited by Europeans in 1568, when Spanish nobleman and explorer

Alvaro de Mendaña y Neyra arrived unexpectedly after a long but far from eventful voyage from Peru. On a quest to find an unknown great southern continent, Mendaña's men instead met with tropical diseases and mostly hostile islanders, who were offended when the Spanish rejected their first offer of a gift, consisting of a quarter of a boy, which they urged Mendaña to eat. In relation to his employer, the governor of Peru, Mendaña had to make the best of what he saw as a dismal discovery. He chose to interpret a glimpse of a shimmering mineral rock as an indicator of rich gold deposits in the inhospitable lands, and daringly named the islands after King Solomon, with reference to that biblical character's legendary lands of Ophir, from which untold wealth had been obtained (Amherst and Thomson 1901; Jack-Hinton 1969).

A new expedition by Mendaña in 1595 to build a European settlement in the islands was lethally unsuccessful for most of those involved, including Mendaña himself, and the 'Isles of Solomon' faded into obscurity in European minds. It was their fate to be 'discovered, lost, and found again' (Amherst and Thomson 1901: i). The islands were in fact not revisited by Europeans until two hundred years after Mendaña's discovery, when official British and French expeditions explored the Pacific Ocean, still searching for a fabled great southern continent. In 1767 HMS *Swallow,* commanded by Lieutenant Philip Carteret, sailed through parts of the Solomons. Carteret's unseaworthy ship and scurvy-ridden crew desperately needed repairs, water and fresh provisions. Encounters with hostile islanders in the Santa Cruz group of the eastern Solomons made it difficult to cover those needs, and Carteret sailed on, not realizing that he was in fact in the fabled Solomons. For his 'rediscovery' of Santa Cruz (thus named by the Spanish visitors of 1595), he provided the short-lived name of 'Queen Charlotte's Islands', then sailed on to find safe landing and provisions in the Bismarck islands off New Guinea.

About a year after, a French expedition led by Louis-Antoine de Bougainville sailed along the major islands of the Solomon Islands group and named several, including the northernmost and largest, for which the expedition leader chose his own name. Further (re)discoveries of the Solomons were made in 1788 by Lieutenant Shortland of the Royal Navy, when part of the First Fleet to Botany Bay sailed along the south coasts of the main islands on its return from Australia. From about 1800 American whaling ships began calling at the large, populous and well-forested islands for water, wood and safe harbours in the tropical cyclone season, and European contact became regular.[3] By 1850, the Solomon Islands group was embedded in an expanding colonial economy that involved the trade of exotic products from the sea and, soon, the recruitment of labourers for sugar plantations in Australia and Fiji. In 1893 the Solomon Islands became a British protectorate, an imperial construction intended to safeguard Melanesians from unregulated labour recruitment, to stop local warfare and attacks on Europeans and to secure British privileges over colonial trade and plantation development. By 1910, following a couple of turbulent decades, warriors had been disarmed in nearly all of the Solomons (partly by colonial power and partly from local initiative), and white missionaries were busy converting the islanders to one of many strands of Christianity. The archipelago drifted into a peripheral existence in the British Empire, with a colonial economy dominated by copra.[4]

From the mid-nineteenth century it had been common knowledge among coastal islanders in the Pacific that European seafaring traders desired bêche-de-mer (dried sea cucumber), turtle shells, mother-of-pearl and so forth from the coral reef, and gradually also oil products of the ubiquitous coconut tree. Soon, it was copra, the oil's dried raw material, that became the significant commodity. Across the Pacific, including in the Solomon Islands, islanders started clearing coastal forest to plant coconut trees. Twenty halves of dried coconut flesh were stringed on a length of fibre rope, and the 'one-string' commodity became a reality. In the Solomons, islanders would typically wait for the next visit by a small sailing vessel of a European trader, who would bring iron and steel tools, weapons, cloth and tobacco. With islanders as crew, traders sailed over stormy seas and among uncharted reefs. Landing was made at village after village for trade, which took place on the beach or with villagers who paddled loaded canoes out to an anchored vessel. It was a risky business. Until about 1900, villagers in most parts of the Solomons were engaged in endemic intertribal warfare and well armed, and attacks on traders were numerous (Golden 1993: 434). Ironically, this danger to itinerant traders was reinforced by the trade itself, which supplied islanders with increasingly effective weapons, including steel axes and firearms.

With purchased goods stowed on board the ship, the trader would sail towards the next village and repeat the trading procedures. Some traders appointed local agents in the form of villagers who received a quantum of trade goods to exchange while waiting for their employer's next visit. With the ship fully loaded with copra and other commodities, a course was set for the trader's local base, which could be a simple house of local materials or a more elaborate trade station with a comfortable house and a trade store. Some financially pressed traders spent most of their time on board their little ships, a life that provided fresh air and seafood, but had its unpleasantries, particularly in the form of the cockroaches that invaded any copra cargo. In the early days, each trader used his own vessel to transport copra to the main ports of the Solomons, at which large sailing ships, later steamers, arrived from Australia to deliver and pick up cargo. Traders had to cover the freight costs to Australia, so profit margins were slim. Later, regular trade routes were established whereby large ships would sail through the archipelago to a selection of smaller ports and purchase copra 'on the beach'. From the late nineteenth century, a number of European traders in the Solomons gained increasing control over the elements of copra trade by purchasing coastal lands, hiring labour and establishing private coconut plantations, while continuing to operate trade stores and small ships, the latter also used for labour recruitment.

In the late 1800s tropical diseases and the danger of attack from islanders gave white men a short life expectancy in the Solomons. But the islands also gained a reputation for being rich in cultivable land, natural resources and labour; somewhat unrealistically, they were seen as a promising place for hardworking and fearless Europeans to accumulate wealth through copra trade, land purchase and plantation development. For adventurous (or desperate) white men those potentials and more utopian rumours balanced the dangers. Although, as previously said, profit margins tended to be thin, from the 1890s there were several successful long-term resident traders who did live comfortably in the Solomons in large houses and with unlimited workforces, and who could afford annual recreational travel to Sydney.

The writer and adventurer Jack London visited the Solomon Islands in 1908 on what would be the last leg of his Pacific 'cruise' with his wife and friends on board the yacht *Snark* (London 1911a). London enjoyed spending time with residential traders and planters and travelled with them throughout the islands. 'The Terrible Solomons', one of several lurid short stories in his *South Sea Tales*, conveyed a particular view of the predicament of the 'white man' in the early twentieth-century Solomon Islands (London 1911b: 135–36):

> There is no gainsaying that the Solomons are a hard-bitten bunch of islands. On the other hand, there are worse places in the world. But to the new chum who has no constitutional understanding of men and life in the rough, the Solomons may indeed prove terrible.
>
> It is true that fever and dysentery are perpetually on the walk-about, that loathsome skin diseases abound, that the air is saturated with a poison that bites into every pore, cut, or abrasion and plants malignant ulcers, and that many strong men who escape dying there return as wrecks to their own countries. It is also true that the natives of the Solomons are a wild lot, with a hearty appetite for human flesh and a fad for collecting human heads. Their highest instinct of sportsmanship is to catch a man

with his back turned and to smite him a cunning blow with a tomahawk that severs the spinal column at the base of the brain.

It is equally true that on some islands, such as Malaita, the profit and loss account of social intercourse is calculated in homicides. Heads are a medium of exchange, and white heads are extremely valuable. Very often a dozen villages make a jack-pot, which they fatten moon by moon, against the time when some brave warrior presents a white man's head, fresh and gory, and claims the pot.

All the foregoing is quite true, and yet there are white men who have lived in the Solomons a score of years and who feel homesick when they go away from them. A man needs only to be careful – and lucky – to live a long time in the Solomons; but he must also be of the right sort.

London himself had to leave 'the terrible Solomons' after succumbing to malaria, festering sores and various consequences of malnutrition. What is not directly evident in his tales of the Solomons is how he and his wife travelled around the islands not on *Snark* but on board the schooner *Minota*, owned by seasoned Solomons veteran Oscar Svensen – a Norwegian captain who had by 1908 been a major actor in the plantation and trade business for seventeen years, living and working in those islands deemed by London to be so 'terrible' to the white man.

Norwegians in the Colonial Solomons: Traces of a 'Different' Sort of Man

When I first arrived in the Solomon Islands in 1986 it was the beginning of eighteen months of anthropological field research that has led to a continued engagement with these islands and their people. In the earliest morning hours of 14 April I was standing on the upper deck of the interisland ferry MV *Iu Mi Nao* as the ship slowly entered the great Marovo Lagoon, an extraordinary place located in the New Georgia group of the western Solomons. I watched the stars in the sky and the bioluminescence that outlined small and large fish in the dark sea while having a conversation in English with Luke Pitu, an elderly gentleman who was a Methodist minister in one of the lagoon villages. He asked me where I was from, and as I started explaining about the distant land of Norway he smiled and said,

> Norway, yes! That is a place we know here, for, you see, we have Norwegians here. Paddle over to an island further along this way called Mahoro. An old man by the name of Erik Andersen lives there. He is from Norway, or rather, his father was from Norway. And then there is the Paulsen family further down west in the Roviana Lagoon. You must go there and ask for Peter Wick, his surname is Paulsen and his father was from Norway, too.

I had no idea that such connections between the Solomon Islands and Norway existed. But I followed Pitu's advice. The Andersen and Paulsen families welcomed me with warm hospitality and a desire to learn more about Norway, a country about which they did not know much but saw themselves as connected to. In the New Georgia islands kinship is reckoned bilaterally and every person belongs socially to, and can claim land and sea rights and inherit from, the kin of both mother and father (Hviding 2003b). Thus, for the Andersens and Paulsens it was logical to look at 'Norwegians' or 'Norway' as one of the lineages from which they descended. This notion has remained through the generations, and being partly 'of' Norway has become integral to the social identity of these families.

In September 1987, as I was about to leave the Solomons, Erik Andersen arranged a grand farewell party for me, during which speeches were held with the expression of hope that I would find their kin in Norway, and also that I would someday return to my Solomon Islands 'family'. I had come to realize that for the Andersen and Paulsen families, their Norwegian connections had a very different meaning from that of the British or Australian ancestry recognized by other 'part European' families I had met. On my subsequent visits I have met islanders who carry the family name Nielsen, descendants of a Norwegian known from Woodford's 1896 census. Others have contacted me with a wish to talk about their forefathers Andy Andresen and Fred Ericksen, whom they thought might be from Norway, or at least Scandinavian.[5]

The seven Norwegians enumerated by Woodford were Julius Walter Andersen, Alec. Ellingsen, Lars Nielsen, J.G.B. Nerdrum, Søfren Nerdrum (referred to in English materials as 'Solfren'), Charles Olsen and Oscar Svensen. The latter's brother Theodor had died of malaria in 1896, just before the census. The Svensen brothers ran their business in cooperation with the two Nerdrum brothers, but in September 1896, just after the census, Søfren Nerdrum also died of malaria. Charles Olsen, who apparently arrived in the Solomon Islands in 1894, is assumed to have died in 1897 (Golden 1993: 288). Little if anything is known about the mysterious 'Alec. Ellingsen', although Woodford's report of 1896 tells us that both he and Olsen were among the few traders who possessed their own ships.

From the turn of the century several more Norwegians arrived in the Solomons, more or less connected to the seven already there in 1896. The three brothers John, Leif and Niels Schrøder are on record as employed in the Solomons from 1905 by Oscar Svensen, as plantation managers and masters of trading vessels. They were from the town of Kragerø on Norway's southeast coast, and having sailed the world's oceans with their father, Captain Schrøder, they settled in Australia in the late 1880s. Niels Schrøder joined the Australian Imperial Force and fought in France during the First World War, but returned to the Solomons to continue his work in plantations and shipping, this time for himself, not Svensen. He retired to Brisbane in 1927. His younger brothers, John and Leif (known in the islands as 'Lafe'), worked in the Solomons for many more years before the Second World War.

In 1905, one Norwegian seaman arrived in the Solomon Islands in an extraordinary way. Nineteen-year-old Anton Daniel Olsen worked on the U.S. four-masted bark *Susquehanna*, then the largest wooden ship in the world. While transporting a heavy cargo of ore from New Caledonia, *Susquehanna* sailed into a storm and foundered without loss of life. The crew and two passengers drifted towards the Solomon Islands. After nine days at sea they sighted the large island of San Cristobal (now Makira) – and soon after they were rescued by Oscar Svensen, who took all twenty of them on board his schooner *Leueneuwa*.[6]

We can only imagine the amazement felt by a nineteen-year-old shipwrecked Norwegian sailor adrift in the middle of the Pacific when he was welcomed on board a vessel with a crew of Melanesians and a Norwegian captain. 'Tony' Olsen was to reside in the Solomon Islands until his death in 1952, the only exception being a few years in Australia during and right after the Second World War. Over the years he worked for a range of employers (including, for a time, his rescuer, Captain Svensen) as a master of trading vessels and as a labour recruiter, was involved in gold prospecting and bought land and developed a plantation on Guadalcanal, while also operating several smaller ships of his own. A heavy drinker, Olsen participated in a particularly disreputable alcohol-fuelled punitive expedition against the Kwaio of Malaita in 1927, following the murder by Kwaio warriors of District Officer William Bell and his islander policemen (Keesing and Corris 1980). From that exploit and associated activities he appears to have become known as 'Devil-Tony' (Støre 1967).

The last Norwegian seaman to settle in the colonial Solomons seems to have been Victor Olaf Vilhelm Paulsen from Oslo. Sometime before 1920 he disembarked from the Swedish steamer on which he worked to arrive in the islands at the dawn of a new era. No longer were there any attacks on Europeans by islanders, and a few large British and Australian companies had taken over most of the trade and plantation business. Paulsen arrived in a well-organized colonial economy that immediately offered him employment.

Only two women of Norwegian background appear in this male-dominated sphere. Henriette Schrøder, the sister of Niels, Leif and John, married Solomon Islands old-timer Oscar Svensen in Australia in 1900, but she was not to spend much time in the islands. Nellie Berg, daughter of a Norwegian sea captain in Oscar Svensen's circle of acquaintances in Brisbane, arrived in the colonial headquarters at Tulagi in 1913 and married John Schrøder at the Anglican mission. John and Nellie had three children, all born in Brisbane, but the family continued to live at their plantation in Ghatere on the north coast of Santa Isabel until 1923, when recurrent malaria among the children made them return to Brisbane. They lived in Santa Isabel again between 1928 and 1931.

Golden (1993: 434) documents that thirty-three resident Europeans were 'killed by natives' in the Solomons between 1878 and 1915. Attacks on the crews of ships that passed through the islands were also numerous but are not included in Golden's estimates of violent deaths of Europeans. In addition, a considerable number of early European residents died of malaria and other tropical diseases. In this bleak context, the Norwegians who settled in the Solomons appear collectively in a remarkable light, since not one was murdered by what were at the time perceived as 'treacherous natives'. The deaths that did occur among Norwegians were caused by malaria, pneumonia and other diseases (perhaps aided by alcohol), with one exception: 67-year-old 'Tony' Olsen died in 1952 on his plantation in Guadalcanal from a gunshot to the head, after yet another alcohol-related quarrel with his Australian wife of forty-three years.

This initial glimpse of an early Norwegian presence in the Solomon Islands portrays the lives and careers of these men as pioneers, founders, entrepreneurs, employers and employees in a fast-growing colonial economy. Whereas some did operate in the 'wake' of colonialism, others assumed prominent roles in building and operating the very movements that ultimately caused that wake. Several of them exploited their diffuse political status in the new colony, as 'expatriates' not associated with the British Empire. While a few developed large plantations and companies, others moved in and out of different types of employment, filling small but important practical niches in one of the empire's least prioritized colonies. Taken together, the lives they were to live in the Solomons provide fascinating insights into cross-cultural encounters and situations on the beach that could be both dangerous and economically rewarding.

The personal histories that follow below also provide a specific perspective on political-economic relations in a peripheral imperial scene over a fifty-year period. From 1870 to 1920 Britain's presence in the Solomons developed from unsystematic trading attempts under threats of local violence, with random punitive expeditions by the Royal Navy against headhunters and other troublesome 'natives', through the establishment of a protectorate, to the colonial operation of a well-regulated commercial system of plantations. That economy was shaken by the international financial crisis in the interwar period and then collapsed altogether as the Second World War descended on the Solomons in 1942. The histories of the Norwegian residents in the early colonial Solomons provide an altogether different account from those based on imperial sources and empire-centric perspectives.

Some of the Norwegian settlers entered into long-term, stable relationships with local women, which is reflected in their many descendants in the islands who still use Norwegian family names. Entering into such relationships, in some cases formalized as marriage after the arrival of missionaries, had been a widespread strategy among European resident traders since the first arrivals around 1870. Living with a local woman could improve trade opportunities and often enhanced security against raids. The woman's extended family had self-interest in the long-term local residence of a trader, who provided reliable access to tobacco, steel axes and other weapons and tools and who could obtain firearms in areas where intertribal warfare prevailed. Although traders had many ways of acquiring land from chiefs, cohabitation or marriage with a local woman in areas where women had their own land rights provided extra strength. In the islands of the western Solomons, Guadalcanal and Isabel, prevailing forms of kinship and land tenure imply that nearly all women have recognized rights in land. A woman from those islands who entered into a relationship with a white trader could thus offer him access to land and would have a powerful position vis-à-vis him, grounded as she was in the immediate social and political circumstances. Should her husband not treat her respectfully, his business and personal security would be equally jeopardized.

Many elders I spoke to remembered Norwegian traders and seamen as somehow different from the majority of white men. They reminded me that, contrary to some of their European contemporaries, no Norwegian ever met a violent death in conflict with the locals. Some lived in the islands for so long that they seemed to have become immune to both disease and violence, and a few even managed to retire with sizeable fortunes at the end of their careers, relocating to Australia. Taken together, these observations point to a perception of early Norwegians in the Solomons as tough men who were also just. Unlike some traders of the time they were not known for belittling, threatening, beating or killing their employees. Some of the Norwegians, I was told, were even so civilized as to rarely even swear. But while behaving well in some respects, they were also known for strict discipline and expectations of hard work from their employees on ships, at trade stations and on plantations. Some Norwegians also drank heavily, at least in periods with easy access to alcohol. During binges they could be rough indeed, singing Scandinavian drinking songs, swearing and being prone to uncontrolled shooting with the pistols and rifles every white man in the Solomon Islands possessed and rarely kept out of sight.

Beyond such perceptive recollections by old islanders who knew them, the early Norwegians in the Solomons are of interest in relation to other resident Europeans. The Norwegians were all experienced seamen. Woodford's 1896 census highlights this by reporting that six out of a total of twenty-one small ships operated by traders were owned by Norwegians. Some, like Oscar Svensen, were qualified master mariners. It is reasonable to believe that long maritime careers across the world's oceans and ports had developed a heightened ability for travel and interaction in unknown, potentially dangerous situations and environments.

The coastal populations of the Solomon Islands were themselves of a profoundly maritime orientation. Like so many other Pacific Islanders, they were able to navigate across the open sea to neighbouring islands by following stars, currents and wave patterns, and it appears that they had considerable respect for hardworking Europeans with solid maritime backgrounds. Of course, many non-Norwegian European residents in the Solomons had similar backgrounds, but a good proportion of them were poorly qualified Englishmen or Australians, for whom boarding a ship bound for the Solomons in an Australian port might have been a last resort. Once in the islands they often met with a strenuous job for which they were ill prepared, perhaps as an established trader's solitary representative on a small, remote trading station. Tales I have been told suggest that experienced seamen like Lars Nielsen, Oscar Svensen and Julius Walter Andersen were viewed by islanders as exceptionally observant people, not easily deceived or taken by surprise. Such qualities were useful in the face of local war strategies that relied on deception, ambush and attack by axe from behind.

Another trait that seems to have set Norwegians apart was the perception that they were not connected to the colonial power. This points to well-known aspects of culture and society in the Solomon Islands and the Pacific Islands more generally: islanders possess effective cultural mechanisms for distinguishing between different kinds of people arriving from the sea (Hviding 2003a). In parts of the Solomons, white people are still referred to as 'people from ships' – a definition that has several subcategories related to practices of power and violence. Norwegians appear not to have been perceived by islanders as linked to the Royal Navy, although Lars Nielsen sold coal to visiting British warships and Oscar Svensen showed lavish hospitality towards visiting Royal Navy officers. In other cases, however, Norwegians were actually allied with the islanders in projects frowned upon by the British colonial power. At Marau Sound, where Oscar Svensen was first based, he is still remembered for helping to arm the local people in their warfare with inland groups between 1891 and 1892 (Bennett 1981). At the time, an act from the British high commissioner in Fiji prohibited the supply of firearms to indigenous people in the Pacific, but Svensen believed this did not apply to him, as he did not see himself or his ships as subject to British law.

The Solomon Islands trading history from 1870 to 1920 contains numerous examples of plantation managers and ships' captains who meted out hard physical punishments to their Melanesian workers and ships' crews. Some even went so far as to shoot and kill local employees. The colonial administration did make some efforts to investigate repeated complaints against violent Europeans, and some were deported. Physical punishment could be particularly humiliating for those who worked in plantations far from home – for example, the plantations of New Georgia had labourers mostly from Malaita. Those workers could not seek support from their fellow tribesmen when punished or otherwise insulted. Some brutal plantation managers were killed by internally rioting employees. Norwegians, however, were viewed as distinctly different from their British and Australian colleagues in that they rarely hit or beat up their employees.

It appears that a large proportion of the resident Europeans were heavy drinkers, and it was quite normal to be foulmouthed when addressing islanders. What Europeans of the time did not comprehend was that in most communities in the Solomons, cursing at someone or addressing a person in derogatory terms was to transgress powerful taboos. Violation of such rules generated demands for compensation, and a deep cultural divide could develop between a trader who cursed at his workers or at islanders he did business with and those affected by his foul mouth. There is little reason to believe that Norwegian seamen were particularly God-fearing or modest in their expressive manners, but a distinct pattern is discernible from the passing mention of the veteran Lars Nielsen's 'calm' way of interacting with the islanders, an old Marovo man's memory of Julius Walter Andersen as 'kind and helpful to the people in the villages' and Bennett's description of Oscar Svensen: 'Unlike so many of his European associates Svensen dealt with Solomon Islanders as human beings' (1987: 54–55).

Versatile Lives: Norwegian Careers in the Solomons

It was a common understanding among European residents in the nineteenth-century Solomons that islanders were not to be trusted. The many attacks that ended in a trader's death (and sometimes the loss of his head) served to confirm this view. Traders often lived on small islands close to the coasts of the main islands but far away from co- lonial powers, and they were at the mercy of local people in relation to both trade and protection. Well into the twentieth century it was of the utmost importance to have good relationships with chiefs, or- dinary islanders and employees from other parts of the archipelago. By about 1920, local warfare had all but disappeared, and other con- siderations became more important. Resident Europeans now had to maintain the local desire for trade by contributing to new projects on the village level, but village initiatives were increasingly in the hands of missionaries and their local followers. Traders also needed to build good relationships with the powerful British and Australian companies that were taking over and centralizing a commodity business that had so far been managed by solitary traders. Every one of the dozen or so Norwegians who appear in the history of this period was in his own way and time involved in the first stages of the colonial period, from the time when the Solomons could be seen as a truly dangerous place (and perhaps 'terrible', as Jack London would have it) until the archi- pelago had become the scene of a stable colonial economy supported by influential churches.

For closer insights into these Norwegian careers I start with Lars Nielsen, the first to settle in the Solomons. I then develop a narrative about some Norwegians whose modest careers reflected the diversity of economic life in the early years of this remote British colony before shifting my focus to the massively successful career of Oscar Svensen, who personified the dreams of success shared by all island traders.

Lars Nielsen was on a ship of unknown nationality that was wrecked in the notorious Bougainville Strait in 1875.[7] With his English shipmate Frank Wickham, Nielsen was rescued by the already legendary captain Alexander Ferguson, who had sailed and traded in the Solomon Islands and New Guinea for ten years and was well connected to the chiefs of the Shortland Islands and southern Bougainville. Nielsen and Wick- ham's immediate employment by Ferguson gave them a good start. When Ferguson was killed by an axe blow on the coast of Bougainville in 1880, both former castaways were already well established. Wickham remained in the western Solomons and became the most prominent trader in the Roviana Lagoon, retiring to Sydney in 1908 as a wealthy man. Nielsen was stationed first on the island of Savo near Guadalcanal to run Ferguson's trade, but soon began operating his own. By 1888, he had set aside enough money to buy the small island of Gavutu in the Nggela group. This gave him considerable privilege when a colonial administration was established in 1896 at Tulagi, a large natural harbour with Gavutu in its centre. Nielsen had previously assisted the new resident commissioner, C.M. Woodford, who had explored the nature and people of the islands during 1886–88 by using Nielsen's ketch *Amelia*. Woodford described Nielsen as a tranquil man with good relationships with the islanders, and the proud owner of a gold watch given to him by the president of the United States for rescuing the crew of an American whaler wrecked in the 1880s. In a footnote Woodford (1890: 22n) wrote incorrectly that Nielsen had recently been 'assassinated by natives'. Nielsen and his crew had in fact been attacked in 1889 while trading copra on Rendova in New Georgia, but he had survived.

And so when Woodford returned to the Solomon Islands in 1896 to establish colonial rule, he may have been surprised to find Nielsen still thriving, with a flourishing business at Gavutu. The Norwegian managed a large trade station and owned a comfortable house, a schooner, a cutter, two islands in Nggela and one in Roviana, and had a lucrative contract with the British admiralty for supplying coal to the increasing number of ships from the Royal Navy that visited the Solomons.[8] When missionaries started arriving Nielsen was helpful towards them, unlike many other traders. He hosted the Catholics who arrived in 1898 while they waited for their mission station to be built on the island of Rua Sura off Guadalcanal, and when the Methodists arrived in 1902 he gave them the island of Banga in Roviana Lagoon. It appears that Nielsen, who had a local wife and probably several children, had planned to stay in the Solomon Islands for the rest of his life. However, around 1902 his health deteriorated and he decided to leave the tropics. He offered his properties, his ships and the Royal Navy coal contract to the Australian company Burns, Philp & Co. for GBP 4,000, an offer the company did not accept. Nielsen then left the Solomons and travelled alone to Sydney, where he sold the whole lot to Oscar Svensen for GBP 3,000. What happened later to Lars Nielsen is uncertain, but it has been suggested that he returned to Norway. He had lived a remarkably calm life for twenty-seven years in a place Jack London had yet to describe as 'terrible'. He had survived tropical diseases and attacks from armed islanders. Nielsen cleverly dispersed economic risk by pursuing a range of activities (the coal contract was essential) so that he could continue in business when copra prices slumped and cargo rates rose.

Another Norwegian seaman, Charles Olsen, arrived in the Solomons in unknown circumstances around 1894 and probably only lived until 1897. He ended up on the small island of Santa Ana east of Makira, where he registered as a copra trader and had a local 'wife'. From Bennett's analysis of colonial trade in the Solomons we learn that in 1896 Olsen managed to buy about twenty-five tons of copra from Santa Ana, a small island with modest copra production and little access to other desired export goods. The copra steamer that visited minor trade stations such as Olsen's gave him a 'beach price' of GBP 2 a ton, which gave him an income in 1896 of GBP 50. Interestingly, Bennett compares Olsen's business with that of Lars Nielsen. In 1896 Nielsen shipped out of Gavutu fifty tons of copra, one ton of bêche-de-mer and a quantity of mother-of-pearl and turtle shells, and made altogether GBP 200 (Bennett 1987: 54–55).

Julius Walter Andersen is a contrast to the Norwegians who established their own trading stations. Andersen appears fleetingly in historical notes and travel accounts, since he worked for long periods as a ship engine mechanic in the colonial capital of Tulagi. My close relationship over many years with his descendants has made it possible to unveil more about his long life in the Solomons. It is believed that he arrived in the islands around 1896. Little is known of his background in Norway or of how he came to the Pacific, but he was certainly a seaman. To his son, Erik, Andersen told stories about first landing in Bougainville – perhaps voluntarily, perhaps after shipwreck – with shipmates who were then dispersed into trade and plantations. In Andersen's case early engagements took him through successive locations – from southern Bougainville to the Shortland Islands, via Rendova and on to the central Solomons, where he was for a time an employee of Lars Nielsen at Gavutu.

Walter Andersen (it seems he omitted 'Julius') maintained a modest but exceptionally long career through forty years as a multipurpose employee for different trading companies, interspersed by unsuccessful attempts to manage his own trade. Andersen worked as copra trader, trade station manager and shipmaster in some of the most violent parts of the archipelago. He was also a mechanic with expertise in the small diesel engines found in most small sailing vessels used by traders and the colonial administration. In Tulagi, Andersen's services as engineer and mechanic were much needed, but he was reputed to work slowly while charging by the hour and to take regular breaks for beer.[9] A man of many talents, Andersen was skilled in forging machine parts. He probably had a profitable monopoly given that there were no other qualified mechanics in the protectorate, and a base at Tulagi provided regular work on the often poorly maintained traders' vessels, which had to call at that central port from time to time. Andersen's career, extending from the earliest colonial times well into the 1930s, thus differs from those of most other resident Norwegians. While the latter lived relatively stable lives on stations and plantations and developed modest or larger-scale business, Andersen remained mobile, with frequent changes of employer and work type. Despite this unstable career, Andersen survived, remained active and did not succumb to disease or violence.

Andersen appears to not have had a family until he settled in Marovo Lagoon around 1920. Soon he had two daughters and a son with Dima, a woman of central Marovo (in order of birth, Jessie, Erik and Gladys). He lived and worked for some years in central and southern Marovo, running a trade station and operating a small ship around the New Georgia islands. But ultimately he left his family and returned to Tulagi. He continued to pay visits to Marovo from time to time, and his son, Erik, remembers him from his childhood as a man past his prime then, at least fifty. In the local traditions of the places where he spent much time and in his children's recollections, Andersen is remembered as a periodically heavy drinker. While he could be rude towards his local workers when drinking, he usually interacted with islanders in respectful and fair ways. But he disliked missionaries and had a continuing feud with the powerful Methodist leader Rev. J.F. Goldie. One Sunday, Andersen sailed past the mission village of Patutiva as Goldie was preaching there, and he took his gun and fired it in the air while yelling insults at the missionary. Andersen also had medical interests, and in Marovo he is remembered for giving injections and other treatments against yaws and other afflictions. His children also recall that he had a large book in which he recorded local knowledge about herbal medicine.

Andersen's long career in the islands was unimpressive in financial terms, but impressive in terms of individual achievement and sheer dedication to survival. Whereas Oscar Svensen saw rapid growth of his business and overall influence in the colony and ultimately operated a small trading empire as a central director, with many submanagers handling 'the field' for him, a man like Julius Walter Andersen was himself constantly out in that 'field' and had to manage at close hand the shifting challenges of unstable, often hostile situations. He had to negotiate and renegotiate conditions for trade with islanders without assistance from outside, since he had no particular connection to the colonial powers or to more powerful European traders. He was probably more than sixty when he died: in the *Pacific Islands Monthly*, April 1935, it is stated that Julius Walter Andersen, old-timer in the Solomons, had died of tuberculosis in the hospital in Tulagi in March that year (Golden 1993: 76). Andersen has many descendants in the Solomons – a quick count in 1987 showed more than eighty.

Victor Olaf Vilhelm Paulsen (1886–ca. 1937) is listed in the 1900 census for the town of Kristiania (now Oslo) as son of Olaf Vilhelm Paulsen (a 'casual worker') and his wife, Elise Paulsen. Paulsen is on record as a seaman resident in the Solomons since 1920. He arrived as crew on a Swedish steamer that sailed regularly from Europe through Australia to ports in the Solomons and New Guinea. According to family traditions in the Solomons, Paulsen's primary motivation for becoming a seaman had been wanderlust. Left behind by his ship in Tulagi after a drunken night at the Chinese hotel, he became enthusiastic about the islands. Notified by the colonial administration that he could not stay unless gainfully employed, he quickly got a job as master of a trading vessel for Burns, Philp & Co., by then the leading company in the Solomons. When Paulsen's ship returned to Tulagi from Rabaul in New Guinea to continue freighting copra between those ports for six months, Paulsen reembarked. However, he got left behind again (this time in Rabaul), and the Swedes gave him up. He wrote to his family in Oslo and explained his plans to settle in the Solomons, was reemployed by Burns, Philp & Co., and worked his way from Rabaul to the colonial station and trading centre of Gizo in the western Solomons. Golden (personal communication) noted that Paulsen may have also worked as a shipmaster for Oscar Svensen's companies, during a time when professional divers were hired to gather mother-of-pearl. Later, Paulsen managed a coconut plantation at Vella Lavella, and then was deputy manager for Burns, Philp & Co.'s office in Gizo. He fell in love with Zaza, a woman from Roviana Lagoon, and paid 'bride-price' to her father in the form of shell money and cash. During the early 1930s they had three sons and lived in a large house in the beautiful Vona-vona Lagoon west of Roviana while Paulsen travelled around to inspect company plantations.

Victor Paulsen's late arrival in the Solomons, when British colonial rule, large British and Australian companies and British, Australian and New Zealand missions were joint operators of practically all economic activities, made for a new kind of story. Paulsen settled in the islands at a time when an established colonial economy offered an experienced seaman a variety of interesting jobs. Concurrently, the opportunities for operating one's own business in the old way, as a solitary trader on one's own little island, had been severely limited. Missionaries encouraged villagers not to sell land to Europeans, and the small islands and coastal strips that had been purchased by small-scale old-timer traders and planted with coconut trees had mostly been taken over by large companies. The Solomon Islands had become a smooth-running colonial economy with its own specific niche in the British Empire and within world trade, geared exclusively to the plantation-based production of copra.

And so Paulsen became a supervisor and manager on the large companies' smaller plantations, carrying out some personal trade on the side, in a situation where individual economic entrepreneurship had been curtailed. As for previous Norwegians in the islands, Paulsen's maritime experience was a definite asset, since his work involved the navigation of small ships around New Georgia and over to Choiseul. Like Julius Walter Andersen, Victor Paulsen is remembered as a hard-drinking man. But while Andersen survived in the islands for forty years, Paulsen's drinking habits seem to have contributed to an early death. His son Peter noted to me that Victor always kept up a steady consumption of whisky and water while steering vessels at sea. Sometime between 1936 and 1938 (the exact date is uncertain), during a voyage from New Georgia to Choiseul, he became seriously ill with pneumonia. His crew tried to bring him back to the hospital in Gizo, but the sea was too rough and he died in the house of the Australian Methodist minister in Sasamungga on the southern coast of Choiseul, where his grave still exists today.

Oscar Svensen and the Norwegian Solomon Islands Trading and Planting Company

None of the Norwegians who came to the Solomons had more influence on the development of the colony than Oscar Svensen (1862–1943). Working initially with his brother and other Norwegian partners, Svensen built what would become the largest commercial enterprise in the early twentieth-century Solomon Islands, well before the arrival of large British and Australian companies. A master of trade encounters, economic interaction and business enterprise, Svensen profited first from dealings with islanders still engaged in intertribal warfare, later from shrewd engagements with the colonial power and ultimately from gaining influence over every link in the chain of export trade. Over more than twenty years of continuous residence in the Solomons, he maintained a central position among the traders and planters. He married a Norwegian woman in Brisbane and appears to have no descendants in the islands, but the scale of his business and his general influence on the colony and its economy has made him a household name in the Solomons. As late as 1978 the people of Marau Sound on Guadalcanal – the place where Svensen set up his first station in 1888 – honoured him by naming their new wharf 'Kapitan Marau, Oscar Svensen' (Bennett 1981: 170).

In the last quarter of the nineteenth century Norway was the world's third-largest shipping nation, after the United States and Great Britain. The family-owned Svensen shipping company owned and operated four sailing ships out of the port of Larvik, and the brothers Samuel, Oscar and Theodor Svensen were all among the ships' masters and mates.[10] But steam was taking over. The four Svensen ships were sold during the winter of 1887–88, and the old family company closed down (on the transition from sail to steam, see the chapters by Nygaard and Sætra, this volume). Samuel Svensen passed away that winter, while Oscar (b. 1862) and Theodor (b. 1867) left Larvik for England and then Australia. While southbound they met Captain Schrøder, from the port of Kragerø near Larvik, and when all had disembarked at Melbourne, they established the ship chandler Svensen & Schrøder in 1888. While Oscar remained in Melbourne to take care of that business, Theodor travelled to Sydney, where he took work as the mate of a steamer on the New Zealand route. Then hired to navigate a private yacht from Sydney to Brisbane, he learned about the intense traffic of labourers between the islands of Melanesia and Queensland's sugar plantations. Theodor purchased the topsail schooner *Archimedes* and made several journeys to the Solomons and the New Hebrides (now Vanuatu). Assisted by such men as the young labour recruiter John Cromar (see Cromar 1935), who worked for a while on *Archimedes,* Theodor acquired expertise both in the labour trade and in the difficult art of conducting business on the beaches of exotic islands. In particular, it appears that he became aware of how easily land could be purchased from islanders. Before long Oscar went to sea again, departing in the schooner *Thistle* with a cargo of coal for the Ellice Islands (now Tuvalu). On the return *Thistle* called at Marau Sound on the eastern tip of Guadalcanal, and Oscar, too, discovered the potential for trade and land purchase in the Solomons.

Further details are unclear, but it seems that Oscar, Theodor and Alex Monrad, a man of unknown nationality, sailed to Marau Sound in *Archimedes* in April 1890. They got along well with the local people, decided to establish a station and made a deal for the purchase of the small island of Tavanipupu. Back in Brisbane, Theodor sold *Archimedes,* Monrad withdrew from the enterprise altogether, and Oscar left the ship chandler business in Melbourne. The Svensen brothers prepared for their new project with two other Norwegian brothers they had met in Brisbane, J.G.B. and Søfren Nerdrum. Together they formed the Norwegian Solomon Islands Trading and Planting Company Ltd.[11] All four sailed to Marau in the forty-ton ketch *Siskin,* and the purchase of Tavanipupu was settled with a quantity of firearms and ammunition and some more conventional trading goods. The ambitious new company considered itself Norwegian, and its owners considered themselves exempt from British imperial restrictions on the profitable provision of firearms to islanders. Another advantage was soon discovered. While the Norwegians had been making preparations in Brisbane, trading possibilities at Marau had been suddenly 'improved' when resident Marau traders Jack Cooper and Charles Ladden were murdered during a copra-buying trip to Malaita.

In a newspaper interview from 1922, Oscar Svensen noted that the Marau people were considered very dangerous, a reputation enhanced by the murder there of the government representative on a labour trade vessel not long before the Norwegians arrived. Although the Svensen and Nerdrum brothers appeared to have established cordial local relationships right from the start, they did build their house at Tavanipupu on four-metre posts for maximum protection. Sailing wide and far in *Siskin,* along the coasts of Guadalcanal, Malaita and Makira and out to the remote atoll of Sikaiana, the brothers traded cloth, knives, tobacco and other goods for copra, 'ivory' nuts (the hard fruits of the sago palm) and turtle shell. Tavanipupu rapidly developed into a significant trading station, with large numbers of islanders coming in by canoe to sell their copra. In a photograph from the time of Oscar Svensen and a Nerdrum brother buying copra on Tavanipupu (see figure 8.1), we see both gentlemen (Svensen to the left) handsomely dressed – Nerdrum is even wearing a bow tie. They are rocking their chairs while bags of copra are offered, and the atmosphere seems relaxed. The photograph depicts the Norwegians' control over the situation: while many other traders were forced to travel out to the villages to buy copra in often-precarious seashore situations, villagers would travel to Tavanipupu to sell the commodity. Considering the fearsome reputation that corner of Guadalcanal had at the time, with the warriors of Malaita just across the channel, the relative tranquillity portrayed in this early photograph is striking.

But things were not all that easy. In 1893 Theodor Svensen died at Tavanipupu from blackwater fever (a complication of recurrent malaria). This was also the year when the Solomon Islands became a British protectorate, and the Norwegians at Marau saw opportunities in connecting to the emerging colonial power. When in 1896 C.M. Wood-

Figure 8.1. Oscar Svensen and one of the Nerdrum brothers buying copra at Tavanipupu in the 1890s. *Source:* Private collection; reproduced with permission.

ford started his work as the first resident commissioner, the Norwegian Solomon Islands Trading and Planting Company had already changed its name to the Marau Company, and company ships flew the British flag. Søfren Nerdrum appears to have been a specialist in tropical farming, and at Tavanipupu he planted cocoa and tobacco and various experimental crops. The Marau Company's dedication to innovation in an otherwise monotonous plantation industry impressed the colonial administration.

The year 1896 was to become particularly challenging: in August Søfren Nerdrum, too, died of the accumulated ill effects of recurrent malaria. Like Theodor, he was buried at Tavanipupu. Another blow came when the good ship *Siskin* was wrecked. Not long after, Theodor's son Karl, who worked at Marau, became seriously ill and had to leave for Brisbane, where he soon died. J.G.B. Nerdrum gave up the Solomons altogether, sold his company shares and returned to Norway, where he published a well-written, detailed scholarly lecture about his Solomon

Islands experiences in the journal of the Norwegian Geographical Society (Nerdrum 1901–2). Despite this adversity Oscar persevered and managed to obtain a credit of GBP 6,000 with his Sydney agent, which enabled him to expand with several new stations and to employ Europeans to operate them. However, as the Marau Company expanded, not all employment of Europeans was well considered. For example, in 1897 Svensen found two French runaway convicts from New Caledonia adrift in a boat, barely alive. He hired them to run a small trading station on the mainland at Marau, but they were violent and treated the natives so badly that they were soon murdered.

As permanent British colonial administration was established in the Solomons, Oscar Svensen was dedicated to getting the resident commissioner, C.M. Woodford, on his side. The relationship between the two men warmed particularly after they carried out a seven-day expedition to the interior of Guadalcanal in November 1898. Svensen provided carriers and guides, equipment, supplies and all transportation. He personally picked up Woodford in Tulagi with his schooner *Sikaiana* and returned him there after the expedition (Woodford 1898: 18–28).

From the very beginning of his many years in the islands, Oscar Svensen cleverly navigated the emerging colonial order. He was one of the sharpest agents in and of the fast-growing colonial economy, buying more land than any other European. On Guadalcanal, in the Nggela group, on Santa Isabel and even in notorious Malaita, Svensen accumulated land through transactions with local leaders, and then continuously established plantations, mainly for copra, but also for crops new to the colony such as cotton, rubber and coffee. In the 1890s Svensen was the largest single employer in the entire Solomons, having thousands of islanders working on his many plantations. His company recruited and managed labour independently, with several small ships sailing between the areas where labour could be easily recruited (especially Malaita and Makira) and the areas with less labour potential where plantations were developed. At the end of their contracts (usually two years), workers were returned to their homes by those same ships, unless they opted to stay for another period, and new recruits were taken on. This smooth-running, large-scale recruitment operation was unique in the early colonial Solomons, and had its roots in the years when the Svensen and Nerdrum brothers sailed around recruiting workers mostly for other plantation owners. They had become experienced operators of this dangerous traffic that relied particularly on ports in Malaita, where mighty 'saltwater' chiefs in coastal strongholds managed the flow of plantation workers from the large inland populations. While quite a few recruiting ships involved in the Queensland trade were attacked, Svensen's vessels involved in the intra-Solomons trade never were.

Oscar Svensen's success with long-term projects in plantations, labour management and other businesses was founded in his enduring ambition of accumulating wealth – succeeding where many other Europeans failed. Before the arrival of the colonial administration, Svensen had already built a network of agents throughout the archipelago, whereas the colonial administration, when it did come, lacked the means for permanent presence in its remoter parts. In 1895 Svensen's annual income was estimated at GBP 6,000, while Woodford earned GBP 300 as resident commissioner. Svensen's control over the protectorate's economic system culminated in 1902, when he bought his countryman Lars Nielsen's island Gavutu, with its trading station, coal depot and steamship wharf. With this stroke, Svensen's business extended right across the Solomons to include primary access to and influence over the shipping connections to Australia that were so essential to the export economy.

But other actors were set to take over as colonialism matured: not long after his Gavutu 'coup', Svensen sold most of his properties and companies to the emerging forces of a more modern colonial economy in whose development he had himself played a central role. Already in 1903 he had offered most of his land, his four ships and twenty years of exclusive rights to copra trade with Sikaiana to Burns, Philp & Co. Svensen demanded GBP 10,000, a price Burns, Philp & Co. found too steep. And so in 1907 Svensen sold 51,000 acres of land and other assets to Burns, Philp & Co.'s British archrival, Levers, for the extraordinary sum of GBP 45,000. This massive land acquisition by Levers left Burns, Philp & Co.'s force in the colony severely reduced. Captain Svensen had reached his goal of becoming a wealthy man, and he now shifted his primary residence to Brisbane, where he bought some acres of centrally located land and built a large home for his family.

Meanwhile, Svensen's nephew Jack Svensen (Theodor's son, known in the Solomons as Zeke Marau), who had worked for Oscar since 1908, continued managing company plantations for many years until setting out in 1920 for a challenging independent life (with his English wife, Edith) on land he had bought on the remote coast of Guadalcanal. Jack and Edith Svensen stayed on in isolated circumstances of illness and poverty for fifteen years until she died; Jack himself even remained in the Solomons when the Japanese invaded in 1942 (Golden 1993: 153–54).

Despite the profitable sale of his assets in 1907, Oscar Svensen was far from done with the Solomons. His agreement with Levers included responsibilities in the management of the plantations he had sold, and he used that opportunity to develop a new crop – rubber trees, imported from Singapore. After a while Svensen again purchased land on which he planted coconut trees, rubber trees and another experimental crop – cotton, which he himself introduced and developed in the Solomons. In 1912 Svensen had reached fifty, and he decided it was time to settle down permanently in Brisbane with his wife Henriette and their eight children. He sold some properties in the Solomons (including his rubber plantations in Isabel) for GBP 16,000 and set up a group of companies for the management of the rest, appointing himself as main shareholder and chairman of the board. As a wealthy and successful businessman he became a prominent figure in Brisbane, where he was also active in land transactions. Svensen's formal connections to Norway reached significant proportions in 1918, when he was appointed honorary Norwegian consul in Brisbane. In 1927 he received the Knighthood (First Class) of the Royal Norwegian Order of St. Olav. His coming and going in the Solomons was noted until 1933, when his son, Oscar Jr, took over responsibility for the most important plantations and lived in the Solomons until 1940. When Oscar Svensen Sr died in Brisbane in 1943 at the age of eighty-one, the Solomon Islands were an intense combat zone, all plantations had been abandoned and several had been razed to become Japanese and American airfields. After the ravages of the Second World War, Oscar Jr and his seven sisters sold all their father's remaining assets in the Solomons to the plantation company R.C. Symes. Their marginalized cousin Jack, still in the Solomons, does not appear to have been part of the picture.

'Norwegian Sea Captain Played Big Part in Developing the Solomons' was the headline of a February 1964 retrospective article about Oscar Svensen published in the long-running regional periodical *Pacific Islands Monthly*. Oscar Svensen was indeed the most important single actor in the development of a colonial plantation economy in the Solomons. His role in the transformation of the archipelago from a 'terrible' place where white men had a short life span to an economically well-managed, although still remote, part of the British Empire cannot be overestimated. When in 1907 he sold his main properties to Levers, that company was destined to lead the development of the plantation economy of the colony to an even larger scale. But those developments were firmly grounded in Svensen's extensive territorial reconfiguration of coastal land throughout the archipelago, and the lands originally purchased by the Norwegian Solomon Islands Trading and Planting Company Ltd in fact provided the foundations for what became Levers Pacific Plantations Ltd.

Svensen's career in the Solomons is also remarkable for his central role in the networks of other Norwegians who spent time there, including his own partners in the early period – his brother Theodor, the two brothers Nerdrum and the somewhat younger Schrøder brothers. Even indirectly, Svensen was connected to other Norwegians in the islands. We recall how the shipwrecked Anton 'Tony' Olsen was rescued at sea by Svensen (later to work for him), and how Lars Nielsen, after no less than thirty-three largely successful years in the islands, sold all his properties to Svensen. In contrast to Oscar Svensen (and to some degree Lars Nielsen), people like Julius Walter Andersen, 'Tony' Olsen and Victor Olaf Vilhelm Paulsen represented the less well-planned island existence, involving diverse entrepreneurship more or less independent from the large companies, unstable incomes, unrealistic expectations and often strong connections to local social life through relationships with Melanesian women. During the early colonial period it was this lifestyle that was the most typical for Europeans in the Solomons.

Norwegian Descendants in the Modern-Day Solomons

From my many conversations with the children and grandchildren of Julius Walter Andersen and Victor Olaf Vilhelm Paulsen, it has become evident that both men were genuinely concerned with their local families – both had three children with their wives from the western Solomons. Although both these Norwegians died while their children were young, their sons and daughters remembered fathers who built large houses, owned books in Norwegian or about Norway and were careful to explain to them where they came from. The Norwegian language was never used, however; the fathers spoke English and Solomon Islands Pijin with their families and learned bits and pieces of local languages. Their children were multilingual from the start, mastering English and one or two local languages, which gave some of them an advantage in the formal labour market that emerged in the protectorate after the Second World War.

While it has been difficult to fulfil very many of the expectations my friends in the Andersen and Paulsen families have had about finding relatives in Norway, I have managed to supply them with Norwegian flags, books about Norway (even a much-desired one entitled *Teach Yourself Norwegian*) and, not unexpectedly, small Viking ships and more or less ugly-looking trolls. During our first conversations in 1986, Erik Andersen and Peter Paulsen were quick to point out that the Viking ships, with their high, decorated prow and stern posts, were remarkably like the war canoes of their Melanesian forefathers, and that Norwegian ideas about trolls almost completely overlap with New Georgian beliefs about dangerous ogres who roam the forest and hunt down and eat people. Once I offered my friend Erik Andersen a ticket to go to Norway, but he already felt that he was too old for a journey of such magnitude. After active and mobile careers in paid employment, the two old men retired into quiet lives on their respective islands in the lagoons of New Georgia.

Erik Andersen (1924-2013) lived since the 1980s on the raised coral island of Mahoro in central Marovo Lagoon (figure 8.2). Mahoro was first sold in 1913 by a relative of Erik's own mother, probably to the Swedish trader known as Fred Ericksen. Having worked since 1949 as a respected manager of several plantations for the company R.C. Symes, mainly on the island of Isabel (including the large Gozoruru plantation originally established by Oscar Svensen in 1905), Erik bought Mahoro island from that company in 1984. He and his wife Vivian wanted to return home to Marovo Lagoon for their retirement years. From Mahoro there is a view across the lagoon to the village of Chubikopi, where one of Vivian's clans resides, a clan that Erik's mother also belonged to. Through the lineage of his mother, and through his sister Jessie, who was married to the late chief of Chubikopi, Erik Andersen had a significant influence on local politics. In the 1990s Victor Paulsen Jr, youngest son of the Norwegian from Oslo, also settled at Chubikopi, since his wife Cylia (who is Erik Andersen's niece) took up work as a teacher at the village school. The Norwegian Andersen and Paulsen families have thus joined together – as expressed in an important local concept, they have 'reconnected' through blood.

Peter Paulsen (1931–2010) lived until his death on Hobupeka, a small island outside the township of Munda by Roviana Lagoon. That island is famous in the colonial history of the Solomons as the place where British sailor Frank Wickham (shipwrecked, we recall, with Lars Nielsen) established a small but profitable local trading empire under the protection of the formidable head-hunting chief Ingava. Peter's marriage to Wickham's granddaughter Betzy brought together two families of descendants from two Europeans who worked and lived in the Solomons at entirely different stages of colonial history. Through his mother's lineage, Peter had significant rights to large tracts on the mainland, where after a long career as plantation supervisor and construction foreman he established a series of agricultural projects.

Peter was about twenty years old when he first met Norwegians, in the port of Honiara. After the Second World War, as the colonial econ-

Figure 8.2. Erik Andersen with wife, children and grandchild at home on Mahoro, 2007. *Source:* Edvard Hviding; reproduced with permission.

omy slowly revived, he had wanted to continue his education, but instead went to work to provide for his mother and two younger brothers. He worked for some years on copra boats and on the old sailing vessels of those traders who returned after the war, but he soon settled in Honiara, an abandoned American military base designated as the new capital after Tulagi's demise during the war. Many ships arrived in Honiara to load leftover war equipment and scrap metal, and among them, Peter told me, was a Norwegian ship that arrived in 1951. He explained:

> In those times it was forbidden for us islanders to drink beer. But we were friends with the workers from Fiji who had come to clean up after the war, and we used to hang around in their houses. The Fijians were allowed to drink, so we drank beer there and became their friends. Visiting seamen also came to those houses, and some came from that Norwegian ship. I was sitting in a corner when a man from Fiji said: 'This boy here is from Norway!' The Norwegians looked at me. A man named Ted, who I believe came from Bergen, asked me where I came from, and I said: 'Not from this island, but from New Georgia. My mother is from there. My father also lived there, and he was from Norway.' Ted touched my hair, which was soft and fair at the time, he smiled and said there was no doubt, I was from Norway and I was one of them.

Ted and his shipmates invited Peter on board the ship, which was anchored in the roads. They drank together and treated him to mutton from the ship's freezer, and Peter also remembered a large cake. None of them knew much English, but they got along anyway. Peter stayed on the ship for a week, until the cargo was loaded and the ship left Honiara. In the early mornings he was taken ashore by the ship's motor launch, and when his working days were over his Norwegian friends picked him up and took him back out to the ship. The night before they left they gave a large farewell party for Peter. This encounter was a powerful experience for a young man from Roviana who had always been a little different from everyone else because of his Norwegian descent. The hospitality of the Norwegian seamen, and their insistence on Peter being one of them, made a big impression. Peter decided, when the time was right, to tell his children as much as possible about their Norwegian connection.

The descendants of Julius Walter Andersen and Victor Olaf Vilhelm Paulsen are still visible in the Solomons today. This is not only because, even in the generation of great-grandchildren, they remain relatively light-skinned in New Georgia, where people are generally jet black. Skin colour is in fact readily talked about and commented upon in the Solomons, without this being degrading. Black is black, and 'red' (a term used for a wide spectre of lighter skin tones) is 'red'. When representatives of the nation's more than eighty different 'ethnolinguistic' groups meet in the capital, Honiara, a short glimpse of a person gives enough information to know approximately where he or she is from, and how to address him or her. People from the Andersen and Paulsen families, however, do not look like they are from any identifiable place in the island group. They have also had a habit of marrying partners of European or Chinese descent, and in Honiara's colourful everyday street life most of them are still recognized as people of 'half descent', with unspecified, usually European elements. 'It is strange how the Norwegian blood remains visible in generation after generation', Peter Paulsen commented to me with reference to the appearance of his beautiful daughters.

In contemporary Solomon Islands society, these 'third-generation Norwegians' whose northern ancestors may have been of modest stock at home have in large measure entered the modern elite of a diverse South Pacific nation. Given the mostly humble origins and challenging local predicaments of the Norwegians who first settled in the Solomons in the nineteenth and early twentieth centuries, meeting well-educated part Norwegians today in middle management positions in the public service and business sector of the Solomon Islands evokes images of vertical class mobility over generations of truly exotic family history. Other Norwegian pioneers who have no descendants in the islands, in particular Oscar Svensen, have left a less tangible but no less important heritage by defining major parameters of the economic development of the archipelago no longer known as 'the terrible Solomons', instead marketing itself in the present as 'the Happy Isles'.

Notes

1. I have worked as an anthropologist in the Solomon Islands, mainly in Marovo Lagoon of New Georgia in the western parts of the islands, for more than three years altogether since 1986, and this long-term fieldwork continues. While I have concentrated on Marovo Lagoon, I have travelled by sea throughout the New Georgia islands, lived for shorter periods in the Western Province capital of Gizo and in the national capital of Honiara, and made brief visits to the islands of Guadalcanal, Nggela and Malaita. This research has resulted in a number of books (Hviding 1993, 1995, 1996, 2005; Hviding and Bayliss-Smith 2000) and several documentary films (Hviding, Scott and Tollefsen 2000; Hviding and Scott 2006).
2. These materials are held on microfilm at PMB 975, 'Papers re Captain Oscar Svensen, 1896–1968' (the years referring not to Svensen's birth and death but to the time span covered).
3. I use 'European' with the meaning conventionally used throughout the Pacific Islands – not as a reference to Europe as a continent, but as a wider term for people, language, artefacts and so forth from European countries as well as from North America and Australia. In this sense, it is that which may generally be understood as 'Western'.
4. The colonial history of the Solomon Islands has been thoroughly examined by historian Judith Bennett (1987). Among relatively recent anthropological studies that give detailed insights into history and present circumstances in different parts of this diverse nation are White (1991), Keesing (1992) and Hviding (1996).
5. Golden (1993) and archive materials suggest that 'Andy' (Albert Molkin) Andresen, a well-known character in the Solomon Islands from 1917 until his death in 1965, was a Swedish sea captain, while Fred Ericksen, described by sources as 'Frederick Ericksen a Swedish seaman', traded in the islands from a ship as early as 1887, bought significant areas of land in Marovo Lagoon from about 1913 and left the Solomons in 1920.
6. *The Adelaide Advertiser*, 18 October 1905, p. 7.
7. While in English sources his surname is incorrectly rendered 'Neilsen', this nonetheless reflects the Norwegian pronunciation of the name.
8. The British navy had from 1885 started to explore the future colony and carry out punitive expeditions on villages they assumed were the place of

residence for murderers of Europeans or attackers of ships. With the excellent harbour at Gavutu, Nielsen was particularly well placed in relation to doing coal trade on a substantial scale with the navy. Logbooks show that typical naval vessels on missions to the Solomons in the 1890s – steam-and-sail corvettes of twelve hundred to fourteen hundred tons or smaller gunboats – routinely loaded one hundred to two hundred tons of coal at a time.

9. In 1932 the South African Roy Struben stayed in Tulagi with his newly purchased schooner *Navanora*. The ship was found abandoned in the Santa Cruz Islands in the east: '[T]he two owners, New Zealanders, had died suddenly some months before, and the crew had returned to their village. It was rumoured that the men had been poisoned by jealous women.' In the absence of an owner Struben bought the schooner from the colonial administration for GBP 400, and found its engine in need of repairs: '[T]he only engineering firm of Tulagi, consisting of Mr. Andersen, a Norwegian, overhauled the Diesel engine. It is said that Europeans cannot do manual work at sea level in the tropics, but here, slap in the middle of the hottest tropics, was a man of the cold north proving that they can. He worked long and hard, a good deal of the time at the forge, hot work in any climate. His charge was seven-and-sixpence per hour, or ten shillings if using a lathe. This became expensive, especially as he had a system of a pause of ten minutes every hour, like the Foreign Legion on the march, but instead of flinging himself down on the desert sands, Andersen threw his head back and sucked in a couple of bottles of beer. That overhaul cost forty-five pounds' (Struben 1961: 25).

10. The account of the Svensen shipping company and of the brothers' first years in Australia is based on information from letters left by two of Theodor's sons (N. Theodor Svensen and Jack Svensen), an interview with Oscar Svensen in *The Daily Mail,* Brisbane (20 July 1922), and an article about Svensen in *Pacific Islands Monthly* (February 1964); all are in 'Papers re Captain Oscar Svensen', PMB 975. The versions of certain events given by different members of the Svensen family do not completely correspond in relation to years and other details, but I have considered their perspectives and tried to create a logical synthesis.

11. J.G.B. Nerdrum was considered a useful partner in relation to the brothers' ambitions to buy land in the Solomons: in *The Brisbane Courier,* 23 February 1891, we can read that Nerdrum is amongst six men who have been approved for work measuring and registering land: '[H]aving exhibited evidence of competency as surveyors, [these men] have been licensed to affect surveys under the provisions of The Crown Lands Act of 1834 subject to the rules of the Surveyor-General's Department.'

Archives Consulted

Pacific Manuscripts Bureau (PMB), Canberra.

References

Amherst, Lord and B. Thomson. 1901. *The Discovery of the Solomon Islands by Alvaro de Mendaña in 1568: Translated from the Original Spanish Manuscripts, Edited with an Introduction and Notes by Lord Amherst of Hackney and Basil Thomson,* 2 vols. London: Bedford Press by permission of the Hakluyt Society.

Bennett, J.A. 1981. 'Oscar Svensen: A Solomons Trader among "the Few"', *Journal of Pacific History* 16: 170–89.

———. 1987. *Wealth of the Solomons: A History of a Pacific Archipelago, 1800–1978.* Honolulu: University of Hawai'i Press.

Cromar, J. 1935. *Jock of the Islands: early days in the South Seas; the adventures of John Cromar, sometime recruiter and lately trader of Marovo, British Solomon Islands Protectorate.* London: Faber & Faber.

Golden, G.A. 1993. *The Early European Settlers of the Solomon Islands.* Melbourne: G. Golden.

Hviding, E. 1993. *The Rural Context of Giant Clam Mariculture in Solomon Islands: An Anthropological Study,* ICLARM Technical Report 39. Manila: International Center for Living Aquatic Resources Management.

———. 1995. *Vivinei tuari pa Ulusaghe: Stories and legends from Marovo, New Georgia, in four New Georgian languages and with English translations,* recorded, translated and edited by Edvard Hviding, with V. Vaguni and others. Bergen and Gizo: University of Bergen, in collaboration with Western Province Division of Culture.

———. 1996. *Guardians of Marovo Lagoon: Practice, Place, and Politics in Maritime Melanesia.* Honolulu: University of Hawai'i Press.

———. 2003a. 'Between Knowledges: Pacific Studies and Academic Disciplines', *The Contemporary Pacific* 15: 43–73.

———. 2003b. 'Disentangling the *Butubutu* of New Georgia: Cognatic Kinship in Thought and Action', in I. Hoëm and S. Roalkvam (eds), *Oceanic Socialities and Cultural Forms: Ethnographies of Experience.* Oxford: Berghahn Books, pp. 71–113.

———. 2005. *Reef and Rainforest: An Environmental Encyclopedia of Marovo Lagoon, Solomon Islands/Kiladi oro vivineidi ria tingitonga pa idere oro pa goana pa Marovo,* Knowledges of Nature Series 1. Paris: UNESCO.

Hviding, E. and T. Bayliss-Smith. 2000. *Islands of Rainforest: Agroforestry, Logging and Ecotourism in Solomon Islands.* Aldershot, U.K.: Ashgate.

Hviding, E. and R. Scott. 2006. *Vincent and the Rainforest: Global Conversations in Rural Melanesia.* Bergen: SOT-Film AS and University of Bergen, in cooperation with Solomon Islands National Museum. DVD, 75 mins.

Hviding, E., R. Scott and T. Tollefsen. 2000. *Chea's Great Kuarao.* Bergen: SOT-Film AS and University of Bergen, in cooperation with Solomon Islands National Museum. DVD, 57 min.

Jack-Hinton, C. 1969. *The Search for the Islands of Solomon 1567–1838.* Oxford: Clarendon Press.

Keesing, R.M. 1992. *Custom and Confrontation: The Kwaio Struggle for Cultural Autonomy.* Chicago: University of Chicago Press.

Keesing, R.M. and P. Corris. 1980. *Lightning Meets the West Wind: The Malaita Massacre.* Melbourne: Oxford University Press.

London, J. 1911a. *The Cruise of the* Snark. New York: Macmillan.

———. 1911b. *South Sea Tales.* New York: Macmillan.

Nerdrum, J.G.B. 1901–2. 'Indtryk og oplevelser under et 7 aars ophold paa Salomonøerne' [Impressions and experiences from seven years' residence in the Solomon Islands], *Norsk Geografisk Aarbog* [Norwegian Geographical Yearbook] 1901–2: 23–58.

Støre, E.H. 1967. 'Devil-Tony og kannibalene' [Devil Tony and the cannibals], in J. Falck-Hansen (ed.), *Nordmenn på eventyr* [Norwegians on adventure]. Oslo: Ernst G. Mortensens Forlag, pp. 144–50.

Struben, R. 1961. *Coral and Colour of Gold.* London: Faber and Faber.

White, G.M. 1991. *Identity through History: Living Stories in a Solomon Islands Society.* Cambridge: Cambridge University Press.

Woodford, C.M. 1890. *A Naturalist among the Head-Hunters: Being an Account of Three Visits to the Solomon Islands in the Years 1886, 1887, and 1888.* London: G. Philip.

———. 1897. *Western Pacific: Report on the British Solomon Islands.* Presented to Parliament by command of Her Majesty. Colonial reports, miscellaneous.

———. 1898. *Annual Report, British Solomon Islands Protectorate.* Presented to Parliament by command of Her Majesty. Colonial reports, miscellaneous.

9

Norwegians in the Cook Islands

The Legacy of Captain Reinert G. Jonassen (1866–1915)

Jon Tikivanotau Michael Jonassen

Taka'i koe ite papa enua
Akamou ite pito enua
A'u ite marae i tapu
I tere ei to'ou rangi.
You step onto solid land
And connect your umbilical cord
Create a safe communal spiritual place
That your world may succeed.

Me tae ki te ora tei akono'ia,
ka tu mai no Iva teta'i tumu pua tei tapoki 'ia
e tōna au tiare kakara.
At the appointed time,
An immense *pua* tree covered with fragrant blossoms
will spring up from the nether world.
[Your destiny is in your hands and is awaiting you.][1]

Ever since Magellan sailed into the Pacific in 1521 as the first recorded European voyager to that ocean and its islands, a wide variety of explorers, navigators and adventurers from the Western world have plied their trades over the Pacific's vast expanses. Initially they came primarily from Spain and Portugal. When in 1768 Captain James Cook started his extensive voyages crisscrossing the Pacific, he was to be followed by many others from the United Kingdom, the United States, France and Germany. By the 1890s, many Norwegian ships were also sailing among the islands of the Pacific (see both chapters by Hviding, this volume). This chapter has a very specific focus on the captain of one of those Norwegian ships: Reinert Godtfred Jonassen, later known in the Cook Islands as Reinhardt Godfrey Jonassen. He was my grandfather. While my chapter tells of his ancestry and descendants, it gives particular attention to his arrival, settling and resident life in the Pacific

Islands.² But the chapter is more than family genealogy and oral history. It is a story of political and social intrigue, of colonial times and independence for a small Pacific Islands nation.³ The story connects two sides of the globe – Norway and the Cook Islands – while inscribing the name Jonassen permanently into the Cook Islands' political, economic and social history.⁴

Captain Jonassen was well liked in the Cook Islands. Living on the island of Aitutaki but voyaging widely throughout the archipelago, he was commonly known as *Te Norue* or 'The Norwegian'. His only son, Michael, grew up with the nickname *Norue* (Norway). When I was born, my father, Michael (known as Ka or Norue), named me Jonassen Michael Jonassen. Captain Jonassen's descendants in the Cook Islands do reflect typical Norwegian names that have reappeared over several generations: Mikal or Michael, Reinert or Reinhardt, Josephine or Josefine, Ragnhild, Theodora, Ane or Anne, Jon – all of course subsumed under the family name of Jonassen.

Reinert Jonassen lived in the Cook Islands during an interesting period in the history of the archipelago. As he was sailing in the Pacific in 1897, not many years had passed since what were then known as the Hervey Islands had been declared a British protectorate in 1888.⁵ He must have been keenly aware of French efforts to claim islands in the Pacific, and once he had settled in the islands he would have lived amongst rumours of growing New Zealand government interest. He was actually in Aitutaki when the New Zealand government finally annexed the Hervey Islands in 1901. The Norwegian captain was part of a quiet though increasingly independence-oriented movement in Aitutaki that occasionally showed some deference to efforts of increased political control by the chiefs of the island of Rarotonga. Reinert's marriage to important women of Aitutaki – first Tauariki and then Ti'avaru – entrenched him in enduring relationships with the traditional chiefly leaders of Aitutaki. Interestingly, his two marriages also connected him to some more infamous individuals in the Cook Islands' history. Reinert's mother-in-law Petirini (Ti'avaru's mother) was a daughter of William Marsters, the well-known polygamous English settler of Palmerston Island, and Ti'avaru was the great-granddaughter of Matakavau, who had been kidnapped and abandoned in Aitutaki by the villainous sandalwood trader Captain Goodenough. Reinert also had some interesting foreign friends in the Cook Islands: Aleck Campbell, a black immigrant businessman on Aitutaki, Emil Georg Piltz, a German sea captain turned trader in Rarotonga, and Viggo Rasmussen, the Danish trader who settled in Mitiaro Island.

From Norway to the South Seas

Reinert Godtfred Jonassen was born on 12 March 1866 on the tiny island of Egerøen in the southern Norwegian seaport of Farsund. He was the second child (but eldest son) of Jonas Mikal Børresen and Grethe Bollette Reinertsdatter. Reinert had a younger brother named Jonas and three sisters: Josefine, Benedikte and Ane. Reinert's paternal grandparents were Børre Egerøe and Johanne Lisabeth Ingralsdatter, while his maternal grandparents were Reinert Rasmussen and Grethe Samuelsdatter. Reinert married his first wife, Jørgine Gabrielsen, in Norway and they soon had Theodora (b. 1893), the first of two daughters.

Reinert was attracted to the sea when very young, as were nearly all men of the Farsund area. He qualified as a master mariner at an early age, and it was no surprise when in 1893, at the age of twenty-seven, he took command of the bark *Gyda*. An unidentified Norwegian manuscript in the author's possession describes the background to that particular event:

> In 1893 the management of *Gyda* changed from Urbye to Brøvig. This took place during the vessel's call at Farsund, Norway. *Gyda* was 627 net tons and was built in Arendal in 1883. During the call at Farsund, a new master took command of the vessel, namely, Reinert Godtfred Jonassen of Korshavn. *Gyda* was one of the many vessels bought by the people of Farsund on a joint ownership basis. A total of eighty people had a share in *Gyda*.[6]

Captain Jonassen sailed as the master of *Gyda* for several years, and in 1897, as his wife was pregnant with their second child, Ragnhild, he set off to the South Seas. Unbeknownst to Reinert, it would be the last time he would see his wife, since during his absence she would die while giving birth to their daughter. Of course, Jonassen was also unaware that *Gyda* was embarking on the ship's last voyage, on what was to become an eventful journey. In 1897 *Gyda* was loaded with a cargo of copra from the Vava'u islands in Tonga for Europe. On the homebound journey the ship did not get far, however; *Gyda* suffered heavy weather damages and had to seek refuge in Pape'ete, Tahiti. The damaged ship was condemned by the insurers in December of that year. The crew took passage back to Norway on other ships, while Captain Jonassen remained in Tahiti to deal with the formalities associated with the loss of *Gyda*.[7]

While at Tahiti, Captain Jonassen received notice that his wife had died in childbirth back home in Korshavn. Having circumnavigated the world, visited so many islands in the Pacific, lost his ship and cargo as well as his wife, and experienced the lure and magic of Tahiti, he soon fell into the arms of the gracious and loving widow Tauariki Teurukura Ariki, herself a paramount chief from the island of Aitutaki, who was visiting her cousin at Tahiti, Paramount Chief Pomare. Reinert and Tauariki fell in love, and she invited him to make his new home on her own island. We might note that Aitutaki means 'god-led', whereas the old name of the island was Araura, 'fragrant flower wreaths for dancing' (Williamson 1924: 250). Aitutaki has a huge lagoon encircled by a coral reef with a main hilly island at one end. It is located 225 kilometres north of the archipelago's main island of Rarotonga (Syed and Mataio 1993: 12). Jonassen arrived at Aitutaki and became Tauariki's new husband at a time when the island's population was declining owing to introduced diseases and out-migration. In 1843 alone, thirty people had died of dysentery in Aitutaki (Maretu 1871: 143).

Jonassen in Aitutaki: Reinert Godtfred Becomes Reinhardt Godfrey

During his marriage to Tauariki (ca. 1898–1909) Captain Jonassen established orange and copra plantations on Aitutaki and tried to improve the island's commercial opportunities (*Pacific Islands Monthly* 1970). Tauariki held the title of Teurukura Ariki, one of the four paramount chiefly titles on Aitutaki (the other titles being Manarangi Ariki, Tamatoa Ariki and Vaeruarangi Ariki). From his wife's powerful position Jonassen had access to all major resources and activities on the island, as well as to traditional leaders and church and government representatives.

Jonassen built several schooners that shipped the island's products to New Zealand, and he became a fairly wealthy man. His marriage produced no new offspring, and so, according to family traditions, Tauariki asked her husband to request for his two daughters, Theodora and Ragnhild, to be sent to the Cook Islands from Norway so that they could be raised in Aitutaki. But it is said that Jonassen's parents in Norway would not allow their grandchildren to be exposed to the 'heathens of the islands'. Ironically, Aitutaki had been the first island in the Cook Islands group to accept Christianity in 1821, and so Christian morals and codes of behaviour were well entrenched by the time Jonassen arrived there. He and Tauariki were regular attendees at the local church. Reinert and Tauariki eventually adopted a 'feeding son' (*tamaiti angai*) from his wife's Aitutaki family – in reality Tauariki's younger brother. Their feeding son later embraced the surname of Natini, coined from

Jonassen. Many Natini descendants live today in Aitutaki, New Zealand and Australia.

The year 1902 witnessed the first labour strike in Aitutaki, when the islanders refused to make copra because the price offered them had dropped too low. The newly appointed first resident commissioner, Gudgeon, reacted negatively, even suggesting that Aitutakians should be poll taxed to make up for the lost revenue (Scott 1991: 96–97). Now referring to himself as Reinhardt Godfrey Jonassen (adopting an English spelling of his first names), the Norwegian captain sympathized with his wife's people, and behind the scenes encouraged a softer approach by the administration.

The travel writer Beatrice Grimshaw visited the home of Tauariki and Captain Jonassen in Aitutaki and added the experience to her 1908 publication *In the Strange South Seas*. Grimshaw ([1908] 1971: 132ff.) declared Tauariki to be 'gloriously married to a white' who could 'teach even the Aitutakians something about boat-building, and she [Tauariki] is travelled and finished, having been [on] a trip to Auckland – the ambition of every Cook Islander'. She described Tauariki as 'a person of importance in her own circle, [who] was allowed by the natives of the town first right to entertain the white woman'. It is apparent from this account that Grimshaw was ignorant of the traditional entitlement of a paramount chief to receive visitors first. Tauariki's title of Teurukura Ariki demanded respect from visitors, whether they were white or not, and so the entitlement had nothing to do with Tauariki being the wife of a white man. Granted, Tauariki's ownership of a local shop did enhance her position on the island, to which was added the marriage to a Norwegian who was much loved by the locals. But it is important to note that Tauariki had often travelled outside Aitutaki before meeting Captain Jonassen in Tahiti. The fact that Tauariki was a powerful and well-travelled woman in her own right was ignored by Grimshaw, blinded as she was by arrogant, self-indulgent ideas of white superiority. Grimshaw's supercilious account described her stay in the Jonassen home in some detail:

> [Their house was located] in the middle of the rambling, jungly, green street of the little town … a wooden bungalow with a verandah and a tiny roof, very ugly, but very fine to the native eyes. There were tables and chairs in the 'parlour'; and the inevitable boiled fowl that takes the place of the fatted calf, in Pacific cookery, was served up on a china plate. A rich woman Tau, and one who knew how the *tangata papa'a* (white folk) should be entertained!

She continues:

> She gave me a bedroom all to myself, with a smile that showed complete understanding of the foolish fads of the *wahine papa*. It had a large 'imported' glass window, giving on the main street of the town, and offering, through its lack of blinds, such a fine, free show for the interested populace, that I was obliged to go to bed in the dark. There was a real bed in the room, covered with a patchwork quilt of a unique and striking design, representing a very realistic scarlet devil some four feet long. … There was nothing else in the room, except a new, gold-laced, steamship officer's cap. … There was nothing to wash in but Tau knew her manners, and was quite aware that I might have a prejudice against sitting in a washtub on either the front or the back verandah, to have buckets emptied on my head in the morning. So she made haste to leave a kerosene tin full of water, before going to her camphor wood chest, and extracting a pink silk dress trimmed with yellow lace, for me to sleep in. (Grimshaw 1908: 133)

While married to Tauariki, Reinhardt befriended a German sea captain turned trader by the name of Emil Georg Piltz. They became very good friends, perhaps enhanced by their common interests in seamanship and the fact that Reinhardt also spoke German, and there is some evidence that at least one of the competing British residents was suspicious, if not envious, of the success of the two non-English residents. Piltz contracted Jonassen to build a two-story building in Rarotonga's main town area, Avarua, and called it simply 'Emil Piltz'. As a store involved in the import of general merchandise and the export of island produce (Captain Piltz himself carried copra between Tonga and San Francisco), the building remained a landmark in Rarotonga for many years (Siers 1977: 16).

After a while Tauariki became very ill. In an attempt to save his wife, Reinhardt sent messages by ship to New Zealand, calling for a doctor. A Norwegian who heard about the call from Aitutaki decided to follow the doctor there, and was very surprised to find a stranded Norwegian captain whose family he knew well. Hercules Weyen Sundt is reported to have stayed at Aitutaki for about a year, returning to Norway in 1910. Tauariki died in 1909, despite the medical assistance obtained by her husband.

Prior to this, while already critically ill, Tauariki had appealed to her cousin Tiini Pare'anga that his daughter, Ti'avaru, should take her place after her death as Reinhardt's new spouse. Tauariki expounded on the personal virtues of the captain, and Pare'anga's Vaeruarangi Ariki and Tamatoa Ariki families also felt that it would be a great loss to the island if the Norwegian were to leave Aitutaki following Tauariki's inevitable death. Jonassen was known as a kind and good man who was also hardworking and extremely productive. He had established a reputation as a skilled builder of canoes, boats and houses, a businessman, a musician and a Pacific navigator. At Aitutaki he was considered a good match for the royal daughter, whose full name was Ti'avaru Sarah Aka-kaingaro Mata Pa Tiini Pare'anga.[8] And so it was that upon the death of Tauariki, her family arranged for Captain Jonassen to marry Ti'avaru, Tiini Pare'anga's daughter, who was also part of their extended family. It should be noted that at the time of the original marriage proposal Ti'avaru was only about thirteen years old. By the time she actually married the captain it seems she was fourteen. The delay of the marriage was a result of New Zealand officials in Rarotonga raising concerns at a mixed marriage between a European and a Māori, as well as their unease about the girl's age, although it was not uncommon for Aitutaki men and women of the time to marry at a young age.[9]

Captain Jonassen and Ti'avaru took their vows in typical Aitutaki traditional style. It began with an official engagement that involved a delivery of pigs and other gifts to Ti'avaru's family, acting as a provisional promise and notification of honourable intentions. It was also in recognition of the impending loss to the Tiini Pare'anga clan of an important working and contributing family member. They were married in the London Missionary Society Church (now called the Cook Islands Christian Church) located in the village of Arutanga. A huge celebration followed with feasting and gift giving (known as *o'ora*) of a scale befitting the only daughter of Tiini Pare'anga, a direct descendant of the paramount chief lines of Tamatoa Ariki and Vaeruarangi Ariki. Immediately after the wedding, Reinhardt vacated the shop that he had operated with Tauariki on her land in her village of Re'ure'u. He moved to Ti'avaru's family's home in the nearby village of Ure'ia and immediately set about helping his new father-in-law, Tiini Pare'anga, expand their housing through major renovations. His good nature showed through the close relationships he soon developed with his new brothers-in-law.

Expanding the Business, Extending the Family

By all accounts, Reinhardt had a wonderful life with Ti'avaru, and they had two daughters and a son, all born in Aitutaki and to whom Norwegian names were given: Anne (Ane), born 14 July 1910, Michael (Mikal), born 9 May 1912, and Josephine (Josefine), born in 1914. The captain established a new store on the island of Atiu and transferred his brother-in-law Andrew there to manage it. Andrew eventually married an Atiuan woman and never returned to Aitutaki, while Atiu became an important extension of Reinhardt's growing interisland business. On Aitutaki, the captain built a seaworthy open sailing boat that he named *Annie*. He would sail in *Annie* from Aitutaki to Atiu to gather candlenuts,[10] after which he would continue via Mitiaro and Mauke for more candlenuts, then delivering the cargo of nuts to Rarotonga for onwards shipment to Auckland. Accompanying him on the boat were often his brothers-in-law, Rau Tangata Tiini and Andrew Tiini, and his best friend, Tatira Tatira. Income from the sale of the candlenuts would be used to purchase goods from New Zealand, which were loaded on *Annie* for the captain's store at Atiu. From Atiu, *Annie* would return to Aitutaki, which continued to be the base for the captain's activities. His voyages included visits to Tahiti, where Jonassen is reported to have bought jewellery gifts for Ti'avaru.

This was a period when a multinational group of sea captains were active in the Cook Islands. They included 'Taylor a typical yankee, Piltze and Engeleke, Germans, and Nagle another American whose half caste son commanded the schooner *Maungaroa* when she was lost between Auckland and Rarotonga in 1901' (Ramsden 1939). Captain Jonassen was among quite a few actually trading throughout the Cook Islands. Unlike the others, who operated from Rarotonga, Jonassen retained his base on Aitutaki, whereas his friend Captain Piltz, for example, had been established as a businessman in Rarotonga already from 1892.[11] In later years Captain Jonassen visited the island of Mitiaro more often, after Viggo Rasmussen had arrived and begun to operate a store there.[12] A businessman named Aleck Campbell, who lived on Aitutaki, was another of Jonassen's close friends, and Campbell and Jonassen even embarked on some joint ventures, including their purchase of a duplex-type house on the hill at Pukutoitoi.[13] Among the small number of other foreigners living on Aitutaki during Reinhardt's time were two Catholic priests from Holland and a London Missionary Society pastor from England.

The life of Ti'avaru and Reinhardt on Aitutaki was a joyous and happy one, surrounded by a supportive and respectful extended family. Together they operated a successful business, which through Ti'avaru's brother Andrew's move to Atiu had expanded to that island. Reinhardt also secured property in Aitutaki next to the main harbour from his wife's family, land called Te-Marae-O-Tangaroa. From here, Reinhardt was able to operate, maintain and supply his boat *Annie*. He planted coconut palms on lands called Mania and Rapae, raised chickens for home consumption and prepared to build a Norwegian-style house on a raised part of Rapae, located in the village of Amuri. For this he ordered timber from overseas. Ti'avaru, too, was busy, especially since despite her young age the family had asked her to accept several traditional chiefly and priesthood titles, including that of Tikivanotau Mata'iapo. She became knowledgeable about genealogy, including the links to her chiefly ancestors on Rarotonga.

Ti'avaru used to recite the story of Captain Goodenough, who came to Rarotonga in about 1814 to gather sandalwood but found none, instead staying on for several months to gather *noni* wood. Villainous behaviour by Goodenough and his crew resulted in the death of some people of the Takitumu district, and the chiefs became upset. Their warriors killed and ate a few members of the crew, including Goodenough's female companion – apparently the only woman recorded to have received such a fate in that part of the Pacific. Goodenough escaped on his ship *Cumberland,* kidnapping the two chiefly daughters Matavakau and Tepaeru, abandoning them at Aitutaki. Matakavau's descendant, Ti'avaru, became the most knowledgeable person in Aitutaki concerning this Takitumu connection, which in the present times of land disputes is denied in Rarotonga. During Reinhardt's time, Ti'avaru was particularly interested in gaining access to her ancestral rights over the Avana reef entrance at Takitumu, which she felt her husband could utilize for his shipping activities.

Ti'avaru played a decisive role in decisions related to the choice of holders of the paramount chief titles of Tamatoa (Warrior Chief) and Vaeruarangi (Spirit of the Heaven Chief). The economic successes that she and her husband had gave them a significant role in the everyday lives of the people of Aitutaki. Ti'avaru was often busy with community affairs as well as assisting her husband, and she established a reputation as a successful healer and herbal medicine specialist. But the lives she and her husband led on Aitutaki were also connected to more global developments. With the advent of the First World War, life became more difficult in the Cook Islands, as it did for more metropolitan parts of the world. Communication between the islands and the outside was difficult, the import and export of trade goods became unreliable and the economy suffered in general. In terms of everyday survival, though, Captain Jonassen was faring better than most people, because he had his own boat *Annie* as a means of voyaging. By all accounts he was unaware of the hardships that his sisters were facing at that time in Norway, and a letter written by his sister Josefine, dated 18 June 1915, apparently never made it to Reinhardt – who, as it turned out, was just then nearing the unexpected end of his life.

As a much-respected master mariner in the Cook Islands, Captain Jonassen was often hired to command various ships and yachts on voyages in the islands. Major business owners on Rarotonga or in New

Zealand recruited him to sail their vessels, and the Aitutaki-owned boat *Araura* also occasionally required Jonassen's command. Safe sailing and landfall in the islands required, and still requires, particular skill. Anchorage and harbour conditions in many of the islands in the Cooks group are very difficult, and in Jonassen's time of intense interisland trade, the loading or landing of cargo at extreme high or low tide required specialized expertise. Safe navigation also demanded special knowledge of conditions in the cyclone season.

During one of Captain Jonassen's voyages to Rarotonga as a contracted captain, the ship was struck by a cyclone and the main mast was split. The boom was broken off by the strong winds, and as fate would have it a part of the damaged spars hit Reinhardt's thigh while he was struggling at the ship's tiller. His friend Tatira watched helplessly. An open wound, soon infected, worsened the problem, and blood poisoning rapidly developed in Reinhardt's leg. There was a suggestion that his wounds could be opened and cleaned on board ship with the use of some cleansed, broken glass. But the captain was afraid of losing his leg and did not welcome any attempts at an operation, which in his view might lead to amputation when the ship reached land. The infected wound and the blood poisoning escalated, and as gangrene developed Reinhardt Godfrey Jonassen died, just short of fifty years old. An eventful life reached its unexpected end much too early on the ocean that he loved. He was put to rest on an unknown date in September 1915 at the main grounds of the London Missionary Society Church in Avarua, Rarotonga (see figure 9.1). His grave remains cared for to this day.

A Glimpse of Family Traditions: Surprising Encounters during the First World War

At this stage, before embarking on a narrative of what happened after Captain Jonassen's death and of the subsequent generations, let me dwell for a while on some of the family traditions of the Cook Islands Jonassens. Many are the tales told, and often is the family's unique Norwegian heritage referred to. One tale in particular deserves to be included here, and it concerns events that took place in Aitutaki just after the captain's untimely death. One of the memories that my father shared with me of his early boyhood years at Aitutaki involves a visit to that remote island by the infamous Graf Felix von Luckner (1881–1966), a German naval officer also known as 'the Sea Devil'. During 1916–17, Graf von Luckner commanded the large three-masted sailing ship *Seeadler* (the Sea Eagle) on a round-the-world cruise as an armed

Figure 9.1. The author by his grandfather's grave, 2012. *Source:* Edvard Hvid-ing; reproduced with permission.

commerce raider, destroying much Allied shipping in the Atlantic and the Pacific (Bromby 1985). In his bold operations von Luckner often slipped through British blockades, frequently masking his crew and ship as Norwegian, well aware that large Norwegian sailing ships still voyaged quite regularly across the world's oceans. In August 1917, how-ever, a combination of adverse weather and surprising slips of seaman-ship caused *Seeadler* to be wrecked on an atoll reef in the Society Islands of French Polynesia. In an impressive open-boat voyage, von Luckner and a small number of crew made their way towards Fiji in an opti-mistic search for a new ship. They sailed through the Cook Islands and called at several islands on the way before being captured by police in Fiji in September 1917. Wherever they made landfall they pretended to be Dutch or Norwegian. The visit they paid to Aitutaki was much more eventful than has been recorded in various official and news reports.

My father, Reinhardt's son, Michael, who was a small boy at the time, reports that von Luckner arrived outside the Aitutaki reef at night, and so had to stand off until morning before attempting to land. Strong cur-rents make any entry through the Aitutaki reef difficult, and in those days local expert harbour masters Tiini Pare'anga (Captain Jonassen's father-in-law) and Ka'u Mapu were usually on hand to assist visiting ships and boats. So it was not surprising that it was these two men who went out to meet the unexpected visiting boat that had been spotted earlier by some fishermen. The two island navigators guided the boat into the lagoon through a pass in the reef, and when told by von Luckner that the visitors were Norwegians, Tiini immediately invited the strangers to his home for a hearty meal, a kind gesture motivated by the fact that Tiini's recently deceased son-in-law, Reinhardt, had been Norwegian. Tiini felt that it was important to host the visiting Norwegians in a typical island feast. Local horse-drawn wagons were used to transport von Luckner and his five crewmen to the home of Tiini Pare'anga, where his wife Petirini was waiting with a sumptuous feast of pork, fish, chickens and other local delicacies. At the time, few people in Aitutaki could speak English. Tiini and Petirini were two of those few, and Petirini in particular, who was a daughter of the Englishman William Marsters, had been raised speaking both the English and Māori languages fluently.[14]

Michael was with his grandparents at the time, and he was captivated by the excitement of visiting strangers from his father's homeland. He kept staring at the visitors, in spite of his grandmother urging him not to do so. In recalling the story, Michael confided that he could not help it, but it was during those moments of staring at the visitors that he noticed one of them carrying a gun hidden behind his back. Michael also noted that the language the visitors spoke amongst themselves was very different from the one he had often heard his father speak. He told his grandmother of his suspicions. She had by then also noticed that the English spoken by the visitors was in fact very poor and heavily accented in a way that was unlike the way in which Norwegians spoke English. Petirini deduced that the visitors were in fact Germans pretending to be Norwegians. So as fate would have it, of all the families to become von Luckner's hosts on Aitutaki, it was people who were familiar with both Norwegian and English. Petirini urged her grandson to keep the information confidential, and after quietly sharing her suspicions with her husband, he, too, advised caution. Somehow, several islanders became aware of the situation, and some began gathering at the harbour with a ready plan to capture the Germans after the feast at Tiini's place. Petirini, however, discouraged such actions, and Ti'avaru, Reinhardt's widow, agreed with her, saying that an intervention would mean unnecessary loss of life.

When the Germans were transported back to the harbour, even more locals were gathered there. At this point von Luckner thanked Tiini for the feast and announced that they were departing. Tiini climbed into the boat with the Germans while his friend Ka'u Mapu trailed behind on a canoe. Once at sea, having safely made it through the reef passage, to the surprise of Tiini, a seventh German revealed himself from under a cover that had hidden both him and a machine gun. He had been left on board to watch over the boat and act as a rear guard. Tiini said goodbye to his 'Norwegian' friends and joined Ka'u Mapu in the canoe to return ashore. It is said that the German machine gunner wanted to shoot them, but von Luckner intervened, saying, 'No, they are good people. They are our friends.'

Back on the beach the Aitutaki people were waiting in anticipation. When Tiini and Ka'u were finally sighted, there was jubilation. They told the crowd about the seventh crewman and the machine gun, declaring that the people of Aitutaki were lucky that no attempt had been made to capture the Germans. Petirini was credited for her wisdom and advice. And so the secretive shipwrecked Germans left Aitutaki without incident, having been warmly received by the islanders. Aitutaki's colonial authorities were notified, and a warning was issued to Rarotonga, towards which von Luckner was now headed. As it turned out, von Luckner did not land in Rarotonga, mistaking a grounded ship on the reef in Rarotonga for a waiting armed schooner. He sailed straight on to Fiji, where he was apprehended. Had he only known that his cover had been so solidly blown by his generous hosts on Aitutaki!

The New Generations: Connections and Reconnections

Ti'avaru's world had been suddenly turned upside down at the death of her husband in 1915. Their youngest child, Josephine, was adopted by a family in Rarotonga. The two older children, Anne and Michael, were raised by their grandfather, Tiini Pare'anga. Upon hearing of Reinhardt's sudden death, his brother Jonas travelled to Rarotonga all the way from Norway to find Michael and take him back to Norway, and if possible to also take with him Michael's sisters, Anne and Josephine. But Tiini Pare'anga objected strongly, and so Jonas is reported to have travelled on to New Zealand and never returned to Norway. The Aitutaki family assumed that Jonas did not want to return to Norway because of the unsuccessful attempt to pick up Michael, and that he therefore preferred to settle in New Zealand. In accordance with Aitutaki custom and in memory of her husband, Ti'avaru's name was changed to Moumou, meaning 'what a waste, what a pity [that we have lost Reinhardt]'. Moumou eventually married again, to Tekotia Tekotia, otherwise known as Te-Pu-O-Te-Rangi, and they had several children. She used the name Moumou for the rest of her life.

Petirini, the captain's mother-in-law and the children's grandmother, became the major caregiver for Anne and Michael. As Captain Reinhardt's children grew up, they were given additional local names: Rakau (for Anne), Ka or Norue (for Michael) and Marū (for Josephine). After Reinhardt's death, his fellow Scandinavian and close friend Viggo Rasmussen often visited Michael to give birthday and Christmas gifts. My father fondly remembered how 'Uncle Vigo' had given him a mouth organ and other toys. The three children of Reinhardt and Ti'avaru were not reunited again until later in their adult lives, but they all yearned to see their father's beloved Norway and the family that they knew still lived there. When the Jonassen family's Betela Dance Troup became globe-trotting performers, more regular contacts with Norwegians (even at home in Rarotonga, see figure 9.2) entrenched what was an inherited desire to visit Norway, even for the third and fourth generations.

The opportunity for Reinhardt's children to actually visit Norway did not arise until after Anne had passed away. When they were ninety and eighty-eight, respectively, Michael and Josephine finally travelled to Norway courtesy of Norwegian State Broadcasting as part of a special television documentary on Captain Jonassen. The visit had been preceded by some of Reinhardt's descendants in Norway visiting Rarotonga and Aitutaki. Ironically, it was Ragnhild, the child that Reinhardt never met, who had offspring in Norway. Not long after the visit to Aitutaki by their Norwegian relatives, Captain Jonassen's two surviving children in the Cook Islands, Michael and Josephine, were invited to visit Norway for a follow-up and to conclude the production of the

Figure 9.2. Michael and Lily Jonassen with three daughters on board the Norwegian cruise liner MS *Bergensfjord,* at Rarotonga, 1967. Left to right: ship's officer, Anne, Michael, Muriel, ship's captain, Lily (mother) and Lily (daughter). *Source*: Collection of J.T.M. Jonassen; reproduced with permission.

documentary. It was my honour to escort them and to witness firsthand their deep love for a family they had never before met and a country they had never seen. Josephine was extremely ill at the time, but insisted that she make the journey she had waited for over eighty years to make. Upon our return from the visit to Norway, Josephine was admitted to a hospital in New Zealand with advanced pneumonia. Her remarkable faith and love had sustained her during the whole two-week ordeal of travel between destinations as far apart as can be. My father, Michael, was also a sight to see as he walked around like a young man, insisting on visiting all of the family-related sights and graves, including his grandfather's original house at Egerøen, a tiny island in Farsund, the visit to which required a boat trip and much walking. From there, he brought a collection of stones home to the Cook Islands.

While it was only his daughter Ragnhild who had descendants in Norway, all of Jonassen's children in Aitutaki bore offspring. The legacy that he left in the Cook Islands was one that reflected trading, music, navigation, diplomacy and simply being a good human being. Ti'avaru, or Moumou, as she preferred to be called, often related how wonderful Reinert was, even long after she had married her second husband, Tekotia. Captain Jonassen was a talented navigator, and several members of Ti'avaru's family became expert seafarers as a result of his direct intervention. His son, Michael, also pursued navigation training, but eventually decided to become a career teacher. But as Reinhardt Jonassen was a trader, so did Michael become one, too, opening shops in Aitutaki and in Rarotonga. The hardworking, industrial character that Reinhardt displayed was obvious in all three of his Aitutaki children. Anne and her husband opened a bakery and pursued a variety of moneymaking ventures. Josephine became a talented seamstress and ran a tourist accommodation business in Aitutaki until the age of ninety-two. Michael opened a variety of ventures with his wife Lily, including a bakery, cinema, taxies and motor vehicle rentals, as well as carrying on many of the traditions established by his father.

Captain Jonassen is remembered as an avid musician who played the violin to an Aitutaki population that had a fondness for music. The violin (called a *kinura* by the Aitutakians) was one of the many artefacts that were passed on to his son, Michael, in addition to photographs, navigation tools and a variety of documents written in Norwegian. Michael himself became an avid musician, choir singer and song composer. In conclusion, Captain Jonassen was multilingual, a great musician, a hard worker, a service-oriented person, a fine teacher and a builder of tangible things as well as of good character. These attributes were found in all of his children in the Cook Islands, and have indeed been passed on to third, fourth and fifth generations. However, Reinert's son, Michael, is perhaps the greatest example of his legacy. I devote the last part of this chapter to commemorating my father and the legacy of my grandfather.

Michael William 'Norue' Jonassen, the Captain's Son

Michael William Jonassen was born in Aitutaki on 9 May 1912 as the second child and only son of Reinert Godtfred Jonassen (also known as Reinhardt Godfrey Jonassen) and Ti'avaru Sarah Akakaingaro-a-Pa-ma-Kainuku Tini Pare'anga. Ultimately there were three siblings: Anne (Rakau), Michael (Ka or Norue) and Josephine (Marū). Michael also had two half sisters in Norway from his father's first marriage (Theodora and Ragnhild), and later on several half brothers and sisters from his mother's subsequent marriage to Tekotia (Tuapo, Peri, Eteta, Taiti, Tua, John, Teina, Mata and Petirini). Michael was raised in Aitutaki by his parents, and later by his grandfather and grandmother when his father passed away. Nicknamed Norue (Norway), he was constantly reminded of his father, in particular when he later emulated his father as a diligent and effective worker. Michael attended Araura's primary school and was awarded the prestigious Pomare Medal in 1928 for being the most outstanding student on the island. He was given a special scholarship to attend school in Rarotonga and so attended Avarua's primary school, where he became their representative in a national scholarly competition in 1929, which Avarua won for the first time. He was later awarded a New Zealand Scholarship, but this was not utilized because of an earthquake in Napier. Michael returned to Aitutaki, where he became an assistant teacher at the very young age of seventeen.

On 28 July 1937, Michael married Lily Teina Tauei-o-Tinomana Napa. Together they had six children: Reinhardt Godtfred (also known as Rena Ariki), Anne Lina Ti'avaru, Theodora Ana, Lily Ngapoko Tutu Ariki, Jon Tikivanotau Michael and Muriel Matakavau. Michael had previously adopted his nephew Nooroa (also known as Nono'o), and later raised numerous nephews, nieces and younger siblings.

Over the years, Michael was involved in many activities, including music, church work, community projects, agriculture, nonprofit ventures, business and sports. His first love, however, was teaching, and he maintained that profession for over forty-five years. Having taught, worked and lived in almost every inhabited island of the southern group, Michael touched the lives of thousands of Cook Islanders. Despite retirement from teaching in 1970, he continued to be an active member of the community. He lived in Auckland during the last years of his life.

Retracing the busy life of Michael William Jonassen makes for interesting reading. From 1927 he held an unbroken succession of teaching posts at schools in Aitutaki and Rarotonga, finally retiring in 1970 from a post as the first principal of Rutaki School, Rarotonga. He was an active citrus and pineapple planter, exporting as well as providing for the local market, and was a long-time member of the Rarotonga Grower's Association. His spiritual activities spanned three church groups, including the London Missionary Society (LMS), the Seventh-day Adventists (SDA) and the Latter-day Saints (LDS). From his birth in 1912 to 1950 Michael was an active follower of the LMS and was given several opportunities for a deacon post, but this was declined for travel reasons. For a time Michael helped translate some of the SDA scriptures, before becoming involved in the LDS from 1969 to 2007 as an active member, becoming president of the Arorangi Branch in 1978–79 and second counsellor in the LDS Cook Islands District in 1980–83. He and his wife allowed the LDS to occupy their land in Arorangi for the construction of a chapel.

Throughout his life, Michael was very dynamic in sports. His rugby involvement began when he played for Amuri in Aitutaki (1927–29). He developed his rugby career as a coach, team selector and referee, also playing for teams in New Zealand. In 1935, Michael formed the Araura Cricket Club, and continued to be active in that sport until 1987. Michael also played tennis, and he initiated the development of a tennis association in 1942.

In the field of music, from 1927 to 1990 Michael was a choirmaster and music teacher. He composed many songs, some becoming national classics, including 'Aue Te Tiare Māori', 'Ngaipu Ngaitua', 'Aue Te Namu ite Manata', 'Akiaki Tupa', 'Ngauru', 'Darling Roti Koe Noku', 'Tapuaetai' and 'Ite Pae Taatai Pakea.' From 1934 to 1942 Michael maintained a very popular mouth organ band in Aitutaki. In 1943–44 Michael and his wife Lily coordinated and organized community concerts to raise funds to buy sacrament cups for the LMS Church in Arorangi, and ultimately those funds also contributed to building the Betela Meeting House. By 1960, Michael and Lily had started the Arorangi-based Betela Youth Club, which eventually became an internationally famous dance team, involving hundreds of Cook Islanders over the years. The Betela Dance Troup won many competitions, toured internationally (including Japan – see figure 9.3), raised money for the Cook Islands delegation to the first South Pacific Games in Fiji and contributed funds to several national and community projects, including the construction of hostels in Rarotonga.

Figure 9.3. The Betela Dance Troup on tour in Japan, 1971. Seen here are Michael and Lily and four of their children; the author is in the middle of the front row. *Source:* Collection of J.T.M. Jonassen; reproduced with permission.

The least known of Michael's activities concerns his many nonprofit ventures. From 1934 to 1942 Michael and Lily carved out orange plantation rental projects in Aitutaki to assist planters in earning cash incomes. In the same period, they went into a local fishing boat venture aimed at creating a bartering service to assist locals in exchanging their agricultural products. For the next seventeen years, 1943–60, Michael and Lily used their trucks to assist in various community programs and projects in Rarotonga. They established a nonprofit venture (1944–50) in which coconuts for copra were exchanged for bread. A trial run in 1958 saw the export of one batch of five hundred hula skirts to California, to investigate the potential for marketing a local cottage industry.

It is in business that Michael and Lily are most renowned. From 1942 to 1968 Michael assisted Lily in her import/export business, which included managing a series of shops in Rarotonga. In 1950–55 they operated a 16 mm movie enterprise active in Arorangi, Titikaveka and Ngatangiia. For the next ten years the movie business was extended to the outer islands, the first introduction of film screenings to most of those islands. They also began 35 mm movie shows. A successful bakery business in Arorangi was established, which serviced the whole island of Rarotonga and employed up to fifty people. During 1950–70 Michael and Lily operated a taxi and rental business, which Michael managed after retirement from teaching. In 1970 the taxi and rental business expanded its operations, initiating the import and marketing of Honda and Yamaha motorcycles from Japan, an activity continued until 1989. Their last business venture was a video rental business that operated between 1989 and 1991.

Though reluctant, Michael was at times drawn into the national political limelight. In 1964 he was elected as the Cook Islands' Māori representative in a board consisting of three members (of which two were Europeans) to assist the New Zealand government with the 'taxation' problems of the Cook Islands Māori people. During 1949–50 he was the elected president of the Cook Islands Teachers Guild and fought for increases in the salaries of local teachers. In this capacity he visited most of the outer islands.

On his ninety-fifth birthday, in 2007, a week after the passing of Lily, his wife for over seventy years, Michael still reminisced about his father and insisted that instead of staying close to him in this final stage of his life, I should continue with an already-planned visit to his own father's beloved Norway. I did travel from New Zealand to Norway at the end of May 2007 to give the lecture on which this chapter is based, and to meet my friends at the University of Bergen. On 1 June, when my sister had confirmed to Michael that I had arrived safely in Bergen, he died peacefully.

Reflecting on what I saw in my father's eyes as I left for Norway that day in May 2007, I envisioned the Norwegian grandfather that I never met. Like his father before him, Michael was a self-taught mechanic, builder and musician who dedicated much of his life to teaching, outdoor activities and business ventures. The legacy of Captain Reinert Godtfred Jonassen continues to live through me, my siblings and cousins, and all our descendants – but we have the challenge of emulating his contributions. My own father and his two sisters in the Cook Islands were certainly able to do so.

Notes

This chapter is a revised version of a presentation originally given at the University Museum of Bergen, 7 June 2007. I would like to express my gratitude to the University of Bergen project 'In the Wake of Colonialism', and to Edvard

Hviding in particular, for the interest and attention given to this particular Pacific story, with its Norwegian connections. An earlier version of this chapter was published in Norwegian. For work on the translation of my writings into Norwegian, as well as editorial work on the present chapter, I am very grateful to Edvard Hviding.

1. These are two Cook Islands Māori traditional chants, translated into English by the author.
2. Other Scandinavians arrived in the Cook Islands after Jonassen. Viggo Rasmussen, who is remembered as Danish (or, by some, as Norwegian), married a young woman from the island of Mitiaro and established a store there. Reinert and Viggo were to develop a close relationship. Another Norwegian by the name of Nielsen also visited Aitutaki and established a family there, years after Jonassen had passed away. Nielsen lived in Reureu village with an Aitutaki woman, and they had a son known as Rima Nielson. Rima's descendants continue to live in Aitutaki and Australia.
3. The far-flung archipelago of the Cook Islands is today a nation-state known by that name. It is a parliamentary democracy that exists in an arrangement of 'free association' with New Zealand, and has a resident population of about twenty thousand. A much larger number of Cook Islands Māori live in New Zealand and Australia. While the Cook Islands' land area is modest, at ca. 240 square kilometres, the nation's exclusive economic zone covers as much as 1.8 million square kilometres.
4. Over five hundred Cook Islands songs have been composed by Michael William Jonassen or Jon T.M. Jonassen. A number of books on Cook Islands history and culture have been written by Jonassen family members, who have also been closely involved in the emerging nation's political issues. Sadaraka (Cookie) Sadaraka, Reinhardt (Rena) Jonassen and Jon T.M. Jonassen have served in high-level positions in government over many years.
5. It is not widely known that it was in fact British citizens living in Rarotonga who first convinced Makea Ariki to fly the British flag in her territory of Te Au o Tonga, essentially only one-third of the island. Another chief, Tinomana Ariki, who controlled Puaikura on the western side, married a Frenchman and so was ready with her French flag. When a French frigate came to Rarotonga on a mission to claim the island, it approached Makea Ariki's side of the island, and the British flag was sighted. The history of this island nation could have been very different had the French ship approached Rarotonga from the west.
6. Translated from unidentified papers in Norwegian, p. 80 (in author's files). According to Michael William Jonassen, his father had shares in *Gyda*.
7. From unidentified papers in Norwegian, p. 241 (in author's files).
8. Ti'avaru means 'eight promises', and her name linked her genealogically to the islands of Aitutaki, Rarotonga, Palmerston, Penrhyn, Manihiki and Mangaia.
9. Government officials at the time in Rarotonga noted that early age marriages were common: 'Cameron (Resident Agent) tells me that his great trouble in Aitutaki was the early marriages of the young people' (quoted in Craig 1985: 124).

10. The *kukui* tree (*Aleurites moluccana*) bears large volumes of nuts rich in oil, which in the Pacific has been used as a light source (hence the English name, 'candlenut'). A well-known ingredient in Asian cooking, the nuts used to be important for the industrial production of vegetable oil, hence Jonassen's trade of the nuts to New Zealand.
11. Document signed by Captain Emil Piltz outlining his work experience, HKP.
12. It was speculated that Viggo may have been Reinhardt's cousin through maternal family links, but some have claimed that they were unrelated and that Viggo was from Denmark. That said, there could also have been kinship relations between Denmark and the southern coast of Norway at the time.
13. Upon Captain Jonassen's death, the ownership of the house was somehow transferred to the Cook Islands Trading Company, but the captain's son (and my father), Michael, later bought the property and transferred it to Te Marae O Tangaroa (a family land; the name literally means 'sacred lands of the sea god Tangaroa'). My father also often talked of Campbell's hidden gold chests somewhere in Aitutaki, which were never found.
14. William Marsters settled the remote atoll island of Palmerston with his three wives from Penrhyn Island, and their descendants continue to live on the island.

Archives Consulted

Harry Kalehua Piltz Jr collection (HKP), Laie, Hawaii.

References

Bromby, R. 1985. *German Raiders of the South Seas*. Sydney: Doubleday.
Craig, E. 1985. *Destiny Well Sown: A Biography of Lt.-Col. W.E. Gudgeon*. Whakatane, New Zealand: Whakatane & District Historical Society.
Grimshaw, B. (1908) 1971. *In the Strange South Seas*. New York: Books for Libraries Press.
Maretu. 1871. *Cannibals and Converts*, trans. Marjorie Crocombe. Suva: Institute of Pacific Studies, University of the South Pacific.
Pacific Islands Monthly. 1970. 'Changes in Rarotonga', November, pp. 57–59.
Ramsden, E. 1939. 'Men Who Knew Yesterday', *Pacific Islands Monthly*, 16 January, p. 19.
Scott, D. 1991. *Years of the Poo-Bah: A Cook Islands History*. London: Hodder & Stoughton.
Siers, J. 1977. *Rarotonga*. Wellington: Millwood Press.
Syed, S. and N. Mataio. 1993. *Agriculture in the Cook Islands*. Rarotonga: University of the South Pacific.
Williamson, R. 1924. *The Social and Political System of Central Polynesia*, 3 vols. Cambridge: Cambridge University Press.

10

FROM ADVENTURE TO INDUSTRY
AND NATION MAKING

The History of a Norwegian Sugar Plantation in Hawai'i

Knut M. Rio

> It is of Kaua'i that this story shall tell, the first of the islands to spring from
> the sea, the oldest and fairest. We shall go back to a time when few white
> people had settled there, when strong, bronzed men still lived in grass
> houses, living simply and happily together. This is the saga of Kaua'i, and
> of Kanuka, the tall, blond Norwegian who became a king.
> – Eric A. Knudsen and Guerre P. Noble, *Kanuka of Kaua'i*

I will in this chapter describe how the Norwegian presence in Kaua'i,
Hawai'i, represents a somewhat different version of colonialism from
the one we encounter in Africa in this volume. I will explain how the
northern Europeans who arrived in Kaua'i not only came to extract resources, but also to build a new nation, accompanied by Hawaiian elites.

As indicated by the above quote, there is a popular Hawaiian understanding of Kanuka, or Valdemar Knudsen, as was his Norwegian
name, becoming an aristocratic Hawaiian when he first started engaging with the Hawaiian population in Kaua'i. But contrary to popular
Western conceptions of the Pacific island as an unchanging paradise,
I wish to argue that to be 'king' of a tropical island became possible
because of massive cultural changes in an era when not only were people moving around the world, but also when cultural institutions were
being destabilized.

In this story of Kaua'i we get a unique perspective not only of colonization itself and the actual settlement of the Hawaiian archipelago,
but also of how Norwegian settlers blended in with other northern Europeans and how these together completely transformed the Hawaiian
landscape. Unlike the stories of the many sailors and settlers who became assimilated into the Pacific world (see the chapters by Hviding
and Jonassen, this volume), these Norwegian enterprises eventually
gained such political and social importance that they are well-docu-

mented in, for instance, the Hawaiian Sugar Planters' Association Plantation Archives at the University of Hawai'i, in biographical books such as *Stories of Long Ago* by Ida Elisabeth Knudsen Von Holt (1985), *Kanuka of Kaua'i* by Eric A. Knudsen and Guerre P. Noble (1999) and *Akamai* by Jon Moe (1975), and in photographic and historical archives at the Kaua'i Museum. These documents illuminate the unique characteristic of what I consider to be the creation of the Hawaiian nation – nation building through northern European ideas about the beautiful country they arrived in combined with stories about Hawaiian authenticity, and through work and cultivation of the landscape as an essential value.

Konohiki Kanuka

Valdemar Knudsen was born in 1820 in Kristiansand, the eleventh child in the family, and his father, Knud Knudsen (1770–1850), was the city's president of the magistrate – today known as the town council. Knudsen studied languages at the University of Copenhagen, and his descendants describe him as impressively multilingual – he mastered Latin, German, Spanish, Italian, French and English, and later on he learned Hawaiian on Kaua'i. He eventually travelled to New York, where he found use for his language proficiency and literary background working for the publisher Henry Holt & Co. Knudsen moved on to California during the gold rush, and in 1851 he was such an established commercial traveller that he was listed as one of the delegates for the Constitutional Convention that declared California a separate state. During one of his trips he developed Panama fever and was advised by a doctor to migrate to a warmer climate. Quite accidentally he ended up on a ship from San Francisco to Hilo on Hawai'i Island, and from there to the island of Kaua'i. He arrived in June 1857 and spent the rest of his life there, dying on his Waiawa ranch in Kaua'i in 1898, seventy-eight years old.

Hence, when Valdemar Knudsen came to Kaua'i at the age of thirty-seven, he was already well travelled. Although not very wealthy, he did have an education that made him suitable to fill a role in the upper levels of the colonial structure. In Koloa – the first site for plantation activities on Kaua'i – he immediately made contact with George Wilcox, the plantation manager for what was to become Grove Farm Plantations. Here Knudsen also got in contact with many of the second-generation immigrants from Germany, Scotland, Denmark, the Netherlands or England. They were children of missionaries or commercial travellers who had close relationships with Hawaiian residents whom they had grown up with and gone to Sunday school with, and they had learned their language. Knudsen was also greatly influenced by the proud indigenous Hawaiians and their traditions. Through these different relationships, he created for himself a home on Kaua'i, also known as the 'Garden Isle' due to its lush vegetation.

Shortly after arriving at Grove Farm, Knudsen heard of another Norwegian in the area, Archibald Archer from Larvik. Archer had for the past few years attempted to grow coffee and tobacco on land at Kekaha and Mana in the west. He learned that Archer had a thirty-year contract on a large area of 'crown land' as a tenant directly under King Kamehameha III. Under the great national splitting of land that happened in the years after 1848, large parts of the country had been divided into smaller pieces of land of which most islanders could become owners. The other part of the land was known as 'crown land' and was still considered the king's land but was managed by royally appointed land tenants, so-called *Konohiki*. In this capacity Archer had attempted to work the land, but due to lack of workers he had decided to join his brothers, who were far more successful with their plantations in northeast Australia.[1] Archer was willing to transfer his land contract to Knudsen, and Knudsen was appointed by the king to be the new *Konohiki*, the land manager of one hundred thousand acres on the west side of Kaua'i. According to his son Eric Knudsen's biography about his father, this gave him the authority of a prince:

> All the natives living on it were tenants-at-will, and subject to the orders of the *Konohiki*. The land extended from the Waimea River to the ocean-bound valley of Nu'alolo, and ran far upland into the mountains and dense forests. There was a large population of Hawaiians, many villages of grass houses, and hundreds of others scattered throughout the entire district. (Knudsen and Noble 1999: 35)

Shortly after his appointment as *Konohiki*, Knudsen invited all the villagers to a meeting to introduce himself. Eric Knudsen's biography demonstrates Knudsen's descendants' almost mythical image of him:

> Then he began to talk, not as a *haole* (foreigner), but fluently in their own tongue. They were at first amazed, then delighted. This man was a true *ali'i*, a chief, one they could trust to lead them, one they would be glad to follow. 'My people', he said, '*aloha*.'
> A stillness spread over the group, intensified by the sighing of the wind and clatter of *hala* branches. The sunlight rested on his shoulder like a steadying bird. A child on the edge of the group whimpered and was quickly hushed by its mother. Valdemar studied the faces turned towards him and found only kindness there. 'Your king, Kamehameha', he continued in a clear, ringing voice, 'has appointed me *Konohiki* of all this western land, over the villages of Kekaha, Pokii, Kaunalewa, Kolo and Mana – and all the lands between, far up into the mountains and the valleys. I want to

be your friend as well as *Konohiki*. I shall ask no more of you than is right and just, and I know you will serve me faithfully and well.'

With one voice they answered him, 'We will serve you well.' One man standing near him, taller than the others, the chief of one of the villages, then spoke, 'We will call him Kanuka, Ali'i o Kaua'i' [Chief of Kaua'i].

'Kanuka, Ali'i o Kaua'i,' they repeated. And that became his name, Kanuka, the Hawaiian for Knudsen. A Viking had become a king of Kaua'i. (Knudsen and Noble 1999: 36)

This obviously rosy and fictional account notwithstanding, there are few sources that might inform us of the real nature of the relationship between Knudsen as *Konohiki* and the Kauaian population. However, despite its hagiographic elements, the above account does present us with something of a mystery: how could a Norwegian receive such a royal title and how did the relationship between the land manager and his people work? The relation between the new European land managers and the indigenous population has not been described very much in historical records, where especially Hawaiians' lives disappear into the background. Most likely, however, they continued their irrigation agriculture, as well as becoming gradually more involved in work at the new plantations that developed from around 1850 onwards.

Knudsen built a ranch in an area previously uninhabited but close to indigenous villages, where he raised horses and livestock. He left a large area of marsh to his Chinese friend Pah On Leong, who arrived from China in 1864 and aimed to cultivate rice.[2] As a result of the activities of Knudsen, Long and others, the Hawaiians in the area watched considerable activity on fields and in terrains that previously had been uncultivated. Presumably inspired by this work, some Hawaiians also attempted rice cultivation, and young men came to Knudsen's ranch and asked for work. As part of his *Konohiki* office Knudsen was to keep a record of the population living on his land. This included births and deaths, and he also had some executive powers, to punish and to banish people from the area if necessary. He was the manager of several thousands of people, and could expel inhabitants who did not follow Hawaiian custom.

His son Eric, who grew up with his father and became an advocate for Hawaiian traditions himself after he finished his training as a lawyer at Harvard Law School, gives us the impression that his father was assimilated into these relations on Kaua'i with the traditional degree of hierarchy in Hawaiian society. Knudsen's close friend and coworker at the ranch, the Hawaiian David Kua, allegedly said to him:

You are one of us, Kanuka, and still you are above all of us, and have been from that first day when you spoke to us. We all have felt it. To us you are truly *ka ali'i,* of Kaua'i. You are no common man, you neither drink nor smoke. You put your religious beliefs into your daily life. I have heard many of the people talk of these things among themselves. (Knudsen and Noble 1999: 57)

Based on this trust Knudsen also joined the political arena in 1860. During King Kamehameha III's rule (1813–54) the political system included a parliament consisting of a house of royally appointed representatives and a lower house with the people's representatives. Knudsen was offered a seat in the upper house due to his role as *Konohiki,* but instead he chose to sit in the lower house as the representative for his district of Kaua'i. There were both Hawaiians and *haole,* 'white men', in this assembly, and they dealt with matters of concern to local inhabitants as well as trade and infrastructure between the islands and with foreign countries. Valdemar Knudsen gained an important role, mainly as *Konokiki,* but also as an influential member of the growing Hawaiian bourgeoisie. This can be recognized through his choice of friends, by his interests and not least by his choice of spouse, Anne Sinclair, around 1867 (see Von Holt 1985). The Sinclair family, originally from one of the larger Scottish clans, had crossed the sea a few years earlier from New Zealand. They had run a plantation there for decades, but after the death of the head of the family, the widow, Elisabeth Sinclair, packed her belongings, sold the entire business and sailed across the ocean to find happiness for herself and her six children, including Anne. They participated in Honolulu social life, and they became acquainted with the court of King Kamehameha V. When he heard of their initial plans to continue their travels to Canada, he persuaded them instead to stay by offering to sell them the whole island of Ni'ihau, and a contract was written for USD 10,000 in gold. The island, which is located west of Kaua'i and close to the Knudsen area, had a population of three hundred people, and the Sinclair family could realize their sheep farming and wool production plans there. Later they also engaged in the sugar industry under the Gay & Robinson Co., which had their plantations located just south of Knudsen's land.

Families such as these, in the process of establishing themselves in Kaua'i, became sociable, both in each other's houses and gardens and up in the hills, where their smaller vacation houses offered refuge from the high coastal temperatures. For these immigrants, originally from northern Europe, Hawai'i was the Promised Land in several ways. While they were all eager to maintain the idea of the land as in itself valuable and affluent in tradition, a dominant perception was that it ought to be developed and refined through mixing with the very best of traditions from the rest of the world. All the families imported different breeds of cattle, horses and sheep: Arabian horses, Hereford cattle and

Merino sheep were among the species they introduced. This coincided with the broader worldviews of these adventurers: the notion of a new land with proud traditions in a fruitful relationship with the best of European history. Breeding, genealogy and honour became recurring themes in the development of the new Hawaiian nation. Until annexation by the United States in 1898, this was also combined with extensive sociability with the Hawaiian royal family.

This imagery of traditions, genealogies and pedigrees runs through almost everything that was written in this period – ranging from epic tales of how the European venerable lineages met and interacted with the Hawaiian royal family, to minor remarks such as this quote about Valdemar Knudsen: 'In his face were the strong markings of dignity and breeding' (Knudsen and Noble 1999: 35). The conception of mixing has arguably also become the popular story about the Hawaiian nation. One example of this is how Eric Knudsen is portrayed in a recent publication from Hawai'i: 'It was remarkable how unassuming and friendly such a notable as Mr. Knudsen could be. Born at Waiawa, West Kaua'i, in the 1870ies, his grandfather had been the last President of Norway when it was under Danish rule, and his mother was the beloved Annie Sinclair of Niihau' (Ashman 2004: 134). In this context, the office of *Konohiki* and being a descendant of the 'last president of Norway' (an imaginative reformulation of town mayor) seems to coincide as two statuses of equal importance, even though the latter part was a very biased translation between the Hawaiian world and the Norwegian.

This historical imagery hence flows out of Valdemar Knudsen's office as *Konohiki* under King Kamehameha IV and V. He was part of the reconstruction of the country, not only by domesticating land and raising cattle and thus cultivating a modern landscape, but also in his network of relationships in Kaua'i and nationally through his political engagement. He became what we could call a Hawaiian nationalist and modernist. He lived well off the land rent he obtained from the growing industry in his area, so well that he was able to send all his children to universities such as Harvard. Eric became the most well-known of these. He finished law school, and moved back to the ranch, and in due course became a member of the U.S. Senate for Hawai'i in Washington, D.C., again extending the pedigree of Knudsen as almost royalty.

A Time of Change and Opportunity

The popular understanding of Norwegians who settled in the Pacific Islands is that the adventurers attained high status in static and immutable societies. Before I return to the development of Knudsen's 'kingdom', I will therefore give a brief introduction to the historical context and structural relations that facilitated his establishment on Kaua'i.

Around 1850 Oceania was characterized by a large flow of people and goods (see also Hviding's chapters and the introduction to this volume). Kaua'i was but a microcosm of this situation, and when Valdemar Knudsen arrived in 1857 the Hawaiian Islands were in the middle of a cultural and political transformation. For centuries the islands had been subject to a centralized kingdom with subdivisions of land tenants. *Ahupuaa,* parcels of land that stretched from the coastline up to a point in the middle of the island, forming a triangle, provided the necessary livelihood for family groups. These areas were subject to chiefs, who again were subject to the monarchy. Ordinary people had full rights to move between *ahupuaa,* and were in that sense free people, but they had no land rights, and had to pay the king with goods and favours for the right to cultivate the soil (Daws 1968). In the two decades immediately before 1800, the Hawaiian Islands had been ridden with intense strife, between the king of Oahu and Maui, the king of Kaua'i and Niihau, and the three kings who shared the southern island of Hawai'i. This situation was to a great extent influenced by the increasing European presence since 1780, as the warring kings constantly tried to acquire modern weapons by strategic engagements with military units and traders. Hawai'i's King Kamehameha I was the most talented within this new emerging political field and by 1795 he had conquered Hawai'i, Oahu and Maui. King Kaumuali'i (1778–1824) on Kaua'i resisted for many years, as he was far superior to Kamehameha in the Hawaiian royal family and because he was in the company of many of Kamehameha's rivals from the other islands. In 1810 King Kaumuali'i travelled together with a commercial travel companion from New England to finally meet with King Kamehameha I at Honolulu Harbour. It was under these circumstances of international trade and diplomacy that Kaumuali'i finally declared allegiance to Kamehameha (Joesting 1984).

This hectic activity, of intergovernmental democracy, commercial travellers who tried to gain positions in the networks of the various kings and chiefs who attempted to access the assets of trade, was driven mainly by an international demand for sandalwood. Sandalwood was abundant in the islands, and for several decades chiefs and royalty used it as their most important currency. Until 1819 the two Hawaiian kings shared the exclusive trading monopoly on this commodity. When Kamehameha I died in 1819, his successor was pressured by chiefs and American interests to leave the trade largely to the chiefs, who became land managers, or *Konohiki.* This shift initiated an accelerated timber sale, because the chiefs were now able to buy sought-after Asian goods under the direct agreement of payment in timber. The chiefs surrounded themselves with velvet, satin, Chinese porcelain, tea and coffee, wine, and canned products and sent their workers into the hills to collect the great numbers of logs that were the price of what they had bought. The chiefs' desire for these goods affected Hawaiian workers adversely, as it took time away from farming. The work was exhausting and excessive, and the villages suffered from imported diseases.

The American traders sold the timber in Canton and received Chinese goods such as tea and porcelain in return, which they could sell at a profit in America. Around 1830, after ten years of intensive logging and the delivery of over ten thousand tons of sandalwood, the islands were denuded of wood. At this point consumption was so high among the royals and nobles that they had accumulated vast debts secured by sandalwood that was no longer available. This was the beginning of the Hawaiian nation's debt to the United States (Joesting 1984).

One could argue that the above political and economic shifts were occasioned by the Hawaiian kings' new access to the Asian market through American traders as middlemen. But seen structurally, this also shifted the chiefs' role to increasingly becoming patrons and economic entrepreneurs. This in turn resulted in a lack of faith in the chiefs' authority, and in another groundbreaking change: the abolition of the religious taboos in 1819. When King Kamehameha I died, his son, Liholiho, was subject to intense pressure, first from his mother and her supporters, to end the traditional taboos – mainly traditional laws that concerned relationships with the gods. The taboos were social regulations concerned with maintaining law, order and hierarchy in the gods' images – having to do with seasons, farming, the relationship between genders and between ordinary people and royalty, and prescribing in detail acceptable forms of everyday socializing among ordinary people. Until 1819 all breaches of taboos had been punishable by death to avoid the gods' punishment. The abandonment of the taboos was a radical measure that occasioned the disintegration of the religious superstructure of the society: images of gods were destroyed, women and men could suddenly eat together freely and it occurred to people that the gods might not wield the powers they used to. This radical decline in trust in the gods may also be linked to experiences with white men in the forty years that had passed since Captain Cook's arrival in 1778, experiences that indicated that the taboos did not apply to white people. With the loss of the taboos, and the loss of the chiefs' authority and credibility during the sandalwood period, some of the basis for royal power and hierarchy faded, perhaps along with the belief in godly influence. After this, the royal house also converted to Christianity and introduced rules of monogamy (Daws 1968).

These historical developments show the magnitude of the changes these islands had gone through *before* Valdemar Knudsen could write home about his kingdom on Hawai'i. By 1835, the American firm Ladd & Co. had signed the first contract leasing land in Hawai'i, to start sugar production on Kaua'i. The contract was signed directly with King Kamehameha III. This became an extension of the cultural system of chiefly titles, where all inhabitants on the piece of land in question were encouraged to work on their plantations as a form of tax. Under this system Ladd paid the king USD 0.25 per worker per month (Joesting 1984: 131). Such innovation meant a profound structural change – from a system with patron-client relations between chief and villagers and toward a system of employment and cash labour and a phasing out of the chief's role to the advantage of plantation managers.

Another major shift that was crucial for Knudsen and his contemporaries was what became known as the 'Great Mahele' – the land division of 1848 (Daws 1968: 124–28) – that reviewed all existing land rights throughout the archipelago. The result was that the king abandoned his godly right to all land and only retained what were called 'crown lands'. Commoners could now for the first time buy small parcels of land and, crucially, foreigners could take up leases on this land. While the purpose of this reform initiated by the kingdom was to benefit islanders by giving them the ability to harvest food on their own piece of land, most private proprietary rights were given to foreign investors who wanted to run large plantations and who paid out the land-owning farmers. For most people at the grassroots level, the new *Konohiki* were now the people who controlled plantations and ranches. A local historian of Kaua'i sums this up as follows:

> The men who ran the plantations and ranches were considered chiefs because of their positions of authority. Not all of them had empathy for the Hawaiians or had gained their respect, but over the years those who had were numbered among the new chiefs of Kaua'i. Valdemar Knudsen, William Harrison Rice, Duncan McBryde, Goodfrey Wundenberg, and Paul Isenberg were among them. (Joesting 1984: 144)

It was after this series of historical events – changes in international trade relations and the offer and demand of commodities, a breakdown of religious taboos, and the modernization and democratization of the kingdom – that Valdemar Knudsen and his Norwegian relatives drifted onto the Kaua'i shores rather coincidentally. We can see from the historical events that Hawai'i was far from an unchangeable Pacific paradise. Furthermore, contrary to dominant Western understandings of the colonies as primitive and peripheral places on the outskirts of civilization, places such as Hawai'i were actually leading lights in historic development and modernization. One might say that it was in such places as Honolulu, Singapore, Canton, Cape Town or Rio de Janeiro that the visible density of 'modern life' was highest, as these places were flooded with international products, new technologies were developed to make sugar, coffee and oil, and modern state formation was experimented with through the laboratories of diplomacy, democracy and international law. This is also visible in the story of Valdemar Knudsen. He was educated in Norway but went to New York and later California, probably hungry for adventure as well as prosperity. As recounted, he took part in the California gold rush and in the politics that led to the establishment of California as a state in 1850. When coming to Kaua'i he went directly into a role as manager of Grove Farm Plantations, became responsible for road construction on Kaua'i and was appointed member of parliament, while also running a ranch and cattle farm. Despite his seemingly coincidental arrival in Hawai'i, he soon discovered that these islands were not remote places but buzzing with opportunity.

The Kanuka Family Expands Further

But we shall move on from Valdemar Knudsen to his Norwegian relatives who followed his lead to Hawai'i. Whereas Kanuka remained a mythical figure – relatively well placed within a frame of nobility and pioneering in the Kaua'ian system – his nephew Hans Peter Faye (1859–1928) played a much greater role as an industrialist and modern citizen of the Kanuka kingdom.[3]

Faye was the son of a merchant family that exported Norwegian timber and imported goods to the European continent. Their warehouse in Bergen had burned down, and the family was already heading towards bankruptcy during Hans Peter's youth. His family therefore moved to the eastern Norwegian town of Drammen, where as a seventeen-year-old he started working as a bookkeeper at the family sawmill. But around 1870 times were hard in Norway, and there were rumours going around about his relatives who had migrated to Hawai'i. Not only his uncle Valdemar Knudsen but also his brother-in-law Christian L'Orange and several others in their circle had now followed Knudsen. Hans Peter's father was married to Ida Knudsen, Knudsen's sister. Hans Peter Faye Sr later became a shipping agent in Germany and is also sometimes referred to in sources as 'consul'. After a while Hans Peter the younger received an offer to go to Hawai'i to work at his maternal uncle's ranch. He arrived in Hawai'i in 1880 and first started working as a farmhand with his elder sister Caroline's husband, Captain Henrick Christian L'Orange, who at this point was running a sugar plantation on the island of Maui. After two years working for his brother-in-law, Hans Peter started his own business close to his uncle, in Kehaka on Kaua'i. This is where he became one of the main actors in the establishment of the sugar industry in Hawai'i. Extending the northern European network, in 1893 he married Margareth Lindsay, who was of Scottish ancestry and who came from one of the most influential families on Kaua'i. One of her brothers supplied the plantations on the northeast coast with store goods, and the other was a judge.

From 1880 and until the end of the nineteenth century, important networks and relations developed between northern European families in Kauai. This era and its activities also initiated what we might call the colonial way of being. What had been perceived as an adventurous adaptation to Hawaiian surroundings and relations during the time of Archibald Archer and Valdemar Knudsen was now increasingly an inter-European collaboration in trying to create industry and generate capital on the islands. On the one hand, newcomers were eager to remake the landscape and to create wealth through Western capital by means of an imported workforce. But they also wished to create for themselves an identity as genuine 'people of the land'.

At this point Irish, Scottish, German and Norwegian families frequently visited each other's homes and married their daughters to each other. There are many Norwegian names in photographic and other records from this time. Anton Faye, Hans Peter's cousin, married a Norwegian woman from the Borchgrevink family, who were also settled in the archipelago. There were also Edward Kraft Bull, Gustav Hansen, Vetlesen, Hjort, Blakstad, Gjerdrum and Brandt. Gjerdrum and Brandt were employed as ranchers, or cowboys, at Knudsen's cattle farm, and later as supervisors in the sugar industry. Hansen took over as assisting manager at Kekaha Sugar in periods when Hans Peter was away from the factory. Kraft Bull also initially worked at Hans Peter's factory, but he was then hired by the Sinclair family in Niihau, and finally he became manager at Kekaha Sugar under Hans Peter again. Norwegian workers and engineers were often brought from Norway to contribute to the construction of dams, irrigation, power plants and railways.

Most of these Norwegians became close friends of the influential German Christopher B. Hofgaard, who ran the warehouse in Waimea and later became a judge. This network comprises, thus, not only family and friends, but also became what could be considered a 'nation' of immigrants: the Norwegians formed close relationships with an emer-

Figure 10.1. Overseeing their new nation, the Knudsens, the Fayes and the Doles on a recreational tour in Waimea Canyon in 1907. *Source:* Chris Faye; reproduced with permission.

gent upper class with names such as Meyer, Kruse, Macintosh, Gruber, Schmidt, Von Holt, Nordmeier, Webber, Mahlum, Lindsay and Isenberg. This nation in the making was self-supporting in economic terms, in their belief in hard work and Christian righteousness, and in social reproduction through marriages and friendships. They also started to develop an interest in narratives about the land, in belonging, and they increasingly produced and narrated stories that were about how they had reshaped the landscape, made it fertile for cultivation and also made it into something beautiful, quite in accordance with the ideas of the cultivated man during the Victorian era. In biographies about key figures from the period (Knudsen and Noble 1999; Von Holt 1985; C. Faye 2006), it is striking how certain ideals are repeated. In these often-romanticized accounts, the men were proud, somewhat introverted, but honest and hardworking; the women were beautiful and loyal to their husbands and the new nation. During this period the locally based Hawaiians disappear from the storytelling, perhaps because of their assimilation into the new nation, which they saw developing on their land. They were assimilated as workers, together with people of other nationalities, who after a while began to arrive in large numbers.

The New Nation Is Populated

Not only entrepreneurs and visionary industrialists arrived in Hawai'i around this period: their arrival initiated large-scale migrations from around the globe to bring sugar production to life. A demand for sugar developed in relation to the gold rush and the settling of California from 1849, and, later, during the American Civil War in the 1860s. Still, the early attempts to grow sugar cane commercially in the 1850s and 1860s had failed due to an insufficient workforce, and this remained the main problem for industrialists. In 1871 there were only fifty-seven thousand inhabitants in Hawai'i – the lowest number ever in the history of the islands. The Hawaiian population had suffered many years of disease and depopulation (Daws 1968).

Around this time the German company H. Hackfeld & Co. was established in both Hamburg and Honolulu. The company supplied the plantations on the islands with European goods, communication equipment and, increasingly, also with manpower. By 1875 these Honolulu agents had, in collaboration with the king, negotiated a trading agreement with the United States to export cane sugar with no tax. The market for sugar was therefore unlimited. The challenge was to get a workforce. During the initial period Hackfeld and other agents approached China, and up to 1866 they had brought 1,306 Chinese people to the archipelago. The Chinese arrived on five-year contracts in exchange for travel, housing, food, clothing and USD 3 per month. This opening of the Chinese labour market was very prosperous, and by 1898 a total of more than sixty thousand Chinese workers had arrived. More labour was required, however, and the plantation owners were also not completely satisfied with the Chinese, who often abandoned their contracts or deserted plantations in order to cultivate their own pieces of land or run a business in Honolulu's growing Chinatown (Dorrance 2000: 127).

In 1880 King Kalakau travelled the world to sign trading contracts for workers from various nations. He visited the Japanese emperor and a delegation from the Chinese emperor, he met the governor of Hong Kong and the king of Siam, and he travelled on to Singapore, Burma, India and Egypt. He then continued to Europe, where he had meetings with King Umberto of Italy, Pope Leo XIII in the Vatican and Queen Victoria from England (Daws 1968: 217–18). His tour ended in a meeting with President Arthur in 1881 in the United States. After this trip several new large labour markets opened. By 1898 close to seventy thousand Japanese had arrived in Hawai'i and almost twenty thousand Portuguese (Dorrance 2000: 128). These numbers testify to the great magnitude of the plantation projects that were developing on the islands. The number of inhabitants in Hawai'i had tripled in only a few decades, and not only the landscape had been transformed but also the entire population structure.

Accordingly, a concern was growing among the northern European settlers of what this would lead to in terms of race relations. As Jon Moe writes in his biography about Captain L'Orange:

> Tens of thousands of new acres were constantly to be put under the plough, and there was a limitless optimism. But at the same time there was a dramatic reduction in the indigenous population, so that one could no longer rely on using them. One could not get sufficient number of immigrants from the islands in the Pacific, the Philippines, China or Japan. It had been attempted with Malays, Hindus and American Negros. But now, many agreed with L'Orange: let us counter the Asian influence on our culture and our working life. Let us rather turn to Europe and get the people of a different founding, such as the tough, blue-eyed and faithful Scandinavians! Others are going for the Portuguese and the Germans. (Moe 1975: 33)[4]

This worry was also expressed in the Hawaiian Sugar Planters' Association and in what was called the Hawaiian Immigration Society when it was established in 1872. A growing concern with race, breeding and regulating the ethnic balance of the modern nation was evident – as well as a concern with class:

> In order to insure the success of this Republic, it will be necessary to build up and foster an intelligent middle-class, who understands the principles and the methods of Anglo-Saxon self-government. To accomplish this desirable object will require more systematic efforts to find settlers of this stamp, and the offer of greater inducements to attract them and keep them there. (Thrum 1896: 124)

The Norwegian Labourer's Limited Experience with Contract Work

Due to such racial considerations, H. Hackfeld & Co. signed contracts with Henrik Christian L'Orange, Consul Faye in Germany and other agents to contract people from the north to balance out what was considered to be a great majority of 'southerners', offering also a discount for women and free travel for children. L'Orange at this point already had experience with the 'purchase and sale' of workers and had even been banished from the British African colonies for mistreating workers during transportation. He was also to a certain extent disreputable in the Pacific. His initiative now resulted in two shiploads of Norwegians on the ships *Beta* and *Musca,* and many others from Germany through Hackfeld's office in Hamburg. Much has been written about these six hundred Norwegians who arrived in Hawai'i in 1881.[5] This literature has stressed what a mistake it was to import Norwegians as plantation workers. The mistake was to confuse the Norwegians with those nations where one normally found workers of the kind called 'coolies' or 'negroes'. These events underscore how concepts of race and cultural identity were developing hand in hand with the plantation economy.

I will summarize the events in short. In 1878 Captain L'Orange negotiated an agreement with H. Hackfeld & Co. in Honolulu regarding a quota of four hundred Norwegians for work on the plantations. The company gave him USD 20,000 credit to finance the journey. Rumours about the adventurous conditions in this Pacific paradise spread throughout Norway, ideas such as that one could live in Hawai'i hand to mouth by picking fruit from the trees and catching wild birds with one's hands. This was also supported by anonymous letters from Hawai'i that were published in local newspapers that boasted about the beauty of the Hawaiian Islands, the benign climate and the abundance of food. It was portrayed as a place where one could easily become one's own prosperous master (Davies and Davies 1962: 6–7). Despite some articles contradicting such visions and discouraging people from signing labour contracts, Norwegians queued up to register. The contract that was to be signed stated that they had to work ten hours a day in the fields or twelve hours a day in the sugar mill, and that the free journey committed them to three years of labour under these conditions. The unemployment rate in Norway was higher in the cities and less among farmers, and L'Orange therefore recruited mostly people who did not know farming at all. Many of them were, however, trained in crafts: the recruits included carpenters, blacksmiths, upholsterers, saddle makers, book printers and barrel makers.

The ship *Beta* arrived in Maui on 8 February 1881 with 327 adults and 65 children. On 4 May the same year *Musca* arrived in Honolulu with 233 passengers. During the long journey on the *Beta* fifteen passengers died, most of them children. Some had apparently become insane, a number of new love affairs had developed and two children had been born. The migrants came to Hawai'i with great expectations. They came from dire poverty and poor living conditions in urban areas and had survived a challenging journey through storms, extreme cold, failing food supplies, fires on board and constant sickness and conflicts. When they finally landed, they most likely had hopes for a new life of light, warmth, lushness and plenty of food. That was not what they met.

The recruits who arrived on Maui saw before them a dry, almost desert-like place, lacking the abundant green vegetation they were expecting from pictures they had seen back home. But the social conditions were even harsher. The newcomers had their contracts stamped by Hawaiian officials, and then all passengers were placed on the deck with a number around their neck. The plantation owners then put in their orders for how many workers they wanted. This bidding went on for days until every worker had been distributed to a plantation. They then got a new note around their neck with their destination. Some were sent to L'Orange's plantation, Lilikoi, or other plantations on Maui; others were sent to plantations on the island of Hawai'i, some to Kaua'i and some to Oahu.

A few months later there was a reaction: some Norwegian labourers wrote a letter to the Swedish-Norwegian consul describing their plight and claiming that they were now slaves under L'Orange and his accomplices (Davies and Davies 1962: 11). This first letter was followed by several others, as well as to Norwegian and American newspapers, in which the workers complained about the small, dilapidated and draughty sheds where they lived and their insufficient meals.[6] These letters were also received by the Hawaiian Bureau of Immigration, which, taking their content seriously, sent two observers to check the conditions. After a quick survey they concluded that the conditions for housing and food were adequate, but that the Norwegians did not make use of the food that they received. It was thus not the plantation owners' fault if they did not appreciate the food that was given to them (Davies and Davies 1962: 18).

But the problems continued. The Norwegian workers continued to write letters to newspapers and officials. A group of them also went on strike after working for just six months. Forty workers at Alexander and Baldwin Plantation on Maui were soon arrested. They refused to go to prison, but agreed to stand in front of a judge in a court of law where they could present their complaints. It ended with one of them being condemned to penal servitude. Eighteen went to jail and the rest went back to work. It was a critical moment for the entire sugar industry – not least because the Norwegians gained support from big newspapers in California, such as the *San Francisco Chronicle*, which used the strike to discredit the Hawaiian sugar plantations. These newspapers, fighting their regional battle, wanted to see an end to the trading agreement that made it possible for Hawaiian sugar producers to outbid Californian ones. In February 1882 a long letter from the Norwegian workers was published in the *San Francisco Chronicle*, in which they described the 'evil plantation owner', the 'corrupt judge', the bad health system and the lack of state control over the plantations' authoritarian justice (Davies and Davies 1962: 21–24). This received so much attention that the Norwegian parliament decided in March 1882 that this needed to be further investigated by a delegation from the Swedish-Norwegian state – supported by a warship.

Johan Anton Wolff Grip, from the Swedish-Norwegian embassy in Vienna, was appointed by King Oscar to conduct the investigation. He made a preliminary study by reading all the letters that had arrived – this also included a lengthy interview with Valdemar Knudsen in the Norwegian daily *Morgenbladet* on 17 August 1882. Knudsen, who was visiting his old country at the time, gave a firm statement that none of the complaints were true. Instead, he blamed the Norwegians themselves, who had been unable to recruit the right kind of workers, gathering people who were unsuitable for physical labour. He claimed that the immigration officials in Hawai'i always kept an eye on the working conditions, and he trusted them to do their job.

In October 1882 Grip arrived in Hawai'i and spent ten weeks investigating the Norwegians' living conditions around the archipelago. He interviewed 256 male workers and some of their wives. In his report from December he rejected much of what had been written: 'The many stories in our own and especially American magazines about being "sold as slaves in an auction" or "appointed by lottery" seems to be completely fictional' (Grip 1883: 8). He likened the Norwegian workers to contracted sailors or soldiers who had joined the army and who could not terminate their contract. Grip stated that those who were good workers even had the possibility to make more money than the minimum salary by taking additional jobs as locomotive drivers, sugar chiefs or engineers on the plantation. One also had to consider that they received free housing, which was satisfactory for the climate, that they had free access to their own garden and that the food supplies they received were of far better quality than the food soldiers in the Norwegian or English army received:

> Many of them complained about not getting enough butter or potatoes; in many of the places it is also difficult to provide these products; however, one has sweet-tasting potatoes and other root vegetables. Our emigrants have thus acquired the reputation of being choosy as well as greedy and picky, and I heard several amazing stories about what some of them would not eat. (Grip 1883: 10)

Grip concluded, as Valdemar Knudsen had done in *Morgenbladet*, that these workers lacked nothing in terms of living conditions. Instead, they did not have backgrounds suitable for the labour conditions. He pointed out that these craftsmen had discovered that if they were freed from their contracts, they could triple their income by doing the work they knew from Norway instead of working at the sugar fields. Grip saw it as dishonest of them to attempt to be freed from the contracts based on this.

Following Grip's report, the political turmoil surrounding the Norwegian workers subsided. However, five years after arriving, only fifty of them were still working on the plantations, while the rest had been freed from their contracts and were assimilated into other occupations. The experiment to get Scandinavians, or northern Europeans at all, to do ordinary plantation work thus failed completely, and they were instead moved out of the plantation realm and into the life of the middle class as independent merchants and craftsmen. This was reflected in a newspaper article in the *Hawaiian Gazette* on 29 June 1881, where an anonymous person writes in defence of Norwegians in relation to the 'inferior' workers of other nationalities:

> They are indeed too good a class to be like our other laborers who are being irregular at their work; in feigning excuses for getting away to visit mythical relatives in sickness; in peddling opium and ardent spirits through the community; in becoming often intoxicated; in frequenting the houses of Hawaiians for improper purposes; in making it necessary for their employers to often bring them before the police magistrates for desertion or refusal of work; in committing petty larcenies or serious burglaries. They (Norwegians) are so good a class of laborers that they perform all kinds of work intelligently; that they meet a great necessity by being admirably fitted for household labor, as well as for the care of horses and cattle; that they are moral and, largely, a religious people; that they are a class with whom we can live, while it is getting to be questionable, whether, with the continual importation of inferior classes to these islands, with all their salubrity and beauty, will long be habitable for us.

As the example of the importation of Norwegian labourers shows – with all its protests, deliberations and explicit and implicit politics – the new Hawaiian nation, or 'Republic'after the United States' annexation in 1898,[7] was not only an experiment in statehood and diplomacy, but also an experiment in race relations.

The Kekaha Sugar Company and Waimea Sugar Mill: The Construction of a Small State

From the above we begin to discern how the plantation may be viewed as a microcosm of the nation-making process. Every plantation had its own central board akin to a 'government', replete with own its state-like apparatuses such as schools, health care services, policing and intelligence units, various churches for different congregations and policies for regulating race relations and segregation. These aspects can be shown by returning to the industrious society that Hans Peter Faye helped build around the Kekaha Sugar Company and Waimea Sugar Mill.

Towards the end of the nineteenth century sugar production in Hawai'i increasingly became scientifically based, especially with the supply of fertilizer based first on Chilean guano and then on Norwegian artificial fertilizers, as well as more widespread use of production machinery and innovative agricultural techniques such as irrigation. It was also an era of expansion following the first crop of sugar around Waimea, which had been planted by Knudsen and L'Orange in 1878 and bought by A. Faye and W. Meier for further processing. In 1886 Hans Peter Faye had planted his own field under Knudsen's land contract in Mana; Knudsen's crown lands under the king now became the scene of a booming business. In addition to Faye's planting, irrigation and cultivation of new areas, the Germans Meier and Kruse also leased land to cultivate sugar in Kekaha. At the same time the German Isenberg brothers and the Scottish Wilcox brothers put up a large sugarmill in Waimea, processing sugar cane into liquid sugar. Several businesses were merged, and the Kekaha Sugar Company (KSC) emerged as a modern industrial company. Around this time, the Knudsen family was not directly involved in the large-scale industrial expansion of plantations. Valdemar Knudsen had been living well on the rental income from the land until his death in 1898. His oldest son, Francis, then returned to Hawai'i after spending two years in India, where he had studied theosophy in an attempt to understand the Hawaiian religion (called 'kahunaism') as a branch of Hinduism. Francis went on to run the ranch for some years, until his brother, Eric, returned from Harvard Law School and chose to take over the ranch instead of becoming a lawyer.[8] The Knudsen family represented a completely different lifestyle and approach to life in Hawai'i. While Knudsen's elder son studied religion and became a vegetarian, Hans Peter Faye increasingly took care of Knudsen's ranch, transformed marsh into sugar land, purchased grazing land connected to Waimea's dairy production, opened a railway to the sugar mill and bought the majority of stock in the sugar mill. Faye was now well established within the Hawaiian Sugar Planters' Association, known as a visionary and an innovator.

For the KSC this was a period of modernization, with an emphasis on developing the irrigation system, expanding their own railway to improve accessibility to the more than seven thousand acres of farmland and the construction of housing for the rapidly increasing number of workers. In 1907 a total of twelve miles of dikes had been constructed, Japanese workers had built a water supply and fifteen miles of rail tracks had been built where two locomotives were running. There were constant innovations – such as the construction of a hydroelectric power supply and experimentation with salt-resistant sugar cane for use in the marshlands to increase production. In the introductory essay about the KSC that is now found at the Hawaiian Sugar Planters' Association Plantation Archives, one reads that while in the 1890s they could harvest around two tons of sugar cane per acre, they reached a new record in 1942, harvesting eighteen tons of sugar cane per acre. Faye was also the first to experiment with burning the sugar fields before they were harvested so the work of removing the foliage was reduced. This became normal procedure in all of Hawai'i after a while, and Faye became very influential in the Hawaiian Sugar Planters' Association.

New workers were constantly recruited in this expanding business. At the turn of the century around one thousand workers had already been employed. The plantation was home to approximately three hundred families, who all lived in the village that had been built around the factory. To serve these families, there were four grocery stores, a hospital, public schools and three different religious communities. To provide food for the workers there were large rice fields, vegetable gardens and grazing areas for livestock, and the factory was self-sufficient in terms of most of its food supplies, policing and entertainment (a public cinema was opened in Waimea in the 1920s). The plantation was a world unto itself, organized around the sugar mill, but with well-regulated relations between ethnicities, classes and functions of production.

During this early period, workers were hired on contracts, and the plantation was based on trust between the management and workers. The workers committed themselves in the contract to work for the salary agreed, and in return for their loyalty they received the state-like services that the plantation offered – health care, schooling for children, and churches and leisure activities.

Still, this trust was sometimes broken, and in the years around 1900 there were constant reports of 'deserters'. In those cases the plantations had their own 'detectives' whose job it was to track down the absentees, in particular in Chinatown in Honolulu or on other islands. They were then brought back to the plantation, where they were fined or jailed. This legal power of punishment was stated in legislation and was essential to keep plantation economy costs low, as evidenced by this letter from Faye to the trustees of the Hawaiian Sugar Planters' Association, Honolulu, 5 February 1898: 'We are in receipt of your circular letter regarding the penal clause in our laborers contracts. Many of the laborers desert now, but should the penal clause in our labor laws be abolished, we would probably not keep any of the laborers who have to work for $12.50 a month, they would simply leave and get work as free laborers at $14 or more.'[9] Faye then suggests in the letter a practice of lowering the salary and adding a bonus paid at the termination of the contract. This measure would help to retain workers and counteract deserters.

In the KSC correspondence from this period, we realize how important the handling of the workforce was at this stage of capitalism and colonialism (see also Bertelsen's chapter, this volume). In regular letters Hans Peter Faye requested his agents at H. Hackfeld & Co. in Honolulu to send him supplies of material and workers. The idea of getting northern Europeans to work on the fields or balancing races was now a thing of the past, as the main concern was acquiring workers at the best possible rate. In every letter there were considerations about how many workers were needed, in between details of mechanical parts for machines, petrol or construction materials. In the beginning there was an ample supply of Chinese labour, as shown by this letter from H. Hackfeld & Co. to the KSC in 1884:

> According to advices by last mail, the P.M. Steamer 'City of Rio de Janeiro' has left Hong Kong on the 1 March with about 600 Chinese laborers on board for our port. We are also notified that the 'City of Tokio' may be expected here shortly with about the same number of coolies. We shall use all our influence to ship of them as many laborers as you may desire to have for your plantation. As to wages we shall try to get them as low as possible, at the same time we shall be glad to hear by return of mail from you how high you want us to go at the outside. It will be well to let the Chinese on your island know that large numbers of their countrymen are on the way, perhaps this will tend to make them more willing to secure a few years contract at moderate wages.[10]

In 1905 restrictions were introduced for access to the Chinese labour market, and Faye writes to Hackfeld: 'We are depending upon the good graces of the Japanese government for the importation of Japanese laborers.'[11] He received an answer from the office in Honolulu that he could also expect workers from northern Italy, the Azores or Madeira. The correspondence continuously contains valorizing reflections about the characters and working capabilities of various groups of men identified as 'Spaniards, Malays, Manila men'. For instance, one could rely on the 'Spaniards', while 'Babola-Indians' were not as industrious as those from East India. The 'Japanese' tended to desert as soon as they had a chance and the 'Chinese' were easily involved in the opium trade, and so on. In the lists of employees workers are listed by nationality, reflecting many years of recruitment, such as this list from 1904:

Figure 10.2. The Kekaha Sugar Company factory, with workers' quarters to the right, in 1920. *Source*: Chris Faye; reproduced with permission.

46 Anglo-Saxon, 307 Japanese, 756 Filipino, 35 Chinese, 56 Puerto Rican, 48 Portuguese, 71 Hawaiian, 56 'Others'.[12]

When I interviewed the old KSC manager's chauffeur in 2009, he had many fond memories about the plantation and its joint arenas for music, entertainment, sports and fun. According to him, it was a lively and safe place to live. But it was also very apparent to him that it was 'bloody unfair' that he had to support his family on USD 4 a day, while he knew how much the manager and the other owners could take out as profits from the factory. The KSC was among Hawai'i's most profitable enterprises in its days of glory. I was told that the manager had cashed in a USD 1 million profits from the enterprise in 1921 alone. In the construction of the KSC and other sugar businesses, profit and growth was always of paramount value; keeping the supply of labour under control was therefore of upmost concern, as we have seen above. However, in the first part of the twentieth century a tension arose between this ideology of the plantation as a self-supporting totality and the emerging notion of human rights and individual freedom. Shortly before the Second World War major labour market reforms were implemented because of strikes and general worker dissatisfaction. The emerging concept of the free individual – the worker who could do without the state-like structure of the plantation and the ideology of welfare and care – also became applicable to the further development of the sugar industry.

At the 'Blue Purple Cliffs' of Pō

I have described a series of events related to a few Norwegians who settled in Hawai'i in the nineteenth century. Their adventures had great consequences for the formation of the new Hawaiian nation and for the modernization of Kaua'i. There are few detailed sources on the specificities of their social life and work, but it is evident that they generally idealized the Hawaiian-ness of their new home. The nation they were part of building both embraced the Hawaiian landscape, traditions, language and people and added some Christian, northern European ideals about pedigree, hard work and pride.

What I find particularly interesting with this story from Hawai'i is how closely attached these emigrants actually became to the land they migrated to, perhaps in contrast to colonialists in other parts of the world. By 'land' I do not only mean the land as agricultural land or as an economic resource. I am referring to the way the land appears in all the biographies from the Knudsen and Faye families, as well as in my conversations with living descendants from these families and others: the joy and enthusiasm with which they describe the landscape, its history and the work that was done to transform it. Tellingly, descendants of Hans Peter Faye would show me a photograph in which we could see Faye standing on a slope before he had managed to cultivate it; it looks stony, dry and inhabitable. In another photograph we see a marshland where one could previously only go in a boat at high tide but that was reclaimed for productive cane fields. However, underlying such a narrative of cultivation and imbuing the landscape with productive capabilities was also a concern with a Hawaiian landscape in which cultivation of the land was an addition to its inherent Hawaiian-ness. Isabel Faye, the daughter of Hans Peter Faye, who lived most of her life on Kaua'I, conveys this sense of belonging directly. It is exciting to see how Isabel frames the narrative of her childhood in an account that weaves the colonial landscape together with mythological notions of an authentic Hawaiian land. She writes:

> All that land at Poki'i, the Hawaiians finally had to sell but all through my childhood that *taro* land was there. That's where the spirits travelled on their way to the underworld. The Hawaiians believed that when you

died, your soul would go to Pō down below and that's were all the *heiau* sacred places were at the very end near Polihale. The cane fields of H.P. Faye and Co. eventually got as far to the west at where it ends and where you go up to the *heiau* up on one of the cliffs there. Eric Knudsen did a lot of archaeological work in that area. Pō was where your soul went down where the blue purple cliffs are and there is also drinking water down there because at low tide, there was a spring of water. (C. Faye 2006: 15)

There are many examples of this kind of description, where the old, mythical Hawaiian landscape mixes with the new, industrial landscape – or rather, where the plantation landscape spreads out like a thin coating of watercolour that only made everything brighter, more beautiful and more unique and authentic:

> We lived under the *pali* steep hill because that is were the *taro* patches used to be in Huluhulunui, just back of Kekaha. That's were the Gladdings lived later on when the plantation started, they had a house there. Where the road crooked out and went along the bottom of the *pali* and up to Kōke'e to the new fencing that was built along the beach and up. Then right in front of that steep *pali* used to be in my childhood a wonderful *taro* patch area. It was what was left of the old Poki'i village. Lots of Hawaiians used to live under the *pali* to the east by the side of the road by Hukipō ride where the little plantation place on top of the hill was. There's a wonderful spring there as well as the Pōki'i area. Father used to laugh and said 'the nice old Hawaiian was having her bath at six o'clock in the morning when I went down to the office. And she would rise from the spring and holler "*Aloha!*".' (C. Faye 2006: 15)

Isabel then tells about the summers that were so hot that they all went high up in Waimea Canyon, where there was a nice, cool wind:

> We went up behind Wai'awa village on a beautiful old road that the Hawaiians had paved with stone. Wai'awa must have been quite an important settlement because there was a wonderful temple in Hō'ea Valley. I remember we stopped in between a bunch of *kukui* trees and had lunch just at the ridge that rounds around the river where the *menehune* [pre-historic, mythical inhabitants] got their shrimps. The ridge was called Pu'u'ōpa'e. To this day I can remember the ridge that we went up the first time. (C. Faye 2006: 25)

In this beautiful way of recalling and narrating both past and present landscapes, what emerges are ways of conceptualizing land that differ significantly from the managerial and economy-oriented language describing factory life in most archival sources. It is clear that the Knudsen and Faye families spoke Hawaiian and, further, that their northern European circle was mixing with Hawaiians more and more. Isabel Faye, for instance, writes that among the people Hans Peter surrounded himself with there were quite a few Hawaiians. These had themselves belonged to old Hawaiian families in the area who had arrived from Tahiti in mythical times and had themselves colonized the country (C. Faye 2006: 16). In this microcosm of a new nation, these Hawaiians secured the continuity between old and new, and in many ways also guaranteed the rootedness of their living on the land.

This is probably why the word *haole* – the word that is used all over Hawai'i to characterize white strangers – is absent from all consulted sources for the Knudsen and Faye families. Instead, I believe, they were assimilated into what we can call Hawaiian-ness, itself an identity reflecting both the multicultural mix of people who came to these islands over the years and the nation-making efforts of the industrialists themselves. Their descendants, therefore, are neither Norwegian nor American but Hawaiian, through their connection to the land as *ili āina* – land conceived as cultural heritage.

Notes

I would like to thank Kirsten A. Kjerland and Anne K. Bang for involving me in the research project 'In the Wake of Colonialism', which enabled me to do this historical work in Hawai'i as a variation of my regular field of research within anthropology and Vanuatu. What is presented here is the result of work in the Hawaiian Sugar Planters' Association Plantation Archives at the University of Hawai'i at Manoa Library in 2006, a visit funded by the Norwegian Research Council. I want to thank everyone who helped me put together the pieces of this puzzle; first and foremost, Chris Faye in Kaua'i and Axel Faye in Norway, who have given me information about their family, plantation history and access to pictures and background material. Chris Newton has given me access to the family history of the Blakstad family in Hawai'i. Rolf Scott, Kirsten A. Kjerland, Espen Wæhle, Narve Rio and Bjørn Enge Bertelsen have given me valuable feedback on this text. I am also most grateful to Eilin Torgersen and Camilla Borrevik for translating my text into English.

1. Colin Archer, well-known ship designer, worked with his brother Archibald in Hawaii around 1850 to save up money to start his own plantation in Australia (Møller 1986: 37–47).
2. He gradually established himself as a major producer with his own rice mill, and he was a good friend of both Knudsen and Faye. He was known as 'the rice king' on Kaua'i (Joesting 1984: 206–7).
3. Most of what I write on the life of Hans Peter Faye is based on interviews with his great-grandchild Chris Faye, a resident of Waimea, Kaua'i.
4. All translations are my own unless otherwise noted.
5. See Semmingsen (1950: 325–33); Moe (1975); Greipsland (2004); Davies and Davies (1962); and Niels Emil Aars, 1881, 'Dagbok over en reise fra Norge til Sandwichsøerne', manuscript, NMM. See also the magazine *Nordmanns-*

forbundet, nos. 5 (1973) and 7 (1979), as well as the magazine *The Norseman,* nos. 4–5 (1999).

6. *Valkyrien,* 16 September 1881.
7. Hawai'i was annexed by the United States in 1898 after comprehensive political manoeuvring between the different parties. Today Hawaiian activists struggle to terminate what they call an illegal annexation of a sovereign kingdom.
8. Interview with Ruth Knudsen Hanner (1971), manuscript, HSPA.
9. KSC 14/1, HSPA.
10. KSC 3/2, HSPA.
11. KSC 2/1, HSPA.
12. KSC 2/9, HSPA.

Archives Consulted

Hawaiian Sugar Planters' Association Plantation Archives (HSPA), University of Hawai'i at Manoa Library, http://libweb.hawaii.edu/digicoll/nikkei/HSPA.html.
Kaua'i Museum (KM), Lihue, Hawai'i.
Norwegian Maritime Museum (Norsk Maritimt Museum, NMM), Oslo.

References

Aars, N.E. 1881. 'Dagbok over en reise fra Norge til Sandwichsøerne', manuscript, NMM.
Ashman, M. 2004. *Kaua'i as It Was In the 1940s and '50s.* Lihue: Kaua'i Historical Society.
Davies, E.H. and C.D. Davies. 1962. *Norwegian Labor in Hawai'i: The Norse Immigrants.* Honolulu: Industrial Relations Center.
Daws, G. 1968. *Shoal of Time: A History of the Hawaiian Islands.* Honolulu: University of Hawai'i Press.
Dorrance, W.H. 2000. *Sugar Islands: The 165-Year Story of Sugar in Hawai'i.* Honolulu: Mutual.
Faye, C. (ed.). 2006. 'Memoirs of Isabel Faye'. Unpublished manuscript.
Greipsland, T. 2004. *Aloha fra glemte nordmenn på Hawai'i: Fra slaveliv til feriepa-radis.* Oslo: Emigrantforlaget.
Grip, A. 1883. 'Indberetning til Hans Excellence Ministeren for de udenrigske anliggender betræffende de svenske og norske emigranters forhold på de Hawaianske øer', Stortingspropotion no. 48. Oslo.
Joesting, E. 1984. *Kaua'i: The Separate Kingdom.* Honolulu: University of Hawai'i Press.
Knudsen, E.A. and G.P. Noble. 1999. *Kanuka of Kaua'i: The Story of a True Pioneer.* Honolulu: Mutual.

Moe, J. 1975. *Akamai: Sagaen om den norske utvandringen til Hawai'i.* Oslo: Gyldendal.

Møller, A. 1986. *Australiafarere: Nordmenn som tok en annen vei.* Oslo: Cappelen.

Semmingsen, I. 1950. *Veien Mot Vest: Utvandringen fra Norge til Amerika,* vol. 2. Oslo: Aschehoug.

Thrum, T.G. 1896. *The Hawaiian Almanac and Annual.* Honolulu : Black & Auld, Printers

Von Holt, I.E.K. 1985. *Stories of Long Ago: Niihau, Kaua'i, Oahu.* Honolulu: Daughters of Hawai'i.

11

SCANDINAVIANS IN COLONIAL TRADING COMPANIES AND CAPITAL-INTENSIVE NETWORKS

The Case of Christian Thams

Elsa Reiersen

In the early 1900s, financially strong Scandinavian businessmen invested in trading and plantation enterprises in various locations in the global south. This chapter will explore investments in Portuguese East Africa (present-day Mozambique), touching also on business ventures in French West Africa. Crucially, it investigates the character of Scandinavian colonial entrepreneurship through focusing primarily on the Norwegian Christian Thams (1867–1948), who acted as a coordinator between and investor in several important Scandinavian colonial companies. Moreover, Thams directed several companies that had been established with French and Monegasque capital but that later came to be dominated by Scandinavian, and especially Norwegian, capital interests.

Two themes are central. The first concerns the Scandinavian investors: Who invested in the business networks in colonial Africa?[1] What were their motives and the driving forces behind their engagements? How actively or directly did some of them participate in the operations? Did they seek long-term or short-term profits? The second theme is first and foremost linked to operations in Mozambique: How did investors gain access to the colonial natural resources, such as land, water and forests, and how did they exploit these areas? What were developments on the ground within these domains? The relations between the colonial developers and their African workers will also be dealt with in brief.

A Cosmopolitan Norwegian Entrepreneur

Prior to his investments in colonial Africa, Christian Thams was best known in Norway and business circles abroad for his involvement in large industrial projects and the construction of Norway's first electrified railway, *Thamshavnbanen*. Formally educated as an architect, Thams became the prime mover in establishing and developing large industrial enterprises in the Norwegian county of Trøndelag, such as Chr. Salvesen & Chr. Thams Communication Ltd (1898) and Orkla Mining Company Ltd (1904). In addition, from the early 1890s he was the director of the family firm M. Thams & Co. (a saw mill, timber and construction company), founded in 1867 (Reiersen 2006: 329–32).

Thams was born in Trondheim and spent his childhood both there and in Orkdal. When he reached the age of twelve, his parents sent him to Switzerland, and at nineteen he graduated from Technicum Winterthur in the canton of Zürich. For a short while he worked in Switzerland before establishing his own architectural firm in Nice, France, in early 1887. By then he had married a Dutch baroness, Eléonore de Spengler. After four years in France, he returned to Norway with his family. Christian and his older brother, Wilhelm August, then took over the running of the family business, M. Thams & Co., which their father, Marentius Thams, had directed for twenty years.

Christian Thams may be characterized as a typical innovator in the sense that he was always focused on new projects, being exceptionally creative and full of restless energy. In a Norwegian context, Thams's career may be characterized as remarkable. From early 1911 onwards he was established in Paris, from where he managed trading and plantation companies in East Africa and, for a brief period, also in West Africa. In the interwar period he also managed mining and investment companies in Ethiopia. All the aforementioned enterprises shared the same office address in Paris – Place Vendôme no. 22, from which he administrated each and every business. He travelled yearly to Africa, both to inspect the businesses and to vacation.[2]

At the beginning of the 1900s it was not very common for Norwegian businessmen to invest in and direct large entrepreneurial companies in Africa (but see the chapters of Bang, Eidsvik and Kjerland, this volume), and Thams's commitments may in this context be described as pioneering. Given that the start-ups were established just before the outbreak of the First World War, they faced many challenges and suffered economically – both in short-term and long-term perspectives.

Entrepreneurs and Networks

As is evidenced in the brief biographical sketch of Christian Thams above, there are links between entrepreneurship and family relations on the one hand, and between entrepreneurship and positive social relations on the other (Hreinsson and Nilson 2003). In preindustrial

Scandinavian society, the individual's economic standing was closely connected to that person's family and relatives. Conversely, a community's collective economy strengthened its individual members. It is necessary for an entrepreneur to develop positive relations in a network to secure and instil trust: the composition of the network may be a decisive factor in the realization of ideas and projects. In this respect the notion of *networking* is not unambiguous.

The entrepreneurs and investors involved in enterprises in colonial Africa are cases in point here. They all participated as much in family and informal social networks as in entrepreneurial and business networks of a more or less formal nature. Furthermore, the concepts 'entrepreneur' and 'founder' are likewise ambiguous. A founder is generally regarded as highly creative, inventive and imaginative, while an entrepreneur turns projects into durable and secure businesses and workplaces. It is not uncommon to find a founder and an entrepreneur being the very same person.

When Christian Thams married Eléonore, he was given access to networks of European nobility (Reiersen 2006). For an ambitious young architect this was certainly not to his disadvantage. He gained, furthermore, from associating with fellow former pupils at the Breidenstein Institute, an international Swiss boarding school in Grenchen, and former students at the technical college in Winthertur.[3] Both institutions admitted pupils from a wide range of countries and recruited mainly from the upper social classes. Such schools comprised forums where youth from wealthy families met and developed long-lasting connections and friendships.

While in Nice, Thams sent his drawings of wooden buildings to the family's construction company in Trondheim, and buildings produced by M. Thams & Co. were delivered as prefabricated houses to commissioners in France, Italy, Spain and the Congo Free State.[4] Through his work old networks were maintained and new ones established. He had continuous access to various customer groups, craftwork and business connections, banks, public administration, and his father's and grandfather's business connections, agents and clients – first in Norway and then in Sweden, England, Belgium and Germany.

Norwegian Industrial Development with Capital from Abroad

For decades the most important export market for M. Thams & Co. was Great Britain, and the closest collaborator there was the Norwegian-born shipbroker and shipowner Christian Salvesen in Leith, Scotland (for Salvesen's importance to Norwegian shipping in this era, see also

Sætra's chapter, this volume). Since the 1850s, Salvesen had collaborated with Christian's paternal grandfather, Wilhelm August (1812–84), and also with his father, Marentius (1836–1907), in the wood and timber construction company M. Thams & Co., the salmon business M. Thams, and the Ørkedal Mining Company (in Orkdal). Furthermore, this collaboration was continued by Christian Thams and Christian Salvesen, who initiated larger industrial projects linked to the old mining industry at Løkken Verk in Meldal Municipality and established Chr. Salvesen & Chr. Thams Communication Ltd and the Orkla Mining Company Ltd.[5]

The establishment of the Orkla Mining Company Ltd was achieved with the help of capital raised from several partners of the Thams family: the two Norwegian-born wholesalers Joachim Mogens Berner, in the firm Berner & Nielsen, located in London and Paris, and Thorvald Olrog, in Thv. Olrog Company Ltd, located in Sweden. Both Berner and Olrog belonged to Marentius Thams's business network and had also formerly been business partners in the marketing company Olrog & Berner in Paris.[6] The Swedish wholesaler Fredrik Loewenadler, based in London, also invested in the mining company through Berner.[7] The circle of investors in Orkla Mining Company Ltd was gradually widened, but the majority was comprised of family members or long-term business contacts. Among the Norwegian owners were Thomas Fearnley Sr and Haaken L. Mathiesen, holding honorary titles as Master of the Royal Hunt and Chamberlain, respectively. From Sweden there were several owners connected to the Stockholms Enskilda Bank (SEB), the most prominent being brothers Knut Agathon and Marcus Wallenberg. With two exceptions, namely, Berner and Loewenadler, all of the aforementioned owners of Orkla Mining Company Ltd invested in colonial trading and plantation companies in Africa following invitations from Christian Thams in 1911.

Interests and Driving Forces

When Thams decided to end his Norwegian commitments in order to focus on an international career in 1910, this followed an interesting offer from Prince Albert I of Monaco to move to Paris. From there he would direct the trading and plantation company Société du Madal in the Portuguese province of Mozambique in East Africa (Reiersen 2006: 284, 340).[8] The company was originally established in 1903 under the name Société du Madal, Gonzaga, Bouvay & Cie.,[9] but had not developed as expected. The owners therefore wished for it to be remodelled from a *commandité* to a limited company. A profitable business for the four owners: three responsible managers and Prince Albert (although passive), who in reality was in sole control.[10] Copra was at the time the company's main product.

There are several reasons why Prince Albert wanted Christian Thams to manage the reorganization of Société du Madal. When they first met in Trondheim and Orkdal in the summer and autumn of 1907 and again in the autumn of 1908, it is evident that the prince already had strong confidence in Thams.[11] At the time Thams was both consul for France and consul general for Belgium and Congo (Congo Free state in 1907 and changed to Belgian Congo in 1908). His relatively all-round business experience from abroad, at that time primarily from France and England, and knowledge of French, English, German and Italian also must have weighed in his favour.

Prince Albert's offer to Thams was extremely generous: an annual salary of 50,000 French francs (corresponding largely to USD 300,000 in 2012), shares in the company worth 1.5 million francs out of a total share capital of 4.5 million, and stock options in excess of 2 million. To use a modern expression, it is evident that Christian Thams was 'head-hunted' to rescue the prince's misguided business in Portuguese East Africa.[12]

There are several reasons why Prince Albert became interested in Mozambique at the very same time as most powerful European nations looked to Africa. One was the overall political and economic situation in Europe around the turn of the century. When he was offered a large piece of land for lease from one of his close associates and friends, the absolute monarch of Portugal, Carlos I, he saw no reason to hesitate. Although Prince Albert is better known for his oceanographic interests, he undoubtedly was also a good businessman. And in this particular case, business and politics were interwoven (Reiersen 2006: 299–300): from a letter in Thams's archive it is clear that the prince's intention was to establish a colony in Mozambique.[13] Prince Albert wanted to start developing a profitable trading company and at a later moment make parts of the northern region of Mozambique a Monegasque colony.[14]

However, while the desire to have a colony in Africa motivated Prince Albert's financial commitment at the time, tiny Monaco as well as Portugal was experiencing considerable political unrest. In January 1911 Monaco obtained a new and more democratic constitution, and the prince's colonial plans for the principality were then abandoned. The privately owned plantation company with privileges, concessions and properties was instead to become a limited company, Société du Madal.

Colonial Rule through Trading and Plantation Companies

Portuguese traders who established themselves on the east coast of Africa in the early 1500s founded small trading posts that also became intermediate ports for gold and spices shipped from Portuguese-controlled Goa. Through marriage, for example with the daughters of local chiefs, such traders acquired both power and large areas of land, such as in Mozambique's Zambézia region. Some became powerful landowners with their own armies, which they used to defend their own land and conquer new territories that were cleared and used to cultivate coconuts and groundnuts. Later on, according to demands in Europe, fruits were grown. However, the most important export commodities were ivory, gold and slaves (Vail and White 1980).[15]

In contrast to other colonial powers, the Portuguese did not develop any significant industry in Portugal itself for the export of goods to markets in Africa. It has been claimed that Portugal, in contrast to England and France, for this reason did not develop extensive trading activities on the African continent (see, e.g., Newitt 1981, 1995). It may thus be argued that the Portuguese did not make use of their advantage to ensure sufficient trading capital, but paved the way for others. From the early nineteenth century most of the trading capital and shipping activities were left to the English and Indian investors. Most Portuguese were small-scale merchants, but those who had acquired land were able to live as feudal lords and demand taxes from the inhabitants.[16]

All the trading companies that came to Mozambique in the nineteenth century were given royal consent. They were known as chartered companies and consisted either of individuals or several companies in partnership.[17] Until the beginning of the twentieth century the Portuguese state could also own companies that had a monopoly on all trade in their territories and rule with the assistance of military units in accordance with the home country's laws.

The land acquired by the companies were called *prazos,* land leased to colonial traders and settlers for either a long or fixed period. The term itself has an Afro-Portuguese origin, although the *prazo* system as such was older (Vail and White 1980: 2–8), first practised by Asians and later by Europeans who had gained access to land through marriage or as traders or mercenaries (Newitt 1995: 217). In the mid-eighteenth century, the system was almost legally established as an exclusive ownership right for heirs or migrant Portuguese and was recognized by the Portuguese state. However, the proprietors had to enter into rental contracts with the Portuguese state regarding the use of the land, for which the state demanded a fixed rent as well as a tithe. In return, the *prazo* owners had the right to demand taxes from the local inhabitants. The size of a *prazo* varied considerably; some had large areas at their disposal[18] (for details, see Bertelsen's chapter, this volume).

The Société du Madal, Gonzaga, Bouvay & Cie. initially leased three large *prazos* in what later became Zambézia Province, land that had previously belonged to a Portuguese count, the Count of Vila Verde. The three *prazos*, Madal, Tangalane and Cheringone, were located on the west bank of the River Rio dos Bons Sinais, between the city of Quelimane and the Indian Ocean (Bonnet 1914).[19] According to Thams, the Portuguese government had given the company a concession in the form of 'a larger tract of land in Mozambique in East Africa'.[20] In reality King Carlos I allowed Prince Albert I to take over the land on especially favourable terms: 2 million francs and no obligations to pay for the lease – 'Libres de toutes charges et hypothèques', free from any charge and encumbrance.[21]

French-Monegasque Colonial Companies with Scandinavian Owners

For tax reasons, Société du Madal was registered in Monaco, but the headquarters was in Paris, at Place Vendôme no. 22. The principality of Monaco also had its diplomatic service's offices there, as did the official envoys to the French president's Ministre Plénipotentaire. In 1921 Thams was given this title (Reiersen 2006: 291).

Perhaps surprisingly, the transformation to a limited company did not reduce Prince Albert's influence on the company. No important decision was taken without his approval. Expressed as follows (and noted in a letter to Thams in January 1911) to his representatives on the board of directors, the financial advisors Mayer and Bernich: 'I will be represented on the Board of Directors by a couple of people of my choice, M. Mayer and M. Bernich.'[22]

In January 1911 Thams was appointed managing director for seven years. He was, however, from the very start given an option to resign from his position at the beginning of 1914, given he provided six months' notification in advance (Reiersen 2006: 299–300).

The share capital of Société du Madal totalled 4.5 million French francs in January 1911. The main shareholder, Prince Albert, had a stake of 3 million, while his financial advisors had shares worth 250,000 at their disposal. Shares worth 1.25 million were at Thams's disposal.

By May 1911 the allocation of shares in Société du Madal was changed in Thams's favour,[23] and that very spring he was able to offer shares to his Scandinavian business partners and colleagues.[24]

From the outset Thams wished to have members of the board of directors in Orkla Mining Company Ltd involved in Société du Madal, and shares were offered to them. Marcus Wallenberg and Thorvald Olrog responded positively, and in June 1911 they applied for shares worth 300,000 and 100,000 francs, respectively.[25] Shortly after Haaken L. Mathiesen and Thomas Fearnley Sr also bought shares worth 300,000 and 100,000, respectively. They were soon followed by Fritz M. Treschow, owner of the large Fritzøhus estate at Larvik (Norway), Thams's successor to Orkla's board of directors, acquiring shares worth 200,000. Marcus Wallenberg arranged also to purchase shares for his brothers Knut Agaton and Oscar Wallenberg, as did Jacob Nachmanson, director of Stockholm's Enskilda Bank, and, lastly, Court Marshall Otto Printzsköld.

Thams was the administrative director and chairman of the board when the aforementioned investors bought their initial shares; he was later joined by Marcus Wallenberg and Fritz Treschow, who were then able to control and manage their own investments better. Thams recommended that Wallenberg and Treschow join Société du Madal's board of directors. His first choice, Wallenberg, agreed without hesitation. At the same time, Thams also became the head of Société des Plantations de l'Afrique Francaise and, later, Anglo-French Sisal Co. Ltd (1921) and Société Anonyme des Cultures de Diakandapé (1922) – issues to be dealt with in brief below.

Originally, Société du Madal's board consisted of two of Prince Albert's advisors (*conseillers*), together with three Portuguese members. The inclusion of the latter was demanded by the Portuguese state. Since Mozambique was considered a Portuguese province, by implication the majority of the plantation company's board of directors should be Portuguese. It was also demanded that Société du Madal's administrative headquarters should be in Lisbon. However, all of this went against the wishes of Prince Albert and was most likely impracticable given the problematic political and economic situation in Portugal after the country became a republic in 1910: between 1910 and 1925 forty different governments and eighteen revolutions and attempted coups occurred. When Société du Madal was registered in Monaco on 29 December 1911, no Portuguese was included on the board of directors.[26] Rather, the newly elected board consisted of Prince Albert's advisors, Louis Mayer and Gaston Moch, and also Marcus Wallenberg and Fritz Treschow, with Christian Thams as chairman.[27] By the end of 1911 sev-

Figure 11.1. The main office for Société du Madal in Quelimane, ca. 1906.
Source: Elsa Reiersen; reproduced with permission.

eral Swedish and Norwegian investors had joined Société du Madal, all close acquaintances of the initial shareholders.

From an early start results were positive. A gratified Thams wrote to Marcus Wallenberg that profits in 1913 would be significantly better than 1912, despite the tight money market.[28] Furthermore, in 1913 Thams managed to pull off sales contracts for 1914 for 'even higher prices' and favourable freight contracts. Very soon the Scandinavian shareholders learned from Thams that the 'Sovereign Prince' would probably approve a future annual dividend of 5 per cent: hence, their investments would give rapid profits. But his expectations for the company were not realized – a fact that created unrest among the shareholders.[29] When they asked for regular updates but were instead informed mainly through annual reports,[30] this added to the mistrust. It is evident, however, that on such occasions, Prince Albert made the final decisions.

Plantation Operations and Export Trade

From the headquarters in Paris, Thams and Prince Albert's administrative advisors, Louis Mayer and Georges Jaloustre, directed Société du Madal as well as other more or less closely related companies that emerged over time. The company's main office in Mozambique was located in Quelimane, where Europeans looked after the owners' interests (see figure 11.1). To begin with, the management positions were occupied by Swiss, but when Thams took over as administrative director, they were replaced by Norwegians. In March 1912, the Norwegian former Belgian Congo judge, Fredrik Arnoldus Parelius, was appointed, and shortly thereafter a relative of Thams, Second Lieutenant Bjørn Thams from Kristiania (now Oslo).[31] Over time, Scandinavians, French, Portuguese and Afro-Portuguese all became involved in the running of the company's numerous properties (stations) and its head office in Quelimane. In addition, the factories (trading stations), several of which were established along the coast, were managed by Europeans.

Société du Madal had, in 1911, four *prazos* in Quelimane Province, including a coconut plantation with about seventy thousand mature palms on the *prazo* Madal (Reiersen 2006: 340). The company's goal was to have one million coconut palms.[32] Ultimately, this number was not reached until after the Second World War (Rønning 2000).[33] Like other plantation companies, Société du Madal planted coconut palms, both on the lands that belonged to the company's *prazos* and some distance away on the free lands that belonged to the state.[34]

The company also had a factory that produced palm oil. The total number of Africans who lived on the land that Société du Madal had gained control over varies according to the different sources, but in an interview in 1912 Thams stated that it was between forty thousand and fifty thousand, an enormous workforce that was of 'the greatest significance for running the plantations'.[35] Furthermore, Thams stated that the local population paid taxes to the company and was entirely under its control. This indicates that the people who lived on the *prazos* could be used as forced labour; they came with the territory, so to speak (see Bertelsen's chapter, this volume).

Right from the start the managers of Société du Madal were keen to expand and establish new coconut plantations on the *prazos*. Soils at the mouth of the River Zambezi were very fertile, but swamp-like. Therefore, large-scale drainage was required before coconut palms could be planted. Hence, the work of cutting ditches and constructing canals was given high priority at the start of 1911, in addition to the construction of roads. The work involved in developing this agricultural industry was highly demanding and difficult, not least because draft animals, primarily oxen, could not be used because of the presence of the tsetse fly. Later on, when thousands of kilometres of ditches and canals were dug manually, the ground gradually became drier, allowing the use of draft animals as well as stock.

The canals and small rivers were also important for transport. Large barges were used to transport wares rapidly from the plantations to the trading stations. They were also used to transport goods to cargo ships anchored some distance offshore from the trading stations. In 1919 the company itself purchased a cargo ship, *Madal,* to transport goods and passengers between ports along the east coast of Africa. *Madal* carried goods that were loaded onto larger cargo ships bound for European and American ports.

Société du Madal also constructed narrow-gauge railway lines, so-called *lignes de Decauville* (see figure 11.2). Fully loaded wagons were manually moved along the tracks from the production sites on the plantations to ports on the riverbanks for subsequent export overseas (Bonnet 1921: 3–9). At Quelimane, the largest trading station, a concrete quay, 70 metres long and 4.3 metres wide, was constructed early on along with a Decauville track, making transport to the quay more efficient.

Coconut palms take approximately five years before they produce, and good mature palm trees can give around one hundred coconuts each year. However, Société du Madal's annual figures up to 1920 show that on average the plantations' trees produced some fifty coconuts an-

Figure 11.2. Société du Madal constructed narrow-gauge railway lines, so-called *lignes de Decauville,* to transport fully loaded wagons manually from the production sites on the plantations to ports on the riverbanks. *Source*: Elsa Reiersen; reproduced with permission.

nually.[36] Most of the copra was refined into coconut oil used in soap and food production (mainly margarine), as well as a lubricant for industrial machinery.

Société du Madal's largest factory and trading ports were in Quelimane, the densely populated island Ilha de Moçambiqe, Parapate (in Angoche), Porto-Amélia and d'Ibo. The factories were responsible for the export and import of produce to and from Europe, to take advantage of local trade and trade with South Africa. Already in 1912 the Société du Madal traded in goods worth several million francs, primarily copra coming from the factory in Quelimane.[37] Another important export was groundnuts; in this case the factory in Ilha de Moçambiqe had the largest turnover. In 1916 the factory in Quelimane had a net profit of more than 736,000 French francs, while the profit from the other two factories in Ilha de Moçambique and Parapate was ca. 435,000 and ca. 610,000, respectively. In the same year, Société du Madal sold ca. 3,700 tons of copra with a sale value of 2.2 million francs. Groundnuts worth ca. 115,000 francs were also sold in 1916.

It is evident from Société du Madal's annual reports for the years 1918–21 that the export from all five factories in Mozambique had increased significantly in terms of the number of products and the volume of trade and earnings. In addition to the main export products, copra and groundnuts, Société du Madal's exports now included maize, sesame seeds, passion fruit, herbs, millet, hides and sea salt, but the turnover on these products was much smaller. In 1918 breeding bulls and draft oxen, dairy cattle, heifers, calves, steers and also mules – in total around six hundred animals – were also kept. Occasionally, the export of hides was included in the annual reports. Likewise, the bark of mangroves and valuable ebony were sometimes included. In 1913 rubber was added to the list, produced by Companies des Cautchouc de Moçambique – again a company of which Thams was a major shareholder.

Corporate Power and Development in Times of Crisis

In present-day literature, the plantation companies in Mozambique are generally described as exploiters of the local populations, and indeed the Africans were treated poorly, as forced labourers subjected to brutal conduct. However, there are certain indications that Société du Madal differed somewhat from larger companies such as Companhia de Boror and Companhia de Zambézia, which practised an aggressive policy involving forced acquisition of coconut palms (Vail and White 1980: 155). Société du Madal allowed, for instance, the Africans to keep their own trees, at least in the early years of its operation, and engaged Indian middlemen to buy the copra produced by local farmers (see, e.g., Ishemo 1995). The authorities encouraged African farmers to produce their own copra, but given that the plantation companies controlled the purchase prices, there was little that the Africans could do to secure a good price for their own produce. Regarding the flight of workers, Société du Madal, like all the other plantation companies, struggled.[38]

However, Portugal's neutral position during most of the First World War largely secured Société du Madal's economy: in 1917 the net profit was ca. 1.6 million French francs, and in 1918 it was ca. 1.7 million francs.[39] Various war-related incidents did occur; the annual report for 1918, for instance, records three large accidents hitting the company hard: in March, an unusually strong cyclone caused mass destruction on the plantations, and then in May and June German soldiers invaded Quelimane Province. In November and December the Spanish flu pandemic raged. Nearly eighteen hundred people died on Société du Madal's plantations.[40] These losses may very well have contributed to the workers being treated better, however: from 1919, for instance, the company took over responsibility for all food supplies in the rainy season. According to the management, starvation had previously been a recurrent problem in the wet season. These measures had positive effects, and the annual reports from 1919 to 1922 have no information about hunger problems.[41]

Société du Madal's administrators stated in the annual reports for 1917 and 1918 that the company was developing well, but claimed that more capital was needed to realize the plans to build up a powerful, vigorous plantation company. In 1917 Prince Albert and Thams proposed increasing the share capital by 5 million francs at a rate of 150 per cent.[42] The increase in capital would then total 6 million, and the total share capital would be 10.5 million. The proposal was approved by the board of directors. Over the course of the next four years the capital increased two times, in 1919 and 1921. In 1921 the total share capital was 20 million francs, and the Scandinavian owners, primarily the Norwegians, had increased their portions significantly.

Branching Out

Already after a couple of years in operation it had been suggested that daughter companies should be formed with close connections to Société du Madal. And from the very outset Madal's directors were thus focused on a wide range of products. The objective was all types of undertakings involving trade, agriculture, industry and so forth in Portugal and abroad, but mainly in Portuguese East Africa. The company's statutes point out that special businesses could be established with individuals or other trading businesses and companies that existed or that were in the process of being created.[43]

The first offshoot from Société du Madal was the share company Compagnie des Cautchouc de Moçambique, formed in 1913. Plants producing raw material (latex) for making rubber were established in Africa, Asia and South America – rubber was in great demand at the time, especially for the new car industry. Thams's hopes for rubber production were high, and in the aforementioned company he became the largest owner, with a stake of 5,910 shares out of a total of 6,130. Société du Madal itself owned 10 per cent of the share capital of 1 million French francs. The other owners were three Norwegians. The company was registered in Monaco, but had the same business address in Paris as Société du Madal and was managed by Thams. The production of rubber was based on the invention of a machine that a Portuguese company, Valour Rubber Extracting Machine Ltd, owned the rights to. Thams foresaw great profits when he was given concessions to use Valour's machine for rubber production in Mozambique.

There were several reasons for the establishment of the rubber company as well as other companies closely connected to Société du Madal. The managers of Société du Madal wanted, for one, to spread the responsibility for the production of the various products. At the same time, there was also potential for additional profits – both for the shareholders and for the administrative leaders. Moreover, if Société du Madal and the daughter companies had a common leadership, the administrative expenses could be spread out. Such an arrangement would also make rapid transfer of capital between the companies possible should an acute need arise.

The fact that there were close bonds between the mother and daughter companies is confirmed by the absence of annual reports for the new companies, and also that the general assembly for all companies was held at the same place and time.[44] Information on the rubber company's activities are mentioned just once in the annual report for Société du Madal – in 1916 – when rubber worth 402 francs was sold from the factory in Quelimane. This indicates that the deliveries of rubber from the main factory to Société du Madal were quite modest.

Overall, the development of the rubber company did not progress as Thams had hoped. He explained this as a consequence of the First World War and the accompanying economic crisis. The company was therefore wound up in the mid-1920s.

The trading company Moçambique Trading and Plantation Co., hereafter referred to as Tradeplant, was founded in January 1914. This company, too, had a share capital of 1 million francs, of which Société du Madal owned 10 per cent.[45] Tradeplant's objective was first and foremost trade but also shipping, plantation business and cattle rearing in the southern part of Portuguese East Africa. Thams was the company's administrative director and, together with Haaken L. Mathiesen, the largest shareholder; Thorvald Olrog and Marcus Wallenberg invested smaller sums.

The directors of Société du Madal thought that Tradeplant could be developed into an interesting business enterprise, such as an executive owner of other large shipping companies with traffic in Asia and America. Tradeplant's special interests did not conflict with any of Société du Madal's interests, and the company operated as Société du Madal's agent in the port of Beira in Mozambique.

Like many other companies, Tradeplant experienced economic problems during the First World War and was forced to receive a loan from Société du Madal.[46] By the end of 1921, Tradeplant had an outstanding debt of ca. 220,000 French francs with Société du Madal. A new loan of GBP 10,000 (ca. 500,000 francs) was granted by Société du Madal in January 1922, this time with Thams acting as guarantor. Towards the end of 1922, however, it was resolved that Société du Madal should withdraw from the company and sell its shares. Tradeplant's value was then set at ca. GBP 10,000, and Christian Thams and Haaken L. Mathiesen took over all of Société du Madal's shares.

Société des Plantations de l'Afrique Française was a sisal company founded by the Swiss engineer Auguste Hütz and the company Hütz & Cie. in 1908. In the early 1900s the world's consumption of sisal was significant: more than one hundred thousand tons were sold to the United States alone, and the Société des Plantations de l'Afrique Française invested in the cultivation of sisal in Upper Senegal and Niger, later named French West Africa.[47] In 1911 the company had a concession of eight hundred hectares, located fifteen kilometres south of the town Kayes on the west bank of the Senegal River. To the north the area was bounded by the same river and the road running between Kayes and Bakel.

Prior to 1911 the head office was in Dar Salam (Senegal) but was moved thereafter to Paris. In the same year the company became a share company, registered in Monaco. After a couple of years in operation the company statutes were changed in 1913, and the share capital of 600,000 francs was reduced to 400,000. Both Prince Albert and Thams were shareholders, and Thams became its chairman. It is likely that

Prince Albert had been a coowner from the start in 1908 but represented by his long-standing advisor Georges Jaloustre, who was registered as an owner in 1910.[48] The reason for the reduction in the share capital was so that the owners could receive higher dividends (pro rata) and more readily obtain further working capital if necessary.

Some of Thams's business contacts in Norway and Sweden were offered to be part of the 'Sisal business', described as small but profitable.[49] In autumn 1912 both Marcus Wallenberg and Thorvald Olrog became shareholders, and Wallenberg was offered shares and primary fund units totalling 50,000 francs, the same amount that Thams himself had invested. From January 1914, Thorvald Olrog, Marcus Wallenberg and Thams's brother, Wilhelm August, were all coowners. Société du Madal did not have ownership interests in Société des Plantations de l'Afrique Française, but over time it supported the sisal company through large business loans.

Auguste Hütz, who was company director of Société des Plantations de l'Afrique Française in Africa, died in May 1914 in a work accident in Dar Salam.[50] According to Thams, it was a great loss for the company: Hütz had all the prerequisites to run a plantation well, both with regard to knowledge of sisal fibres and also as a leader. A new managing director was appointed and shortly after carried out a large-scale reorganization process, including expansion of the plantation areas. Unfortunately for the company, the First World War broke out in 1914 and the next four years of war meant that the owners did not receive their anticipated profits. Nevertheless, there were fresh attempts at expansion of the plantations and new planting efforts in order to be positioned well when the war was over.

In 1916 the company was given a concession of four hundred hectares (four square kilometres) in the border areas towards Senegal, and thus now had more than twelve hundred hectares at its disposal. Experimentations were also carried out with the production of *da,* also known as Guinea hemp, in order to find a substitute for Indian jute, the fibres used in the production of sacks and canvas. In 1918 more than 110 persons worked on the company's plantations.[51]

Despite sales profits in both 1916 and 1917, the company's accounts showed negative profit, and like Société du Madal it had freight problems, including lack of tonnage. Lack of capital forced the company to borrow NOK 280,000 (ca. 400,000 French francs) from Wilhelm August Thams in 1917, but this did not have any positive effects. In January 1918 the two Swedish large investors expressed strong dissatisfaction with the company's development, but Thams reminded them that in 1911 they had accepted the report Hütz had prepared on the company and had become coowners based on this. Thams, however, offered to take over both Olrog's and Wallenberg's shares at 'cost price with five per cent interest in France' (i.e., in French francs), but both Swedes only wanted to sell in Swedish kronor, which at that time gave a favourable exchange rate. Thams was unwilling to satisfy their request.

From 1918 Thams was a majority shareholder in the company. However, the problems continued, and in 1921 the company's losses had exceeded three-quarters of its capital. According to the company regulations, the managers then had to deliberate on whether the company was viable. The total debt had increased to over 3 million francs, of which 1.86 million belonged to Société du Madal. In autumn 1921 Prince Albert's advisor, George Jaloustre, took over the chairmanship from Thams, who for reasons of health had withdrawn from all work responsibilities. In letters to Mathiesen and Wallenberg, Jaloustre informed them that the company's capital had been lost, and that his main task was to ensure that the borrowers' demands could be met after a state of bankruptcy had been declared.

During 1922 the company was liquidated and all assets taken over by the company Société Anonyme des Cultures de Diakandapé (SACD),[52] a French company registered in Bordeaux in April 1919. In the course of ten years its share capital of 900,000 French francs increased sevenfold, to 6.5 million. Originally the company had had a land area of nine square kilometres at its disposal, but within a few years the concessions had increased to thirty square kilometres (three thousand hectares). In 1927 sisal was cultivated on twenty-four square kilometres, while the remaining land was used for groundnuts, *da* and cotton. Among other uses, the groundnuts were further refined into groundnut oil and for use in the manufacture of soap. All production was for export. By that time the company had secured an additional ninety square kilometres for clearance and the production of diverse crops.

From the annual report for SACD in 1927 it is evident that Thams was a member of the board and also had large ownership interests in the company. Included among the board's eight members was, unsurprisingly, G. Jaloustre, Prince Albert's advisor.[53]

Long-Term Results of Investments in Colonial Companies

SACD was a daughter company of the large colonial company Maison Devès, Chaumet & Cie., founded in 1807. In 1927 it had equity of 30 million French francs. The holding company Maison Devès, Chaumet & Cie. was one of the oldest companies operating in West Africa, and had specialized in valuations of African agriculture in regions in which Maison Devès wanted to operate. Maison Devès's accounts for 1926 showed a profit of 4.7 million francs. In this company, too, Thams was among the large shareholders.[54]

The lists of members of the board in the companies in which Thams had interests reveal that some names recur. The Frenchmen Max Begouën and George Jaloustre were among men Thams collaborated with, both in the African colonies and in free Ethiopia. Both were coowners of Société du Madal. To be a chairman in large companies or concerns was clearly important for the members of the networks under discussion here; the position signalled both a good reputation and economy. When in 1929 the major French bank Banque de Paris et des Pays-Bas wanted to appoint Thams to manage a plantation company in Ethiopia – the Société Minière des Concessions Prasso en Abyssinie – they arranged for an independent evaluation of him as both a private person and a businessman.[55] At the time, his connections with SACD were emphasized as being especially advantageous.[56]

The information gathered from several private archives reveal that Thams held the chairmanship of many French plantation companies in which he was engaged, but especially companies that operated in areas which from 1922 were called Afrique Occidentale Française (French West Africa). The production in these areas mainly consisted of sisal, cotton and groundnuts. Thams was also a coowner of the company Société Coloniale de Gerance et Études (SOCOGET), whose main objective was to develop land use, especially sisal plantations, in the colonies.

In 1921 Christian Thams had taken the initiative to form the Anglo-French Sisal Company in Kenya, and was also a member of its board of directors. When in 1930 the company became a limited company,[57] he resigned as chairman due to problems of loyalty regarding his involvement in SOCOGET.[58] It is probable that most of the investors in the Anglo-French Sisal Company were French, but since information has also been found on the company in the archives of both Haaken L. Mathiesen and Marcus Wallenberg, this may indicate that they, too, had strong connections with the company. In addition to sisal, the company was to produce coffee, maize, cacao, tobacco, tea, sugar, fruits, rubber and other products for export. Among the many proposals for products were tinned meat and fruits. It is thus interesting that the large multinational company Del Monte, which today is a major producer of tinned and fresh fruits, has roots in the Anglo-French Sisal Company.

Haaken L. Mathiesen and Christian Thams collaborated closely in several colonial companies, as well as in a rubber and coffee company in Uganda, Uganda Rubber & Coffee Estates Ltd (URCEL). Among the owners of URCEL were two of Christian Thams's nephews and one of his cousins.[59] The company may have been a subsidiary of the Anglo-French Sisal Company, but operated independently in the 1930s and 1940s.

The Anglo-French Sisal Company is one of several examples of colonial companies that remained viable and that had been established with capital from Scandinavian investors. The best example in this respect is Société du Madal (now named Grupo Madal), which today consists of many companies.[60] The business group is the largest of its kind in Mozambique, and Norwegian capital interests are still strongly represented. Shipowner Niels Høegh is among its dominant shareholders and also a member of the board (Reiersen 2009: 143).

Epilogue

Christian Thams withdrew from managing Société du Madal in 1922 and gradually sold off his shares. Internal disputes between the owners following the death of Prince Albert in the summer of 1922 were the most important reasons behind his withdrawal (Reiersen 2006). Thams's business problems seem particularly connected to his relationship with the Swedish business magnate Marcus Wallenberg, who both directly and indirectly had great influence on the board of directors of Société du Madal – especially after Prince Albert died. It was on Wallenberg's initiative that the former finance minister and minister of foreign affairs of the Russian Provisional Government (1917), Michael Terestchenko (in Russian, Mikhail Tereshchenko), succeeded Christian Thams as Société du Madal's managing director in 1922.[61] Some years later Société du Madal was transformed into a holding company for the very large plantation and trading company Compagnie du Madal.[62]

The choice of Terestshenko and his acceptance indicates that Société du Madal was a most interesting trading company and undoubtedly a company with possibilities of great dividends for the shareholders. His acceptance also confirms that the Scandinavian 'colonization' entrepreneurs mentioned in this article operated in a worldwide financial network. The company developed very successful under Terestchenko's management, and in the years following his death in 1956.

From 1928 until the mid-1930s Christian Thams managed three companies in Ethiopia that prospected for gold and platinum for industrial production. He died at home in Ville d'Avray, outside Paris, in May

1948. This marked the end of the history of an energetic, cosmopolitan and creative businessman and founder of industry – and a first-class network builder.

Notes

1. Mainly men were active as investors, and women did not participate in board meetings (although they could be shareholders).
2. Thams left behind a large archive in Paris, which the author has had access to. The archive included notebooks and letters that testify to his extensive business trips.
3. It was not unusual for the Norwegian upper middle classes to send their sons abroad to be educated. Many sons of renowned business families in Trondheim attended the business school Green Row Academy (now Greenrow Academy), in Abbey Holm near Silloth, Carlisle, in the U.K. (Reiersen 2006: 58).
4. In the period 1890–1910, M. Thams & Co. (Trondheim) exported timber, prefabricated houses and log-built houses to countries in Europe, Africa, India and South America, as well as custom-built crates for the house parts. The Congo Free State belonged to King Leopold II of Belgium from 1885 to 1908, thereafter changing its name to the Belgian Congo.
5. For information on Løkken Verk's production of especially copper and sulphur, see Reiersen (2006).
6. Thv. Olrog (1840–1928), who migrated from Kristiansand (Norway) to Stockholm, went into partnership there with Astrup as Olrog & Astrup. In the 1870s the timber merchants Astrup & Sørensens aktiebolag was established, and the marketing company Olrog & Berner (Paris) was represented there by the timber merchants Thv. Olrog and M.M. Astrup & Sørensen. After some time, Olrog withdrew from the marketing company, and the firm Berner & Nielsen replaced him (Reiersen 2006: 107–9).
7. See Gasslander (1959). Loewenadler was a negotiator for several Swedish matchstick factories, a close friend of the brothers Knut and Marcus Wallenberg and participated in hunting expeditions together with, among others, H.L. Mathiesen and Thomas Fearnley Sr (Reiersen 2006, with reference to SEB and MEV).
8. Portuguese East Africa became the colony Mozambique in 1920.
9. Gonzaga, Bouvay & Cie. was an oil and soap company in Marseilles.
10. Letter from Prince Albert I of Monaco to Chr. Thams, 16 May 1911, TAP.
11. According to Jacqueline Carpine-Lancre, chargée de recherches historiques au Palais princier de Monaco, their first meeting took place in 1907. Letter from Carpine-Lancre to the author, 8 September 2002.
12. The prince and Christian Thams also shared several common interests outside their business affairs, including science, technology and large game hunting.
13. Letter from Chr. Thams to H.P. Krag, 27 April 1911, SEB.

14. This is reminiscent of King Leopold II's argument in favour of the Congo Free State, which in 1908 became the Belgian Congo (Morell [1919] 2002); Jenssen-Tusch 1902–5).
15. From 1830 as many slaves were exported from Mozambique as from Angola.
16. See also Bertelsen's chapter, this volume.
17. The Portuguese differentiated between large companies (*companhias majesticas*), such as Companhia de Moçambique, and minor companies (*companhias arrendatárias*), such as Société du Madal, Sena and Luabo.
18. See Sequeira (1944); TAT.
19. See Bonnet (1914). At the end of the 1920s Bonnet was a board member of Société du Madal.
20. *Søndre Trondhjems Amtstidende*, 22 March 1912. 'Kokos, kautschuk, ibenholt' (coco, rubber, ebony).
21. 'Note sur la Société du Madal', 1912, SEB.
22. Letter from Prince Albert I of Monaco to Chr. Thams, Paris, 16 May 1911, TAP. The prince lists eight points on how the former company should be wound up and the new one run.
23. Letter from Prince Albert I of Monaco to Chr. Thams, Paris 16 May 1911, TAP; court papers from Orkdal County Court, 22 June 1928, Public Record Office in Trondheim, Statsarkivet.
24. Letter from Chr. Thams to Hans P. Krag, 27 April 1911, SEB.
25. Letter from M. Wallenberg to Chr. Thams, 7 June 1911, SEB.
26. Letter from Chr. Thams to M. Wallenberg, 3 December 1911, SEB. There had also been discussion on whether the company should be registered in England or Belgium. The company's statutes were adopted 21 December 1911: 'Statuts dressés suivant actes recus par M. Le Boucher, Notaire à Monaco, le 21 Décembre 1911', SEB. Letter from Chr. Thams to M. Wallenberg, 14 January 1912, SEB.
27. Prince Albert had in this period four advisors working with affaires related to Soc. du Madal, namely the four mentioned in this text: Louis Mayer, Emile Bernich, Gaston Moch and Georges Jaloustre.
28. Letter from Chr. Thams to M. Wallenberg, 12 November 1913, SEB.
29. See also Reiersen (2006: 366) on power struggles.
30. Letters were also exchanged between the members of the board and shareholders. Letter from Thv. Olrog to Wilhelm Thams, 24 November 1914, copybook, 1911–, TOA.
31. F.A. Parelius was a well-known author in Norway in the interwar period. Bjørn Thams was the son of Lieutenant Colonel Brynjulf Birger Thams.
32. 'You know our program is to reach 1,000,000 coconut trees on our own plantations', Thams wrote to Wallenberg on 28 January 1918, SEB.
33. According to Rønning (2000), the company had around eight hundred thousand palms in 1940 and more than 1.8 million in the year 2000. Each year storms and bad weather accounted for much destruction on the plantations and reduced the number of palms significantly.
34. Per Rygh, 'Indberetning' [Report], 26 March 1923, SEB; Vail and White (1980: 147). The Portuguese authorities claimed that the free lands were for

Africans to use and therefore should not be used by the plantation companies, yet the authorities did nothing to prevent the companies from exploiting them at will.

35. *Søndre Trondhjems Amtsavis*, 22 March 1912.
36. Société du Madal, annual report for 1918 and 1920, TAT.
37. 'Note sur la Société du Madal', 1912, SEB.
38. For a development of this argument, see Bertelsen's chapter, this volume.
39. Société du Madal, annual report for 1917 and 1918, SEB.
40. Between 1.5 and 2 million people died of the Spanish flu in Africa south of the Sahara.
41. The author has not examined reports from 1922 to 2000.
42. Letter from Chr. Thams to M. Wallenberg, 30 September 1917, SEB.
43. Article 3, pt. 4, Société du Madal Statutes, Notaire à Monaco, 21 December 1911, TAP.
44. *Journal de Monaco*, 1 June 1915, 30 May 1916, 29 May 1917, 11 May 1920, 27 September 1921, all in TAP.
45. Note from H. Mathiesen to the shareholders in Société du Madal, 30 March 1921, SEB.
46. C. Selmer and H. Wetlesen, 'Rapport ad Société du Madal', 20 May 1922, SEB.
47. Letter from Chr. Thams to M. Wallenberg, 28 January 1918, with enclosure, SEB. Upper Senegal and Niger from 1900 to 1922; French Sudan (French West Africa) from 1922 to 1959.
48. Brochure on Société des Plantations de l'Afrique Française dating from 1913, SEB. File marked Wallenberg, Société du Madal and Société des plantations de l'Afrique française, TAT.
49. Letter from Chr. Thams to M. Wallenberg, 18 August 1912, SEB.
50. Rapport du conseil d'administration de la Société des Plantations de l'Afrique Française a l'assemblee generale extraordinaire du 16 Decembre 1921, SEB.
51. Société des Plantations de l'Afrique Française, annual report, 31 October 1918, SEB.
52. Letter from G. Jaloustre to H. Mathiesen, 29 August 1925; copy in M. Wallenberg's archive, SEB.
53. Prince Albert I died 26 June 1922.
54. Financial overview of Maison Devès, Chaumet & Cie., which was a daughter company of Compagnie de Bordeaux, 30 April 1926, TAP.
55. Banque de Paris et des Pays-Bas is known today as the bank BNP Paribas.
56. Copy of information on the Société Anonyme des Cultures de Diakandapé, 20 July 1929, BNP Paribas Arch. Hist. Secr. de Mr. Roudy, ref. 58, no. 2, 1925–33, TAT.
57. Memorandum & Articles of Ass. of Anglo-French Sisal Co. Ltd, 27 February 1930, SEB.
58. Letter from Chr. Thams to M. Begouën, 1 August 1929, TAP.
59. The nephews were Marentius and Wilhelm August Thams and the cousin was Carl Selmer.

60. Information from the administrative director, Rogerio Henriques, 11 January 2007. In 2007 Madal had about sixteen thousand hectares of coconut plantations, ninety-four thousand hectares of timber plantations, seventeen thousand hectares of game farms and thirty-nine thousand hectares used for diverse agricultural use: cattle, groundnuts and so forth.
61. Born 18 March 1886 in Kiev, died 1 April 1956 in Monaco. A biography of Terestchenko, 'The First Oligarch', written by his grandson Michel Terestchenko, was published in Ukraine in 2011.
62. Per A. Arneberg, 'Sociedade Agricola Do Madal/Michael Terestshenko', note to the author, 3 February 2009, TAT.

Archives Consulted

Mozambican Historical Archives (Arquivo Histórico de Moçambique, AHM), Maputo.
Archives of the Mathiesen Eidsvold Værk (MEV), herunder the archives of Haaken L.Mathiesen and the Mathiesen/Tostrup family, Eidsvoll.
Archives of the Stockholms Enskilda Bank (SEB), hereunder the archives of the Wallenberg family, Stockholm.
Historical Archives, BNP Paribas (Archives Historiques, BNP Paribas, BNP), Paris.
Regional State Archives in Trondheim (SAT), (Statsarkivet i Trondheim).
The archives of Christian Thams, Paris (TAP).
The archives of Christian Thams, Trondheim (TAT).
The archives of Thorvald Olrog, Swedish National Archives (TOA) (Riksarkivet), Stockholm.

References

Bonnet, T. 1914. *Monograhie de la Société du Madal*. IIIe Congrès International d'Agriculture Tropicale, London.
———. 1921. *Monographie de la Société du Madal*. Lisbon: Casa Portuguesa.
Gasslander, O. 1959. *Bank och industriellt genombrott: Stockholms Enskilda Bank kring sekelskiftet 1900*, vol. 2. Stockholm: Esselte Aktiebolag.
Hreinsson, E. & Nilson, T. (eds). 2003. *Nätverk som social ressurs: Historiska exempel*. Lund: University of Lund.
Ishemo, S.L. 1995. *The Lower Zambezi Basin in Mozambique*. Aldershot, U.K.: Avebury.
Jenssen-Tusch, H. 1902–5. *Skandinaver i Congo: Svenske, norske og danske mænds og kvinders virksomhed i den uafhængige Congostat*. Copenhagen: Gyldendal.
Morell, E.D. (1919) 2002. *Kongelig Slaveleir*. Nesbru: Fritt og vilt.
Newitt, M. 1981. *Portugal in Africa: The Last Hundred Years*. London: Hurst.
———. 1995. *A History of Mozambique*. London: Hurst.

Reiersen, E. 2006. *Fenomenet Thams.* Oslo: H. Aschehoug.

―――. 2009. 'Skandinaviske entreprenører og investorer i det koloniale Afrika, 1911–1948: Deltakelse i kolonisering gjennom handelsselskap og kapitalsterke nettverk', in K.A. Kjerland and K.M. Rio (eds), *Kolonitid: Nordmenn på eventyr og big business i Afrika og Stillehavet.* Oslo: Scandinavian Academic Press, pp. 221–48.

Rønning, M. 2000. *Utvikling eller utbytting? Grupo Madal i Mosambik.* Oslo: NorWatch.

Sequeira, J.R. 1944. 'Palmares da Zambézia: A Société du Madal', *Documentário Trimestral* 38: 61–74.

Terestchenko, M. 2011, *The First Oligarch.* London/Den Bosch: Glagoslav Publications Ltd.

Vail, L. and L. White. 1980. *Capitalism and Colonialism in Mozambique: A Study of Quelimane.* London: Heinemann.

⤜⤜ 12

COLONIALISM IN NORWEGIAN AND PORTUGUESE

Madal in Mozambique

Bjørn Enge Bertelsen

In 1909, owners of large plantations in the provinces of Zambézia and Tete in what was later to become Mozambique made a radical move: in writing they accused the colonial secretary of native affairs (*Secretário dos Negócios Indígenas*), Francisco Ferrão, of presenting a skewed account of their activities to the general consul for Mozambique, Alfredo Augusto Freire de Andrade. This protest revealed disagreement over how the plantation owners both administered their properties and levied taxes from the African population. The owners commented on the secretary's account:

> Whoever reads the account of Sr. Secretary of Native Affairs will be left with the impression that naught or near naught beneficial has been undertaken in Zambézia after the current owners took over the plantation properties [*os prazos*]. … His understanding is that the plantation owners are little more than parasites living off taxation and repression of the natives. [There is] little in his account which prevents Zambézia from becoming a Congolese inferno which merits international intervention. … In all his writings, Sr. Secretary of Native Affairs underlines the principle that all interests shall be second to the interests of the colonial state. But His Excellence the General Consul will certainly know that in Zambézia the state, in its key functions, is constituted by the plantation owners. (Prazos da Coroa 1909: 562)[1]

Printed as a booklet in Lourenço Marques (now Maputo), the protest was signed by the major plantation owners of the time. Among them were the owners of what was in the booklet entitled Société du Madal, which a year later would become Norwegian-owned under the entrepreneur Christian Thams.[2]

The quote from the protest illustrates several intriguing aspects of plantation colonialism. For one, it is abundantly clear that the plantation owners see themselves as de facto and, perhaps, de jure authorities over the territories they control, with a distinct autonomy within the Portuguese colonial framework. It is also evident that the production regimes of the plantations significantly include what one might call nonprimary forms of accumulation – more precisely, the Portuguese taxation system of *mussoco* (head tax) and *imposto de palhota* (hut tax).

Madal's[3] participation among the 1909 signatories signals that we are not only looking at a colonial actor in a narrow economic sense, but also a player within the colonial political field. From 1910 and throughout the century, Madal was to have a strong Norwegian presence in both ownership and management (see also Reiersen's chapter, this volume). As key Norwegian entrepreneurial families have had significant interests in Madal from 1910 until at least 2013, the plantations' political and economic dealings assumes importance in the writing of the colonial history of Mozambique, Portugal and Norway.[4] Furthermore, given the involvement of the Norwegian Christian Thams in 1910, the centenary of Norwegian presence in Madal constitutes a long-term case of Norwegian colonial and postcolonial African history.

Analysing this long-term Norwegian involvement in what was to become Zambézia Province following Mozambican independence in 1975, this chapter outlines three characteristics that are, to some extent, also recognizable in the 1909 protest. First, Madal may be seen as instance of a *total institution* (Goffman [1961] 1991; see also Foucault [2004] 2007) in the sense that it controlled and structured nearly all aspects of the African subjects under its command. Second, the plantation may not only be analysed in isolation, but must be approached as a *node* – a singular point in a network – in the vaster economic and political colonial system. Last, the chapter argues that Zambézia's plantation regime – of which Madal comprised a part – was an integral part of Portuguese colonial rule and strategy in Mozambique.

For the history of colonial participation, these aspects of Madal imply that Norwegian entrepreneurs and capitalists may not merely be analysed as agents opportunistically following in the wake of larger colonial processes. Contrarily, Norwegian colonial participation in Madal was at times characterized by an extensive use of violence, a politics of territorialization and a regime of forced labour and taxation that one would associate with the colonial state order.[5] This chapter focuses mainly on the period before 1930, when Madal demonstrates the large-scale and expansive Norwegian colonial plantation regime and the Portuguese politics of pacification and domination to which they were integral.

Portuguese Colonialism: An Opening for Norwegian and International Capital

Arguably, the Portuguese colonial state failed to attain sovereign control in a conventional sense of the term until the late 1800s and, in some places, well into the twentieth century. Besides Mozambique, this pertains to Angola, Guinea-Bissau, São Tomé e Príncipe and Cape Verde – to name the African colonies later to become independent nation-states (Chabal and Birmingham 2002). Such a weak development of colonial control crucially resides in the Portuguese colonial orientation towards resource extraction on the one hand and its largely maritime-based administration and trade on the other. As Young points out, the early Portuguese colonial state was 'a loose-knit mercantile state … based on domination of the Indian Ocean trading routes, and a nucleated string of outposts at key commercial intersections whose central base was Goa' (1994: 50).

This Portuguese maritime orientation is visible in concrete colonial settings such as the central parts of Mozambique, including Zambézia Province, where Portuguese traders from the 1500s onwards often used routes previously established by Arab traders. In addition, the Portuguese tentatively established a minimum of political, economic and military control solely on the coast and through coastal fortifications, such as Sofala, Kilwa and Ilha de Moçambique, without making any concerted attempts at gaining control over the interior. This strategy made the Portuguese, to a large degree, dependent on the politics of African chiefdoms and their impositions of regulations on trade.[6] Early Portuguese coastal towns may therefore be conceived of as a system of *nodes* and *routes* rather than based on aspirations towards achieving territorial control in sovereign terms.

The Portuguese approach was, however, challenged by other colonial powers' increased grip on African territories manifested through the politics of the Berlin conference (1884–85), where de facto territorial and sovereign control was decided to be the key to achieving international legitimacy vis-à-vis the colonies. As a comparatively impoverished European power in the late 1800s, the post-Berlin political order challenged Portuguese colonial politics, especially as it was nearly impossible to establish such control solely through the Portuguese state's resources. In Zambézia Province the solution for Portugal was to attempt to reform and redevelop the so-called *prazo* system.

The *prazo* system, initiated by Portugal already in the 1600s, allocated land to Portuguese settlers based on the idea of establishing a landowning elite of Portuguese heritage in the colonies. However, after establishing themselves in Zambézia, social and political dynamics emerged that the colonial authorities neither desired nor had foreseen revolving around it being opportune for the aspiring landowning settlers to marry into local African political organizations. Conversely, without matrimonial ties with the existing African landowning elite, the Portuguese newcomers were prevented from accessing resources to defend themselves and their properties, to expand, to introduce taxation and to mobilize labour. Due to these dynamics, the *prazo* system radically changed character in Zambézia and came to be dominated by what has been described as an Afro-Portuguese elite that, unsurprisingly, lacked aspirations towards defending or upholding institutions of the colonial administration. Vail and White (1980: 8) characterize the system during the mid-1800s:

> The result was the growth of a small but powerful settler population, mainly of mixed race, living off tribute and the gold and ivory trades, forming its own alliances, executing its own laws, conducting its own wars, and subject more to its economic and cultural involvement with the indigenous African population than to attempts at political control by Portuguese administrators at Quelimane or Moçambique Island [Ilha de Moçambique].

From having been envisaged as bridgeheads of Portuguese civilization, the *prazos* from the 1850s to 1900 had evolved into 'statelets' based on trade, warfare, forced and bounded labour, the and slave trade that were integrated into encompassing and autonomous African polities – and without much contact with the Portuguese colonial authorities (Isaacman 1972: 124–63; see also Newitt 1969, 1973).

In addition to the transformed *prazo* system, the slave trade is also key to understanding Zambézia at the inception of the twentieth century. During the nineteenth century the slave trade grew dramatically in volume, and before 1846 some three hundred thousand slaves had been caught and exported from Zambézia alone (Vail and White 1980: 23).[7] The slave trade has been documented to have represented an important income in Zambézia well into the 1900s, when the Hova and Sakala kingdoms of Madagascar reportedly were the last purchasers of slaves (Capela 1995; Sheriff 2005). Both the slave trade and the transformation of the *prazo* system led the Portuguese authorities to see the interior of Zambézia – as other parts of Mozambique – as beyond (or inimical to) colonial control, leading Serra (1983) to point out that Mozambique had powerful African localized military units that effectively prevented Portuguese control until around 1920.[8] Similarly, Newitt (1995: 364) characterizes the situation in Zambézia around 1890 as one of 'internal anarchy'.

While politically unruly and militarily volatile Zambézia worried Portuguese politicians throughout the 1800s, the post-Berlin international politics provided a strong incentive to finally act on the problem of what the *prazos* had become.[9] The solution was to allow the establishment of concession companies in the area that would, it was hoped, both develop and, crucially, pacify the *prazo* areas. Concession companies were therefore bestowed with the authority of local administrations as well as the opportunity to collect *mussoco* (head tax) – a colonial distortion of earlier African forms of tribute to African polities and chiefdoms (Newitt 1995: 365).[10] For undertaking the brunt of the work of pacification and establishing control, the companies were also allowed to keep so-called *cipais* – African mercenaries, policemen or guards – used primarily for organizing and implementing the forced peasant labour. Often known as *tchibalo*, this frequently assumed the form of imposing tax burdens on peasants that they were unable to meet, which led to being incorporated into a system of forced labour (Newitt 1995: 367).[11] Various forms *tchibalo* were sanctioned by the Portuguese colonial state until the last decades before independence in 1975.[12]

With African countries increasingly gaining independence following the Second World War, the Portuguese continuation of *tchibalo* received much international attention, a fact prompting Ghana to complain about Portugal to the International Labour Organization (ILO) in the early 1960s. Interestingly, during the hearings related to its commission that was sent to investigate the charges, Count Carlos de Bobone, Madal's general manager at the time, was summoned to Geneva in September 1961. In the official 1962 report from the commission, Count Bobone expressed that 'he thought it was a habit in the Zambezia district for the workers to come for six months, then to be replaced by other natives, and to come back for a further period of six months, and so on [*sic*] for many years' (ILO 1962: 241).

The fact that Madal's Count Bobone as late as 1961 refers to a system of compulsory or forced labour is indicative of its duration within the Portuguese colonial regime. Further, as was generally the case in Mozambique, the concession companies of early 1900s Zambézia to a large degree depended on *tchibalo* in the comprehensive development, restructuring and expansion of plantations and their infrastructure throughout most of the twentieth century. 'From the 1890s to 1930, most of the district was under the quasi-governmental control of four large plantation companies', according to Vail and White (1983: 883). Put differently, by pursuing a politics of concession companies, Portugal not only opened Zambézia to international capital, including Norwegian, but also paved the way for totalizing plantation regimes.[13]

The powers vested in plantation companies by the colonial authorities were by no means lost on their owners. For instance, these powers and the politics of pacification in Zambézia remain the central elements in Count Géorges Stucky de Quay's memoirs (Quay 1938). In the period from 1898 to 1927 he was director general of one of the four companies Vail and White referred to above, Companhia de Boror. The count's memoirs give a glimpse of the formation of plantation companies in Zambézia and, in summing up Boror history, it is therefore revealing that he emphasizes the importance of the company's own *cipais* in gaining territorial control. For instance, he recounts with great pride how Boror helped pacify the districts of Zanga and Haut-Boror and underlines how Boror's *cipais* executed such pacification without having to ask the colonial authorities for assistance (Quay 1938: 133). As the count's memoirs illustrate, the landscape of Zambézia in the early twentieth century was one of ongoing campaigns of pacification and violence – shaped by complex and long-term relations of exploitation and domination relating to *prazos* and the slave trade. It was in such circumstances that commercial companies such as Madal and Boror were established and expanded.[14]

Madal: Sovereignty, Pacification and the Crisis of the First World War

> This area [Zambézia] was under the so-called *Prazos da Coroa* regime, a form of colonialism attempted from the 1890s onwards which consisted in deferring all political, economical and administrative power over vast areas to certain well-capitalised companies that developed agriculture on their *prazos* simultaneously as collecting taxes and maintaining law and order by a corps of native soldiers – *cipaios* [*cipais*] – which the companies arm and pay.
>
> – Manoel de Lancastre Bobone and Carlos Lourenço Bobone, *Genealogia dos Condes Bobone*[15]

Such was the retrospective characterization of the Zambézia system by a representative of yet another family of nobles, the Bobones, who from 1903 were central to the administration and ownership side of Madal (Chichava 2007: 102ff.).[16] Given Zambézia's violent past, Count Bobone's account to the ILO makes asking whether the establishment of control by companies such as Madal continued *prazo*-related forms of taxation (as in tribute) and forced labour a valid question. Historians certainly argue for such a continuation – as does the account to which the *prazo* owners were opposed that opened this chapter (Newitt 1995:

356–86). Also, the fact that companies like Madal and Boror appropriated the armies of *cipais* that were formerly used by the previous *prazo* owners subscribes to such continuity. At the time of appropriation, the *cipais* had established practices of taking slaves during raids, imposing forced labour and violently extracting taxes for the *prazo* owners. Based on a stay at the Micahune plantation station controlled by Madal and reflecting on its *cipais*, the German travel writer Emil Ludwig (1913: 171) tellingly notes that while there are no recruiting agents for Madal, the system is very effective, as 'the police force brings the Negro to work'. The sovereign right of Madal to recruit and force those that are variously called 'natives' (*indfødte*) or 'negroes' (*negre*) to work for 180 days each year, is also asserted directly several times in reports, for instance Norwegian entrepreneur Wilhelm Nicolaysen's from 1919: 'These are recruited, as it is called, which in reality means: they are forced to work' (1919: 6; see also 27).[17]

Beyond the continued use of *cipais* for concession companies, there is also more direct evidence of the violence and brutality characterizing the working environment of plantations such as Madal. In a private letter to her newlywed husband Ernst Meyer, a Swiss foreman at Madal for several periods from 1915 onwards, Cläry Ernst proclaims horror at the violence she is witnessing at Madal's station in Angoche. The letter, from 4 May 1920, contains several paragraphs such as this:

> The bloody day of yesterday was not over. In the morning Carvalho [a foreman] had hit an old nigger so that he had a hole in his head. I suppose, he had opposed his work. He (the nigger) was crying and bleeding, and he was running to Lehmann [head foreman] – but Carvalho made clear his own position to Lehmann. Oh Aeschi [Ernst], to see such things, that's nothing for me.

Written in 1920, the letter is revealing both of the working environment as well as the wider violent colonial context within which the companies operated. For instance, the companies' use of *cipais* to violently enforce control of their workers occurred while the colonial state was also using soldiers to quell rebellions. Pélissier (2004: 298ff.) describes how the governor of Beira in 1917 ordered his military commander to crush what was later known as the Barúe rebellion by placing an additional fifteen thousand African Nguni warriors at his commander's disposal.[18] The governor's orders, quoted below, starkly illustrate the instrumental approach Portuguese colonial authorities had to using violence in attempting to pacify their unruly African subjects: 'You must burn all the rebel villages destroying all the fields, confiscating all their cattle and taking as many prisoners as possible including women and children. It is indispensable that these actions be carried out as rapidly and violently as possible in order to terrorize the local population and prevent further revolts' (quoted in Isaacman 1976: 170). Portuguese violence concerned even, for instance, British colonial authorities, who reported of the Barúe rebellion that '[a]ll leaders of the rebels who are caught are beheaded and their heads given to their wives to carry home, if the wives are caught with them' (quoted in Isaacman 1976: 170). Generally, the Portuguese colonial state's use of violence to quell resistance illustrates that Zambézia at the time was seen as characterized by rebellions and attacks on colonial institutions.[19] For Madal and other companies, this situation necessitated the maintenance of military and paramilitary forces so that threats to property and personnel could be minimized and the local population kept under control. In sum, the concession companies' use of *cipais* for these purposes in this period is largely consistent with their usage under the previous *prazo* owners (Ishemo 1995: 248; Hedges 1999: 61).

Another element of continuity pertains to how concession companies appropriated *labour resources* as well as territories through campaigns of expansion and pacification. When the companies first came to Zambézia, African households there had been part of systems of forced labour and slavery connected to the *prazos* for centuries. Such practices were to a large degree continued by the concession companies, and in 1899, while illegal enslavement was still ongoing and while there was widespread unrest in Zambézia, Portugal issued a new law that gave the companies extensive powers relating to securing labour power. The Labour Law of 1899 ties the idea of the civilizing mission of presumably primitive Africans to the duty to work. In a comparison with the French and British colonial systems, Roberts and Mann (1991: 30) comments that the Portuguese 1899 law made Africans 'liable to compulsory labor either for the colonial state or for the private sector. Failure to work in Portuguese Africa was thus a legal offense, contributing simultaneously to the criminalization of the bulk of the African population and to the emergence of myriad forms of resistance to colonialism.' Throughout Mozambican territory, including in areas formerly under the control of large companies such as Companhia de Moçambique, the 1899 law was extensively used both to recruit ordinary workers as well as to impose forced labour (Allina 2012; Neves 1998).

Together these elements of the concession companies comprise a continuation, appropriation and redeployment of *prazo* practices and mechanisms of control (see also Serra 1980). The attractions and possibilities of such continuities for international investors were by no means lost on the Portuguese authorities, and these features were therefore regularly communicated: for instance, as late as 1944, the *prazo* system

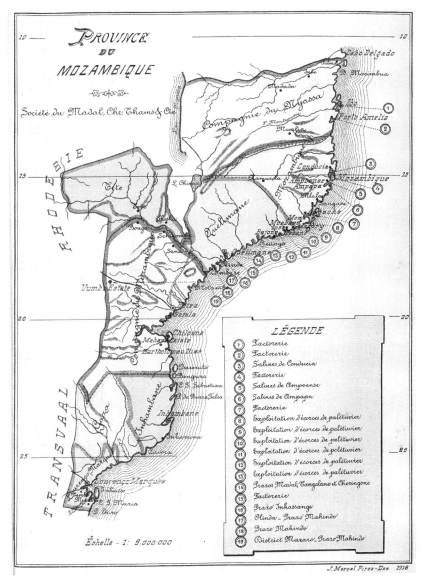

Figure 12.1. 'Province Mozambique' in 1918, showing Madal's possessions highlighted by numbered points to the left. *Source:* Hans Peter Fyhn Kragh archives; reproduced with permission.

was marketed as central to Madal's success in clearing large tracts of forests, draining wetlands and establishing a great number of coconut plantations for copra production (Sequeira 1944). In their bid to attract more investment to Zambézia in general and specifically to Madal's areas, the Portuguese authorities reiterate the benefits of the *prazo* system (Sequeira 1944: 68): 'The regulation of native labour power, which still is in full operation, continues to be tied to the ancient and very interesting *prazo* institution which allows for a simple and large-scale recruitment of labourers.'[20]

However, it was not only in the glossy colonial advertisements that the Portuguese authorities emphasized the continuities of the *prazo* system and the wide-ranging liberties thereby bestowed upon concession companies such as Madal. In a number of letters between Madal and the Portuguese Ministry of Finance in 1943, the subject of Madal's size and relative strength are discussed in relation to the colonial state–dominated Companhia de Zambézia.[21] The exchange starts with a letter dated 19 April 1943 that Madal's Lisbon office sent to the Ministry of the Colonies in Lisbon offering to purchase 135,000 shares in the Companhia de Zambézia, owned by the Portuguese state. In a letter the following day, the Ministry of the Colonies recommends that the Ministry of Finance accept Madal's offer. However, in a letter of 28 June 1943, the Ministry of Finance flatly and directly refuses to accept the proposition, emphasizing instead the ideal of further nationalization of colonial companies. Crucial to the argument is that the Portuguese state and business presence is still weak in Mozambique. Consequently, if Madal, a company based largely on non-Portuguese capital, were to impinge on and gradually take over the Companhia de Zambézia, this would undermine state interests.

There are, of course, large differences between Madal in its formative years of pacification and consolidation from 1910 onwards and the mature and expansive company we see in the documents from the 1940s. However, and as evidenced by the worry in the Portuguese Ministry of Finance, Madal was a colonial total institution in several aspects from the 1910s onwards. First, Madal's (and other companies') activities must be seen as a totalizing effort combining the Portuguese aim of attaining territorial control of rebellious zones with international capital's perennial aim of profit. Second, Madal (and other companies) largely maintained the violent systems of taxation/tribute and forced labour – for instance, through the unclear distinction between the slave labour of the 1800s and early 1900s and the forced labour that the 1899 law enacted (see also Nicolaysen 1919). Finally – as demonstrated in the chapter's opening quote – the concession companies' wide-reaching control of people, land, law and production amounted to de facto if not de jure sovereign formations within the wider Portuguese colonial order.

In the case of Madal, this is also ascertained by Elsa Reiersen's (2006: 353) work about Christian Thams, where, based on a wide range of sources, she points out that Madal was the predominant colonial power in its area of operation. Mirroring Reiersen's observation on a general level and reflecting the fragmented nature of Portuguese colonial state power during the era of the concession companies, Pélissier (2004) even asks whether Mozambique may be described as one or several colonies during the time of the First World War. Pélissier's general question is also supported by contemporary French diplomatic sources – in particular a French official report from 1914 on the labour force in Mozambique made by the French vice-consulate in Lourenço Marques. Commenting on Madal, Luabo and Lugella in particular, the French report denotes the directors of these companies *petits souverains* – minor sovereigns – and as ruling minor states.[22] While noting further the companies' nearly complete territorial and administrative control, the report also launches a strong critique against Portuguese colonial politics, sardonically summing up the aims of Portuguese rule:

> The goal [for the Portuguese administration] is always the same: It is to pursue immediate profit. Building for the future, preparing for an orderly development and regulation of agricultural and other resources of the Province of Mozambique, following the example we give in our colonies, is not yet the dominant practice of the Portuguese government. They work only for the present, believing perhaps that this is the best mode to exploit their possessions overseas.[23]

However, the Portuguese pursuit of 'immediate profit' and little or no development of general infrastructure or facilities for its population, in the eyes of the French diplomat, benefited both companies such as Madal as well as the Portuguese colonial state, which attracted significant foreign investment. Similarly, in 1919 the Norwegian entrepreneur Wilhelm Nicolaysen also remarked that the *prazos* under Madal's control had surprisingly few facilities for its population of over forty thousand people, including no doctors, only a handful of teachers and huts for the labourers in such a condition that 'they under no circumstance would pass inspection if the question in the future came up' (1919: 27).

The liberty allowed such concession companies – ruled by *petits souverains* – was, however, not unproblematic. This was especially the case during the First World War, when northern Mozambique was increasingly contested, exposing the numerous foreign administrators, representatives and owners in this area to suspicions of being spies by the Allied powers. For Madal this had the consequence of Christian Thams being suspected of having dangerous German sympathies during the First World War; he is mentioned specifically in Consul E. Savoyo's letter from the French vice-consulate in Lourenço Marques to the 'Direction des Affaires Politiques et Commerciales' on 10 October 1918.

Savoyo's concerns are rooted in what the ministry also acknowledges in its response: Thams (in cooperation with the Norwegian shipowner Thor Thoresen) from 1915 onwards was believed to have profiteered from trade during the First World War in a manner nonbeneficial to Allied interests.[24] However, while recognizing Savoyo's and other French sources' concerns based on suspicions of Thams's alleged war profiteering, the French Ministry of Foreign Affairs responds to Savoyo via a letter to his superiors at the French embassy in Lisbon:

> I would like to add that Mr. Thams, of whom our Consul at Lourenço Marquez proved to be most suspicious and, as you know, was indeed once considered suspect also by the [French] General Staff of the Army, was rehabilitated entirely following an inquiry made by our legation in Christiania [now Oslo], the result being that no substantial complaint against him should be made.[25]

Although Thams was officially cleared of the suspicions against him by this letter from the French Ministry of Foreign Affairs, the Portuguese and British authorities nonetheless continued to view powerful foreigners in northern Mozambique with suspicion. This was also fuelled by the de facto lack of Portuguese control over the concession companies.

As an accepted (but not revered) part of Portuguese colonial strategy, Madal evolved along with the transformation of Portuguese colonialism from a system of nodal control and exploitation of resources – via trade routes, a seaborne political and military dominance and a control of markets – to involve, at the turn of the twentieth century, territorialization and pacification through non-Portuguese concession companies and international capital. Madal was, then, clearly a small (and sometimes suspect) sovereignty within a Portuguese colonial order – as well as internationally suspect during times of crisis such as the First World War. But how did Madal operate in the areas under its dominion? How were the 'immediate profits' – in the words of the French vice-consul to Mozambique – made for Madal?

Taxation, Forced Labour and Considerable Profits in Zambézia

> They are completely black, of the Kaffir race, totally subordinate to the rule of the company and pay taxes etc. to this.
> – Elsa Reiersen, *Fenomenet Thams*[26]

This bold statement was made in 1912 by Christian Thams about Madal – a company he was instrumental in setting up and managing and, in 1912, in which he was also a large shareholder. Reminding us of the derogatory European view of Africans of his time, it also came merely three years after the *prazo* owners' protest that opened this chapter. However, more interesting than reflecting contemporary racial slurs is that Thams was aware of Madal's control over labour power and the crucial part taxation played in gaining profits from such control (see also Chichava 2007: 99). Indeed, the companies' income from such taxation *surpassed* the money generated from production and trade (Ishemo 1989, 1995).

The Norwegian-controlled Madal was among the companies that, through the help of *cipais*, in the early part of the twentieth century thrived on taxation of Africans within its realm of domination. For instance, in 1912 in the district of Quelimane, the Portuguese colonial authority had only approximately 300 soldiers and 150 marines at its disposal to control a registered (and unruly) African population of 434,549 (Pélissier 1994b: 168). Put differently, Madal and other concession companies' rule were employed to enforce a colonial state-like order that the Portuguese state's military and administrative presence clearly could not itself furnish. This was also recognized by Savoyo, the French vice-consul to Lourenço Marques quoted above, when summing up that Madal, Luabo, Lugella and other companies must be understood in the context of taxation and forced labour. Savoyo emphasized specifically how the lack of money or goods is beneficial for the companies by turning 'the native' into a *travailleur forcé* – an 'unfree' labourer – noting that 'the native's' lack of money guarantees these companies continued exploitation as well as ample labour power.[27] He goes on to ask: 'Should we not say that this form of slavery still flourishes in this part of Africa? … Given the many abuses in the *prazos* the conditions of the natives there are nothing less than precarious.' Savoyo's impression is also sustained by the German travel writer Emil Ludwig (1913: 175), also quoted above, who notes that Madal used *cipais* to capture those unable to pay *mussoco* and subjected these to forced labour.

The fact that companies like Madal relied greatly on taxation can be exemplified statistically. In 1913 – the year following Thams's explanation to his fellow Norwegians about how those of 'the Kaffir race' were under Madal's dominion and paid taxes to the company – the Portuguese authorities surveyed land in Zambézia. The survey showed that out of a total 9 million hectares of land in Zambézia, 5.4 million were controlled by the concession companies and less than half (3.6 million hectares) was retained by the colonial state and under its nominal control. This ratio shows that not only in the domain of policing power but also in terms of land ownership the *prazo* owners *comprised* the colonial state in the area – as the *prazo* owners also reminded the

Portuguese colonial authorities in the opening quote of this chapter. In terms of profitability and production, the survey showed another interesting feature: out of the 5.4 million hectares under *prazo* owner control, a mere 0.5 per cent (45,000 hectares) was registered as agricultural land – a very small number given the Portuguese authorities' keen interest in showing control, development and success in these areas (Ishemo 1995: 160).

Given the vast areas left uncultivated in 1913, we can assume there was little money to be made from ordinary types of agricultural production normally associated with plantations. The key to profits lay in taxation. As also reflected in Savoyo's report above, from the early 1900s onwards the concession companies steeply increased the taxes levied on the African population while simultaneously retaining poor salaries. The prospects of considerable *mussoco* income therefore naturally figures prominently in the report made by Nicolaysen, who boldly states that 'the prazo concessions is merely a tax instrument … whose importance relates to this providing the prazo holder administrative right within the district as well as, if the taxes are not paid, to demand this paid through work on the properties of the prazo' (1919: 23f).[28] Tellingly, Nicolaysen goes on to detail in various of Madal's *prazos* the total number of able men and women as well as the mussoco income for each of these (24–26).

While this was a violent and repressive regime, at a systemic level it comprised an interweaving of the African peasants' livelihoods and crop production with the low and seasonally varying salaries provided by the companies – labour that the taxation regimes obliged the peasants to undertake following the 1899 law (see also Negrão 1995). For companies like Madal, this system proved to be very profitable, and the system was continued far into the 1930s (Ishemo 1995: 269). Taxation was particularly important for Madal because the copra price between 1911 and 1930 was relatively low, stable and consistent along the East African coast. For instance, from Zanzibar in 1911–15 copra was exported at GBP 19.00 per ton, 1916–20 at GBP 28.00, 1921–25 at GBP 24.00 and 1926–30 at GBP 22.00 – falling dramatically to GBP 10.00 per ton in the period 1931–40 (Ferguson 1989: 39). Vail and White (1980) provide similar prices, confirming the overall trend of price stability interrupted only by a minor rise during the First World War and followed by a slump back to prewar prices in the 1920s.

The argument of taxation – and in particular *mussoco* – as the backbone of the economy of the concession company has been underlined by Serra (1980) and Jones (2005). Both argue that, in general, for concession companies and Portuguese colonial authorities, the violently enforced

taxation regime integrated peasants into a capitalist mode of production and societal order from the end of the nineteenth century onwards.
Barry Neil-Tomlinson's (1977) extensive analysis of the Nyassa Chartered Company in the area bordering Zambézia (now known as Niassa
Province) supports such a reading: 'The Nyassa Company, which originally had grandiose plans for the capitalist development of its territory,
soon saw hut tax receipts as its major source of income' (1977: 109).

Portuguese colonial authorities' policy on taxes also was a strong incentive for Madal, Nyassa and other companies to focus on 'tax farming' instead of expansive agricultural production. In 1890 the *mussoco*
(head tax) was 1.20 escudos and 1.60 in 1913; it then increased dramatically from 2.50 escudos in 1921 to 10.00 in 1923 (Serra 1980: 38). At
the same time, weekly wages at the *prazos* in Zambézia were low: 0.4
escudos per week at the end of the 1910s and 0.61 per week from 1919
to 1924 (Negrão 1995: 63).[29] With drastically increased taxes, relatively
stable wages and low copra prices, one clearly sees the incentive for
Madal, which controlled from thirty thousand to fifty thousand people in the period 1910 to 1930, to focus on the collection of *mussoco* in
addition to expanding copra production and other ventures, such as
sisal and cattle rearing.[30] An example provided by Negrão (1995: 78)
from 1927 in Zambézia clarifies the burden of taxation for the African
household: the hut tax of 42 escudos was equivalent to 111 days of work
of both husband and wife. So, if the concession companies to a large
degree were used to pacify an African population and to force peasant
livelihoods into a largely extractive form of production based on cheap
and forced labour, how did the Portuguese colonial authorities and the
African population react?

For the Portuguese colonial authorities, the report made by 'Sr. Secretary of Native Affairs', to which the opening letter in this chapter
refers, is indicative: Madal and other concession companies did not fo-
ment the kind of economic development, large-scale investments and
modernization of production that the Portuguese colonial authorities
had envisaged. However, until the establishment of the Portuguese so-
called *Estado Novo* (New State) from 1930, which corresponded with a
stronger colonial state apparatus, the authorities had little alternative
but to let the concession companies have their way (Mahoney 2003).
Also, the fact that Madal and other companies' contracts were, indeed,
not terminated demonstrates their value as strategic assets for the colonial government's political and economic aims (see also Pitcher 2003).

The African population reacted to the harsh realities of the concession
companies by simply fleeing: in the period 1900 to 1920 an estimated
one hundred thousand people emigrated to Malawi from Zambézia

(Ishemo 1995: 170).[31] Even though this is a large number, it is not unusual. In the same period, similar numbers emigrated from the repressive regimes of the concession companies in, for example, the central Mozambican province of Manica.[32] The large numbers emigrating from diverse areas of colonial Mozambique speaks volumes in terms of how surrounding colonies (or other areas in Mozambique not under concession company rule) were viewed as more attractive. A key factor here is also that the pay African workers in Zambézia received – for forced labour and for their copra produce – was comparatively speaking very low. It also seems there was no real incentive to raise the pay at Madal – at least according to Nicolaysen (1919: 17): 'The negroes are difficult people; in general more or less unintelligent. The work is for most of them forced and one would surely neither get more work out of them nor make them more willing to work by paying a higher salary.'[33]

In his magisterial survey of a hundred years of peasant households in Zambézia, José Negrão shows that the salaries of Madal, Boror and Lugela during the 1920s were much lower than that of the large-scale factory Sena Sugar. Owned by British businessman John Peter Hornung, it produced sugar for the international market: '[C]ompared to Hornung & Co [Sena Sugar], the wages paid by Madal, Boror, Lugela and Companhia de Zambézia were "miserable". People doing the same work received in one year what others were earning at Sena Sugar in one month, and all paying the same *mussoco* amount' (Negrão 1995: 63–64).

Sena Sugar was the largest company operating in the area, and the salary discrepancy was most probably due to the comparatively greater need for skilled labour in sugar production. In addition to using their labourers for copra production, Madal frequently earned money by leasing seasonal labour to Sena Sugar (see also Head 1980).[34] In this way, under Madal, African peasants' subsistence agricultural production was integral to a so-called *dual economy* in which the labour force of the African household was at the mercy of seasonally varying production at the concession companies.[35] Concession companies exploited the flexibility of the dual economy system. In addition to making large profits on taxation, African peasants' salaries were very low. This situation made the alternative for the African population of emigrating to Malawi seem very attractive.

Another aspect of the brutal labour and taxation regime is exposed in Vail and White's (1980: 158) detailed study of the Quelimane district – the heart of Madal's realm. 'Child labour, for example, was paid by both Madal and the Boror Company at the rate of five litres of rotgut spirit per week.'[36] Related to child labour, alcohol and the embroilment

Figure 12.2. At Chinde, one of Madal's plantations. Following the shelling of coconuts, scraping is done manually, as seen in this image from the author's visit in 2007. *Source:* Bjørn Enge Bertelsen; reproduced with permission.

of the whole African household in the regime of labour and concession company rule, it is also widely documented that *mussoco* in Zambézia could be paid in alcohol, foodstuffs or other products (Ishemo 1989, 1995). This represents a shift from when alcohol in the precolonial and early colonial period was integral to noncommercial ways of organizing communal work – in, for example, work parties with beer. Like *mussoco*, the *prazo* system and other aspects of the sociopolitical landscape of Zambézia, it seems reasonable to assume that alcohol use, as an object of taxation as well as payment, was also altered by the concession companies' co-optation of precolonial practices and institutions. It is also well-known that large companies, such as Sena Sugar, produced large quantities of alcohol for both export and local consumption from the late 1890s (Collin 1973: 38, 50).

As in the case of Madal – and supported by references to other companies like Sena Sugar, Boror, Lugella, Companhia de Zambézia and Companhia de Niassa – the plantation encompasses and encapsulates nearly all aspects of its subjects: enforcing labour, integrating households into its economy, imposing a heavy taxation regime, appropriating the practices associated with the former *prazo* institutions and aggressively policing its territory with *cipais*. For these reasons, the plantation regime of Madal in the period until 1930 may be viewed as a total institution (Beckford 1972; see also Cooper 1977; Ishemo 1995; Negrão 1995). Its establishment was crucial to Portuguese colonialism as a colonizing and pacifying force – Madal being also a node in the global capitalist system.

Pacification, Consolidation, Expansion: Colonial and Postcolonial Norwegian Madal

The ownership and entrepreneurship of the Norwegian Christian Thams was imperative for Madal's growth and consolidation. For Thams such a colonial venture was very profitable, and between 1910 and 1920 Madal's profits were large; Reiersen (2006: 353) notes that the net profit in 1917 was F 1.6 million and F 1.7 million the next year. However, Thams was not the only Norwegian to profit from being involved in Madal; in 1920 Norwegian shareholders were a majority and dominated the board. Likewise, a Norwegian administration was established in Quelimane that consolidated the Zambézian base of Madal's expansion.[37] While underresearched, this Norwegian dimension has not been lost on economic historians. Commenting on the situation of concession companies and plantations around Mozambican independence in 1975, Pitcher (2002: 28) writes:

> Foreign investors from the United Kingdom, South Africa, Switzerland, and Norway controlled many of the powerful agricultural undertakings that were on private hands. Companies such as the Sena Sugar Estates, the Boror Company, or the Madal Company had operated in Mozam-

bique since the turn of the 20th century and dominated the production of export crops such as sugar, tea and copra.[38]

The fact that Norwegian investors are listed together with well-known colonial profiteers (South Africa, the United Kingdom and, perhaps surprisingly, Switzerland) underscores Madal's position within the colonial state formation of Portuguese East Africa. Put differently, while Norwegians in many contexts may be cast as colonial microentrepreneurs – many examples appear in this anthology – in Mozambique Norwegian investors were influential throughout the twentieth century. As late as 2007, during a visit to Madal's headquarters in Quelimane, the sheer volume underscored the company's continued importance. With around five thousand seasonal labourers in 2007, Madal exported between five thousand and seven thousand tons of coconut oil, mostly to Switzerland and the factories of the multinational company Nestlé.[39] The areas under Madal's control in 2007 were still enormous: sixteen thousand hectares of coconut plantations, ninety-four thousand hectares of timber concession areas, seventeen thousand hectares of game farms (in Chinde) and thirty-nine thousand hectares devoted to other uses, such as cattle rearing and the (at the time) new business of jatropha biofuel production. These areas are so considerable that Madal in some texts is portrayed as the largest private landowner in Mozambique (Mackenzie 2006; Rønning 2000). Given this long-term perspective, Madal's impact and its colonial Norwegian character may be tracked along a number of dimensions, including *administration, communication and transport* and *land ownership*.

First, in terms of *administration,* throughout Madal's more than century-long presence in Zambézia, the local administrators, foremen and general managers of the plantation have been largely European and often Norwegian. This racial or European feature was frequently publicized proudly during the colonial era: in 1921 an overview made by Madal boasts that its administration had 'tout ce personnel de race blanche' and that it governed more than fifty thousand Africans (Bonnet 1921: 3, 8).[40] In addition to the Norwegians at Madal's base in Quelimane, a total of forty-seven Swiss worked there until 1970 – most of these in the period from its start until the Second World War (Linder 2001) – including Ernst Meyer.

Economic ties to Norwegian interests are, perhaps, most visibly traced through its long-standing *communication and transport* links – especially shipping at several Mozambican ports – in keeping with the intimate links between the maritime domain and the colonial order. Even in the 1950s ownership was dominated by Norwegian interests, together with the Portuguese Carlos Francisco F.P.B. Bobone (Count Bobone V). Its scale of production was significant: more than one million coconut palms were under its control, producing ten thousand tons of copra per year, as well as over eleven thousand head of cattle (Chichava 2007: 102). During this period the copra Madal produced was transported on Norwegian ships to Europe (Botte 1985–86: 51). Such transport was based on long-standing Norwegian sailing along the Mozambican coast. As early as 1912, in an annual report to the Norwegian Ministry of Foreign Affairs, the Norwegian consulate at Lourenço Marques reported that in that year fourteen Norwegian vessels called at the harbour – eleven steamers and three sailing ships.[41] In 1915 in the central city of Beira Norwegian ships made twenty calls, some several times.[42] The trend continued, and in 1946 the Norwegian ships consisted of nine motor ships and two steamers visiting Lourenço Marques, six motor ships and two steamers calling at Beira and one steamer registered for Ilha de Moçambique, according to official Portuguese statistics (República Portuguesa 1948: 194, 202, 210). Later on, according to the protocols of the Norwegian consulate in Quelimane, between 1958 and 1970 Quelimane had 117 Norwegian ships calling at its harbour – most of these taking on board cargo there.[43]

The third central feature relates to the gradual territorial expansion of *land ownership* in periods with Norwegian dominance within Madal, at the expense of peasant holdings. Negrão's (1995) work shows that the company's territorial expansion must be understood on two levels. First, such expansion occurred through purchasing *prazo* rights from former owners through the colonial administration. This process secured Madal fifteen such rights prior to 1930, and at Mozambican independence in 1975 it controlled a total of forty-one (Negrão 1995). However, equally important was more direct expansion, and Negrão details how Madal adapted to (but also evaded) the laws and regulations to pursue this. Specifically, he documents how Madal expanded by occupying land and then afterwards attaining rights for the properties either through the local colonial legal system or by using *mussoco* claims to get peasants and minor *prazo* holders to cede the land to Madal (Negrão 1995: 134–37). This form of murky expansion through legal and illegal means may also be the reason why Nicolaysen complains extensively in 1919 about the lack of documentation over the properties Madal controls (1919: 30–32).

Given these three general traits, one may argue that the Norwegian character of Madal was a not insignificant part of the expansion of de facto Portuguese colonial control in the historically unruly Zambézia Province. Through its century of operation, Madal must therefore be seen as both a Norwegian and a Portuguese colonial creation – an enterprise still thriving around four decades after independence.

Conclusion

This chapter has analysed various aspects of the formative years of a Norwegian colonial institution. Interestingly, a mainstay of Madal – from the colonial era to the postcolonial era – is the way in which its owners and managers have managed to be both internal to large-scale political projects – as it was in the early years – as well as the owners' ability to weather political storms. Cases in point, and only alluded to in the above, include Thams's navigation through the politically troubled waters of doing business during the First World War and the controversy surrounding Madal's desired expansion into Companhia de Zambézia's territory in the 1940s. In more recent years, such navigation is evidenced by the fact that Madal was neither nationalized during the era of Mozambique's radical postliberation politics following 1975, nor have its relations to the Mozambican political and business elite in the 2000s and 2010s been severed.[44] In retrospect, the Norwegian-dominated plantation company may be evaluated as having adapted surprisingly well to dramatically changing historical circumstances: from being initiated on the basis of limited agricultural production, to engaging in large-scale tax farming through *mussoco* collection and with nearly sovereign powers, in the twenty-first century Madal attained a position as a regular and consolidated agribusiness. It is still globally oriented, still employs seasonal labour and is still profitable for a changing international consortium of owners.

Notes

The text is based on Norwegian, French, British, Portuguese and Mozambican archival sources at the archives provided above the bibliography. Further, some private letters from Swiss former workers at the plantation Madal – kindly provided by Simon Steiner – a field trip to Quelimane and Madal in 2007, an extensive report from Norwegian entrepreneur Wilhem Nicolaysen (Nicolaysen 1919 in the reference list) kindly made available by Knut Olav Krohn Lakså and several pilot studies on Madal history carried out by Mozambican researchers Carmeliza Rosário, Celso Inguane and José Adalima under the guidance of Professor Gerhard Liesegang also inform this text. Thanks are extended to all archives above, particularly to Arquivo Histórico de Moçambique, to Elsa Reiersen and Elin Folgerø Styve for sharing their photographic material and to, in no particular order, José Adalima, Jason Sumich, Inês Galvão, Adolphe Linder, Erlend Eidsvik, Kirsten Alsaker Kjerland, Anne Synnøve Nilsen, Øystein Nilsen and Knut M. Rio for having commented extensively on various drafts or aided in other ways. I also extend my gratitude to Aline Afonso and Sandrine Mansour-Mérien, who assisted me in some of the archival work at AHU and CADN, respectively. I am also grateful to three anonymous reviewers, who all provided valuable insights when revising this chapter.

1. All translations are by the author unless otherwise noted.
2. Prazos da Coroa (1909: 569) provides a complete list of signatories. For an overview of Thams's international and Norwegian businesses, see both Reiersen's contribution, this volume, and Reiersen (2006).
3. 'Madal' here denotes the wide range of names and companies that characterize a particular area in Zambézia in terms of continuities relating production regimes, properties, labour and so forth. Beyond simply 'Madal', names used in archival sources and literature include 'Société du Madal, Gonzaga, Bovay & Co.', ' Société du Madal, Chr. Thams & Co.', 'Société du Madal, Fearnley, Bobone & Co', 'Société du Madal, Bobone, Bonnet & Co.', 'Société du Madal', 'Société Agricole du Madal', 'Empresa Madal' and 'Grupo Madal'. Crucially, 'Madal' is also the term used in Zambézia, as noted in historical sources and by scholars (see, e.g., Rufino 1929; Ishemo 1995; Newitt 1995; Isaacman and Isaacman 2006; Chichava 2007).
4. These include Christian Thams (1867–1948), as well as Thomas Fearnley Sr, Haaken Mathiesen, Fritz Treschow, Hans Peter Fyhn Krag, Halvor Nicolai Astrup and Leif Høegh, who all were involved at different periods during the 1900s. See also the extensive 44 page report based on a five month trip to Madal's Mozambican holdings in 1919 (Nicolaysen 1919) which illustrates the profound interest considerable Norwegian businessmen such as Wilhelm Andersen had in colonial ventures like Madal.
5. Portugal's struggle for some level of territorial control was, as other colonial processes, characterized by extensive violence; Pélissier (2004; see also 1994a, 1994b), for one, documents how Portugal was in an almost permanent state of war between 1844 and 1941. As Young (1995: 93) has argued for colonial processes in general, 'Major nuclei of resistance to colonial expansion were subdued by force. Pure military conquest had the advantage of leaving no semblance of rights in the hands of the dominated community.' The notion of 'territorialization' as a key aspect of these violent campaigns is often identified as central to (colonial) state formation (Deleuze and Guattari [1980] 2002; Foucault [2004] 2007).
6. See Bhila (1982), Chanaiwa (1972), Liesegang (1966, 1996) and Mtetwa (1984) for sound historical studies of trade under Portuguese colonial rule, as well as Strandes ([1899] 1961) for a classic study of Portuguese colonial presence. Central works that survey or reproduce key primary sources for the period and that have been consulted here include selected volumes from NAZ, UEM and IICT (1962–89), as well as Theal ([1898] 1964).
7. Portugal's incomplete control over its territories, great local variation and various forms of slave trade – to mention a few factors – mean that diverse

dates are provided for when slavery may be said to have been abolished within Portuguese colonies. For two views, see Harries (1981) and Newitt (1972), as well as Marques's (2006) analysis of the politics of Portuguese nonintervention in the nineteenth-century slave trade. More detailed explorations of the slave trade are found also in Capela and Medeiros (1987), Isaacman and Isaacman (2006), Newitt (1972) and Zimba et al. (2006).

8. While being 'beyond control' has been seen as comprising part of both violent and nonviolent resistance to colonial domination, others argue that it is difficult to support such a perspective of resistance based on the historical material. For two contrasting positions, see Isaacman (1976) and Serra (1983).

9. The Portuguese also developed a number of development plans for Zambézia in this period, although none of them were fully implemented (Newitt 1973).

10. While *mussoco* previously was integral to a hierarchical system where taxes, often in the form of food, were collected and subsequently redistributed during periods of crisis (e.g., hunger), its character shifted when appropriated by the colonial system: it then became a mechanism for accumulation, and aspects of relationality and redistribution largely disappeared.

11. See Quay's (1938) detailed description of his use of *cipais* in what he, quite literally, describes as a process of pacification.

12. For analyses of *tchibalo,* see also Head and Manghezi (1981), Ishemo (1989), O'Laughlin (2002), Penvenne (1981) and Roesch (1991).

13. Unsurprisingly, there were also other economic interests in Zambézia in this period, as exemplified by Teixeira's study of the impact of Indian traders (2008).

14. Throughout most of the 1900s, Boror was superior to Madal in size, territory and modes of production. However, after the end of the Mozambican civil war (1977–92), Madal expanded considerably and in 1997 bought three large former Boror plantations. See Louro (2003: 66) for details.

15. The quote in Portuguese, taken from Bobone and Bobone (1996: 111), is as follows: 'Essa área estava sujeita ao regime dos "Prazos da Coroa", forma de colonização experimentada na Zambézia desde a década de 1890, consistindo em entregar toda a gestão política, económica e administrativa de extensas regiões a companhias particulares que dispunham de grandes capitais e faziam a exploração agrícola dos prazos sob a sua administração, enquanto cobravam os impostos e mantinham a ordem pública com um corpo de soldados nativos – os cipaios – que armavam e sustentavam à sua custa.'

16. The Bobones were regularly given representative roles vis-à-vis the Portuguese colonial state also. For instance, in a letter dated 29 June 1915, signed by Christian Thams and sent from Madal's Paris office to the Portuguese Ministry of the Colonies, Carlos Jeronymo Humberto Bobone was named Madal's Lisbon representative (letter, folder 810 13 DOCOR 1906–21 [third box], AHU).

17. The Norwegian original reads: 'Disse rekruteres – som det heder – det vil i virkeligheden sige: tvinges til at arbeide' (Nicolaysen 1919: 6).

18. An extensive analysis of the Barúe rebellion and its leader, Chief Makombe, is provided by Artur (1996). The event was perhaps the last major rebellion before the liberation movement Frente de Libertação de Moçambique (FRELIMO) resurfaced five decades after to initiate the armed struggle for independence in 1964, culminating with Mozambican independence in 1975.

19. J.P. Hornung, the founder of Sena Sugar, which was set up at the end of the nineteenth century, repeatedly refers in a biography to the problems of 'native attacks' (Collin 1973: 29, 35).

20. Capela (2010: 111) notes that until very recently the lands of Madal were popularly still represented as *prazos* and that the person governing these was still represented as a count (*conde*), underlining the protracted nature of colonial hierarchy and social and political order.

21. The letters in this section can be found in the folder 536.2-GN-NÇ, 23 – 1939–43, Sala 6, DOC 'Processo número 19/46 – Société du Madal', AHU.

22. Expressed in the report 'Le main d'oeuvre dans la colonie portugaise de Mozambique', written by the French vice-consulate in Lourenço Marques, 10 March 1914, and submitted to the French ambassador to Portugal, 'Lisbonne Ambassade A 40', CADN.

23. Ibid. The French text quoted is: 'Le but poursuivi est le même: C'est la recherche du profit imédiat. Edifier pour l'avenir, préparer de loin un développement méthodique e réguler des richesses agricoles ou autres de la Province de Mozambique, en suivant l'exemple que nous donnons dans nos colonies, n'est pas encore le souei dominant des gouvernements portuguais. Ils travaillent uniquement pour le présent, persuadées peut-être que c'est le meilleur mode d'exploitation de leurs possessions d'outre-mer.'

24. 'Compagine de Boror et Socitété du Madal', report by Consul E. Savoyo, 10 October 1918, 'Lisbonne Ambassade A B385', CADN.

25. Letter from the French Ministry of Foreign Affairs to 'Le Ministre des Affaires Etrangeres, A Monsieur Daeschner, Ministre Plenitpotenitaire de la Replublique Francaise a Lisbonne', 14 June 1919, 'Lisbonne Ambassade A B385', CADN. The original quote reads: 'J'ajoute que M. Thams, à l'égard duquel notre Consul à Lourenco Marquez fait preuve de la plus méfiance et qui, comme vous le savez, avait été en effet considéré autrefois comme suspect par l'Etat-Major de l'Armée, a été entièrment réhabilité à la suite de l'énquête effectuée par notre Légation à Christiania dont le résultat n'avait permis de retentir aucun grief substantiel contre lui.'

26. Translated from Reiersen (2006: 350–51). The original quote in Norwegian reads: 'De er helt sorte, av kafferracen, helt underlagt selskapets styre og betaler skatt m.v. til dette.'

27. 'Le main d'oeuvre dans la colonie portugaise de Mozambique', written by the French vice-consulate in Lourenço Marques, 10 March 1914, and submitted to the French ambassador to Portugal, 'Lisbonne Ambassade A 40', CADN.

28. The Norwegian original reads: 'Prazokoncessionen er som før nævnt alene en skatteforpagtning … men det væsentlige er at denne skatteforpagtning giver prazholderen administrativ ret inden districtet samt til, forsaavidt

skatten ikke betales, at kræve den betalt ved arbeide paa de inden prazoen erhvervede eiendomme' (Nicolaysen 1919: 23f).

29. As Serra (1980) provides the figures in escudos and Negrão (1995) in the old currency of réis – Portugal changed the currency to escudos in 1910 – I have converted Negrão's figures to escudos for comparative purposes at the standard conversion rate of 1 escudo being equivalent to 1,000 réis.

30. The figure of thirty thousand to fifty thousand people is taken from Reiersen (2006: 350) and builds on Madal's own reports. Nicolaysen's 1919 report mentions a total of population of all the *prazos* as being 44,185 (1919: 25).

31. Pélissier (1994b: 162–63) provides a similar figure, writing that 235,616 people fled from 1900 to 1930 due to forced labour, heavy taxation and forced military service.

32. Works on Manica show that where Companhia de Moçambique, the largest Mozambican concession company, operated, vast groups fled forced labour, the *mussoco* regime and poor labour conditions. Contrary to the Zambézia peasants heading to Malawi, in Manica these often went either to Zimbabwe (then Southern Rhodesia) and South Africa to work, for instance, in the mines or they went to the port town of Beira to either work there or to engage in construction work on the railway to Southern Rhodesia (Neil-Tomlinson 1987; Neves 1998; Allina 2012).

33. Translated from Norwegian, the original reads: 'Negrene er vanskelige folk; ialmindelighet mer eller mindre uintelligente. Arbeidet er for de fleste av dem paatvunget og man faar visselig hverken mere arbeide ud av dem eller gjøre dem mer arbeidsvillige ved at betale høiere løn' (Nicolaysen 1919: 17).

34. Writes Collin (1973: 64), commenting on Sena Sugar around 1910: 'Labour was not required at the same extent all the year round. The peak period was when the [sugar] crop was being harvested and crushed. Afterwards the natives returned home to till their own plots.'

35. José Negrão (1995) has detailed this dynamic for the Zambézia region, confirming Serra's (1980) much earlier study. This dual economy system and its importance for especially migrant labour is well-known for a wide range of sub-Saharan African contexts, as Wolpe's (1972) classic study of apartheid South Africa, African households and migration demonstrated. For specifically southern Mozambican perspectives, see also the classic studies by Ruth First (1983), Marvin Harris (1959) and Katzenellenbogen (1982).

36. Linder's meticulous documentation of the many Swiss working in Mozambique also contains a number of photographs documenting child labour at Madal and other Zambézian concession companies at the time (2001: 59–69), while Negrão (1995: 58ff.) shows how alcohol were long-standing means of payment for labour.

37. For early critiques of the Portuguese colonial system, see Anderson (1962) and Harris (1958).

38. For instance, Madal produced in Tacuane in Zambézia 621,870 kilos of tea in the agricultural year 1961–62 (Artur and Xavier 2003: 139); as documented by also Louro (2003) and Chichava (2007), Madal's activities must be approached as heavily diversified throughout the 1900s.

39. All figures kindly provided by Madal's managing director in Quelimane, Rogério Henriques, in an interview on 10 February 2007.
40. Reiersen (2006: 350) holds that the number of people under Madal's control varied between thirty thousand and fifty thousand people; Gustave Bovay, Madal's managing director between 1893 and 1913, claims that in 1913 he was 'king over 40 000 inhabitants' (Linder 2001: 59) and Nicolaysen lists 44,185 people in Madal's prazos in 1919 (1919: 25). Linder's, Nicolaysen's and Reiersen's figures thereby concord roughly with Bovay's estimate.
41. 'Lourenço Marques. Aarsberetning 1912. Sak 54/12. Royal Norwegian Consulat, Lourenço Marques, 20 February 1914', RA.
42. 'Lourenço Marques. Aarsberetning 1915. Sak 54/11. Royal Norwegian Consulat, Lourenço Marques, 21 July 1916', RA.
43. The ships with frequent calls included MS *Tanafjord*, SS *Idefjord*, MS *Eidanger*, MS *Kongsfjord*, MS *Drammensfjord*, MS *Ravnanger* and MS *Tyrifjord*. 'Register of Norwegian ships calling at, or departing from the port of Quelimane, P.E.A.', Royal Norwegian Vice Consulate, Quelimane, Protocol no. 6, RA.
44. Narandás (2009: 26), based on an interview with Vicente Onofre, former director at Madal's Quelimane headquarters and employed by Madal for thirty-nine years, claims that because the major shareholder in the 1970s were Norwegian and the Norwegian government supported the postindependence FRELIMO government, Madal was not nationalized. For an overview of the period of transition for colonial companies through different phases of the Mozambican postcolonial state, see Pitcher (2003). For a critical report on Madal's activities, see Rønning (2000).

Archives Consulted

Mozambican Historical Archives (Arquivo Histórico de Moçambique, AHM), Maputo.
Central Office of the National Archives of Norway (Riksarkivet, RA), Oslo.
Portuguese Overseas Historical Archives (Arquivo Histórico Ultramarino, AHU), Lisbon.
French Centre for Diplomatic Archives (Centre des Archives Diplomatiques de Nantes, CADN), Nantes.
National Archives (NA), London.

References

Allina, E. 2012. *Slavery by Any Other Name: African Life under Company Rule in Colonial Mozambique*. Charlottesville: University of Virginia Press.
Anderson, P. 1962. 'Portugal and the End of Ultra-Colonialism', *New Left Review* 15: 83–102.
Artur, D. do R. 1996. *Makombe: Subsídios á Reconstituicão da Sua Personalidade*. Maputo: Arquivo do Património Cultural (ARPAC).

Artur, D. do R. and E. Xavier. 2003 *Cidade do Guruè: Heranças e Continuidades.* Guruè: Núcleo de Investigação Cultural.

Beckford, G.L. 1972. *Persistent Poverty: Underdevelopment in Plantation Economies of the Third World.* New York: Oxford University Press.

Bhila, H.H. 1982. *Trade and Politics in a Shona Kingdom: The Manyika and Their African and Portuguese Neighbours 1575–1902.* Harlow, U.K.: Longman.

Bobone, M. de L. and C.L. Bobone. 1996. *Genealogia dos Condes Bobone.* Braga: Livraria Bizantina.

Bonnet, T. 1921. *Monographie de la Société du Madal.* Lisbon: Casa Portuguesa.

Botte, T.C. de S.P. de S. 1985–86. *Memórias e Autobiografia: 24 Anos em Portugal e 60 em África,* vol. 3. Maputo: Minerva Central.

Capela, J. 1995. *Donas, Senhores e Escravos.* Oporto: Edições Afrontamento.

———. 2010. *Moçambique pela sua História.* Lisbon: Editora Húmus.

Capela, J. and E. Medeiros. 1987. *O Tráfico de Escravos de Moçambique Para as Ilhas do Índico, 1702–1902.* Maputo: Universidade Eduardo Mondlane.

Chabal, P. and D. Birmingham (eds). 2002. *A History of Postcolonial Lusophone Africa.* London: Hurst.

Chanaiwa, D. 1972. 'Politics and Long-Distance Trade in the Mwene Mutapa Empire During the Sixteenth Century', *International Journal of African Historical Studies* 5(3): 424–35.

Chichava, S. 2007. 'Le "vieux Mozambique": Étude sur l'identité politique de la Zambézie', PhD dissertation. Bordeaux: Université Montesquieu – Bordeaux IV.

Collin, B.M. 1973. *J.P. Hornung: A Family Portrait.* Kent, U.K.: Orpington Press.

Cooper, F. 1977. *Plantation Slavery on the East African Coast.* New Haven, C.T.: Yale University Press.

Deleuze, G. and F. Guattari. [1980] 2002. *A Thousand Plateaus: Capitalism and Schizophrenia.* London: Continuum.

Ferguson, E. 1989. 'Value Theory and Colonial Capitalism: The Case of Zanzibar, 1897–1945', *African Economic History* 18: 25–56.

First, R. 1983. *Black Gold: The Mozambican Miner, Proletarian and Peasant.* Brighton, U.K.: Harvester Press.

Foucault, M. (2004) 2007. *Security, Territory, Population: Lectures at the Collège de France, 1977–1978.* Basingstoke, U.K.: Palgrave Macmillan.

Goffman, E. (1961) 1991. *Asylums: Essays on the Social Situation of Mental Patients and Other Inmates.* London: Penguin.

Harries, P. 1981. 'Slavery, Social Incorporation and Surplus Extraction: The Nature of Free and Unfree Labour in South-East Africa', *Journal of African History* 22(3): 309–30.

Harris, M. 1958. *Portugal's African 'Wards': A First-Hand Report on Labour and Education in Mozambique.* New York: American Committee on Africa.

———. 1959. 'Labour Emigration among the Mozambique Thonga: Cultural and Political Factors', *Africa* 29(1): 50–65.

Head, J. 1980. 'Sena Sugar Estates and Migrant Labour', *Mozambican Studies* 1: 53–71.

Head, J. and A. Manghezi. 1981. 'Interviews: Forced Labour by Those Who Lived Through It', *Mozambican Studies* 2: 26–35.

Hedges, D. 1999. *História de Moçambique,* vol. 2, *Moçambique no Auge do Colonialismo, 1930–1961.* Maputo: Livraria Universitária.

ILO (International Labour Organization). 1962. *Report of the Commission Appointed under Article 26 of the Constitution of the International Labour Organisation to Examine the Complaint Filed by the Government of Ghana Concerning the Observance by the Government of Portugal of the Abolition of Forced Labour Convention, 1957 (No. 105).* Geneva: ILO.

Isaacman, A.F. 1972. *Mozambique: The Africanization of a European Institution, the Zambesi Prazos, 1750–1902.* Madison: University of Wisconsin Press.

———. 1976. *The Tradition of Resistance in Mozambique: Anti-colonial Activity in the Zambesi Valley 1850–1921.* London: Heinemann.

Isaacman, A.F., and B.S. Isaacman. 2006. *Escravos, Esclavagistas, Guerreiros e Caçadores: A Saga dos Chicundas do Vale do Zambeze.* Maputo: Promédia.

Ishemo, S.L. 1989. 'Forced Labour, Mussoco (Taxation), Famine and Migration in Lower Zambézia, Mozambique, 1870–1914', in A. Zegeye and S.L. Ishemo (eds), *Forced Labour and Migration: Patterns of Movement within Africa.* London: Hans Zell, pp. 109–58.

———. 1995. *The Lower Zambezi Basin in Mozambique: A Study in Economy and Society, 1850–1920.* Aldershot, U.K.: Avebury.

Jones, B.G. 2005. 'Globalisations, Violences and Resistances in Mozambique: The Struggles Continue', in C. Eschle and B. Maiguashca (eds), *Critical Theories, International Relations and 'the Anti-globalisation Movement': The Politics of Global Resistance.* London: Routledge, pp. 33–73.

Katzenellenbogen, S. 1982. *South Africa and Southern Mozambique: Labour, Railways and Trade in the Making of a Relationship.* Manchester: Manchester University Press.

Liesegang, G.J. 1966. *'Reposta das Questoens Sobre os Cafres' ou Notícias Etnográficas Sobre Sofala do Fim do Século XVIII.* Lisbon: Centro de Estudos de Antropologia Cultural.

———. 1996. *Ngungunyane: A Figura de Ngungunyane Nqumayo, Rei de Gaza 1884–1895 e o Desaparecimento do Seu Estado.* Chimoio: Arquivo do Património Cultural (ARPAC).

Linder, A. 2001. *Os Suiços em Moçambique.* Maputo: Arquivo Histórico de Moçambique.

Louro, M. do C.A. 2003. 'Modelização da produção de coco e copra em Moçambique: Uma aplicação à produção da Empresa Madal', master's thesis. Lisbon: Universidade Tecnica de Lisboa.

Ludwig, E. 1913. *Die Reise nach Afrika.* Berlin: S. Fischer Verlag.

Mackenzie, C. 2006. *Forest Governance in Zambézia, Mozambique: Chinese Takeaway.* Quelimane: FONGZA.

Mahoney, M. 2003. 'Estado Novo, Homem Novo (New State, New Man): Colonial and Anti-colonial Development Ideologies in Mozambique, 1930–1977', in D.C. Engerman et al. (eds), *Staging Growth: Modernization, Development, and the Global Cold War.* Amherst: University of Massachusetts Press, pp. 165–97.

Marques, J.P. 2006. *The Sounds of Silence: Nineteenth-Century Portugal and the Abolition of the Slave Trade.* Oxford: Berghahn Books.

Mtetwa, A.H. 1984. 'A History of Uteve Under the Mwene Mutapa Rulers 1480–1834: A Re-evaluation', PhD dissertation. Chicago: Northwestern University.

Narandás, J.M. 2009. 'A Companhia de Madal e o campesinato: A produção e comercialização de copra entre os anos 1970–1986, na Localidade da Madal, Zambézia', PhD dissertation. Maputo: Universidade Eduardo Mondlane.

NAZ (National Archives of Zimbabwe), UEM (Universidade Eduardo Mondlane) and IICT (Centro de Estudos de História e Cartografia Antiga do Instituto de Investigação Científica Tropical). 1962–89. *Documentos Sobre os Portugueses em Moçambique e na Africa Central, 1497–1840: Documents on the Portuguese in Mozambique and Central Africa, 1497–1840*. Lisbon: NAZ, UEM and IICT.

Negrão, J. 1995. 'One Hundred Years of African Rural Family Economy: The Zambezi Delta in Retrospective Analysis'. PhD dissertation. Lund: Lund University.

Neil-Tomlinson, B. 1977. 'The Nyassa Chartered Company: 1891–1929', *Journal of African History* 18(1): 109–28.

———. 1987. 'The Mozambique Chartered Company: 1892–1910', PhD dissertation. London: University of London.

Neves, J.M. das. 1998. 'Economy, Society and Labour Migration in Central Mozambique, 1930–c.1965: A Case Study of Manica Province', PhD dissertation. London: University of London.

Newitt, M.D.D. 1969. 'The Portuguese on the Zambeze: An Historical Interpretation of the Prazo System', *Journal of African History* 10(1): 67–85.

———. 1972. 'Angoche, the Slave Trade and the Portuguese c. 1844–1910', *Journal of African History* 12(4): 659–72.

———. 1973. *Portuguese Settlement on the Zambesi: Exploration, Land Tenure and Colonial Rule in East Africa*. London: Longman.

———. 1995. *A History of Mozambique*. London: Hurst.

Nicolaysen, Wilhelm. 1919. *Beretning om Advokat Nicolaysens reise til Portugisisk Østafrica. Mai–september 1919*. Oslo.

O'Laughlin, B. 2002. 'Proletarianisation, Agency and Changing Rural Livelihoods: Forced Labour and Resistance in Colonial Mozambique', *Journal of Southern African Studies* 28(3): 511–30.

Pélissier, R. 1994a. *Historia de Moçambique: Formação e Oposição 1854–1918,* vol. 1. Lisbon: Editorial Stampa.

———. 1994b. *Historia de Moçambique: Formação e Oposição 1854–1918,* vol. 2. Lisbon: Editorial Stampa.

———. 2004. *Les Campagnes Coloniales du Portugal: 1844–1941*. Paris: Éditions Pygmalion.

Penvenne, J. 1981. 'Chibalo and the Working Class: Lourenço Marques 1870–1962', *Mozambican Studies* 2: 9–25.

Pitcher, M.A. 2002. *Transforming Mozambique: The Politics of Privatization.* Cambridge: Cambridge University Press.

———. 2003. 'Sobreviver a transição: O legado das antigas empresas coloniais em Moçambique', *Análise Social* 38(168): 793–820.

Prazos da Coroa. 1909. *Protesto da Arrendatorios de Quelimane e Tete contra o Rala-tório de Secretário dos Negocios Indigenas e Resposta D'este.* Lourenço Marques: Imprensa Nacional.

Quay, G.S. de. 1938. *La Compagnie du Boror en Zambézie – Mozambique. Ses Orig-ines, 1891–94. Sa Création, 1898. Son Développement, 1899–1934. Souvenirs de Georges Stucky de Quay.* Marseilles: Moullot.

Reiersen, E. 2006. *Fenomenet Thams.* Oslo: Aschehoug.

República Portuguesa, Colónia de Moçambique, Repartição Técnica de Estatís-tica. 1948. *Estatística do Comércio externo e da navegação.* Lourenço Marques: Imprensa Nacional de Moçambique.

Roberts, R. and K. Mann. 1991. 'Law in Colonial Africa', in K. Mann and R, Roberts (eds), *Law in Colonial Africa.* Portsmouth, N.H.: Heinemann and James Currey, pp. 3–58.

Roesch, O. 1991. 'Migrant Labour and Forced Rice Production in Southern Mo-zambique: The Colonial Peasantry of the Lower Limpopo Valley', *Journal of Southern African Studies* 17(1): 239–70.

Rufino, J. dos S. 1929. *Quelimane: Aspectos Gerais. General Views of the District of Quelimane. Vues Géneraux du District de Quelimane.* Hamburg: Broschek.

Rønning, M. 2000. *Utvikling eller utbytting? Grupo Madal i Mosambik.* Oslo: Nor-Watch.

Sequeira, J.R. 1944. 'Palmares da Zambézia: A Société du Madal', *Moçambique, Documentário trimestral* 38: 61–74.

Serra, C. 1980. 'Colonial Capitalism in Zambezia 1855–1930', *Mozambican Stu-dies* 1: 33–52.

———. 1983. *Para a História da Arte Militar Moçambicana (1505–1920).* Maputo: Cadernos Tempo.

Sheriff, A. 2005. 'Slave Trade and Slave Routes of the East African Coast', in B. Zimba, E. Alpers and A. Isaacman (eds), *Slave Routes and Oral Tradition in Southeastern Africa.* Maputo: Filsom Entertainment, pp. 13–38.

Strandes, Justus. (1899) 1961. *The Portuguese Period in East Africa.* Nairobi: East African Literature Bureau.

Teixeira, L.P. 2008. 'The Workings of the Indian Traders of Zambézia, Mozam-bique, 1870s–1910s', *Lusotopie* 15(1): 39–58.

Theal, G.M. (ed.). (1898) 1964. *Records of South-Eastern Africa: Collected in Various Libraries and Archive Departments in Europe,* vols 1–9. Cape Town: C. Struik.

Vail, L. and L. White. 1980. *Capitalism and Colonialism in Mozambique: A Study of Quelimane District.* London: Heinemann.

———. 1983. 'Forms of Resistance: Songs and Perceptions of Power in Colonial Mozambique', *American Historical Review* 88(4): 883–919.

Wolpe, H. 1972. 'Capitalism and Cheap Labour-Power in South Africa: From Segregation to Apartheid', *Economy and Society* 1(4): 425–56.

Young, C. 1994. *The African Colonial State in Perspective.* New Haven, C.T.: Yale University Press.

Zimba, B., E. Alpers and A Isaacman (eds). 2006. *Slave Routes and Oral Tradition in Southeastern Africa.* Maputo: Filsom Entertainment.

⤻ 13

NORWEGIAN INVESTORS AND
THEIR AGENTS IN COLONIAL KENYA

Kirsten Alsaker Kjerland

Yara Estate, 6 May 1912[1]

Dear Father

Thank you for your letter dated 31 March together with letters from
Mother, Alf and Auntie. The post to Europe unfortunately passed me by.
I arrived at the plantation on Sunday 28 April and thought that I would
write from here but then I found that the mail service is only three times
a week.

From Nairobi it is 20 kilometres to Yara. I live in a stone house with
plastered walls both inside and outside. There are five rooms and a ve-
randa. The kitchen is in a separate building. The roof is made of thatch,
not nice to look at, but when the rainy season is over it will be replaced by
corrugated iron. The surrounding countryside is undulating and covered
by low bush with a few big trees. Between here and Nairobi there is some
forest, but not beyond. It takes about 30 minutes to get to the nearest
farm, and around 50 minutes to the other neighbouring farm. On both
of these farms the owners have made beautiful gardens and built cosy
homes.

I have already worked as manager here nearly two weeks. The first
manager, a Swede, had to leave as he was useless. The next one, a very
hardworking Englishman, is now managing a farm about one hour away.
He helped me here in the beginning. His name is Bell, married but with
no children. I visited him last Sunday. He was so kind as to send a boy
with his mule in the early morning, so I could ride over. The boy followed
behind us with a second boy who carried my raincoat on his arm. One
should always have a boy when going out. They are fleet of foot and
move as fast as a horse.

I really enjoyed myself there. They are both very nice people. It was
the first decent meal I had since leaving Norway. The Bells live comfortably for 75 Rupees a month, which I must say is reasonable. You can buy a
two kg. leg of lamb for one Rupee, and 22 eggs for the same price. Almost
every day one of the locals comes with a bird, always alive, as it has been
caught in a trap. I pay about a penny each and they taste good. Right now
I am clearing some acres of land free of weeds, in order to plant beans in
between the rows of black wattle, as they fetch a good price.

I have about 90 natives working for me. I call out their names, just like one does in the army, to mark off their employment cards. After 31 working days they get their pay, which varies from three to five Rupees.

I have two black foremen to watch over the native workers. One of them gets six Rupees and the other, who is a headman, is paid 10 Rupees. He is looked up to by his people. He has three huts and three wives. Recently he sold one of his daughters to get another wife. He is quite stubborn and wants the workers to do things his way, not mine. I told him one day I would punish him if he disobeyed, and since then he has been like a lamb. They have great respect for corporal punishment, so it is usually enough to threaten such action.

My cook is not very good, but he is reasonably honest – which is an unusual trait, so I think I will keep him. I have noticed that he eats my sugar. At six in the morning he sends a boy in to me with a cup of tea. I think this is a humane way of starting my day. At 06.20 I yell through the window for the bell to be rung by one of my three servants. *Piga kengene,* as it is called, is done by the man beating on a big iron triangle hanging outside the house. It is a signal for the workers to come up to the house. I stay in bed until 06.30, than get dressed in five minutes, by which time all the natives have come. When they have been given the necessary tools – machetes or hoes – they are ordered to set off to work. I then have time until about 08.00 to shower and have breakfast, when I go out so that the houseboy can tidy up the house. I go to check the labour about every hour, occasionally needing to scold some lazy worker. In between I go in to read some English or perhaps half an hour studying Swahili, the local language.

The lingo here is a bit problematic, as the locals do not speak proper Swahili, but rather use the Kikuyu dialect. Luckily most of the workers understand some Swahili. However, they do not like to speak it, which leads to misunderstandings. The previous manager had ordered four hut owners to move their buildings to another part of the farm as the land was to be ploughed up. A deputation arrived one day to ask me where they should relocate and with the help of one of my houseboys, who is quite good with Swahili, I was able to grasp what they wanted to know. I showed them a suitable place, and believe they can remain there for some time to come. Another time one of the natives appeared holding his stomach and said that he was feeling ill. I presumed that it was diarrhoea so gave him 40 chlorine drops. It took a little while before he swallowed the drink, and you should have seen how he grimaced, it would have made a good photo. Some hours later, on asking him how he was, he said he felt fine. You never know, maybe I will get a reputation for being a medicine man.

As the farm covers 640 acres the labourers often have to work in several different areas, and it takes quite some time to walk to each workplace so the day passes quite quickly. Work stops from 12.00 noon till 1.10 p.m., when it resumes until 5.20 p.m. Tools and equipment are handed in and counted, as the blacks are apt to steal. One has to be strict in dealing with them, and any misdeed must be firmly acted upon, preferably by setting a warning example. They have to be dealt with in the same way as punishing children or dogs. It is usually near six o'clock before all is done, and when darkness falls 15 to 20 minutes later I have a long and lonely evening ahead of me. Dinner is at 7 p.m., after which I sit and read for a while, go to bed some time between 8.30 and 9 and read a little more. Evenings are quite chilly so I am glad that the fireplace is alight and pretend that I am somewhere up in the Norwegian mountains.

I get to feel a bit lonely living on a farm with only natives around. Daytime is ok, as one has work to do, but mealtimes and evenings I feel a bit sad. It would be so much nicer here with my Sarah. You must wish Alf good luck in his exams. Tell him that I would really appreciate it if he could send me a package with newspapers once in a while, unless postage becomes prohibitive. It would really be great to have the organ here with me. Do you think Alf could contact Karl Lassen about how much the freight would cost? It would have to be packed very carefully in a strong case with many labels showing 'Handle with Care'.

With much love to Mother and my best to Alf, Auntie and all in No. 52. Hope all is well with everyone. Hearty greetings from your devoted Eivind.

This letter, slightly shortened and translated, is the first written by the then 24-year-old Eivind Eriksen recounting his early impressions of living on a farm in the White Highlands of British East Africa a century ago.[2] Between May and September of 1912 he wrote a total of fifteen letters containing details on how he had to adapt to his new surroundings and all the difficulties therewith – all addressed to his father and

Figure 13.1. Some of the labourers at Yara Estate just before the First World War. *Source:* Photo courtesy of the late Bjørn Eriksen; reproduced with permission.

mother (Hans and Agnete Eriksen) and his brother Alf, who was three years younger than him.[3] When the stream of letters subsided during the autumn it was not due to him having less news to write home. The main reason was that Sarah, his longed-for bride-to-be, had arrived in Nairobi on 29 August. In Sarah's first letter to her parents-in-law, Eivind added a paragraph on the last page: 'No problem at all being at Yara now.'

As it turned out, Eivind Eriksen was so content managing Yara and living on East Africa's soil that he continued doing so for the next forty-five years. But before we venture into details, let us take a look at who sent him to Africa, and why he was chosen for the job.

Azania Ltd

On 19 April 1911 a company named Azania Ltd[4] was inscribed in the company register of Kristiania (Oslo after 1 January 1925). Initially it was endowed with a capital of NOK 150,000 divided into 150 shares, its aim being to establish plantations in East Africa. Three shareholders were nominated to the board: Nils Backe Børresen, Karl Klaus Nordskog and Hans Peter Fyhn Krag, the latter as general manager. As with the other shareholders, they were members of the then eastern Norwegian *Haute Finance*.[5] Three of the capitalists involved (Hans Peter Fyhn Krag, Haaken L. Mathiesen and Elias C. Kiær) had already made investments on the African continent for nearly two decades, for instance, by selling lumber products and building materials in northern as well as in southern African countries.

It is believed that a Norwegian by the name of O.M. Rees (employed by Krag, Mathiesen and Kiær in Cape Town) was the initiator of this new venture. After numerous notices in South African newspapers, he was convinced that land was productive and available for a giveaway price in the Eastern African highlands, and furthermore, in contrast to South Africa, that labour was almost unlimited and very, very cheap. Rees's suggestion to do a survey and report his findings to his Norwegian bosses at the end of 1909 received an almost immediate go-ahead; his employers – ever ready to make profits – fully supported a field trip to be undertaken the following year.

What Rees then saw convinced him. His report was virtually ecstatic about the development possibilities existing, not forgetting to mention that the British colonial administration warmly welcomed representatives from all European nations to take part in agricultural development in the Nairobi region. Rees was summoned to Norway and asked to make a cost survey of annual income and expenditure, and to calculate expected profit and prospects as far ahead as the next forty years. Near the end of 1910 Krag, Mathiesen and Kiær received a final draft of his 'Calculations for the projected East African Company'.[6]

In May the following year one of the board officials of Azania Ltd, Nils Backe Børresen, travelled to Nairobi to purchase land,[7] and four months later the first of the title deeds was signed. Within one year Azania Ltd owned four farms (estates) in the same district, north of Nairobi: Yara, Kizembe, Njuno and Gigirie. Before long the company also made further investments in East Africa (Uganda Plantation, Kilindini Sites Ltd, Simba Syndicate, Namenage Estates Ltd, and Berlin Gold Mine & Development).[8] The present text, however, deals only with the four farms.

The character of the project was such that it had given rise to considerable optimism from the very beginning, and by May 1915 the share capital had been increased by NOK 450,000. Well-known Norwegian shipowners like Fred. Olsen and Sigvald Bergesen had by then involved themselves in the business. So, too, had Christian M. Thams, a leading industrialist, businessman and diplomat. Krag had hoped to have Thams invest from the start, but Thams's major interest at the time was Société du Madal, a large company with plantations located in northern Mozambique (see Reiersen and Bertelsen's chapters, this volume).[9] By 1915 the major shareholders of Azania Ltd were Kiær (49 shares), Mads Wiel (60), Mathiesen (109) and Krag (111).

There is much evidence to show that Krag was the key person involved in getting Azania Ltd established, and therefore carried a particular responsibility for the well-being of this company from the very start.[10] Moreover, when the company ran into financial difficulties, he came to its rescue. In the meantime, the shareholders were filled with such optimism that the Azania share capital was further subscribed by NOK 200,000 in the middle of the First World War. By 1916 the paid-up shareholders were credited with an annual dividend of 10 per cent, an arrangement lasting until 1924.[11]

Azania Ltd Becomes Krag Estates Ltd

Right up to 1920 the number of shareholders increased, and at the beginning of that very year the company was capitalized by a further NOK 200,000.[12] When optimism turned to despair towards the end of the year due to a worldwide economic crisis, documents record that Azania Ltd was unable to borrow money in foreign banks.[13] The situation became so bleak that the board of directors was forced to discuss whether to dispose of the farms by bank auction and take an expected loss.

When, in April 1925, the company books showed a deficit of NOK 925,000 (equivalent to some GBP 3 million in present-day values), Krag proposed – to the great relief of the board of directors and its share-holders – that he personally assume responsibility for the company's debts, pledging personal bank guarantees to shore up the liquidity of the company. In the financial agreement that was drawn up, all the original shareholders were to be paid out within the following fifteen years, unless the share capital had been repaid in full within that time. However, in 1928, Krag chose to settle with all the creditors, and the business was taken over by a newly formed company, Krag Estates Ltd.[14] On 23 November 1931 Azania Ltd was formally deleted from the Oslo company register.

The difficulties facing the company were due to the fact that most of the shareholders had run into financial problems following the sudden end of the economic upswing many capitalists in neutral Norway had experienced through the war years. The bright outlook during that period suddenly came to an end in the winter of 1920–21 and most gilt-edged securities were now hardly worth the paper they were printed on. The Norwegian krone, which all along had maintained parity with the pound and the dollar, crashed (see Christensen 1934: 9–19).

The reason for prospects becoming so gloomy was neither to be found in the geographical location of the company nor the particular product (coffee) that had been chosen: the highlands of Kenya had proven very suitable for coffee growing and, indeed, coffee was considered to be truly a wonder crop.[15] Between 1850 and 1910 world consumption quadrupled.[16] When, in 1913, it had been decided to grow only coffee on Azania Ltd's farms, it was fully in conformity with British strategy for development of the colony. Between 1909 and 1919 coffee exports climbed from ten tons to thirty-five hundred tons. The area north of Nairobi had proved successful for growing arabica coffee due to its good soil, sufficient rainfall and climatic conditions. The fact that coffee planters, regardless of nationality, were encouraged to settle in the area by the colonial authorities was also an important factor. They had re-served some of the best land for white settlement and adopted a policy of not allowing the indigenous African population to grow coffee for export. This policy continued to be enforced until the early 1950s.

Instead, it was the point in time when the venture was started that had been unfavourable. The first year of significant production on the Norwegian-owned farms was 1917, but the market for coffee and other produce was at a low point due to war conditions hindering trade. Immediately after the end of the First World War so much coffee came on the market that there was a glut, with a consequent sharp fall in price levels. Whereas coffee was sold at around GBP 150 per ton on the London Exchange in 1920, only GBP 60 per ton could be obtained the following year. It was only after the Second World War that prices rose to a stable and satisfactory level. Krag, who died in 1938, did not live to see this. In the last ten years of his life he constantly regretted that he had ever bought out the other shareholders in Azania Ltd.[17]

Overseas Stationing

From the very start of business in 1911 and right through until the company ceased operating in the mid-1970s, the head office of Azania/Krag Estates was located in Kristiania/Oslo. The farms in Kenya were run as a group by a managing director, a Norwegian based in Nairobi, with a general manager, mainly Norwegian, on each farm responsible to the Nairobi office. This management organization was common in Africa during colonial times. While individuals with limited capital invested in smaller plots and nearly always ran their businesses themselves, large-scale enterprises were operated by others (see also Reiersen's chapter, this volume). As such, management was liable to get out of control and was more open to abuse, leading to problems. Thus, Krag – who himself appointed his managerial staff – had reason to be wary, and put in a lot of time and effort to find the right people. The fact that Rees was chosen to be Azania's first managing director was due to Krag and several of the board members knowing him from an earlier job relationship. Moreover, Rees was the one who had suggested the already mentioned survey to decide if a company was viable. Krag would systematically take on only people he knew well (including relatives) or, as in the case of Eivind Eriksen, a youth from his own neighbourhood in Norway. He thus had a higher probability of securing loyal employees.

As the venture into Kenya involved heavy investment, there is little doubt why, by 1913, a kind of controller arrived on the scene. It was said that Krag had arranged for his nephew, William, to go to Nairobi to manage a farm that his uncle had bought privately, but Krag's many letters to William indicate that he was to keep an eye on what was happening on the company farms. However, the nephew found almost nothing to be critical of in his reports, suggesting that most managers were satisfied with their salaries, working conditions and housing.

Although the manager at Njuno Estate was provided with the best of the four farmhouses, none of the Azania/Krag Estates managers had any reason to complain. A manager was entitled to six months leave every three years with full pay. Passage home and back was paid for him as well as his family. This was a benefit generally provided by all employers to practically all their administrative staff members working in British East Africa. When Krag and his board chose to follow such regulations, it was because it was generally accepted that white people could endanger their health if they lived for long periods in equatorial climatic conditions.

Some of the Norwegian employees, directors and managers worked for Azania/Krag Estates for an exceptionally long time. Rees, for one, worked for three decades; Bernhard Aagaard, the last of the Krag Estates managing directors, stayed for almost forty years. But it is Eivind Eriksen – with his forty-five years as manager at Yara – who holds the record. His early letters to his family and to the company (along with a tale towards the end of this chapter by his second wife) provide a microlevel example of Kenyan colonial agribusiness history from 1912 to 1957.

The Early Years at Yara Estate

In the early spring of 1912 Eivind travelled on the German passenger vessel *Windhuk* to Africa, and apart from a minor storm in the Bay of Biscay nothing of note occurred. He was met by Rees in Mombasa on 17 April and escorted to Nairobi by train.

All Eivind's first letters are written on Azania's official letterhead, showing his address as PO Box 53, Nairobi. The company was in the making, and the office, although situated on Government Road, comprised a single room for which they paid a monthly rent of GBP 23.[18] When Eivind first arrived Rees was still staying at the Stanley Hotel.

Eivind found life in Nairobi really enjoyable, exclaiming that 'the air is pure and fresh, just like it is in the mountain areas of Norway', further assuring his parents that 'there are no lions, nor mosquitoes or malaria here'. He found many of the recently constructed buildings (like the large store Whiteway Laidlaw and Nairobi House at the corner of Government Road and Sixth Avenue) in the new colonial capital to be beautiful, and was indeed fascinated by the large number of white women who had already found their way to East Africa. The white population in Kenya swelled from some 400 in 1897 to almost 5,600 towards the end of the First World War. This group contained some 2,500 men and an equal amount of women and children – 1,523 and 1,554, respectively (Nicholls 2005: 59). As very few whites arrived in the country during the war, this number of women is probably only slightly higher than that of 1912.

And with women in mind, Eivind immediately decided to bring to Africa Sarah, his fiancée. Luckily she was keen to relocate, too. Sarah arrived in late August accompanied by her sister, Margit, who turned out to be a most supportive family member. In the next ten years Sarah gave birth to four boys.

To cover their travel Eivind had to borrow 400 Indian rupees from the company. Well aware that this amounted to more then two months of his salary, he assured his parents that he would never marry again. (As they already knew what he earned, there was no mention of this in any of his letters. He probably had the same salary as his predecessor, Ernst Lekander, who was paid 180 Indian rupees, equivalent to GBP 12, per month.[19]) And money seemed indeed to be enough: food was cheap and Eivind paid neither tax nor rent, and details regarding reasonable living conditions are much repeated in his letters.

Eivind started thinking on the ship of how it would be to lead a life 'all alone' on a 640-acre farm outside Nairobi, and the thought of being in charge of a large number of workers with whom he could not communicate bothered him. But as we have seen in his first letter, things worked out quite well. He found that he adapted to a daily routine and a regular schedule of work and mealtimes, where his precisely set bath time. 'The three kitchen boys probably think, as Auntie does, that I waste a lot of water. They must think I am a really odd screw.'

Rees initially instructed him to give priority to black wattle and black beans,[20] but soon he was ordered instead to plant forty acres with coffee. This met with Eivind's approval, as he, too, believed strongly in this crop. Within a short time in 1913, a diversity of fruit was also planted at Yara: seventy-five each of apples, pears, plums, peaches and almonds, followed by gooseberries and some orange and lemon trees.

The outbreak of war in 1914 caused concern, both for private reasons and in terms of business.[21] White farmers were unable to dispose of their coffee crops, and the forty tons produced at Yara in 1917 had to be retained in storage for the next two years. Throughout the war years money transactions were problematic, and much of the correspondence between the head office in Norway and the managers in British East Africa went astray.

Eivind never mentioned Rees as a friend; he was the boss. Rees dealt with salaries and financial matters. As managing director, he made the decisions about how the business was to be run and handled farm product sales. He was frequently travelling, either to Norway for meetings with the board of directors or in Uganda or South Africa to check on the company's many other ongoing projects. At Christmas Rees would visit each farm, bringing bonuses to the employees and presents for the managers' wives and children. But before the actual celebration began he always returned to town.

The managers, however, socialized extensively. Eivind and Sarah met with the others to celebrate Christmas and the New Year, and often also on weekends or other holidays. Two of their close friends were Alf de Roepstorff Thomé, who came to British East Africa in 1914 to be manager of Njuno Estate,[22] and Christian Aubert, who arrived two years later to manage Gigirie Estate.[23]

Most of Eivind's letters, however, concerned Marius Riis, a relative of Rees,[24] who settled down on Kizembe Estate near the end of the First World War and became a close friend of the family. No one could measure up to jovial 'Tubby Riis', as he became known, who was the life and soul of a party, with his rotund and smiling countenance. The four Eriksen boys referred to him as 'Uncle'. Marius Riis, full of fun and tricks, may very well also have had a certain ability to see the more comic side of grand nationalism and white supremacy. The fact that he staged the 1930-scene in the photograph on the front cover of this book, does point in this direction: Six-year-old Bjørn Eriksen posing regally over the houseboys, seated on the Norwegian flag.

As with most good friends, they joined together to eat, drink, sing, play or take part in informal sports. They pulled together as the occasion demanded. A typical example of this solidarity is when Alf fell ill with Spanish flu in the autumn of 1918.[25] Sarah insisted that he be nursed at Yara instead of in a hospital.

Sarah and Eivind spent some thirty years together at Yara, until she passed away in 1943. He later remarried a young Danish widow, Ulla Berg, who bore him two additional sons and lived with him at the farm until he died in 1957. The tale given below is based on a conversation with her from 29 August 2000. She provides us with details regarding the running of all the farms and describes the routines of everyday life on Yara itself. Although her tale makes a strong contrast to Eivind's opening letter to his parents from May 1912, traces of continuation regarding the almost feudal-like structure on such farms may be read between the lines; real rupture strikes when Ulla describes her sewing classes. After the First World War, the number of white women settlers involved in voluntary social welfare work grew steadily (Van Tol 2013), and in the 1950s, when Ulla began such activity at Yara, this was probably driven both by personal need to create space and meaning and by her upbringing in a European country where ideals of hierarchies of power began to be challenged. While a certain cultural and political mind-set seem to have been the common denominator for people

Figure 13.2. Ulla Eriksen with her pupils in one of her sewing classes in the mid-1950s. *Source:* Photo courtesy of Ole P. Eriksen; reproduced with permission.

(like Eivind) who had spent years in a colonial setting, whites arriving towards the end of the colonial period (like Ulla) often brought with them 'fresh' attitudes. A number of young Scandinavians arriving on the Kenyan scene right before, during and after the Second World War make it clear that they were shocked by how the 'colonial old-timers' treated their employees (see, e.g., Kjerland 2010: chap. 18).

Ulla states that conditions were favourable for the managers who worked for the Norwegian company. She also reveals that the running of the farms and the entire agent-based system established in the beginning was retained, a system followed until the last of the four farms was sold in the mid-1970s.

Ulla's Saga

Eivind was twenty-three years older than me. When we met during the Second World War I was a widow and he was a widower. He was unusually tall, well over six feet. Some of the other Norwegians were even taller, for example, Olaf Johansen. Once when Olaf came to visit I called out, 'Oh, I didn't realize that I had married such a small man!'

I came to Tanganyika in 1938 together with my first husband, but two years later he died.[26] The war had already started, so I went to Nairobi, and that is where I met Eivind.

Krag had four farms. Lagerberg, who was a Swede, was manager of Gigirie, the farm situated closest to Nairobi. It was further to Yara, but only about twenty kilometres from the city. When I lived there only coffee was grown. Next to Yara was Njuno, and this farm was managed by a Norwegian, Bernhard Aagaard, who was married to an English woman. I believe that tea was planted there in later years. The fourth farm, Kizembe, was situated not far from Yara, but a bit higher up. It did not have a manager in my time, and periodically lay fallow. Eivind and I went up there occasionally to talk to one of the boys living on the farm.

My husband had four sons by his first marriage. I met them only after the war ended. I myself did not have any children with my first husband. Eivind's first four children had been sent home (to Norway) when aged six to eight years, for their schooling, whereas our two sons went to school in Kenya. Eivind died when our boys were nine and seven, respectively. The only one of Eivind's children that I got to know well was Bjarne, the eldest. It was our intention to invite the three living in Norway to visit Kenya when Eivind was to be seventy, but he fell ill and passed away before anything was arranged.[27]

Eivind and I never had our own place. We never talked about that. Eivind had good terms and conditions at Yara. We had a lovely house and I had a beautiful garden. We even had our own tennis court. As with all the other managers, we got overseas leave with full pay every three years, also for the family.

My husband was very thoughtful and kind, and loved the natives as much as I did. Once, when we travelled abroad, an English couple looked after the farm. My husband's first wife, Sarah, who died in 1943, had a lot of silverware and sets of porcelain placed openly around in the house. The English lady did not dare to let them be on display, but we insisted that they could remain in place. We were sure that they would not be touched. Things in the house would definitely be safe. Our cook had been at Yara since he was a child and had worked for Sarah for very many years, and could be trusted.

The two of us led a quiet life. I am the quiet type of person, and Eivind had experienced most things before he met me. So we stayed mostly at home, more so than most others. One of the things that added spice to my life there was that I held many sewing classes. I had a nanny who constantly came to me with clothing that needed mending or buttons sewn. After a while I began to realize that I had some spare time when the boys were at school, so I started a small class for the girls on the farm. The first time only two came, the next time six came. Thereafter, more and more turned up. It ended up with me having to have two classes a week, as I didn't want more than thirty in a class. It was really fun, and a few of them did quite well. One in particular was amazing, and I certainly could not sew like her. She showed me something she had done: a little sewing bag in which she kept her sewing kit, so neatly made that I had to ask if she had used a machine. Everyone in the class protested loudly: she had sewn it herself!

Yara funded the materials that we used in the classes, but I paid for the scissors as well as the thread needed for embroidering. The Africans were particularly fond of red yarn and red knitting wool.

Once, when class work had come to a finish, one of the cutting scissors was missing. I announced that unless it was handed in before I was to go, the following sewing class would be cancelled. This caused quite an uproar, with much talk in Kikikuyu, which I didn't understand. Many of the women had attended my courses over a long time, married women bearing small children on their backs. These went around inspecting the pockets of those who were younger. In the end they found the missing scissors, and so we could all sew on the next occasion.

I can say that most of the natives were appreciative to those who gave them help or who showed that they cared. Once, when thirty people had come for the sewing class, I had to ask the gardener to announce that the class was full. Of course, it so happened that one had come who declared that I had to let her be included because she had walked nine kilometres to get to my house.

Another time, when the wife of the British district commissioner of Kiambu District asked to be present at one of my sewing courses, I requested all the women to wear the white aprons they had sewn. On the appointed day I could hardly believe my eyes when I looked out to the garden and saw them all standing ready, dressed in their white and clean garments. Right then I was close to tears.

At the End of an Era

Ulla emigrated from Kenya shortly after Eivind's death in 1957, mainly because she now had an opportunity to start a new life in Denmark. Some forty years later, she insisted that this was why she decided to leave Africa. However, there were certainly other reasons for leaving then: one was widespread fear amongst the white settlers due to the warlike situation between the Kenyan freedom fighters (Mau Mau) and the British colonial authorities, which escalated towards the latter part of the 1950s.[28] As a consequence of this unrest and the British government preparing to lead the country towards independence, many whites feared for the future and decided to flee the country. By December 1963, when Jomo Kenyatta was declared president of independent Kenya, many of the sixty thousand whites who had been living in the country in the early 1950s had already left (Nicholls 2005).

It is reasonable to believe that Eivind Eriksen would have stayed on in independent Kenya – if he had lived. The Norwegian owners (now with Jan Helmer, the grandchild of Krag, heading the company) had no immediate plans to give up the business. Over the years, coffee prices had remained favourable,[29] and the current local managing director, Bernhard Aagaard, was also convinced not only that coffee growing would continue to be profitable, but also that it would be possible to live on peacefully for some time ahead.

Helmer and Aagaard were right, although the going was not very easy. In 1974, some ten years after independence, the Norwegian owners were inclined to dispose of the last of the four farms positioned in the very heart of Kikuyuland. By then most white owners had been forced to give up their farms in the area near Nairobi years before. The fact that Aagaard was a Norwegian citizen and the owners of Krag Estates lived in a country generally believed to have good intentions towards the liberated colonies in Africa is likely to have postponed Jomo Kenyatta's decision to 'take' the farms. Moreover, the entire business was settled in an orderly manner: while the same Norwegians investors lost all their money when they were forced to leave Algeria four years earlier, in 1970, all the four farms outside Nairobi were compensated for by the Kenyan government. Although such money was under restriction and could only be taken out of Kenya in minor portions, the company was able to do so with the help of Norwegians in official, diplomatic positions.

Notes

1. The present text is just one example of which types of activities Norwegians involved themselves in in colonial Kenya. For a full overview, consult the present author's book (in Norwegian) *Nordmenn i det koloniale Kenya* (Norwegians in Colonial Kenya), published in 2010. It deals with the Norwegians living, working and investing in the country from the 1890s until Independence in the early 1960s. A modest group indeed; during the peak period in the 1950s they counted one hundred adults and children only. Like the rest of the whites finding their way to East Africa in the aforementioned period, Norwegians, representing all social strata, sought a better life. A small group of very wealthy capitalists dwelling in Norway looked to the colonies for investment only, and the present chapter deals with the

first company that bought coffee farms in the highlands outside Nairobi in 1911. The four farms in question were bought by agents and operated by white managers until they were sold in 1974. Hans Peter Fyhn Krag, the main investor (who took over all the shares of the company in the 1920s), never even visited the country. To him and other investors Kenya was one of many eggs in a full tray, investments that were scattered all over colonial Africa and the rest of the world.

2. The country known today as Kenya was formally the East Africa Protectorate and after 1920 the Kenya Colony. Otherwise known as British East Africa.

3. The author is indebted to the late Bjørn Eriksen, the youngest son of Eivind and Sarah Eriksen, who allowed her to copy part of the family's collection of historic letters (ABE).

4. In old Greek scripts, 'Azania' referred to the eastern seaboard of the African continent.

5. The other shareholders were Magnus Blikstad, Johs. G. Heftye, Elias C. Kiær, Haaken Larpent Mathiesen, Viktor Mønichen Plahte, Otto Keyser Thoresen, Th. Thoresen and Mads Wiel. Krag had secured twenty-five shares for himself; Heftye, Mathiesen and Nordskog each had twenty shares. The others held fifteen, ten and five. Each share counted as one vote, so Krag, the company's managing director, effectively had the most power.

6. Official letter with a caption 'Invitation to subscribe to shares. Annual reports. Circulars etc.', AHLM.

7. According to correspondence between two Norwegians who lived on Zanzibar, Børresen came to the island on 11 May 1910, with the intention of proceeding to Nairobi to purchase farms for Azania. This is mentioned in a letter from Oscar Chr. Olsen to Christian Janssen dated 1 June 1911, ANSS.

8. A number of letters from the mid-1920s reveal information about documents (now owned by the Helmer family, AJH), including a balance sheet of accounts from 1924 for the properties in Kenya, a financial statement as of 31 March 1925, notes from an extraordinary board meeting for Azania dated 29 April 1925 and, finally, an extract from the company register in Oslo dated 13 May of that year.

9. Christian M. Thams has been well documented in Reiersen (2006). All of the largest shareholders of Azania Ltd took up shares in one of the largest plantations in Portuguese East Africa, Société du Madal, and Norwegian investors are dominant in that company even now. See also the chapters by Reiersen and Bertelsen, this volume.

10. The author is currently writing a book on Krag's business interests on the African continent.

11. Minutes from an extraordinary general meeting held on 29 April 1925, AHLM, as well as AJH.

12. Wilhelm Arvesen, Arne Christensen, G. & G.M. Coward, Hermine Eckbo, Eivind and Louise Krohn, and Thor Thoresen Jr all invested in Azania Ltd in 1920.

13. A number of letters from the mid-1920s reveal information about documents (now owned by the Helmer family, AJH), including a balance sheet

of accounts from 1924 for the properties in Kenya, a financial statement as of 31 March 1925, notes from an extraordinary board meeting for Azania dated 29 April 1925 and, finally, an extract from the company register in Oslo dated 13 May of that year.

14. The purchase price of three of the four farms can be compared with the price that Krag paid when he took over the company in 1928. Yara had originally cost GBP 1,350, Njuno 4,410 and Kizembe 5,858. Seventeen years later Krag paid GBP 6,500, 5,000 and 3,000, respectively, showing that Yara was then regarded as the most valuable of the three. Details obtained from the notary public letter through the law firm Hamilton, Harrison and Matthews, Nairobi, Kenya, dated 1 September 1965, 13/MRK/MISC, AJH.

15. All the facts and figures relating to coffee are obtained from Clarence-Smith and Topik (2003) and Wrigley ([1965] 1982: 208–64).

16. During the Napoleonic Wars coffee became a popular drink in the Western world. Consumption in the United States amounted to half a kilogram per person in 1783, and by 1883 that had increased to 4.5 kilograms per person. A ninefold increase is in itself remarkable, but considering the huge population increase in America over that period, the consumption escalation was phenomenal. The United States had become and still is the world's principal coffee consumer, and Brazil soon became the leading producer, a position it has maintained.

17. The diaries of Hans Peter Fyhn Krag, AJH.

18. According to a letter from Rees to Krag, 'Subscription of Shares, Annual reports, Circulars etc.', dated Nairobi, 8 July 1911, AHLM.

19. According to a letter from Rees to Krag, dated Nairobi, 29 July 1911, AHLM.

20. These were products in great demand at this time throughout the world. The bark of the black wattle tree – a kind of acacia – was used in the tanning industry. The black beans were sold to France, serving as food for the military.

21. Near the end of the war Eivind and Sarah feared that their two eldest children might be hindered from going to Norway for their schooling.

22. According to conversations with Thomé's daughter, Tove Dreyer, on 17 August 2000, 15 October 2003 and 4 October 2006, Thomé stayed in British East Africa/Kenya for twelve years. He subsequently went to Argentina, where his Danish wife, Jenny, had grown up. He was educated at Ås Agricultural College outside Kristiania and took up farming on his arrival in Argentina in 1925. He later became involved in running a hostel, combined with the sale of antiques. The name of his establishment – Kenya House – reflects how important to him his earlier life in Africa had been.

23. Aubert was twenty-four years old when he came to British East Africa in 1916. During a holiday in Norway in 1919 he married Sonja Charlotte Bødker Dorenfeldt, who accompanied him back to Africa. The following year their first son, Knut, was born. In 1922 Sonja decided to return to Norway, and Christian followed in September of that year.

24. Riis (who in contrast to his half brother did not anglicize his name) never got married. It would seem that he died during the Second World War.

From his arrival during the First World War until his demise he was manager of Kizembe Estate.

25. Spanish influenza took the lives of 160,000 people in British East Africa; a total of between 1.5 and 2 million died in Africa south of the Sahara (Paice 2007: 395).

26. Ulla's husband, Lasse Berg, was a qualified engineer and came to Tanganyika to take up employment with a Danish firm.

27. According to a conversation with Didrik Krag on 6 January 2001, Fridtjof Lagerberg (a Swede) became the manager of Yara Estate after the death of Eriksen. He knew the farms from his childhood days: his father, Gustav, was manager of Gigirie Estate for a number of years.

28. The freedom fighters killed thirty-two white farmers between 1952 and 1956. This caused not only a steady exodus of whites from Kenya but also motivated the British colonial government to react with military force, resulting in a death toll of between twelve thousand and twenty thousand Kenyans. Of these, just over one thousand were brought to trial by the British authorities and sentenced to be hanged – an action never before carried out under British colonial rule. About a million local inhabitants were forced to leave their homes and several hundred thousand were interned in concentration camps. The first of these camps was opened in 1953; the last remaining camp was closed in January 1960. For further details, see Anderson (2005) and Elkins (2005).

29. Coffee growing became profitable in the mid-1940s, and revenue from exports for the year 1952 amounted to GBP 150.7 million. By the mid-1950s Kenya's coffee exports accounted for 6 per cent of the world trade in coffee. Although Brazil continued to be the dominant coffee-producing country, Kenya's arabica coffee became renowned for its good quality and commanded a higher price than robusta coffee, which was more widely grown, for instance, in Uganda (Hyde 2008: 3–4).

Archives and Sources Consulted

Archives of Norske Skog Saugbrugsforeningen (ANSS), Halden, Norway.
Private archives of Bjørn Eriksen (ABE), Oslo.
Private archives of Haaken L. Mathiesen (AHLM), Eidsvold Verk, Norway.
Private archives of Jan Helmer (AJH), Oslo.

References

Anderson, D. 2005. *Histories of the Hanged: The Dirty War in Kenya and the End of Empire.* New York: W.W. Norton.
Christensen, C.A.R. 1934. *Det hendte i gaar: En skildring av efterkrigstidens Norge.* Oslo: Tanum.

Clarence-Smith, W.G. and S.C. Topik. 2003. *The Global Coffee Economy in Africa, Asia and Latin America, 1500–1989*. Cambridge: Cambridge University Press.

Elkins, C. 2005. *Imperial Reckoning: The Untold Story of Britain's Gulag in Kenya*. New York: Henry Holt.

Hyde, D. 2008. *Global Coffee and Decolonization in Kenya: Overproduction, Quotas and Rural Restructuring*, Commodities of Empire working paper 8. London: London Metropolitan University.

Kjerland, K.A. 2010. *Nordmenn i det koloniale Kenya*. Oslo: Scandinavian Academic Press.

Nicholls, C.S. 2005. *Red Strangers: The White Tribe of Kenya*. London: Timewell Press.

Paice, E. 2007. *Tip and Run: The Untold Tragedy of the Great War in Africa*. London: Weidenfeld & Nicholson.

Reiersen, E. 2006. *Fenomenet Thams*. Oslo: Aschehoug.

Van Tol, D. 2013. 'The Heart of a Stranger: Voluntary Work and European Settlement in Colonial Africa', paper presented at Queen's University, Kingston, Ontario, April. Retrieved 16 June 2014 from http://papers.ssrn.com/sol3/papers.cfm?abstract_id=2252614.

Wrigley, C.C. (1965) 1982. 'Kenya: The Patterns of Economic Life', in V. Harlow and E.M. Chilver (eds), *History of East Africa*, vol. 2. Oxford: Oxford University Press, pp. 208–64.

ᴏ⟫ 14

Scandinavian Agents and Entrepreneurs in the Scramble for Ethnographica during Colonial Expansion in the Congo

Espen Wæhle

King Leopold II of Belgium's Congo Free State (1885–1908) earned disrepute due to the brutal mistreatment of the Congolese peoples and plunder of natural resources. The Free State exported ivory, rubber and minerals to the world market, disregarding that the ostensible purpose of the colonial endeavour was to free them from slave traders and bring Christianity, civilization and commerce to the region. The Congo Free State became one of the greatest international scandals of the early twentieth century.[1]

Significantly, the colonial administration of King Leopold II recruited noncolonial colonials from countries seldom mentioned in the imperial rush for Africa: Denmark, Finland, Norway, Sweden, Switzerland and Italy. Between 1885 and 1930 around fifteen hundred to two thousand Scandinavians worked in the Congo, among them about two hundred Norwegians.[2] In the river traffic Scandinavians constituted 90 per cent of the workforce. Others served as officers, medical doctors, civil engineers, judges or missionaries.

The formative period and marked growth of ethnographic museums coincides with the period of high imperialism, the 1870s to the 1930s, and these collections offer a different but distinctive window onto this extraordinary example of colonialism. Indeed, Scandinavian museums house such collections, consisting of Congolese artefacts and a considerable range of diaries, correspondence, maps, photographs, drawings, ethnographic and linguistic notes, newspaper articles and interviews, and travelogues and unpublished manuscripts. The sources are spread across a range of museums and archives, and some are still in private hands.[3] In this particular case colonial interests directed neither the process of archiving nor the publishing – and as such the material may offer interesting perspectives on the colonization of the Congo Free State and the geopolitics of Central Africa at the time. Further, the holdings of the

University Museum of Bergen in western Norway and other Scandinavian museums point to what is virtually unknown outside expert circles: King Leopold II's dream of expanding the colony northeastwards to control the Nile valley and beyond, in stiff competition with African empires, slave traders and other Western colonial powers.[4]

This chapter views the University Museum of Bergen Central African ethnographic collections in a Scandinavian and wider European setting.[5] The material is used as an inroad to the growth of colonial ethnographic collections, colonial history, colonial entrepreneurship and ethnography. It illustrates how exploration and exploitation was matched with a frantic but short-lived entrepreneurial market in Congo ethnographica. Both Danish and Norwegian ethnographic entrepreneurs were providers to Norwegian museums: while the Danish and Norwegian sea captains Andersen[6], Martini and Schønberg as well as the engineer Scharffenberg largely serviced the early phase of general exploration and exploitation of the Congo Free State, in the next phase of colonization the Danish gun maker Hansen and the Norwegian engineer Johannesen and the officer Schumann Krüger were part of King Leopold II's secret endeavours to expand the Free State into the Nile valley. Lastly, an explanation as to why the collecting continued after the museums only seldom purchased ethnographica from the Congo is presented.

Colonial History and the Scramble for Congo Collections

The flamboyant duo Chr. Martini and Chr. Schønberg were the first Scandinavians that went beyond acquiring smaller collections of souvenirs that could be brought home as personal luggage.[7] Martini and Schønberg became entrepreneurs trading in Congo ethnographica and masters in marketing themselves and their colonial goods. Their participation in the early exploration of the Congo gave them an initial advantage; both had in addition a nose for marketing and publicity and financed and arranged blockbuster Congo exhibitions in Copenhagen and Kristiania (now Oslo). They toured Europe often, lecturing on their Congo adventures, and published their first travelogue in 1890.[8] They were widely cited, got invited to the royal court in Copenhagen and were true celebrities for some years.

In 1889 the stage was set for an almost feverish urge to boost the Kristiania collection with 585 objects. Director Yngvar Nielsen embarked on what has probably been the most considerable sponsored hunt in the history of the collections (Gjessing and Krekling Johannesen 1957;

Figure 14.1. In Gothersgade in central Copenhagen, Denmark, A. Jacobsen's Naturaliehandel specialized in natural history specimens and ethnographica. The postcard, with handwritten announcements of new acquisitions, was distributed to Scandinavian museums. *Source*: Bornholms Museum; reproduced with permission.

Bouquet 1996). In Bergen curator Gabriel Gustafson followed the same strategy three years later.[9]

The archives, yearly reports, acquisition protocols and other sources reveal hectic activity in Bergen and Kristiania aiming at securing basic collections and later supplementing them as resources and opportunities arose. The Norwegian collections were comparatively small and had fewer resources than sister museums in Copenhagen, Denmark, and Stockholm, Sweden – and again tiny in comparison with the metropolitan colonial museums of the main colonizing powers, which were funded as the show window of imperial governments. Germany was not only the academic centre, inspiring the development of ethnographic museums in Norway, but also presented the stiffest competition, as city bourgeoisie fought to create the best and most impressive of the fashionable ethnographic museums (Penny 2002). Collectors tried to boost prices by attempting to play off one museum against the other. In Bergen and Kristiania the directors and curators demonstrated creativity in straitened circumstances and were by no means isolated in an ivory tower. They traded duplicates and copies with other museums and traders and pleaded for extra funds from the government or went into larger fund-raising campaigns with sponsors to cope, at times paying from their own pockets until funds became available. They travelled and researched the market, subscribed to catalogues from auction houses or from trading companies and had an extensive correspondence with sister museums (see figure 14.1). In Kristiania they appealed to Norwegians to help build the nation with international collections and used the media and the possibilities of royal decorations to develop a prestige sphere around donations to the museum. While the situation was tough, there was hardly any competition from private collectors in Norway. Contrary to developments elsewhere in Europe and the United States, Norway had no significant collectors' market after the modernist painters started celebrating 'exotic art' in the first decades of the 1900s. The few with financial means gave priority to 'Norwegian ethnographica', the peasant antiquities celebrated in the national romantic age (Wæhle 2001).

While substantial parts of the Martini and Schønberg collections came to be the core of the great ethnographic collections in Copenhagen and Kristiania, they probably also sold more than one thousand objects to museums abroad. One source mentions two thousand objects in their collection exhibited in Kristiania and Copenhagen.[10] The success story of Martini and Schønberg created immense interest in the Scandinavians, who had 'followed in the footsteps of Livingstone and Stanley' (Wæhle 2002, 2004).

Congo: The Last Big White Spot on the World Map

What was so special about the Congo? From the 1870s Central Africa was one of the few remaining white spots on Western maps of the exploration of the world: the surface of the moon was better mapped than conditions on the ground in the Congo. The exploration and ensuing colonization of the area led to massive public interest, and museums soon acted to get their hands on collections from this hotspot. Ethnographic museums could neither miss the chance to take advantage of the public attention on the Congo nor the opportunity to add Congo artefacts to their 'ethnographic laboratories', along with collections from, for example, the Zulu of South Africa, Madagascar, imperial Japan, Netsilik Inuit, peoples of Siberia and the Santali of India. What were formerly primarily exotic souvenirs and memorabilia could wisely be transformed to have market value and prestige for entrepreneur collectors. As Congo ethnographica were among some of the most sought-after objects, competition between researchers, museums, cities and collectors arose.

Only 696 African items can be documented in Western collections from 1400 to 1800. From the kingdom of Kongo[11] and the present-day Democratic Republic of the Congo (DR Congo), only seventy-two arte-facts are known globally. Several of these have been lost since they arrived in Europe, but documents on the artefacts remain. As many as twenty-three of the world stock of early Congo artefacts can be found today in the collections of the National Museum in Copenhagen. No other museum has such large and varied early Congo collections. Two further objects later ended up in ethnographic collections in Oslo (Bassani and McLeod 2000; Gjessing and Krekling Johannesen 1957). For the DR Congo, Schildkrout has maintained that from the 1870s to the 1930s 100,000 art objects left the Congo area (Schildkrout and Keim 1998). This is certainly grossly underestimated, as the Royal Museum for Central Africa in Tervuren alone houses around 250,000 artefacts.[12] Adding other collections in Brussels, Antwerp, Namur, Ghent and so forth as well as museum holdings in Germany, France, the Netherlands, Switzerland, Italy, the United Kingdom and the United States, one would calculate at least 500,000 to 1,000,000 objects. For the Nordic countries, the present author's investigations point to 38,500 Congolese artefacts in museums and collections, and of these at least 6,500 are in Norway. The majority of the objects are with the University of Oslo, the rest mostly in Bergen, Trondheim, Stavanger, Arendal and Tromsø (Tygesen and Wæhle 2007).

Since Norway was a small country on the outskirts of Europe, only harbouring two specialized ethnographic museums (one in Kristiania and one in Bergen), collectors were forced to market artefacts in Germany, Belgium – and possibly also the UK. But all in all, what initially might have looked like a golden opportunity to obtain extra income soon decreased to a puff of wind.[13]

A Stiffening Competition among Providers of Congo Ethnographica

In December 1893 the Bergen Museum (Bergen University Museum after 1946) received a letter with a sales prospect of a collection from Central Africa[14]:

> A month ago I returned from a three-year expedition in Africa: from the Congo River to the Nile along the Uelle River. I brought with me a size-able collection comprising spears, bows, shields, arrows, axes, musical instruments, ivory items like horns, arm rings and headpins, tools and a number of other forms of artefacts. The collection includes artefacts from

the following tribes: Djabbir, Ababua, Niam Niam, Mobanka, Mambuttus, Tikke Tikke (the dwarf people), Momfu, Tangamonanki, Mengsje. I would prefer to sell the 200 artefacts as one collection, but I am also willing to consider selling individual pieces. I can also offer to photograph the collection, without costs for the museum. I have already sold artefacts to the museum of this town [Copenhagen], but as there are doublets, this will not reduce the quality of the collection.[15]

The Danish gun maker F. Hansen presented an arsenal of arguments to make his collection attractive. By referring to what later became known as the Van Kerckhoven expedition of 1891, he borrowed glory from Henry M. Stanley and David Livingstone. The Congo, Nile and Uele Rivers tied his collection to a grand geographical mystery. At the time, collections from the upper Uele River were still extremely rare (Grootaers 2007). In Bergen Director Gustafsen wrote a detailed list ordering artefacts from Hansen, The Ethnographic Collection of the National Museum of Denmark in Copenhagen, one of the most prestigious ethnographic museums at the time, had already purchased artefacts from Hansen.[16] While the 1880s was a time when ethnographic museums were anxious to acquire collections from the Congo, in 1893 the competition was already stiffening, and Hansen was the third Dane to approach the comparatively small museum on the Norwegian west coast.

A few years prior to Hansen's arrival in the Congo, only a few Europeans had been inside the vast territory. After reports in the 1870s from explorers like Henry M. Stanley, V. Cameron and H. von Wissmann, King Leopold II noted promising descriptions of the richness of Central Africa. After securing the territory in 1885, Leopold immediately sent off small expeditions to make a statement of presence in relation to rivalling claims for territories from France, Germany, Britain and Portugal. Subsequently, the king dispatched his own associates to map resources. Already during the early explorations of the colony, Scandinavians took part: Albert Christophersen, Martin Mortensen and Anton Emmanuel Andersson for Henry M. Stanley, and Jes Bugslag for H. von Wissmann (Tygesen and Wæhle 2007).

Several expeditions had failed to navigate and chart the Ubangi River and its connection to the Uele River in the far northeast: a major geographical mystery at the time. It was only after the Danish sea captain Chr. Schønberg and engineer Hans Hansen participated, along with seventeen Hausa and Zanzibari soldiers and sixteen Congolese paddlers, in the Alphonse Vangele expedition with *En Avant* in 1889 that the Uele-Ubangi-Congo River confluences were confirmed (Coosemans 1951; Lederer 1965). The borders with the French colonies were established some years later, thanks to the charting carried out during this expedition (Ndaywel è Nziem 1998; Lederer 1965; Lotar 1937). In 1888 the Danish-Norwegian sea captain Chr. Martini was at the helm when a five-month expedition commanded by Alexandre Delcommune chartered the Kasai, M'Fimi, Lukenie, Sankuru and Lubefu Rivers, as well as Lake Leopold II (now Lake Mai-Ndombe). After Delcommune's expedition, Compagnie du Congo pour le Commerce et l'Industrie (CCCI) decided to launch La Societé Anonyme Belge pour le Commerce du Haut-Congo (SAB), which developed into one of the larger commercial operators in the colony. CCCI and SAB were examples of companies chartered by the Congo Free State to exploit, transport and export resources and maximize profit. Over the years close to a hundred Scandinavians found work with SAB. Almost eighty were employed by one of the twenty other chartered companies. The notorious concession companies hired at least sixty-five Scandinavians, while the largest employer was the Free State itself, with more than one thousand employees from Scandinavia.[17]

The collections of people like Andersen, Schønberg and Martini stem from what has been called the time of the pioneers (Lederer 1965), and artefacts and collection histories both reflect life situations and cultures in the Congo and expose European individuals' characters, such as differences in approaches between female and male collectors and peaceful exchange versus violent confiscation of artefacts. The range of colonial encounters was sadly expanded with the next phase of intense and brutal resource extraction, in particular the infamous rubber years (Ndaywel è Nziem 1998).

A King Dreaming of Adding the Nile Basin to the Congo Colony

King Leopold II's Congo Free State was the largest private property in modern times. Being his own spin doctor, the king managed, amid scenes of enthusiasm in the Western world, to rally support for Livingstone's credo and thus secure for himself the Congo in order to bring Christianity, civilization and commerce to the inhabitants, and furthermore promising to fight slavery and slave traders. In reality, it was a trading- or military-based colony (Reinhard 2011) geared towards first and foremost maximizing profits for its sole owner: the king. The Congo Free State itself was clearly understaffed, and it was a daunting task to colonize and manage the 2.3 million square kilometres. Few imagined, therefore, that Leopold had plans for immense territorial expansions beyond this. In secret the king revealed to the Belgian prime minister that the glory of his career would be to include Sudan, the Red Sea coast, Eritrea and Egypt in his empire and become the pharaoh of Egypt (Daye 1934: 413).

From the Emin Pasha Relief Expedition in 1887 and via the Van Kerckhoven expedition in 1891, the push towards the Nile was a dominating factor in Leopold's colonial ambitions. As Belgian losses to disease and war threatened to expose what was a hidden agenda, the administration started recruiting Scandinavians: first by transferring those already in service in the Free State and from 1886–87 through comprehensive recruitment campaigns in Scandinavia (Jenssen-Tusch 1902–5). About 180 Scandinavian medical doctors, officers, judges and sailors were attached to the offensive in the northeast.[18] There was an attempt at recruiting 500 Swedish soldiers in 1890 but apparently the Swedish government regarded this as too delicate an undertaking, as both France and Great Britain had geopolitical interests in the region.[19] The offensive in the northeast needed more weapon makers like Hansen, which led to the recruitment of twenty-five Swedish experts, travelling in small groups not to attract attention (Collins 1968: 168).

The Congo Free State's war against Zanzibari slave traders and the Batetela rebellion, described below, probably increased the number of Scandinavians in the Congo/Uganda/Sudan border areas to between 250 and 300. As the expansion was prepared on the ground and offensives were launched in the Congo, Hansen's collection became the first in a stream of artefacts from northeastern and eastern Congo and southern Sudan that reached Scandinavian museums at a period in which collections from other geographical areas had started to saturate the market for ethnographica.[20]

While the world economy was expanding during colonialism, hundreds of thousands of Norwegians were in dire straits at home and consequently emigrated (mainly to the United States) or ended up as international migrant workers. They established themselves worldwide as traders, plantation managers, trappers, bankers, farmers, accountants, insurance agents, custom officers, marine pilots, judges, medical doctors, officers and missionaries – just to mention a few of the professions turning up in the files of our museums (and exemplified in articles in this volume). The Congo Free State was, in spite of inherent dangers, an interesting labour market for a number of Scandinavians. Congo was a free state: individuals, companies and states could freely engage in trade and export without tax barriers.

The first Scandinavians in the Congo reported in public speeches, papers and magazines about extraordinarily rich natural resources and the 'willingness of the Congo Negro to engage in trade' (Fuglede 1918). Denmark and Sweden-Norway took part in the Berlin conference of 1884–85, with a view to the economic potentials (Martini and Schønberg 1890; Tygesen and Wæhle 2007; Yngfalk 2005). The Norwegian government wanted to promote trade and shipping in the wake of colonialism and announced international trade scholarships.[21] One of the applicants, Johannes Scharffenberg, dreamed of establishing a trading house in the Congo. Like others who worked in the Congo, he also tried to make a business out of selling ethnographic artefacts.

An Entrepreneur with a Trading House in Matadi, Congo

Engineer Johannes Scharffenberg (1864–99) was one of the early Norwegian sailors in the Congo (Wæhle 2008). In general, mariners have left little documentation of their experiences in colonial service, compared to missionaries, officers and judges. Scharffenberg not only stands out because he conveyed detailed information on trading opportunities, river traffic and ethnographic descriptions; his position in early Congo colonial history is also rare because he publicly described and denounced the atrocities he saw and exposed the true nature of the 'philanthropic' undertaking of the Congo Free State. Starting as an engineer for SAB, Scharffenberg went on to head the SAB workshop and yard at Kinshasa outside Leopoldville and was for a time one of the main recruiters of Norwegian sailors to the Congo (Godøy 2010). When Scharffenberg arrived for his first term in 1889, the initial exploration of the territory was finished and he thus joined the early phase of exploitation: servicing steamers that brought soldiers, weaponry and trade goods to the interior and that shipped the first riches, like ivory, copal, corn, caoutchouc and palm oil, for export to Europe (Lederer 1965).

The documentation accompanying his collections at the University Museum of Bergen and the Museum of Cultural History in Oslo reflect how widely these early sailors travelled in the immense Congolese territory.[22] The original Scharffenberg collection may have been more varied and complex than what is reflected in the Bergen holdings. Director Gabriel Gustafsen made a strict selection among the artefacts offered and used the Scharffenberg collection to supplement what was already bought. The correspondence between Scharffenberg and Gustafsen clearly reflects that the director had the upper hand in negotiations and could dictate his own terms as to which artefacts he desired and at what price. In all, Gustafsen bought 78 artefacts from Scharffenberg. Shortly before Gustafsen had acquired 151 objects from the Danish sea captain Rasmus Christian Andersen. Proudly presenting the Andersen collection in 1893, Gustafsen stressed that it was from an area that had received much attention in the preceding years, thanks to explorers like Livingstone, Cameron and Stanley. Further, he mentioned the founding of the Congo Free State and also the colonial pursuit of the French and the Germans. The Andersen collection was the first from this significant area, and in Gustafsen's opinion among the most attractive in the museum (Bergens Museum 1894: 55–56).[23] Newly acquired Congo collections were immediately put on display – the museum's protocols suggest that years passed before the acquisition entries and proper cataloguing took place. Scharffenberg obviously had a larger collection than the selection he offered the Bergen museum. Museum protocols in Germany, Belgium and Scandinavia reveal that several Scandinavians tried to sell collections, or parts of them, to museums outside their native country. When the estate of Scharffenberg was put up for auction in 1899, the Ethnographic Museum in Oslo bought fourteen artefacts. So far, no other trace of his collection has been found.

Scharffenberg had served three terms in the Congo when he received a scholarship in 1896 to establish a trading house and market Norwegian goods.[24] With his wife, Anna (née Siewerts), he built the first stone house in the port of Matadi on the lower Congo River and launched La Société Norvegienne au Congo. Scharffenberg expected that when the railroad in progress replaced the caravan route from Matadi to Kinshasa, the economic opportunities would increase significantly. Before launching the trading house, Scharffenberg gave two public lectures at the Norwegian Geographical Society (Scharffenberg 1896) and interviews in the dailies *Morgenbladet* and *Dagbladet* (Godøy 2010).

The First Rebellion against Colonization Offers an Opportunity for Joseph Conrad

In Scharffenberg's Congo lectures at the Norwegian Geographical Society, the killing of the Danish sea captain Johannes H.F.F. Freiesleben was casually intertwined in the narrative. This is notable for several reasons. First of all, it must have been a shocking experience for Scharffenberg himself, only twenty-six years old, to witness the captain of the ship he was sailing on being killed. Today we can add that it was notable because in the history of the colonization of the Congo, Freiesleben was the very first European killed in an uprising against the intruders. And finally, it is also notable because when Freiesleben died, SAB company director Albert Thys reluctantly accepted a mariner that later would become famous for describing the horror during the Congo Free State years: Joseph Conrad.[25]

Freiesleben lost his life in the village 'Tchumbiri of the Bajenshi people',[26] and Scharffenberg introduced the episode with a surprising remark: 'I will briefly recount this episode as a proof of how easy you can end up in a war – against your own will' (1896: 66). Scharffenberg's contemporaries among Scandinavian mariners regularly detailed attacking villages, revenge attacks and uprisings, setting ablaze whole communities, pilfering food and shooting at villagers displaying aggressive behaviour against the colonial intruders. As Blom (2006) has noted, the diaries or writings of the sailors have a striking lack of opinion or protest relating to the many unwarranted and meaningless incidents they participated in. In Sigfried Duhst's diary, for example, one entry read: '15th of March. Left Bangala together with SS *Stanley* [Duhst was on board SS *Ville de Gand*] to wage war in different localities' (quoted in Blom 2006: 90). Although similar cases in point from the late 1880s and early 1890s are found in the writings of Amdrup (1888–90, published in Wæhle 2010), Kit and Will (1891), Jenssen-Tusch (1902–5) and Schønberg and Martini (1890), none of them demonstrate a level of reflection similar to Scharffenberg.

On 28 January 1890 Scharffenberg and Captain Freiesleben were heading for Stanley Falls aboard SS *Florida*. They landed in Tshumbiri to secure provisions for the fifty-man crew and themselves. When members of the crew went ashore, they ended up in a fight with the chief of Tshumbiri, and one was wounded. Arriving to investigate the incident, Freiesleben and Scharffenberg received the following explanation: 'I don't want any strangers in my village. You have probably arrived here to plunder, return to your vessel or you will all be killed' (quoted in Scharffenberg 1896: 67). The conflict escalated as Freiesleben and Scharffenberg demanded compensation. They took the chief captive and headed for the steamer. Along the way the *Florida* crew was attacked. Freiesleben was killed on the spot, while a wounded Scharffenberg managed to flee to the steamer after killing the chief with his revolver. When the Bajenshi had reloaded their muzzle-loading guns, the crew was already guarding *Florida* with their modern breech-loading rifles until the engine produced enough steam to leave the shore. One month later the Congo Free State sent soldiers to attack the village, several men were taken prisoners and the houses were set ablaze (Scharffenberg 1896: 66–68).

A Trading House Owner with Sharp Criticism of the Congo Free State

Today it may seem both false and paradoxical to simultaneously express deep sympathy for the Congolese and launch strong criticism against the colonial system while at the same time preparing for business in the Congo Free State, as Scharffenberg did. However, like many of his contemporaries, Scharffenberg was convinced that trade was key to assisting the Congolese in development. He condemned the policies and practices, but he still believed in a more humane form of colonialism. Scharffenberg continued his lecture with some quite remarkable comments compared to other reports from the Congo in 1896. Starting with a reminder of how Europeans for three hundred years had enslaved the Congolese, he continued to describe the labour policies and recruitment in the Congo Free State, which he regarded as a new form of slavery. In his view the main motive of the government of the Free State was to transfer its riches to Europe and to create as high a profit as possible. The most famous of similar reporting from the field is the 1903 report of the British consul to the Free State, Roger Casement (Ó Síocháin and O'Sullivan 2003; Ó Síocháin 2007), and those of the Swedish Baptist missionary Edvard Vilhelm Sjöblom ([1907] 2003), who started reporting in the early 1890s (see Hochschild [1998] 1999).[27]

As Nancy Rose Hunt (2002) has pointed out, one-sided terror narratives from the Congo tend to depict those who participated in the colonial project as a single social category, excluding us from exploring some of the individuals who, like Scharffenberg, came away with an insightful analysis and thorough critique of the form of colonial exploitation that took place. Importantly, Scharffenberg also depicted the Congolese resistance to colonization. We can thus see the Congolese as agents, sometimes offering resistance to the colonization and violent exploitation of their lands.

After a few years, Scharffenberg's business in Matadi was in financial trouble.[28] In 1899 his wife, Anna, left for Norway to look for more capital. One month later Johannes Scharffenberg died after a spell of malaria. During her stay in Kinshasa, Anna had already experienced the death of her brother, SAB engineer Axel Siewers, who was twenty-two years old (Coosemans 1958). Now her husband was dead at thirty-five. The trading house was thereafter liquidated.

The explanation for the demise of the trading house may be found outside Scharffenberg's business. A peculiar credit system made it almost impossible to retrieve money from customers (Godøy 2010). In addition, it is likely that Scharffenberg's denouncement of the Congo

Free State's economic policies led the colonial administration to create difficulties for him. This is a strategy that is well-known, in particular, from the case of Nigerian trader A. Shanu, who was instrumental in providing information to the British Consul Roger Casement and his investigations on the abuse of the Congolese and to E.D. Morel (Ó Síocháin 2007; Vellut 2005), the leading campaigner against the atrocities in the Congo. King Leopold II and a few of his allies devised an ingenious system of chartered companies and large concession companies, establishing a number of secret decrees with a single goal: to prevent all forms of competition. In violation of the General Act of the Berlin conference, obstacles and discriminatory practices were systematically put into place. Protectionism and a state monopoly made the Congo Free State the most profitable colony ever: only the king and a few helpers reaped the rewards. The system was a catastrophe for small Western entrepreneurs like the Scharffenbergs, and the administration further imposed devastating measures on the economic opportunities for the Congolese: local and long-distance trade was curbed. All areas except cultivated land were declared state property. In another decree, all natural produce was defined as belonging to the state. A monopolistic 'Free State', enforced labour, hostage taking, killings and other methods created widespread suffering and death but increased profits in the harvesting of the Congo's natural resources (Ndaywel è Nziem 1998).

Collecting in the Upper Uele River under a Shroud of Secrecy

When the Danish gun maker F. Hansen, who offered a collection to the Bergen Museum in 1893, arrived in the Congo in 1890, his travel and tasks were shrouded in deep secrecy. Shortly after returning to Copenhagen from the Congo, Hansen also presented his arduous expedition in a well-orchestrated newspaper article[29] (see also Lotar 1937; Jenssen-Tusch 1902–5), associating himself with what had been described as significant world events. Much has been published on King Leopold II's greed for profits and how this came to dominate colonial policies in the Congo, but there was one exception: the king would not 'let good business interfere with his Nile quest' (Collins 1968: 145). This aspect of Congo history is rarely examined but is fundamental in understanding why there are so many ethnographic collections from the northeastern Congo in Scandinavian museums. The Van Kerckhoven expedition was King Leopold II's early contribution to the Fashoda crisis – the 'Cuba crisis' of high imperialism that had been underway for years. In July

1898 it peaked when a group of French soldiers, under the command of Major Jean-Baptiste Marchand, arrived in Fashoda (today Kodok) on the White Nile with the intent of forcing the British out of Sudan and Egypt and gaining control of the strategic Nile River. A British flotilla under the command of Sir Herbert Kitchner arrived to face the French while the situation was negotiated in Paris and London. In November the British won a diplomatic victory, and the ensuing agreement marked the borders between French and British spheres of influence in that part of Africa (Levering Lewis 1987; Pakenham 2002).

Hansen was the first Scandinavian hired for an expedition, unprecedented in the Congo Free State when it came to staffing and equipment (Gilliaert et al. 1952). The notorious Guillaume Van Kerckhoven headed the secret thrust to seize border areas between present-day Sudan, Uganda and DR Congo and to plant the Congo Free State flag along the Nile River (Collins 1968). Together with Stanley, Van Kerckhoven had already participated in the dubious river expedition (1879–84) in which local chiefs ceded their sovereignty to King Leopold II's International African Association. Van Kerckhoven may have introduced the idea ultimately giving the Congo Free State property rights to soil not occupied by the Congolese (the *terre vacante* ideology, assuming that all land outside village bounds were unused and thus to be regarded as state property). This decree and later ones meant that the Congolese were in reality trespassers and poachers when harvesting, fishing and hunting in areas surrounding their villages.

Hansen started his newspaper report by providing information on the punishing of rebellious Congolese, stressing also his participation in avenging the death of Freiesleben.[30] After sailing up the Congo and Itimbiri Rivers, the expedition continued overland through dense rain forest. From here on there is no doubt about the nature of the expedition: a Belgian geographer simply described their violent approach as an epidemic (A.J. Wauters, quoted in Levering Lewis 1987). As the expedition approached the Uele River, the rain forest was replaced by gallery forest, and they arrived in one of the many sultanates in northeastern Congo:

> We received a royal reception as all Sultan Djabir's soldiers were on parade and fired a salute. The Sultan was presented with costly gifts such as guns, gunpowder, pearls, watches, silk etc. In exchange, the expedition received one ton of ivory and large amounts of provisions. While King Leopold had promised to eradicate slavery, this was forgotten when a strategic alliance with a slave trader was instrumental in his strategies to expand the colonial territory. (Hansen 1894)[31]

Halting Zanzibari Expansion that Threatened the Colonial Project

As the expedition left Djabir, a war of conquest under the disguise of exploration and expedition was initiated (Ndaywel è Nziem 1998). Hansen's account mixed ethnographic observations on forms of dwellings, clothing, weapons and agriculture with reports on how the expedition either waged war or managed to forge further alliances with local chiefs or sultans. He associated himself with the achievements of the Van Kerckhoven expedition, failing to mention that he was detached from the expedition for long periods. For a while he was left behind as head of the Angu station in the Makua zone, and later he was sent all the way to the Atlantic coast to recover from illness. The push to the Nile took seventeen months after Djabir. The expedition was busy establishing a rudimentary administration and presence in a vast territory. Posts were established in Bima, Bomokandi, Amadi, Niangara, Dungu, Angu and Surur. Simultaneously, it was essential to gather intelligence on the whereabouts, nature and activities of competing forces in the northeast. On several occasions the expedition met heavy armed resistance.

The Congo Free State had impressive competitors in the scramble for riches and strategic positions along the Uele: the area had for ages been raided by slave and ivory hunters from the Nile valley and the Chad systems (Levering Lewis 1987). Some Congolese associates of Sudanese trading empires converted to Islam and started their own operations. These became known as sultans, and they increased in number after the 1881 Mahdi revolt blocked export opportunities along the Nile. The Mahdists waged holy war against the Anglo-Egyptian rule in Sudan and ruled large parts of Sudan until 1899. As the Van Kerckhoven expedition continued northeast, they met yet another challenging force: slave and ivory traders from Zanzibar (Northrup 1988).[32] In the largest battle at the confluence of the Uele and Bomokandi Rivers, 1,800 Zanzibaris and their allies were killed and 250 taken prisoner, and ivory worth 1 million gold francs was confiscated. After this so-called Bomokandi battle, the Zanzibaris retreated to their well-established base in Riba-Riba, west of Lake Tanganyika. Their attempt at expanding into the northeast was effectively halted by the Van Kerckhoven expedition. As long as they did not threaten King Leopold II's ambitions for the Nile, they continued for a while as strategic allies in the eastern Congo, most prominently represented by Tippu Tip (also known as Hamed ben Hamed ben Juma Marjebbi), the slave trader that the king named colonial governor of Stanleyville (Kisangani). How Tippu

Tip and his sons built personal relations with the Scandinavians can be seen both in the University Museum of Bergen and other ethnographic collections.[33]

A King's Megalomania and the Geopolitics of the Nile Basin

Leaving the Uele River, the expedition continued along the tributary Kibali. In what is today northwestern Uganda, Van Kerckhoven died from an accidental shot during an attack. A few days later Captain Milz, second in command, led the expedition as they arrived at Fort Albert on the Nile in 1892. Here they forged an alliance with the Egyptian soldiers of Emin Pasha and managed to build four stations and link two thousand Makraka people to the garrison.[34] For a while, King Leopold II had managed to gain a foothold in southern Sudan and northwestern Uganda. The newspaper article on Hansen ended with a note that the task was now accomplished. Although the Mahdists soon drove the Congo troops out of Sudan, the king's megalomania proved unstoppable. Analysing the tactical moves of King Leopold II, one gains a perspective on the Fashoda incident (1894) in southern Sudan, where the British and French were pitted against each other: if they had gone to war in Africa, it would most certainly have led to war in Europe.

> [T]he 'race to Fashoda' ... has generally been considered little more than an historical footnote, it is in fact one of the great galvanic moments of the last century, a cynosure of the imperial energies of several European states and (ignored by both African and European students) an equally energizing moment in the defensive strategies of several African states. ... [T]hey set in motion a vast international and interracial drama. (Levering Lewis 1987: xi)

Levering Lewis sums up by stating that the incident was 'a piñata of previously unexplored facts, motives, and ramifications' (1987: xiii).

After some four months at home, Hansen wrote a letter to the colonial administration in Brussels demanding to know what plans the colonial administration had for his collection (underlined three times).[35] He suggested an auction in Boma (at that time the capital of the Congo Free State) so that he could receive payment. He further insisted on being reinstalled in service, this time as an engineer on a steamer. Hansen's letter has an intriguing form. Between the lines he admits having done something wrong, but he also wishes to return to the Congo. It was possibly his lack of training in French that makes the style what one today would describe as current French, as opposed to the bureaucratic and intricate official French of colonial times. While he may have seen his writing as direct and it may have been replete with unintended clumsiness, the administration probably read it as blunt and provocative.[36] At any rate, his Congo career was at an end; his career continued abroad, in Thailand, Singapore and Vietnam.[37]

After examining documents on Hansen's collection, it was startling to learn that there were no objects in the store.[38] The explanation for this was buried deep in the Belgian colonial archives in an 1893 document titled 'Punishment'. Here it was revealed that the administration withheld one month's salary and declared Hansen noneligible for the decoration l'Etoile de Service. Hansen was characterized as undisciplined and brutal. He could only achieve results by threats and was unable to lead African soldiers. The document goes on to state that his boss disliked him and that he had operated outside the control and command of his superiors. The only positive remark is that he was a skilful gunsmith. There had been an official enquiry into an alleged killing of a black man 'without legitimate reasons'. Instead of awaiting further documents on the suspected murder, the administration decided to send Hansen back to Denmark. Apart from artefacts belonging to the Ethnographic Collection of the National Museum in Copenhagen, no trace of Hansen's artefacts in European collections has been found. Hansen's collection may have been incorporated into the collection of a Belgian officer or bought by traders searching the Antwerp harbours for goods.[39]

Further Collecting Linked to the Quest for Expanding into the Nile Valley

Archives and protocols in museums in Denmark, Finland, Norway and Sweden reflect the many Scandinavians engaged in the offensives towards the Nile valley. The northeast of Congo and parts of southern Sudan and western Uganda are well represented in the Central African collections. In the following, some examples from the University Museum of Bergen are presented.

In 1901 a collection of thirty-eight daggers, knives, swords and spears from engineer A.J. Johannesen from Laksevåg (a borough of Bergen) reached the Bergen museum.[40] Johannesen left for the Congo in 1899 (Jenssen-Tusch 1902–5; Lederer 1965). A part of his collection is mentioned as coming from Mangola – probably a misspelling of Mongala, a tributary of the Congo River and an important transport route for the offensive towards the northeast. There is scant information on this engineer, but he was in the Congo twice. There are indications that he participated in the arduous transport of sixteen hundred parts for a river steamer all the way from the Atlantic coast to the Redjaf station on the Nile: on the fourteenth anniversary of the Congo Free State the steamer was launched and baptized SS *Vankerckhovenville*. Johannesen sold a few pieces from Redjaf to Bergen.[41]

The museum also houses a collection of sixty objects from the officer Daniel Schumann Krüger. He served both in the Congo Free State and in the Belgian Congo, after King Leopold II relinquished control of the Free State. In the archives of the Norwegian Congo Veterans Association in the National Library in Oslo, there is mostly information on Krüger's complaints about not receiving a pension from Belgium (he lacked a few weeks of service).[42] Krüger arrived in the Congo for the first time in 1905 and again in 1909 and served for eight and a half years total. Only the protocols in Bergen document that he was part of the offensive towards the Nile, particularly in the collections from the Aruwimi district and from the Mangbetu people.[43]

For years King Leopold II orchestrated a frenetic and exhausting diplomatic campaign trying to drive in a wedge as Britain, Anglo-Egyptian Sudan, the Mahdists, France, Russia, Ethiopia and Germany struggled and competed to control the upper Nile. In 1894 the British agreed to a lease of parts of southern Sudan and northwestern Uganda: the so-called Lado enclave. During his campaigns in the northeast, Leopold (from the 1890s to his death in 1908) assembled the largest concentration of troops in colonial Africa, after the war between Britain and the Boers. Troops and workers, some under Scandinavian command, were busy establishing firewood posts for steamers, building bridges and roads, and extending and expanding the network of colonial posts and stations – with a view to further expansion along the Nile (see figure 14.2).

As the military and colonial apparatus in the Congo grew steadily stronger, the opportunity arose in 1892–95 to drive the Zanzibari out. This campaign is known as the only war Belgium ever won (Catherine 1994). The Zanzibaris represented fierce competition and finally provided King Leopold II with an opportunity to demonstrate that he was fighting slavery. The Congo Free State forces were better equipped, but it took a long time to overcome the many pockets of resistance. Local Congolese suffered under the Sudanese, sultanate, Mahdist, Zanzibari and Free State forces – and yet in the short periods in between the series of offensives they could enjoy short-lived pockets of power vacuum. 'Foreigners have always deceived us', a Mangbetu chief commented at the time:

> We have been the prey in succession to the Zandes, the Turks, and the Arabs. Are the whites worth more? No, beyond doubt. But whatever they are, our territory is today freed from the presence of any foreigners, and

Figure 14.2. The artillery of the Congo Free State was the largest in colonial Africa. *Source:* Photo album made by Martin Engh in author's possession, received as a gift from his son, Ole Engh, and to be deposited in the National Archives of Norway; reproduced with permission.

> to introduce another would be an act of cowardice. I do not wish to be a slave to anyone, and I will fight the whites. (Boulger 1925: 2:197, quoted in Levering Lewis 1987: 69)

Widespread warfare and fighting continued. As the follow-up expedition to Van Kerckhoven's expedition was about to enter southern Sudan in 1895 and expand the few and small Free State positions, the Congolese troops started a mutiny. They managed to seize large amounts of weapons and ammunitions. The uprising, called the Batetela rebellion, against Baron Dhanis's expedition ended King Leopold II's dream of expansion. Instead of securing a foothold in southern Sudan, Free State officers and troops had to engage in four years of fighting in the eastern part of the colony to quell the rebellion. When the Batetela rebellion was at an end, it was too late to present further claims on the Nile valley.

Collecting: Always a Crucial Part of Colonial Encounters

Artefacts collected in the distant Congo could be converted to economic profit – or donations, which equalled prestige in the academic world and contributed to building Norway as a nation. And yet such factors only partly explain why collecting took place. In the Congo, artefacts may have served to open eyes, minds and doors: artefacts came to be an opportunity to be introduced to and culturally socialized in a foreign and challenging world. In short, they acted as a way to navigate a range of Congolese orders. Apart from being commodities, artefacts were a means to create colonial meetings, relations and confrontations and also functioned as heuristic devices in colonial service.

As Hansen was steaming home after his expedition, the next contingent of Scandinavians was heading south to join the push for the northeast. Swedish officer Axel Svinhufvud offers a glimpse into the practical importance of understanding Congolese material culture and exchanges, and thus suggests that field collecting continued to be of crucial importance even as the market opportunities in Scandinavia waned. As Svinhufvud had dinner one night, along the Uele, a large number of Congolese with spears and shields appeared out of the dark. Svinhufvud reached for his revolver, but the leader of his crew intervened: the strangers arrived as guests and merely wanted to greet the white man. Watching him closely as he ate, they parted after having been presented with the appropriate gifts – or *pamba,* as the Swede later wrote (Svinhufvud 1942: 105).⁴⁴

In big pompous ceremonies, as with Hansen's introduction to Sultan Djabir, or the modest Uele encounter for Svinhufvud, colonial encounters were characterized by intricate forms of social, political, religious or material modes of exchange, most often through elaborate ceremonies and rituals (Fabian 1998; Roberts 2013). In the sources we learn how the Scandinavians soon realized what the local currencies were (cotton, brass rods, copper crosses, cartridges or gunpowder for hunting, cigarettes or, glass pearls) or how even waste could become a resource: Svinhufvud mentioned that used bottles were highly popular among local people in the Uele region. In the Museum of Ethnography in Stockholm we find a beautiful harp, Chief Musere's farewell present to Svinhufvud, while a photograph in Svinhufvud's book (1942) documents the proud Mangbetu chief wearing the officer's pyjamas. After arrival in Africa we see that Scandinavians gained insight in how alliances and trust could be built through exchanges, and how knowledge could be acquired.

In most forms of colonial encounters artefacts were changing hands: 'Objects were consistently used, along with verbal exchange to challenge, placate, seduce and test each other, not only in friendly encounters, but in the brandishing of weapons, the firings of guns and the extending of a green branch in peace' (Henare 2005: 35). Although there are museum artefacts documented as having been robbed or confiscated, this was not sustainable: 'Trade and gift giving were also crucial ethnographic methodologies, allowing extended periods of interaction, examination of each other's practices, material culture and beliefs, and the sharing of food and entertainment' (Henare 2005: 36).

Field Collecting as a Heuristic Device

It is evident that artefacts and the collection of them was useful for the Scandinavian official while in the field. We have already seen how Hansen announced the provenance of his collection: 'Djabbir, Ababua, Niam Niam, Mobanka, Mambuttus, Tikke Tikke (the dwarf people), Momfu, Tangamonanki, Mengsje'. Put in other terms, he was listing artefacts from important places like Djabir (Bondo in DR Congo) and Tangamonangi (in Uganda). He mentioned the following peoples: Boa (Ababua), Azande (Niam-Niam), Banza (Mobaka, Mobanka), Mangbetu (Mambuttus), Pygmies (Tikke Tikke) and Mamvu (Momfu). These groups can still be found in the corner where the Central African Republic, DR Congo, Sudan and Uganda meet. Hansen's collection is a sign of the many ethnic groups and language families that are scattered along the Uele: Bantu, Ubangian, Central Sudanic and Nilotic. The collection further covers a vast range of political organizations, from stateless societies (Pygmies) and hereditary chiefdoms (Banza), via house societies or big-man societies (Momvu), to the Uele's forms of kingdoms (Mangbetu), empire builders (Azande) and enslaving sultanates (Djabir). Hansen's collection is thus a mental map covering the complex ethnical, political and societal variation in the Uele region. For the young Scandinavians in the Congo, artefacts were 'good to think with' (Fabian 1998), serving as pegs of memory when mapping and understanding a complex landscape of military, political and ethnographic factors (for a similar argument on German-speaking expeditions, see Fabian 1998).

Congo Free State decrees were issued aiming at monopolizing trade in ethnographica, while other decrees sought to channel the artefacts into Belgian collections (Vangroenweghe 2005). However, little was done to enforce these policies, and any attempt would have been difficult. The trade in ethnographic items was exceptionally dynamic and well established, as was trade in daily objects, tools, magical instruments and medicine in Central Africa in precolonial times. Thus, the Europeans did not initiate such exchanges; they joined, expanded and changed an existing market according to their particular interests and needs. In the restricting economic policies of the Congo Free State, trade in ethnographic artefacts was more or less the only unrestrained and free economic strategy available to the Congolese (Wæhle 2000). The incoming colonizers saw many reasons to make purchases of local artefacts. Early on the Congolese started providing goods reflecting the ideas, fascinations and desires of the incoming customers and soon learnt to forge aging and use in newly produced items (Wæhle 2000). There was a considerable market in the Western world for what initially was part of local religious, political, social and practical needs in the colony (Fabian 1998; Harms 1981; Schildkrout and Keim 1998; Wæhle 2000).

Colonial Entrepreneurship Leading to Collections for Research and Display

Ethnographic collections have mainly been studied as part of scientific museum collecting, documentation in evolutionary and cultural historic schemes or as examples of how the budding ethnographic museums represented the cultures of colonized regions. Sailors and travellers had for ages brought souvenirs and memorabilia from faraway places, but the intensity and drive of such efforts exploded in the latter parts of the 1800s. During the final race for colonies, demand for foreign artefacts reached an all-time high: from the 1870s to the 1930s enormous amounts of artefacts ended up in museums (O'Hanlon and Welsch 2001).

There are more than a few explanations for this development: the same time period is when scientific disciplines were created and diversified and museums became central research institutions and laboratories. The need for collections for research and display within geography, ethnography and cultural history coincided with a colonial expansion accompanied by unprecedented economic growth and prospects for entrepreneurship. Modern mass communications (postal boat services, telegraphs, newspapers and magazines) brought explorations and colonization close to an emergent public, and museum displays offered authentic 'closeness' to famous explorers and native peoples recently discovered by the West. For colonial powers, ethnographic museums also became handy display windows to rally support and understanding and to highlight the 'primitive nature' of foreign peoples and the need for 'civilisation by way of colonialism and commerce' (Wastiau 2000).

Notes

Heartfelt thanks for inspiration to all in the 'In the Wake of Colonialism' project. Special thanks to Sonja Inselset, Inger-Alice L. Loftesnes, Knut M. Rio and

Frode Storås at the University Museum of Bergen; Kirsten Alsaker Kjerland and Bjørn Enge Bertelsen at the former Unifob Global; Jesper Kurt-Nielsen, Bodil Valentiner and Anne Bahnson at the Ethnographic Collection of the National Museum of Denmark in Copenhagen; Bert Blom in Elsinore, Denmark; Lilian Nielsen in Wezembeek-Oppem, Belgium; Pierre Dandoy from the African Archives, Brussels; Bjørn Are Godøy and Elisabeth Solvang Koren in Oslo; and Marie-Laure Legouy in Høvik.

1. See Godøy (2010); Hochschild ([1998] 1999); Morel (1906); Ndaywel è Nziem (1998); Nelson (1994); Northrup (1988); Tygesen and Wæhle (2007); and Vangroenweghe (2005).
2. In international sources, Norwegian colonial agents are listed under the generic term 'Scandinavians' – no distinction is made between 'Scandinavians' (Denmark, Norway, Sweden) and the 'Nordic countries' (Denmark, Faroe Islands, Finland, Greenland, Norway, the Saami areas, Sweden and Åland Island).
3. I focus on sources from the 1870s to the 1930s. Later sources include business archives, missionary activities, contingents of United Nations soldiers and nongovernmental organization interventions – such sources are still arriving. A recent Danish book examines writings on the Congo, including lesser-known Danish texts, and demonstrates the colonial roots of representation and its perpetuation and differentiation today (Andersen 2010).
4. Collections and accompanying documentation may also help to better understand Congolese resistance to the European and 'Arabic' scramble for resources and slaves, but this aspect is not treated here.
5. The Bergen Museum was founded in 1825 and became a part of the founding of the University of Bergen in 1946.
6. R. C. Andersen's collection, BME 563–65, BME.
7. Schønberg was Danish, Martini was born while his Danish parents worked in Norway. After Martini worked in the Congo Norwegian authorities acknowledged him as Norwegian. He was seen as a Danish citizen in Denmark.
8. After Denmark had to cede Norway to Sweden in 1814, Danish writing conventions continued to be the rule in Norway, as well as for some time after independence from Sweden in 1905. At the time of the Congo Free State and later, books on the Congo for the Norwegian market were mainly published in Danish.
9. In Kristiania there were two pre-1800 Congo raffia cushions stemming from the royal treasure collections in Copenhagen. A missionary and a sea captain provided the next few items. Bergen had no Congo artefacts prior to 1892.
10. *Nordstjernen,* 1889.
11. The Bakongo lives, and has historically lived, in an area that is today covered by DR Congo, The Republic of Congo, Angola and the Angolan enclave Cabinda, north of the mouth of the Congo River.
12. One of Schildkrout's PhD students has pointed out that the figure cited was not a quantification, but was meant to illustrate the magnitude of the trade (Martin Skrydstrup, personal communication, Seoul, South Korea, August

2006). Schildkrout's term is 'Congolese art', excluding a range of the arte-facts in museums and collections. But even if we restrict the figure to what many scholars describe as African art, the estimate is still too low.

13. Norwegian museums continued to acquire a few Congo artefacts, such as offers from collectors with a particular link to the city. Increasingly, dona-tions became more important than purchases. For many Congo collectors and their relatives, prestige could be as convincing as cash, and artefacts from the Congo Free State and the early decades of the Belgian Congo con-tinued to arrive in museums until the 1950s.

14. All translations are the author's own unless otherwise noted.

15. Letter from F. Hansen, dated Copenhagen 21st December 1893, to Bergen Museum, BME.

16. Aquisition Protocol, 1912, NMD.

17. The figures are based on Jenssen-Tusch (1902–5), Tell (2005) and Morgen-stierne (2002), as well as documentation in the Scandinavian ethnographic museums and archive materials in Oslo, Copenhagen and Brussels.

18. The figures are based on Holm (1987), Jenssen-Tusch (1902–5), Lotar (1946), Svinhufvud (1942) and acquisition protocols in ethnographic museums in Bergen, Oslo, Copenhagen, Stockholm and Helsinki.

19. Letter, accompanied with one newspaper clipping, from Consul General H.H. von Schwerin for Sweden-Norway referring to non-confirmed news on the five hundred soldiers. Letter no 1036, to the Administrator General of the Colonial Office in Brussels, dated July 22nd 1890. Consulats et lega-tions. Consulats de L'Etat Independent du Congo dans les pays etrangers, AE 154 (223), BMFA.

20. How colonial archives may have biased our understanding of colonial-ism has been discussed in Dirks (2002) and in the introduction to Stoler, McGranahan and Perdue (2007). The many Scandinavian ethnographic col-lections from northeastern Congo and southern Sudan and accompanying documentation are sources that may contribute to a fuller understanding of this particular offensive as part of the colonization of the Congo and southern Sudan. This material may potentially also be an inroad to study local societies and their history.

21. See Angell (this volume) on the nature of conflicts and Norwegian inde-pendence initiatives within the Swedish-Norwegian union.

22. In Oslo the collection is housed in the Ethnographic Collection, which is part of the Museum of Cultural History of the University of Oslo. When established in 1857, the then Ethnographic Museum was also part of the university, normally it was referred to as being part of the Historic Mu-seum, which was actually the name of the building and not an organiza-tional level.

23. The third Dane to contact the Bergen Museum was the son of Christian Schønberg; he took up contact while his father was serving another term in the Congo.

24. Scharffenberg's application and other documents related to the scholarship are to be found in: S-1125 Indredep., A ktr Serie E, Hyllenr. 3A 131 2/4, Eske 0038 Søknader om 'kommersielle stipendier', 1896–97, Folder: Afrika, RA.

25. While Blom (2006) has done a detective's work to locate sources linking Conrad and Danish mariners, he has not, however, included the full description of the only European eyewitness to Freiesleben's death: Johannes Scharffenberg, whose first term in Africa, 1889–91, coincided with Conrad's short stay in the Congo (see Wæhle 2008).

26. It is somewhat unclear which group of people he is referring to, as the terms the Congo travellers used do not always easily translate to contemporary terms. Today the Batiene people live around Kwamouth and the Kwa River's confluence with the Congo River, and they are linguistically related to the Bayansi/Bayanzi – hence the reference to Bajenshi by Scharffenberg.

27. Another fascinating example is Jacobsen's (2010, 2012) story on Daniel J. Danielson (1871–1916) from the Faroe Islands. Danielson assisted Roger Casement during his Congo journey and was the first to organize mass meetings on the atrocities in the Congo in the United Kingdom, meetings that eventually resulted in the Congo Reform Association in 1904.

28. Hartvig Thån: 1946 letter to Bernt Ludvig Hedemark, NBO Ms.fol. 2588 1939–1946, Correspondance, NCVA.

29. Frederik Ferdinand Hansen: 'Dansk Kongofarer', supplement to the periodical *Nationaltidende* number 6437, Monday morning March 19th 1894.

30. This is the first instance of peculiar and incorrect information in the article. Hansen describes avenging Freiesleben in Bolobo, which is sixty kilometres north of Tshumbiri. More important is the fact that the punitive expedition launched to take revenge on the killing of Freiesleben took place in March 1890, seven months before Hansen arrived in the Congo. No Bolobo punitive expedition is mentioned in Lotar (1946).

31. Like his fellow Scandinavian colonial officers, Hansen belonged to the first generations that had learned to read and write. Combined with modern communications (telegraph, postal service, magazines, newspapers), this provided a basis for popular interest in the Congo. At this time there were no strict writing conventions yet, especially for foreign terms. While I spell this 'Djabir', as most sources today, Hansen rendered the place as 'Djabbir'. In Hansen's time centres and villages were named after rulers and chiefs; one may thus struggle to find the first important centre they arrived in on a map: Djabir, later known as Bakango, today Bondo.

32. In contemporary sources slave traders are often referred to as 'Arabic'.

33. R.C. Andersen's collection, 1893, ivory horn, spear, BME 563–65, 'Gift to capt. Andersen from the famous Arab trader and chief Hamed Ben Muhammed Marjebi, known as Tippu Tip' (acquisition protocol, University Museum of Bergen). Several similar examples can be found in other Scandinavian collections and in unpublished and published documents.

34. The Emin Pasha Relief Expedition of 1887–89 was the fourth and last African expedition under Stanley's command. While Emin Pasha and others accepted evacuation by Stanley, a contingent of soldiers remained – isolated in southern Sudan, barred from contact to the north and constantly threatened by Mahdist forces.

35. Frederik Ferdinand Hansen, R.M. 657 (865), SPA 10.019 (K 1839), BMFA.

36. Ibid.

37. Based on Frederik Ferdinand Hansen, 1030-001, C.F. Schiöpffes Samlinger vedrørende Danske som officerer i fremmed krigstjeneste 1815–1965, 826–70 boks 43, D.S.O.-I.F.KH Nr. 868 Frederik Ferdinand Hansen, DSA.
38. Due to construction work at the University of Bergen buildings in the area where the stores were situated, it took some time to compare information in ledgers to the actual holdings. Although Hansen never answered the letter from Director Gustafsen ordering a number of objects, we had expected to find the artifacts in the storage.
39. NMD's protocols list a seven-piece collection bought from Hansen's widow in 1912 (1752–57) and a collection of forty-four artefacts bought after his return from the expedition (Gb 529–45, Gc 775–83 and Gd 312–23). A letter (Journ 700/12) listed has since become missing. These artefacts may have been part of Hansen's personal luggage, while the rest awaited a later transport opportunity.
40. A.J. Johannesen's collection, BME 1076112.
41. Based on Jenssen-Tusch (1902–5), Lederer (1965) and A.J. Johannesen's collection, BME 1076–112. A.J. Johannessen was born in Bergen or Laksevåg on 1 March 1860, went to the Congo for the first time on 6 October 1889 and returned home 3 February 1901.
42. Based on Daniel Schumann Krüger, Ms. fol. 2588. II, 1947 NCVA; see also the NCVA for the years 1947–57.
43. D.S. Krüger's collection, BME 2418–76.
44. *Pamba* is the Swahili term for cotton, a common currency in early colonial trade in the Congo.

Archives and Sources Consulted

African Archives, Belgian Ministry of Foreign Affairs (BMFA), Brussels.
Ethnographic section, National Museum of Denmark (Nationalmuseet, NMD), Copenhagen.
Ethnographic section, University Museum of Bergen (Universitetsmuseet i Bergen, BME), Bergen.
Norwegian Congo Veterans Archive, National Library (Norske Kongoveteraners Arkiv, Nasjonalbiblioteket, NCVA), Oslo.
The Central Office of the National Archives of Norway (Riksarkivet, RA), Oslo.
The Danish State Archives (Rigsarkivet, DSA), Copenhagen.

References

Andersen, F. 2010. *Det mørke kontinent? Afrikabilleder i europæiske fortællinger om Congo.* Aarhus: Aarhus Universitetsforlag.
Bassani, E. and M. McLeod (eds). 2000. *African Art and Artefacts in European Collections 1400–1800.* London: British Museum Press.

Bergens Museum. 1894. *Bergens Museums Aarbog for 1893.* Bergen: Bergen Museum.

Blom, B. 2006. *Dagbøger og Breve fra Mørkets Hjerte: Mareridt & Inferno.* Copenhagen: Thorup.

Boulger, D.C. de K. 1925. *The Reign of Leopold II, King of the Belgians and Founder of the Congo State, 1865–09,* 2 vols. London.

Bouquet, M. 1996. *Sans og Samling: Bringing it all back home.* Oslo: Universitetsforlaget.

Catherine, L. 1994. *Manyiema: De Enige Oorlog die België Won.* Antwerp: Hadewicjh.

Collins, R.O. 1968. *King Leopold, England and the Upper Nile, 1899–1909.* New Haven, C.T.: Yale University Press.

Coosemans, M. 1951. *Schönberg (Christian-Victor-Rask),* Biographie Colonial Belge (2). Brussels: Institute Royal Colonial Belge.

———. 1958. *Siewers (Axel),* Biographie Coloniale Belge (5). Brussels: Académie Royale des Sciences Coloniales.

Daye, P. 1934. *Léopold II.* Paris: Arthème Fayard.

Dirks, N.B. 2002. 'Annals of the Archive: Ethnographic Notes on the Sources of History', in B.K. Axel (ed.), *From the Margins: Historical Anthropology and its Futures.* Durham, N.C.: Duke University Press, pp. 47–65.

Fabian, J. 1998. 'Curios and Curiosity: Notes on Reading Torday and Froebenius', in E. Schildkrout and C. Keim (eds), *The Scramble for Art in Central Africa.* Cambridge: Cambridge University Press, pp. 79–108.

Fuglede, N. 1918. *Hvide og Sorte: Oplevelser i Congo.* Copenhagen: E. Jespersens Forlag.

Gilliaert, A., et al. (eds). 1952. *La Force Publique de sa Naissance à 1914: Participation des Militaires à l'Histoire des Premières Années du Congo.* Brussels: Institut Royal Colonial Belge.

Gjessing, G. and M. Krekling Johannessen. 1957. *De Hundre År: Universitetets Etnografiske Museums Historie 1857–1957* [Studies Honouring the Centennial of Universitetets Etnografiske Museum Oslo, 1857–1957]. Oslo: Etnografisk Museum.

Godøy, B. 2010. *Solskinn og Død: Norge og Kong Leopolds Kongo.* Oslo: Scandinavian University Press.

Grootaers, J.-L. (ed.). 2007. *Ubangi: Arts and Culture from the African Heartland.* Brussels: Fonds Mercator.

Harms, R.W. 1981. *River of wealth, river of sorrow. The central Zaïre Basin in the era of the slave and ivory trade, 1500-1891.* New Haven, C.T.: Yale University Press.

Henare, A.J.M. 2005. *Museums, Anthropology and Imperial Exchange.* Cambridge: Cambridge University Press.

Hochschild, A. (1998) 1999. *King Leopold's Ghost: A Story of Greed, Terror and Heroism in Colonial Africa.* London: MacMillan.

Holm, E. 1987. *Dansk Kriger i Kongo.* Egå: Illerup.

Hunt, N.R. 2002. *Rewriting the Soul in Colonial Congo: Flemish Missionaries and Infertility.* Ortelius-lezing 2002. Wassenaar: NIAS; Antwerp: University of Antwerp.

Jacobsen, Ó. 2010. *Dollin: Havnarmaðurin sum broytti heimssøguna – the Faroese who changed history in the Congo*. Tórshavn: Forlagið Tjørnustova.

———. 2012. 'Daniel J. Danielsen (1871–1916): The Faeroese who changed history in the Congo', *Brethren Historical Review*: 8:13-45

Jenssen-Tusch, H. 1902–5. *Skandinaver i Congo. Svenske, Norske og Danske Mænds og Kvinders Virksomhed i den Uavfhengige Congostat*. Copenhagen: Gyldendalske Boghandel – Nordisk Forlag.

Kit and Will [C.A.C. Christensen]. 1891. *Blandt Sorte: Skildringer fra en Rejse i Kongoegnene. Feulleton til 'Sjællands-Posten' og 'Hadslev Avis'*. Ringsted: Ludvig B. Hansens Bogtrykkeri.

Lederer, A. 1965. *Histoire de la Navigation au Congo*. Musée Royal de l'Afrique Centrale – Tervuren, Belgique Annales, Series IN-8°, Sciences Historiques, (2). Tervuren: Musée Royal de l'Afrique Centrale.

Levering Lewis, D. 1987. *The Race to Fashoda: European Colonialism and African Resistance in the Scramble for Africa*. New York: Bloomsbury.

Lotar, L. 1946. *La Grande Chronique de l'Ubangi*. Mém: Institute Royal Colonial Belge. Section des Sciences Morales et Poltiques (7)2. Brussels: Institut Royal Colonial Belge.

Martini, C. and C. Schønberg. 1890. *To Danske Kongofarere: Erindringer fra vårt Første Ophold i Kongostaten*. Copenhagen: V. Pontoppidans Forlag.

Morel, E.D. 1906. *Red Rubber: The Story of the Rubber Slave Trade that Flourished in Congo in the Year of Grace 1906*. London: Allen & Unwin.

Morgenstierne, S. 2002. 'Hundre År Senere', in *Kongelig Slaveleir: Historien om et Terroregime*. Asker: Fritt og vilt.

Ndaywel è Nziem, I. 1998: *Histoire Général du Congo: Du l'Heritage Ancien à la Republique Democratique*. Paris and Brussels: De Boeck & Larcier-Duculot.

Nelson, S.H. 1994. *Colonialism in the Congo Basin 1880–1940*. Athens: Ohio University Center for International Studies.

Northrup, D. 1988. *Beyond the Bend in the River: African Labor in Eastern Zaire, 1865–1940*. Athens: Ohio University Center for International Studies.

O'Hanlon, M. and R.L. Welsch (eds). 2001. *Hunting the Gatherers: Ethnographic Collectors, Agents and Agency in Melanesia, 1870s–1930s*. Oxford: Berghahn Books.

Ó Síocháin, S. 2007. *Roger Casement: Imperialist, Rebel, Revolutionary*. Dublin: Lilliput Press.

Ó Síocháin, S. and M. O'Sullivan (eds). 2003. *The Eyes of Another Race: Roger Casement's Congo Report and 1903 Diary*. Dublin: University College Dublin Press.

Pakenham, T. (1991) 2002. *The Scramble for Africa: White Man's Conquest of the Dark Continent from 1876–1912*. London: Abacus History.

Penny, G.H. 2002. *Objects of Culture: Ethnology and Ethnographic Museums in Imperial Germany*. Chapel Hill: University of North Carolina Press.

Reinhard, W. 2011. *A Short History of Colonialism*. Manchester: Manchester University Press.

Roberts, A.F. 2013. *A Dance of Assassins: Performing Early Colonial Hegemony in the Congo*. Bloomington: Indiana University Press.

Scharffenberg, J. 1896. 'Congo: Foredrag den 29de januar og 5te februar 1896', *Det Norske Geografiske Selkabs Aarbog 1895–96* 7: 40–72.

Schildkrout, E. and C. Keim (eds). 1998. *The Scramble for Art in Central Africa.* Cambridge: Cambridge University Press.

Sjöblom, E.V. (1907) 2003. *I Palmernas Skugga: Själfbiografi, Dagboksanteckningar m. fl. Efterlämndade Manuskript.* Stockholm: Svenska Baptistsamfundet.

Stanley, H.M. 1890. *In Darkest Africa: The Quest, Rescue and Retreat of Emin Governor of Equatoria.* New York: Scribner.

Stoler, L.A., C. McGranahan and P.C. Perdue (eds). 2007. *Imperial Formations.* Santa Fe, N.M.: School for Advanced Research Press; Oxford: James Currey.

Svinhufvud, A. 1942. *I Kongostatens Tjänst.* Stockholm: Lindfors Bokförlag.

Tell, P.E. 2005. *Detta Fredliga Uppdrag: Om 522 Svenskar i Terrorns Kongo.* Umeå: H:ström.

Tygesen, P. and E. Wæhle. 2007. *Kongospor: Norden i Kongo, Kongo i Norden.* Oslo: Universitetets Kulturhistoriske Museer.

Vangroenweghe, D. 2005. *Voor Rubber en Ivoor: Leopold II en de Ophanging van Stokes.* Leuven: Van Halewyck.

Vellut, J.-L. (ed.). 2005. *La Mémoire du Congo: Le Temps Colonial.* Tervuren: Musée Royal d'Afrique Centrale; Gand: Snoeck.

Wæhle, E. 2000. 'Skandinaviske kongofarere: Etnografisk røveri i barbariets år?', *Jordens Folk* 4: 24–32.

———. 2001. 'A Congo Story from Oslo: Reflections on the Absence of an Exotic Art Market in Norway', *Folk* 43: 137–50.

———. 2002. 'Monganga Makazzi, Judchi og andre nordmenn under Kongostjernen 1885–1918', in K.A. Kjerland and A. Bang (eds), *Nordmenn i Afrika – afrikanere i Norge.* Bergen: Fagbokforlaget, pp. 189–208.

———. 2004. 'Kulturforskjellenes orden og omstendighetenes dans: Museumsantropologiske blikk på kongo-samlinger og -utstillinger ved de Etnografiske Samlinger i Oslo', *Tidsskrift for Kulturforskning* 3: 27–45.

———. 2008. 'Historier bak kongosamlingen', in *Årbok for Bergen Museum 2007–2008.* Bergen: University Museum of Bergen/Universitetet i Bergen, pp. 54–60.

———. 2010. 'Brev fra Kongofloden … og andre skatter fra kolonitiden', in Annette Hobson (ed.), *P2-Akademiets Bokserie XLIII.* Oslo: Transit, pp. 108–23.

Wastiau, B. 2000. *Exit Congo Museum 2000: A Century of Art with/without Papers.* Tervuren: Musée Royal d'Afrique Centrale.

Yngfalk, C. 2005. 'Sverige och den europeiska kolonialpolitiken i Afrika: En studie av Utenriksministeriets och opinionens bemötande av Berlinkonferansen 1884–85 og Kongofrågan 1903', PhD dissertation. Stockholm: Stockholm University.

 Afterword

HER OG NÅ (HERE AND NOW)
History and the Idea of Globalization
Peter Vale

Explanation always precedes confession. My purpose in what follows
is not to intrude on the excellent introduction offered by Bjørn Enge
Bertelsen, who, to remind the reader, situated these wonderful chapters
and made sense of their collective direction. This done, let me turn to
a confession: I'm no historian, and this makes me wonder what sense
I can – indeed, should – make of these chapters. I am, however, interested in ideas and how we use them to make the world and, especially,
how the idea of the 'international' manifests itself across time. Moreover, where there is explanation and confession, we will invariably find
caution: there are some words and ideas that are used to explain the
international, like 'globalization', that are of no use at all.

So why, the reader might ask, should I devote an afterword to an
anthology of fourteen engrossing chapters on a century of Norway's
engagement with different parts of the world by reflecting on a concept
that is limited and limiting? It's a good question, and, as a reading of
this chapter will show, it requires a longish answer – one that is rooted
in a critical reading both of our times and of language.

Let's begin with 'the drawing card' – that land of milk and honey –
that many Norwegians during the century under discussion in these
pages migrated to, namely, the United States. The link between the idea
of globalization and this country has been a persistent analytic theme
for the past three decades – indeed, globalization is seen as the triumph
of the United States' way in the world. But what is wrong with the word
'globalization'?

The central issue is that it has become the kind of word that the
United States' twenty-sixth president, Theodore Roosevelt, would have
called a 'weasel' word, by which he meant a word that has been emptied of any meaning in the same way that weasels empty eggs of their
contents. An Australian sceptic, Don Watson, put it this way: weasel
words 'are shells of words: words from which life has gone … facsimi-

les, frauds, corpses' (2005: 5). The danger with weasel words is not that they are emptied of any meaning that they once may have had, but that they also 'bob about' in everyday understandings and, as they do, obscure many pointed understandings of social reality. This happens because weasel words are easily folded into a prevailing (or dominant) ideology. So, and not to put too fine a point on it, globalization is a key word in neoliberal ideology, which why it is not very helpful in any serious analysis.

Let me illustrate this by relating a personal story. In the mid-1990s, my son, Daniel, who was then in his fourth year of schooling, asked me what I thought of the decline in the value of South Africa's currency, the rand, which was then 'under pressure' – in the metaphor-speak so beloved by economists – because of statements made by South Africa's first democratically elected government. I was elated by the boy's question, thinking that I had obviously fathered a genius and that this meant, surely, all my financial worries were behind me. So, I asked him, 'What's causing the fall in the rand?' He looked at me in total disbelief. 'Dad', he said, 'haven't you heard? It's caused by *globalization.*'

At one level, the ideological one, he was correct. Globalization has been used to explain a plethora of cross-border issues without any recourse to thought. But, in a general sense his question was, probably, prompted by bits and pieces of the garbled understandings of the world picked up from his schoolmates and also, probably, from television news bulletins or the car radio. This was a clear case of the commanding narratives of ideology leaking, as catchphrases and throwaway lines, into everyday speech – or, in this case, the playground speech of children. Just to close the immediate story – today, Daniel is a very serious law student who is interested in a career in international legal issues and, I'm happy to report, never mentions globalization.

The word itself enjoyed a meteoric rise to prominence in the conceptual confusion that followed the fall of the Berlin Wall in early November 1989. This bewilderment followed the sudden removal of those two anchors of social thinking and organization, 'East' and 'West'. Of course, and this seems to be a wholly unnecessary explanation to the readers of these pages, the notions of 'East' and 'West' were encryptions of deeper and far more sinister forms of real-world social organization that was itself reinforced by military strength, which, as we were told so often, were capable of destroying the planet itself.

Moreover, considerations of destructive power and its ideological twin, irreconcilable division, reinforced a complex social condition known by in shorthand as the Cold War. More than anything else, the usefulness of the ideology relied on simple binary explanations both at the micro and the meso level. As a result, there could be nothing outside of a Cold War gaze.

My intellectual interests in the ending of the Cold War were linked to the discipline of international relations, which, in my view, had been complicit in constructing a blinding ideology. It did this in several ways; one was to reduce entire nations to simple stereotypes. My political interest in the end of the Cold War, however, was tied up with the struggle to end apartheid, which, at the time, was engaging much of my energy.

I first heard the news of the famous breach in the Berlin Wall on Friedrichstrasse on an early summer night in Lusaka. During those years, that city was a place of refuge for many South Africans – especially the then exiled African National Congress (ANC), which had established its headquarters in Zambia. But the increasingly fluid politics in southern Africa meant that many, myself included, crossed the ideological divide into Zambia to talk to our long-exiled countrymen. The German family with whom I was staying was animated about the impact of events in Berlin for the future of their own divided country. And, unsurprisingly, we talked all night about the possible changes in the world until the first rays of the sun peeked through the central African sky.

I have long forgotten the many predictions that we made that night, but I wager that most of them were wrong, because they were long on dreams and short on history. I am, however, absolutely certain that the word 'global' never once crossed our lips. And yet, five years later, every conversation about how the world had changed was governed by *globalization* – the noun-cum-verb that was tapped from the root 'global'.

This outcome confirms how readily our thinking and our everyday discourse can become imprisoned by catchphrases and the conceptual encrustation that forms around them. But issues around philosophy of language were not in my mind as I thought about the flap and fury of political change on a grand scale that, even in the full light of the Zambian sun the next day, seemed to be promising, if not quite as earth-shaking as they turned out to be.

But, as we now know, that was the night that the world as we knew it irrevocably changed: the Soviet Union was to fall apart, the communist bloc fragmented, and the Cold War paradigm, which had dominated almost all thinking about the social world, shifted in a way that, perhaps, would have flummoxed even the brilliantly incisive philosopher of science Thomas Kuhn (1922–96).

Closer to home, of course, apartheid ended, and my two children would never again – certainly formally – experience the racial division that had marked the childhood lives of their mother and myself. But discrimination was not wholly over, as we have seen: as Kuhn once wisely cautioned, the 'historian of science may be tempted to exclaim that when paradigms change, the world itself changes with them' (Kuhn [1962] 2012: 111).

Superficially, of course, it was easy to understand change primarily because, much like the jackhammers on the Berlin Wall, we have been able to see and, yes, hear change. But explaining all this has proved to be very difficult, because we were led up several conceptual garden paths before we recognized that (as my friend, and sometime collaborator, Ken Booth, put it) '[o]ur work … [was] … words but our words … [didn't] … work anymore'.

The primary iteration of what form the post–Cold War world might take came from the Japanese American thinker Francis Fukuyama. The timing of his article 'The End of History?' (1989) was propitious – coinciding, as it did, with the fall of the Berlin Wall. Its catchy title hid a serious philosophically centred argument that took, as too few political pundits do, seriously the Kantian notion that ideas are the drivers of history. Fukuyama's assertion was that governments across the world had come to appreciate that what mattered most to their survival were the inherent rights and the dignity of their citizens. This stage of human evolution had been made possible by the triumph of liberal democracy as a form of government and by the ascendency of the market as the arbiter of social intercourse. This was, as Fukuyama's many disciples saw it, the end stage in the development of the organized human community.

It was an *ideal* moment: a condition upon which it was impossible to improve. Furthermore, it was not the result of a single event – say, the end of the Cold War – it was the outcome of a long historical sweep in human affairs, in which the rule of law, representative government and the acceptance of democracy had changed the nature of politics. In other words, it was the triumph of destiny – the end point of human social evolution, which is why history had 'ended'.

In the triumphalism of the moment, there was no place for the old philosophical squabbles about dialectic; there was only space for the triumph of capitalism. It was in this fertile soil, which was watered by the liberal idea of progress, that globalization – idea, first; ideology, next – took hold.

As these things do, it began with the appropriation of language – in this case, the stealing of words and ideas from elsewhere and seamlessly settling them within a narrative that meant exactly the opposite. A key move in the development of globalization was to adopt an old economic notion, 'free trade', in the discourse that was making and remaking the idea of the international. The allure of a borderless world was strengthened by the promise of new technologies that, so the reasoning went, would carry the world to the salvation once promised by organized religion. This was a stroke of political genius because, like Thatcherism, which had prepared its way, the notion of globalization was prompted by an axis that understood that 'it is ideas, not vested interests, which are dangerous for good and evil' – to use the phrase famously used by the interventionist economist John Maynard Keynes (1883–1946). Keynes favoured the idea of free trade, but certainly not in the sanctified form it enjoyed under the cult that developed around globalization.

Very soon, the everyday intellectual paraphernalia upon which ideology feeds took form: the founding of a think tank here, the publishing of a learned journal there. These promoted the idea of a public realm that was hungry for post–Cold War explanations of the international. Greater and greater popularization of the idea took it wider and wider through books like the *New York Times* columnist Thomas Friedman's two books, *The World Is Flat: A Brief History of the Twenty-First Century* (2005) and *The Lexus and the Olive Tree: Understanding Globalization* ([1999] 2012). Very soon globalization-speak became the set form of discourse for every pundit willing to be interviewed in the news cycle that considered itself as both 'global' and as operating on a sequence that was dubbed '24/7' – two neologisms that suggested that man and the world had shaken off those old enemies of social progress, time and space.

If these thoughts encapsulate my frustration with the idea of globalization, what is their relevance for the finely crafted chapters between these covers? As the Austrian philosopher (and sometime resident of Norway) Ludwig Wittgenstein (1889–1951) famously suggested, words are the boundaries in our search for knowledge, and the sheath around words, what we call language, show how far we can reach into the unknown.

The tongue of globalization has been, more than any other, English. This is a language whose own borderlines are intimately linked to control and surveillance, and it has used its command of the word 'globalization' to close off the possibility that this 'new' word could be used as a tool for emancipation in the Enlightenment sense of the term. This move stripped globalization of its potential to replace the idea of the 'international', which was brought to the analytic lexicon by the English philosopher and social reformer Jeremy Bentham (1748–1832), who first used the word in 1789.

It is certainly so that the idea of globalization might encapsulate both the spirit and the fact of the outreach that run through each of these deliciously fresh chapters on Norway and the world. But it is a decided strength of these chapters that 'globalization' is not often used in this anthology, even though what is discussed in each of the chapters could be readily captured under its shade. So while maritime transportation, shipping routes, markets, technological advances, geopolitics and collective or singular entrepreneurship, which help to bring each of the chapters to life, could be within the narrative arsenal of globalization devotees, they are used in these chapters with great subtly and impact. For the reader, their inclusion points towards understanding and explanation, rather than towards the death knell of social control that is intrinsic to globalization. The chapters in this book are written in the tradition of the finest historical essays, in the tradition espoused by the American writer William Faulkner (1892–1962) when he said that 'the past is never dead. It's not even past' (1951: 80).

Indeed, the thicket of history is caught within the human flows, social tensions, political contestations and power of reciprocity that is written into the very heart of these chapters. And this makes them illuminating, clear-sighted and – unlike globalization-speak – very, very relevant to understanding our times. The ideas in these pages stand in sharp juxtaposition to the endless expert knowledge of how to live in a world constantly marked by human encounters: they are as relevant today as when Norwegians first sallied forth to discover their destiny in Africa and Oceania – even if, as we know from these pages, the country was not exempt from the temptations of European-style colonialism.

These chapters have brought forgotten periods and foreign places to life by thorough research, careful analysis and clear writing. By doing so, they abrogate globalization's claim that scholars should only produce utilitarian knowledge. Not only is their prose different from the self-styled 'useful knowledge' said to be the right of Facebook and Twitter; these chapters peer into the past in order to both make sense of our own times and give us hope for the future.

References

Faulkner, W. 1951. *Requiem for a Nun.* New York: Random House.

Friedman, T. (1999) 2012. *The Lexus and the Olive Tree: Understanding Globalization.* New York: Picador.

———. 2005. *The World Is Flat: A Brief History of the Twenty-first Century.* New York: Farrar, Straus and Giroux.

Fukuyama, F. 1989. 'The End of History?', *The National Interest,* Summer: 3–18.

Kuhn, T. (1962) 2012. *The Structure of Scientific Revolutions,* 50th anniversary ed. Chicago: University of Chicago Press.

Watson, D. 2005. *Watson's Dictionary of Weasel Words.* Melbourne: Vintage.

⚛️ Contributors

Svein Ivar Angell is a historian, doctor of art and associate professor at the University of Bergen and affiliated senior researcher at Stein Rokkan Centre for Social Studies (Uni Rokkan Centre). He has researched issues such as nationalism, modernization and identity formation, foreign relations, public sector reforms, resource management, and local history. Angell's publications contain several books and articles in national as well as international journals.

Anne K. Bang is a historian and a senior researcher at the Chr. Michelsen Institute. She has worked on Islamic intellectual history in East Africa and in the Indian Ocean region, and has published widely on the subject. She has also been involved in the study of Norwegian overseas history, and has recently published the book *Zanzibar-Olsen: A Norwegian Timber Trader in Zanzibar, 1895–1925*.

Bjørn Enge Bertelsen, associate professor, Department of Social Anthropology, University of Bergen, has researched issues such as state formation, violence, poverty and rural-urban connections in Mozambique since 1998. Bertelsen's articles have appeared in *Ethnos, Journal of Southern African Studies, Social Analysis, Anthropology Today* and *Urban Studies,* and he has authored the monograph *Violent Becomings: State Formation, Culture and Power in Mozambique* (Berghahn Books, forthcoming) and coedited the anthology *Crisis of the State: War and Social Upheaval* with Bruce Kapferer (Berghahn Books, [2009] 2012).

Dag Ingemar Børresen is a historian and curator at the Commander Chr. Christensen's Whaling Museum, Sandefjord, Norway. He has published a series of articles on political and social history, labour history and whaling. Børresen is currently working on a doctoral thesis on transnational labour history and modern whaling, focusing on whaling activities in African waters.

Erlend Eidsvik is a geographer and associate professor at the Faculty of Education at the Bergen University College. He has researched and published on issues related to Scandinavian involvement in the colonial arena, with a geographical focus on South Africa. His PhD dissertation was part of the broader research programme 'In the Wake of Colonialism', funded by the Norwegian Research Council.

Edvard Hviding is professor of social anthropology at the University of Bergen, director of the Bergen Pacific Studies Research Group and currently coordinates the European Consortium for Pacific Studies, a network of European and Pacific research institutions funded by the European Union. Since 1986, Hviding has been engaged in long-term anthropological research in Solomon Islands, on the basis of which he was in 2010 awarded the Medal of the Order of Solomon Islands. Among his publications are the monographs *Guardians of Marovo Lagoon* (1996), *Islands of Rainforest* (2000, with T. Bayliss-Smith) and *Reef and Rainforest: An Environmental Encyclopedia of Marovo Lagoon* (2005), and the edited volumes *Made in Oceania* (2011, with K.M. Rio), *The Ethnographic Experiment* (2014, with C. Berg) and *Pacific Alternatives* (2014, with G.M. White).

Jon Tikivanotau Michael Jonassen retired in 2013 from his position as professor of political science and Pacific studies at Brigham Young University–Hawai'i, and now resides in Rarotonga. He has a PhD in political science from the University of Hawai'i at Mānoa, and his research interests focus on international relations, small island states, cultural policy and intellectual property in the Pacific region. Jonassen is a Cook Islander, and has served as that country's high commissioner to New Zealand, Australia, Fiji and Papua New Guinea and as the Cook Islands government's secretary of foreign affairs and secretary of cultural development. He has also served as the programme director of the South Pacific Commission. As well as a scholar, diplomat and senior civil servant, Jonassen is an accomplished drummer, performer and composer of Cook Islands traditional music, and a prominent composer of popular Pacific music.

Kirsten Alsaker Kjerland is a historian with a PhD (1995) from Kenya based on research on agricultural history during the colonial period. She has also worked on development aid issues and the implications of global trade on African local agriculture and commerce. From 1999 she was part of a team of historians writing a history of Norwegian development aid (published in three volumes, 2003). From 2005 to 2010, she headed a large-scale research project called 'In the Wake of Colonialism'. She is presently attached to UiB Global at the University of Bergen and is funded by the Norwegian Author's Association to write a book about

Hans Peter Fyhn Krag (1857–1938), who traded and invested on the African continent during the colonial period.

Knut M. Nygaard holds a PhD from the University of Bergen. His research interests are in economic maritime history. Nygaard's doctoral dissertation examines transnational Scandinavian cooperation in the liner trade between the Nordic countries and South Africa in the period 1900–40, while his earlier work has analysed the shipping company Fred Olsen & Co.'s transition from sailing ships in tramp trade to steamers in liner trade, in the period 1886–1904.

Elsa Reiersen is a historian and former senior researcher affiliated with Norwegian University of Science and Technology (NTNU), Department of History and Classical Studies. She has researched issues such as banks and finance institutions and the history of industry and organizations, as well as authored several books on these topics, such as on the history of the Norwegian State Housing Bank (1996) and Fokus Bank (2000), and a biography about the industrialist and businessman Christian Thams entitled *Fenomenet Thams* (2006).

Knut M. Rio is professor of social anthropology at the University of Bergen and is responsible for the ethnographic collections at the University Museum of Bergen. He has worked on Melanesian ethnography since 1995, with fieldwork in Vanuatu. His work on social ontology, production, ceremonial exchange, witchcraft and art in Vanuatu has resulted in journal publications and the monograph *The Power of Perspective: Social Ontology and Agency on Ambrym Island, Vanuatu* (2007). He has also coedited *Hierarchy: Persistence and Transformation in Social formations* (with Olaf Smedal, 2009) and *Made in Oceania: Social Movements, Cultural Heritage and the State in the Pacific* (with Edvard Hviding, 2011).

Gustav Sætra is an associate professor in history at Agder University in the Department of Religion, History and Philosophy. He has participated on projects for the Norwegian Research Council and for the shipping industry, and has published articles and books about maritime history and political issues within the Danish-Norwegian state, especially peasant revolts in the eighteenth century. Sætra has authored two books for the shipping companies Arnt J. Mørland in Arendal and O. T. Tønnevold in Grimstad, as well as for the Aust-Agder Ship Owners' Association.

Peter Vale is professor of humanities at the University of Johannesburg and the Nelson Mandela Professor of Politics Emeritus, Rhodes University, South Africa. Vale's research centres around social thought, intellectual traditions in South Africa, critical theory, the future of the humanities, the origins of international relations in South Africa and the politics of higher education. He has held a number of visiting appointments, including UNESCO professor of African studies at Utrecht University, fellow at the International Centre for Advanced Studies, New York University, and professor of politics, Macquarie University, Sydney, Australia. Vale publishes extensively in international journals as well as books, such as *Security and Politics in South Africa: The Regional Dimension* (2003).

Espen Wæhle is a social anthropologist and acting director at the Norwegian Maritime Museum. He has undertaken field studies in the Ituri region of the Democratic Republic of Congo and written on the hunter-gatherers of the rain forest, colonial history and museum collections. He has worked for the ethnographic collections of the Bergen University Museum and the Museum of Cultural History in Oslo and has been keeper of the ethnographic collections of the National Museum of Denmark.

🌊 Index